A handbook on
Legal Languages

*and the quest for linguistic equality
in South Africa and beyond*

Zakeera Docrat
Russell H Kaschula
Monwabisi K Ralarala

A handbook on Legal Languages and the quest for linguistic equality in South Africa and beyond

Published by African Sun Media under the SUN PReSS imprint

All rights reserved

Copyright © 2021 African Sun Media and the authors

This publication was subjected to an independent double-blind peer evaluation by the publisher.

The authors and the publisher have made every effort to obtain permission for and acknowledge the use of copyrighted material. Refer all enquiries to the publisher.

No part of this book may be reproduced or transmitted in any form or by any electronic, photographic or mechanical means, including photocopying and recording on record, tape or laser disk, on microfilm, via the Internet, by e-mail, or by any other information storage and retrieval system, without prior written permission by the publisher.

Views reflected in this publication are not necessarily those of the publisher.

First edition 2021

ISBN 978-1-991201-26-3
ISBN 978-1-991201-27-0 (e-book)
https://doi.org/10.52779/9781991201270

Set in Warnock Pro Light 10/14.5

Cover design, typesetting and production by African Sun Media

SUN PReSS is an imprint of African Sun Media. Scholarly, professional and reference works are published under this imprint in print and electronic formats.

This publication can be ordered from:
orders@africansunmedia.co.za
Takealot: bit.ly/2monsfl
Google Books: bit.ly/2k1Uilm
africansunmedia.store.it.si *(e-books)*
Amazon Kindle: amzn.to/2ktL.pkL

Visit africansunmedia.co.za for more information.

CONTENTS

List of Figures and Tables iv
List of Acronyms and Abbreviations vi
Acknowledgements ix
About the Authors x
Preface xii
Foreword xiv

1 Introduction:
  Discussion map, research question and objectives 1
     Context of the research 1
     Research area: forensic linguistics or language and law 7
     Study area 9
     Research problem 11
     Goals of the research 14
     Conclusion 15

2 The Language of Proceedings in Courts on the African Continent:
  Kenya, Nigeria and Morocco 17
     International jurisprudence 18
     Kenya's sociolinguistic landscape 20
     Nigeria's sociolinguistic landscape 31
     Morocco's sociolinguistic landscape 43
     Conclusion 49

3 Insights from International Case Studies on Language and Law:
  Australia, Belgium, Canada and India 53
     Australia's sociolinguistic landscape 53
     Belgium's sociolinguistic landscape 66
     Canadian sociolinguistic landscape 72
     India's sociolinguistic landscape 85
     Conclusion 95

4 The Monolingual Language of Record in South African Courts:
  The complications of court interpretation and the introduction of
  administrative law 97
     Defining the language of record 97
     History of the language(s) of record in South African courts of law 99
     Administrative law as an enabling framework 110
     Language of record directive 114
     The legality of the language of record directive 118

		Interpretational rights and the failures of social justice	120
		The problem with interpretation: quality versus efficacy	123
		Conclusion	127
5	The Language Question in Legislative and Policy Instruments: A forensic linguistics approach to language planning and legislative drafting		129
		The relationship between forensic linguistics and applied language studies	130
		Defining language planning	132
		Ideologies underpinning language planning in South Africa	140
		Legislative drafting	144
		Conclusion	158
6a	Part One: South Africa's Constitutional Language Rights and Provisions: A language right or an interpretational right?		161
		South African constitutional framework	161
		South African constitutional language rights	164
		The enforceability of the constitutional language framework	169
		Section 35 imposing language or interpretational rights	172
6b	Part Two: Linguistic (In)equality in South Africa's Legal System: Linguistic equality for African language-speaking litigants		175
		Language equality in the South African legal system	175
		The limitations analysis: sliding scale formula	179
		South African language demographics: statistics	180
		English language limitations of South African litigants	190
		Conclusion	194
7	The Language Question before Courts: Selected South African case law		197
		South African case law	197
		Conclusion	222
8	South Africa's Legal Practitioners and Judical Officers: Language qualifications and competencies		225
		Legislative language requirements for legal practitioners	225
		A transformed legal profession: Legal Practice Act	227
		Legal professionals: racial demographics	228
		Attorneys' views on languages other than English	231
		Conclusion	235

9   The Relationship between South Africa's Legal System and Higher Education Institutions:
    A policy-based approach 237
        Language planning in higher education 238
        Transformation and decolonisation 242
        Higher education legislative and policy framework 245
        Selected university language policies 247
        A critique of selected university language policies 257
        The language question at selected universities 263
        Language as part of the LLB curriculum 264
        Analysis of the higher education language policy cases 268
        Conclusion 270

10 Conclusions and Recommendations:
    The way forward 273
        Introduction 273
        Overview 273
        Recommendations 275
        Conclusion 287

References 291

LIST OF FIGURES

Figure 2.1	An overview of the Nigerian courts (based on Olanrewaju, 2009)	33
Figure 6.1	National language statistics (Census, 2011)	179

LIST OF TABLES

Table 3.1	Constitutionally scheduled languages arranged in descending order of use	85
Table 6.1	National language demographics of South Africa (Census, 2011)	180
Table 6.2	Eastern Cape Province language statistics per district municipality (Census, 2011)	182
Table 6.3	Free State Province language statistics per district municipality (Census, 2011)	182
Table 6.4	KwaZulu-Natal Province language statistics per metropolitan and district municipalities (Census, 2011	183
Table 6.5	North West Province language statistics per district municipality (Census, 2011)	184
Table 6.6	Northern Cape Province language statistics per district municipality (Census, 2011)	184
Table 6.7	Western Cape Province language statistics per metropolitan and district municipality (Census, 2011)	185
Table 6.8	Limpopo Province language statistics per district municipality (Census, 2011)	186
Table 6.9	Mpumalanga Province language statistics per district municipality (Census, 2011)	186
Table 6.10	Gauteng Province language statistics per metropolitan and district municipality (Census, 2011)	187
Table 6.11	Primary spoken language in criminal matters (Language Survey, Legal Aid South Africa, 2017:2)	189
Table 6.12	Primary spoken language in civil matters (Language Survey, Legal Aid South Africa, 2017:3)	189
Table 6.13	English proficiency in criminal cases (Language Survey, Legal Aid South Africa, 2016:4)	191

Table 6.14	English proficiency in civil cases (Language Survey, Legal Aid South African, 2017:5)	191
Table 8.1	Racial demographics of the practicing attorneys per law society from April 2014 to April 2015 (Law Society of South Africa, 2015:34-43)	227
Table 8.2	Racial demographics of the practicing advocates per Bar recoded in April 2014 (Law Society of South Africa, 2015:49)	227
Table 8.3	Racial demographics of High Court judges per division in each province as at April 2015 (Law Society of South Africa, 2015:50)	228
Table 8.4	Racial statistics of magistrates in South Africa as on April 2015 (Law Society of South Africa, 2015:52)	229
Table 8.5	Clients' English proficiency: The legal practitioners' perspective (De Vries & Docrat, 2019:98)	230
Table 8.6	Survey results: Attorneys' language attitudes, needs and choices (De Vries & Docrat, 2019:100)	230

LIST OF ACRONYMS AND ABBREVIATIONS

AC	Area Court
AIATSIS	Australian Institute of Aboriginal and Torres Strait Islanders Studies
AJ	Acting Judge
ANC	African National Congress
ASP	Assistant Superintendent of Police
BCLR	Butterworths Constitutional Law Reports
BOR	Bill of Rights
CA	Court of Appeal
CC	Constitutional Court
CCA	Customary Court of Appeal
CJ	Chief Justice
CODESA	Convention for a Democratic South Africa
DC	District Court
DCJ	Deputy Chief Justice
DOJ	Department of Justice
DOJCD	Department of Justice and Constitutional Development
DPP	Director of Public Prosecutions
EC	Eastern Cape Province
FS	Free State Province
GP	Gauteng Province
HCA	High Court of Appeal
HE	Higher Education
HEA	Higher Education Act 101 of 1997
ICT	Information and Communication Technology
J	Judge
JP	Judge President
JSC	Judicial Service Commission
KZN	Kwa-Zulu Natal Province

LANGTAG	Language Task Plan Group
LLB	Legum Baccalaureus/ Bachelor of Laws
LOLT	Language of Learning and Teaching
LP	Limpopo Province
LPHE	Language Policy for Higher Education
MC	Magistrates' Court
MCom	Magistrates Commission
MP	Mpumalanga Province
NAATI	National Accreditation Authority for Translators and Interpreters
NAIDOC	National Aborigines and Islanders Day Observance Committee
NC	Northern Cape Province
NCHE	National Commission on Higher Education
NCOP	National Council of Provinces
NDPP	National Director of Public Prosecutions
NP	National Party
NPA	National Prosecuting Authority
NRF	National Research Foundation
NW	North West Province
PAJA	Promotion of Administrative Justice Act 3 of 2000
PanSALB	Pan South African Language Board
PhD	Doctor of Philosophy
ROL	Rule of Law
RU	Rhodes University
SA	South Africa
SAPS	South African Police Service
SC	Supreme Court
SCA	Supreme Court of Appeal
SCC	Supreme Court of Canada
Sharia CA	Sharia Court of Appeal
SLC	Senate Language Committee
SOP	Separation of Powers
SRC	Student Representative Council

SU	Stellenbosch University
UCT	University of Cape Town
UFS	University of the Free State
UKZN	University of Kwa-Zulu Natal
UNESCO	United Nations Educational, Scientific and Cultural Organisation
UNISA	University of South Africa
UP	University of Pretoria
UWC	University of the Western Cape
WC	Western Cape Province
Judicis est dicere non dare	It is the judge's duty to enunciate the law, not to make it
(Court) *a quo*	(Court of) first instance
Viva voce	Oral (evidence)
Amicus curiae	Friend of the court (A person or a group who is not a party to the action, but has a strong interest in the matter and can offer an (expert) opinion)
Stare decisis	A legal doctrine that obligates courts to follow precedents set by previous decisions

ACKNOWLEDGEMENTS

We began conceptualising this book in 2019 during the finalisation of Dr Zakeera Docrat's PhD (the leading author of this book), the findings of which informed the initiation of the book project.

Dr Zakeera Docrat is the first to obtain a PhD at Rhodes University (RU) with a particular emphasis on forensic linguistics/language and law. The work of linguists and legal scholars on the intersection of language and the law is a prime example of how research in the humanities can situate parallel studies in the sciences within a social and cultural context for the advancement of knowledge and upholding of language rights. This is the direction of research in this book.

Several individuals deserve acknowledgement and recognition for their respective contributions to this book. We are grateful to Mrs Pangalay Glenda Docrat (Zakeera's mother) for her unfailing support of Zakeera from the commencement to completion of this book. We owe the same thanks to our families, colleagues and friends for their words of encouragement and inspiration throughout our journey.

This book would never have taken its present form and shape without Dr Jenny Wright's valuable editorial comments. Her critical reading and meticulous editing has significantly improved our work.

We acknowledge the financial assistance provided by the National Research Foundation's (NRF) South African Research Chairs Initiative (SARChI); Chair in the Intellectualisation of African Languages, Multilingualism and Education towards this book. Opinions expressed and conclusions are those of the authors and are not necessarily to be attributed to the NRF.

This work is based on the research supported by the National Institute for the Humanities and Social Sciences (NIHSS). Opinions, findings and conclusions or recommendations expressed in this publication is that of the authors, and the NIHSS accepts no liability in this regard.

ABOUT THE AUTHORS

Dr Zakeera Docrat is an Andrew W Mellon Foundation post-doctoral research fellow in forensic linguistics (language and law) at the University of the Western Cape (UWC), based in the Department of African Language Studies. Dr Docrat was Rhodes University's first post-doctoral research fellow in forensic linguistics (language and law), under the auspices of the NRF SARChI Chair in the Intellectualisation of African Languages, Multilingualism and Education. Dr Docrat holds the following degrees: BA, BA Honours (*cum laude*), LLB, MA (*cum laude*) and a PhD. She has presented at international and national conferences including: The International Association of Forensic Linguists (IAFL) conferences in Portugal and Australia; and at the World Congress of African Linguists (WOCAL) conference in Morocco. She has published widely in accredited national and international journals and books. She has penned opinion pieces in several press forums. As an expert, she has been interviewed on national media. She is a member of the International Association of Forensic Linguists (IAFL), the African Languages Association of Southern Africa (ALASA) and Vice-Chairperson of the Indigenous Languages Action Forum (ILAF). She developed and co-lectured the first course module in African Forensic Linguistics at Rhodes University's (RU) School of Languages and Literatures. Dr Docrat was one of the *Mail & Guardian* 200 Young South Africans in 2018 (Justice and Law category) and received numerous awards, including most outstanding Master's Thesis (African Languages Association of South Africa) and the Women in Science Award – Albertina Sisulu Doctoral Fellowship (Department of Science and Technology), recognising her outstanding academic and research ability.

Prof Russell H. Kaschula is a registered advocate of the High Court of South Africa. He has a PhD in African literature. His research interests are multidisciplinary in that they cover both linguistic and literary issues. He is particularly interested in matters pertaining to applied language studies, sociolinguistics, education, second language acquisition, multilingualism and forensic linguistics. He also has a special interest in intercultural studies, as well as literature. He has presented conference papers and has published widely in these fields, both nationally and internationally. His forthcoming book, published by Routledge, is titled *Languages, identities and intercultural communication in South Africa and beyond*. He has taught at five South African universities and at an institution in the United States of America. He is also a creative writer and has published several award-winning novels.

He has held leadership positions at a number of institutions, including the University of Cape Town and Rhodes University where he was Professor of African Language Studies. He was previously Head of the School of Languages & Literatures, administering six different language sections. He held the seconded position of NRF SARChI Chair in the Intellectualisation of African Languages, Multilingualism and Education until 2020. In 2008, he was awarded the Vice-Chancellor's Distinguished Senior Teaching Medal; and in 2017, he was awarded the Vice-Chancellor's Distinguished Senior Research Medal at Rhodes University (RU). In 2019, he was the recipient of the Mellon Global South Senior Fellow, AUC, Egypt. In January 2021, he was appointed as a professor in the Department of African Language Studies at the University of the Western Cape.

Prof Monwabisi K. Ralarala is Dean of Arts and Humanities at the University of the Western Cape. Previous positions include: Director: Fundani Centre for Higher Education Development (CHED) (Cape Peninsula University of Technology [CPUT]); Director: Language Centre (University of Fort Hare); Director of Research and Policy Development (Commission for the Promotion and Protection of the Rights of Cultural, Religious and Linguistic Communities); and Lecturer at the University of Stellenbosch's (SU) Department of African Languages. Apart from being a Canon Collins Educational and Legal Assistance Trust Alumnus, he received the Neville Alexander Award for the Promotion of Multilingualism in 2017. He holds two PhDs (Stellenbosch University and University of the Free State respectively) on persuasion in African languages; and language practice (emphasis: forensic linguistics).

His diverse research interests follow three lines: language rights and multilingualism in higher education; forensic linguistics; and translation studies. He has held visiting scholarships, nationally and internationally, for teaching and research. He has also published articles and book chapters, mainly in forensic linguistics and translation studies. His co-edited books are: *African language and language practice research in the 21st century: Interdisciplinary themes and perspectives* (2017, CASAS); *New frontiers in forensic linguistics: Themes and perspectives in language and law in Africa and beyond* (2019, African Sun Media) and *Knowledge beyond colour lines: Towards repurposing knowledge generation in Higher Education in South Africa and beyond* (2021, UWC Press). He is founder and Chief Series Editor of Studies in forensic linguistics: Language and the law in South Africa and beyond.

PREFACE

Historically, language has been used as a tool to divide, marginalise and discriminate against persons where the majority of African language-speaking South African citizens were excluded from mainstream society. The Constitution of the Republic of South Africa (1996a) was to charter a new direction of freedom, dignity and equality for all. Theoretically, however (though, of course, in many aspects of life this happened), the challenges to linguistic equality in South Africa remain entrenched in both the legal and higher education systems. The language rights and constitutional language provisions are often restrictively interpreted where phrases such as "equitable" and "where practicable" are used as excuses for failing to implement and use the African languages in high status domains.

The insurgence of English as a global language, one with significant economic and political power, continues to be imposed on African language-speaking litigants, legal professionals and students at higher education institutions. This trend is perpetuated through policy and legislative means favouring a monolingual approach to language planning, as evidenced in the monolingual language of record policy directive for High Courts in South Africa (Docrat & Kaschula, 2019). Monolingual language planning and legislative drafting becomes exclusionary where the majority of litigants and witnesses accessing courts of law cannot speak, read, write or understand English. Reliance is then placed solely on interpretation services in South Africa. The interpretation system presents with many challenges: non-regulation; poor quality of interpretation; a shortage of interpreters; a lack of legal-linguistic qualifications; as well as interpreters being underpaid. In this book we offer solutions, guidelines and new thought processes grounded in the discipline of forensic linguistics with the aim of creating a legally and linguistically inclusive society.

By highlighting the South African linguistic issues plaguing the legal system and the inherent failures of not including language as part of the transformational and decolonisation processes, we provide a broader African and international comparative study. As South Africans, we have an important role to play in informing the language planning process on the African continent where the indigenous languages are developed, promoted and used, with the purpose of ensuring access to justice and the attainment of linguistic equality, which we understand to be linguistic inclusion and equal access to higher education and the courts.

The African comparative case studies from Kenya, Morocco and Nigeria illustrate that Eurocentric language planning models are favoured to the exclusion of developing and using indigenous languages. The African case studies illustrate that the role of language in legal processes is perhaps the most underrated field of inquiry, especially within the discipline of forensic linguistics. In fact, it should be at the forefront of any court case, as the entire legal system is premised on the ability to argue cases in a persuasive way through appropriate use of language that is understood by all parties before court.

The international case studies provide insight into the global approach where the many linguistic injustices that occur mimic those on the African continent. For example, there is an exclusionary legal system in Australia where the Aboriginal peoples' plight for linguistic inclusion and equal access to justice is a daily struggle. As is clear from the Indian case study, language proves to be used decisively as a political, social and economic tool to exclude persons and create an unequal divide in society, a divide which is subsequently endorsed in higher education and legal systems. The global approach therefore also creates vast disparities. Forensic linguistics, as a developed area of research, has not yet reached many such countries and positively influenced legal discourse. In countries such as Canada and Belgium, linguistic inclusion and equal access to justice is synonymous with bilingual teaching and learning language policies of higher education institutions. These case studies serve as models that can be emulated by South Africa and other countries on the African continent for the development and use of indigenous languages in courts and higher education. Some of the cases and sources referred to in this handbook date back more than two hundred years and we are therefore unable to provide online references for these items.

We wish this to be a handbook that is accessible to everyone, particularly students, legal professionals, language planners, legislative drafters and those with a general interest in language and law, as they are introduced to the discipline of forensic linguistics.

Dr Zakeera Docrat

Prof Russell H. Kaschula

Prof Monwabisi K. Ralarala

January 2021, Cape Town, South Africa

FOREWORD

The overarching objective of *A handbook on Legal Languages and the quest for linguistic equality in South Africa and beyond* is to transform the legal linguistics landscape from being exclusionary to inclusive, and to improve the delivery of justice. The authors bring together their extensive knowledge, research and experience of language on the one hand, and the South Africa legal context on the other, to offer solutions to what ought not to be intractable problems.

The contributions include the imperative of a sensitive and purposive interpretation of language rights by the courts; a revisiting of the Chief Justice's (CJ) monolingual language of record policy; legal and policy reform involving court challenges where necessary on pertinent infringements of language and or interpretation rights; the enhancement of interpretational skills; astute language planning against the background of necessary language audits and needs adjustment; linguistic sensitivity training of all role players in the legal system; and the use of legal linguistic experts (forensic linguists) to ensure that the language rights of African language speakers are promoted and implemented in practical situations. At the heart of the transformational agenda explored in this book is the implementation of second language training in school and university curricula, the goal being to produce LLB (Legum Baccalaureus/Bachelor of Laws) graduates who are linguistically competent in African languages.

The history of our country is replete with instances of language being foisted on its people. My own experience, as an English language speaker, who had Afrikaans foisted on from an early age as a dominant language of engagement and learning, is no different from many others. My father's work at Spoornet took my siblings and I to many little towns all over the country where we were slotted into either dual-medium or single Afrikaans medium schools. This did not inconvenience me in the least, but my brothers found the adjustment particularly challenging – like most students who have to access education in a language that is not their mother tongue.

When I commenced my undergraduate law degree at the Nelson Mandela University (formerly the University of Port Elizabeth) 40 years ago, the institution was touted as one of academic bilingualism and linguistic equality (English and Afrikaans being the only official languages back then). However, my experience was that the scales were somewhat tilted in favour of Afrikaans as the medium of instruction. I soon gave up translating my lecture notes into English. I wrote all my essays, tests, and exams in Afrikaans. As hard as it was, nevertheless, this adaptation stood me in good stead when I commenced my career in law as a public prosecutor in Queenstown in 1984 because the language medium of that court was decidedly Afrikaans.

At Queenstown, the statements in the police dockets were taken down in Afrikaans. The magistrates spoke Afrikaans. I precognised, led and cross-examined witnesses in Afrikaans. I also addressed the court in my second language, and judgments, including sentences, were delivered in this language as well. Even the medium of administration of the court was Afrikaans although a fair number of practitioners who represented accused persons in that court and who were themselves indigenous language speakers preferred to communicate in English.

There, I learnt the importance of interpretation within the criminal justice system. I had the privilege of working alongside the late Mr Kaizer Fezile Siwa, an extremely competent interpreter in service of the state at the time, who translated the mother tongue isiXhosa of most of the accused persons and witnesses who came through the portals of the court into Afrikaans and back.

I realise in hindsight the important role the late Mr Siwa played in making non-Afrikaans speaking users of the court feel at ease in what was a most intimidating space (he did so with such kindness, empathy, and subtlety). In the process, he also shaped my own journey, causing me to become sensitive to, and understand, the stark language barrier that a monolingual court imposes upon a speaker of another language.

I transferred to the Durban magistrate's court in 1985 where the demographic is somewhat different to that of the Eastern Cape. I noticed that, although English was more commonly spoken by the users of that court, magistrates (invariably trained in Afrikaans-medium institutions) often conveniently reverted to Afrikaans. I returned to the Eastern Cape in 1986, still employed by the Department of Justice (DOJ), to prosecute at the magistrate's court in Makhanda (where I was quite serendipitously reunited with the now late Mr Siwa) until I took up articles with Netteltons Attorneys in 1989. English and Afrikaans were more or less equally spoken in the city and in that court.

The issue of forensic linguistics did not weigh on me much when I practiced at the Side Bar in Port Elizabeth (1991), or later on when I made the move to the Bar (2000). My bilingualism was a definite plus and came in exceptionally handy when I needed to consult with Afrikaans speaking clients or witnesses, or interpret documentation framed in the language. It also meant that I could attract more clients because of my dual language proficiency.

By the time I made the transition to the Bar in Port Elizabeth in 2000, following a number of years at the Side Bar, democracy had ensured a much-needed change to the dominant role of Afrikaans in the criminal justice system. As Afrikaans receded, English became the language of the day. Because English had jousted for an equal place during apartheid, this was a welcome transformation. I confess that, notwithstanding the advent of the constitutional era, I was somewhat impervious to the language barrier that continued to remain in place for African language speakers. For the majority of our fellow citizens, the battle to understand English, and to read, write, or speak it, continued within the criminal justice system and, particularly, in the domain of the court, where legalese involving unique legal terminology confounds even proficient English speakers.

It is right, especially in the context of criminal prosecutions, that the fair trial rights of an accused person include the right to be tried in the language he or she can understand and relate to and, if that is not practicable (which self-evidently has proven to be the case given the recent adoption of English as the formal and only language of record in our courts), to have the proceedings interpreted (properly and professionally) in that language.

The same bar to understanding must surely also apply to English second-language speakers seeking to assert their rights in court within the realm of administrative law.

Anyone from South Africa who ventures abroad appreciates the sense of anxiety when arriving in a country where airport and street signs, instructions by officials, and even a coffee shop menu are in an unfamiliar, foreign language. It is worse when nobody is prepared to engage with one in any of the official languages of South Africa! Amidst feelings of being disconnected and disempowered, overwhelmed, somewhat undignified, and very unwelcome, one may well cry out, "How dare you?"

Imagine how much more anxiety-provoking the already traumatic legal setting must be for African language speakers to make their way through a domain which, for all intents and purposes, is alien; and yet, one where the meaningful utility of fundamental language rights must surely matter the most.

It is not surprising, given the historically diminished use and status of the indigenous languages of our people, that our Constitution endorses means and measures by which the 11 official languages of our country (including English) are required to be elevated, respected, their use developed and promoted, treated equitably, and are expected, in that exquisite turn of phrase, to "enjoy parity of esteem". Our Constitution also sensitively recognises that beyond the official languages, the Khoi, Nama and San languages, and sign language, must also (again somewhat poetically expressed) be given their places of reverence, with conditions being created for their development and use.

We are not an inward-looking country either. Our Constitution recognises our interconnectedness globally and our unique composition as a iversely cultured nation in that it calls on us all to promote and ensure respect for all languages commonly used by our communities, including German, Greek, Gujarati, Hindi, Portuguese, Tamil, Telegu, Urdu, Arabic, Hebrew, Sanskrit, and other languages used for religious purposes in our country.

Why then are we still wrestling with "the language question" problematised by the authors of *A handbook on Legal Languages and the quest for linguistic equality in South Africa and beyond?* Why, when in our collective perception of the apartheid era, we understand how language was among the devices used to discriminate against and exclude from white society the majority of South African citizens who spoke an African language? Why, when our Constitution was expected to usher in a new era of freedom, dignity and equality for all, do challenges to linguistic equality (entailing linguistic inclusion and the right to use the official language of one's choice in court – the scope of the handbook) remain entrenched in our country? Why, when our Constitution self-evidently recognises language rights as vital to transform our multicultural and multilingual society, do we continue to restrictively interpret these rights, employing phrases such as "equitable" and "where practicable" as facile justification for failing to implement and use our African languages in high status domains? Why do we forsake the aspirations of language equality in our approach to language usage and planning in critical domains of engagement (in the context of the handbook, read courts and higher education settings) and instead resort to an English only bias? Also, why especially have we settled for English as the sole official language of record in our courts at the expense of African languages and bilingualism, or multilingualism even more broadly? By settling for English as the sole official language of record in our courts, we have sacrificed our country's African languages and kyboshed multilingualism, even bilingualism, in our courts.

The authors to this volume, eminent forensic linguists and social justice activists in their own right, are uncompromising in calling out and drawing attention to how language equality in South Africa is being undermined. Their critique of the recent directive of Mogoeng CJ declaring English to be the language of record in the country's courts requires engagement. It bears pointing out that the directive, although applicable to the higher courts, by obvious implication filters down to the lower courts where the majority of litigants and witnesses accessing these courts are unable to speak, read or understand English with sufficient levels of proficiency to understand complex legal proceedings.

The authors further highlight several challenges to the current system of interpretation in our courts. The effect of these challenges is to render interpretation services as wholly inadequate, and to nullify the default interpretational right which is available to those who are disadvantaged by the English medium of proceedings in court. Several examples of the manner in which our courts across the country have approached language and/ or interpretational rights are held up for analysis and critical review. These are useful insights for anyone willing to take a different approach. Importantly too, they consider the shortcomings in the legislative and policy framework which are essential in supporting and giving meaningful effect to the constitutional language rights in court and higher education institutions.

The authors share their rich research of linguistic challenges experienced by other countries in their particular legal systems, and the juristic linguistic solutions which have been introduced in those jurisdictions which could be emulated, avoided, or adapted for our own purposes.

The proposal that law students should be expected to have a language qualification in an African language at the time of graduating is, to my mind, most practicable. Many will recall that in earlier times, the curriculum prerequisites for graduating with a law degree included either one of the (then) two official languages, together with preliminary Latin. In my case I chose English and went on to do Latin 1 simply because the course ignited a passion to go further.

I suspect that the official African languages of our country are already offered as courses in most universities. They should also be more easily assimilated by South Africans, hearing them being more spoken than Latin was by the graduates of yesteryear.

I recognise the irony in writing this foreword since I am not professionally proficient in ten of the official languages. However, while language results from complex neurological and cultural systems, like every other element of our socialisation as humans, the capacity to speak a language is a learned attribute. Learning must never cease, especially for one who purports to engage with the law in the interests of asserting the constitutional rights of all. To do that competently in the home language of the people who are served in our courts is an ideal worth achieving.

The "language question" can never remain rhetorical, even if this handbook, by its nature, offers a forceful argument for reconsideration of the rights of speakers of all official languages in South Africa.

Honourable Mrs Justice Belinda Hartle
Senior Judge of the Bhisho High Court, Eastern Cape Division, South Africa

INTRODUCTION

Discussion map, research question and objectives

This book aims to lay bare the exclusionary South African legal system that perpetuates English as the sole official language of record, entrenching monolingualism at the expense of African languages and bilingualism, or multilingualism more broadly. This book was motivated by the undermining of the principles of linguistic equality, bilingualism and multilingualism and the lack of importance placed on African languages as potential languages of record.

This chapter introduces the research and discussions presented in this book. Although the book uses a comparative approach by looking at forensic linguistics in the context of a number of countries, the primary emphasis remains on the South African context, given the challenging multilingual nature of the country. The chapter commences with the contextualisation of the current legal and linguistic frameworks in which this interdisciplinary research was undertaken. The interdisciplinary nature of this research is expounded upon in the sections comprising the purpose of the study, research area, and research problem where the term 'forensic linguistics/language and law' is introduced.

Context of the research

The historically hegemonic legislative position occupied by English and Afrikaans as the two official South African languages, as discussed in Chapters 4 and 5, has resulted in the marginalisation of use and development of African languages (Bambust, Kruger & Kruger, 2012). The bilingual official languages of English and Afrikaans have been reflected across disciplines, including the legal system (McLean, 1992).

With the commencement of the new democratic era, the Constitution of the Republic of South Africa 1996a (hereinafter referred to as the 'Constitution') ushered in a constitutional democracy founded upon dignity, equality and freedom. With a progressive, all-encompassing transformative Constitution, implementation thereof was essential for redressing past discriminatory injustices. The legal system was, and is, central to the implementation and realisation of constitutional rights and ideals. The legal system is mandated to ensure the non-infringement of rights and any form of linguistic discrimination perpetrated by either the state or private citizens. It therefore ensures protection of all citizens, regardless of race, ethnicity, culture, religion, sexual orientation or language, as underpinned constitutionally.

The discriminatory redress envisioned in the Preamble of the Constitution resonated in the drafting of Section 6, the languages section in the Constitution. The common thread in Section 6 is discriminatory redress, envisioned through the recognition of 11 official languages, as opposed to the previous two. In accord with the 11 official languages, Section 6(2) elevates the status of African languages with a positive obligation conferred upon the state to adopt measures to ensure redress. Through our discussions in this book, we engage with Section 6 in more depth in Part One of Chapter 6. The research examines the provisions of Section 6, the effect thereof, and their implementation thus far. In doing so, we engage in a critical analysis, first of Section 6, where the issues of the constitutional framework are discussed and substantiated through scholarly works such as those of Perry (2004) and De Vos (2008), amongst others, and then of case law in Chapter 7.

Chapter 2 of the Constitution, The Bill of Rights (BOR), establishes specific language rights in Sections 9; 29(2); 30 and 35(3) (k) within disciplines to provide practical implementation and the realisation of Section 6. Section 35(3) (k) of the Constitution provides that an accused person has the right to be tried in a language that they understand; and, where impractical to do so, proceedings are to be interpreted accordingly. Given that the right in Section 35(3) (k) is applied within the legal system, the research explores the parameters of this right. The theoretical discussions pertaining to the right in relation to the constitutional and legislative frameworks (Currie & De Waal, 2013) is discussed extensively in Chapters 5 to 8.

A clear disjuncture exists between Section 35(3) (k) and the new language of record policy directive, exacerbated by the monolingual language policies of universities that are graduating English-only LLB graduates. The first step towards addressing the deficient legislative language requirements for legal practitioners would be to ensure that LLB graduates are linguistically competent when they leave universities. In 2017, the Parliamentary Justice and Corrections Oversight Committee chairperson at the time, Mathole Motshekga, made such a proposal, namely that all LLB students pass one of the indigenous languages before being awarded a law degree (Ndenze, 2017:4). This proposal forms an integral part of our discussions; and is discussed in further detail in Chapters 8 and 9.

Cognisance must be taken of the fact that, although the right in Section 35(3) (k) exists squarely in the legal system, the broader rights framework applying to language, both directly and indirectly to the legal system, is of relevance, given the holistic approach of this book and its discussions. The rights framework referred to includes the legal determination of the fairness of decisions taken in implementing the right, as well as where infringements of rights are alleged. This analysis is undertaken with the purpose of determining the sociolinguistic effects on the broader citizenry in a constitutional democracy. Furthermore, it provides insight into the equality-based approach to limiting constitutional rights in the form of the limitations analysis in Section 36 of the Constitution and the language-specific limitations analysis, namely the sliding scale formula (Currie & De Waal, 2005).

As part of limiting language rights, demographics and other relevant sociological data have to be considered; this must, in turn, influence the language of record policy. To this effect, Legal Aid South Africa's Language Survey (2017) revealed that, in civil and criminal cases, English was spoken by a minority of litigants, but the majority were African language speakers. The study found that, across all nine provinces, English language proficiency of litigants in criminal and civil court systems was either poor or merely satisfactory in the categories of understanding, speaking, reading and writing English. Thus, it would probably be impractical for the language of record to be English only; and this would mean that African language litigants would rely solely on interpretation and translation services, with the potential of placing the litigant at a disadvantage in the South African context where interpretation services are unreliable and of a poor quality. Although the following quotation by Gibbons (2003:202) focuses on the non-existence of interpreters in courts, the quote expressly mentions the disadvantage faced by second language speakers when they cannot speak the language of the court:

> A second language speaker who does not speak the language of the court, and who is not provided with interpreting services may receive the same treatment as native speakers, but such a process is clearly unjust, in that s/he can neither understand the proceedings, nor make a case.

In South Africa, Hlophe (2004:46) states that interpreters lack consistency due to their inadequate level of training, resulting in the possible miscarriage of justice. The Section 35(3) (k) right could then be curtailed due to the limited linguistic competencies of legal practitioners and court personnel (Ndlovu, 2002). Given that the legal system is attempting to navigate its way regarding language rights and the determination thereof where infringements are alleged, comparative foreign and international jurisprudence may assist. Section 39 of the Constitution acknowledges the need to consider international law and confer a discretion on courts to consider foreign law when interpreting the rights in the Bill of Rights (BOR). In light of this constitutional position, we engage in a comparative language rights analysis, focusing on the Belgian, Canadian and Indian jurisprudential models. The theoretical framework comprising the comparative analysis is advanced in Chapter Four where scholarly views, such as those of De Vos (2001) and Cowling (2007) are advanced on how and why a comparative approach is necessary. The comparative study brings to the fore innovative means of how language rights are implemented across disciplines and how a fully bilingual legal system is possible.

The comparative approach also illustrates the linguistic challenges with which the legal systems of the respective countries continue to grapple in maintaining a linguistically inclusive legal system. The comparative studies serve as models which can be emulated and where there are lessons on how to implement language rights successfully in a legal system in a multilingual country. Furthermore, in doing so, there is guidance on what needs to be avoided and how one may skilfully subvert challenges that could hinder the successful implementation of such models.

A legislative and policy framework is essential in supporting the constitutional framework as it provides further interpretation of the constitutional provisions and language rights, as well as discipline-specific directives for implementation. Given that the Apartheid legislation concerning language in the legal system was adopted into the democratic dispensation, legislative and policy reform were needed. In response to this call, the Legal Practice Act 28 of 2014 and the Use of Official Languages Act 12 of 2012, hereinafter referred to as The Languages Act (2012), become relevant. According to the preamble of the Legal Practice Act (2014), it is aimed at providing a framework for the transformation of the legal profession in accordance with the constitutional provisions to ensure that the diversity of South Africa's demographics is represented within the legal profession. The Languages Act (2012) provides a framework for the successful implementation of Section 6 of the Constitution across disciplines. This creates an onus on government to adopt certain measures and create structures with the aim of realising the language rights conferred upon South Africans. This legislative framework emphasises the importance of transformation of the legal system and the role of language therein (Pretorius, 2013).

By engaging with the legislative and policy frameworks, we advance and discuss the various types of legislation in accordance with Turi's (1993) categories and Du Plessis's (2012) sociolinguistic analysis thereof. In applying the categories and sociolinguistic analysis, the Higher Education Act 101 of 1997 (HEA) also arises as the legislative framework enabling the drafting of university language policies. This links back to the research area of forensic linguistics/language and law, where legislation is at the centre of regulating language usage in the legal system. In explicating the theoretical discussions underpinning language planning and policy formulation at universities, practical examples of relevant case law are provided in Chapter Seven. These cases include: *AfriForum and Another* v *University of the Free State* (2018); *AfriForum and Another* v *Chairperson of the Council of the University of Pretoria and Others* (2017); and *Gelyke Kanse and Another* v *The President of the Convocation of the Stellenbosch University* (2017). In all instances, the courts reaffirmed the English-only approach, entrenching monolingualism at the expense of bilingualism or multilingualism.

The practical effect and implementation of the right in Section 35(3) (k) in relation to the legislative and policy frameworks, as well as the current language of record policy directive, is analysed with reference to case law. At this point, however, it can be noted that the legislative and policy frameworks fail to acknowledge that African languages can be used as languages of record. Evidence of this is the cases of *State* v *Matomela* (1998) and *State* v *Damoyi* (2004) which were conducted in an African language, giving effect to the accused's Section 35(3) (k) language right. The accused persons in both instances were isiXhosa and isiZulu speakers. The cases illustrate that, where there are linguistically competent legal practitioners and judicial officers, cases can be heard and recorded in an African language where the litigant is a mother tongue speaker.

What is needed is a thorough engagement of the language of record policy directive in relation to monolingual language planning in the legal system and at universities. Such critique and engagement need to take place in accordance with McLean's (1992:153) four ideologies underpinning language planning. In the context of this research the ideology of assimilation is closely linked to internationalisation given that English is an international language. Based on language statistics, it was idealistic and there remains an urgent need for language planning in the legal system to be informed by the ideologies of pluralism and vernacularisation. These two ideologies of pluralism and vernacularisation conform with the language statistics which require citizens to conform to the linguistic diversity of the country and government to commit to the maintenance of these diverse languages (McLean, 1992:153). Emphasis would be placed on centralising the role of African languages in the legal system through practical implementation of discipline-specific policies (Docrat, 2017a:39).

What would be required is a new, inclusive, language planning process for the legal system and universities, where language is seen as a resource and a right rather than a problem (Ruíz, 1984). A fourth tier of language planning, namely opportunity planning (Antia, 2017:166), would be relevant, allowing for marketing and reinforcement of the institution's language policy in addition to coercive legislation which is often ineffective (Antia, 2017:166). Opportunity planning is "understood and offered as a framework that foregrounds implementation in language planning and policy" (Antia, 2017:166). Opportunity planning provides strategies for the implementation of a language policy in a specific domain. In doing so, opportunity planning addresses incentives and directives on implementing such a language policy, including infrastructure and training (Antia, 2017:166).

An inclusive language planning process for both the legal system and universities will ensure a transformed system where engagement with African languages is seen as a tool to enable transformation. Wesson and Du Plessis (2008:2) define transformation as "a change from a state of affairs that existed previously". Wesson and Du Plessis (ibid) provide that transformation will not carry one meaning only but, instead, may be defined according to the various themes in the discipline in which it is being applied. The legislative position regarding language as part of the broader process of transformation must be engaged with, given that language is integral to racial demographics (Lubbe, 2008:4) which the Legal Practice Act (2014) seeks to develop. We argue that transformation of the legal system must include language, alongside race and gender, if a transformative agenda is to emerge following the implementation of the Legal Practice Act (2014) and the Languages Act (2012).

The process of transforming the legal system, guided by the legislative and policy framework, requires the proposal of legal reform, which can be advanced through the constitutional concept of meaningful engagement. Meaningful engagement was conceived in the socioeconomic rights spectrum with specific reference to eviction (Muller, 2011). Meaningful engagement has since been expanded upon and developed in the realm of ensuring successful implementation of language policy by Docrat and Kaschula (2015a:8-9). In the case of *Occupiers of 51 Olivia Road, Berea Township, and 157 Main Street, Johannesburg* v *City of Johannesburg* (2008:212), meaningful engagement was defined by the court as a two-way process in which government and the affected persons are required to find common ground where issues are addressed and solutions found or agreements forged, and outcomes are favourable to all stakeholders. Meaningful engagement should occur in good faith, transparently, with mutual understanding and sympathy and the necessary skill to achieve the objectives (Chenwi & Tissington, 2010:4).

The primary purpose of this book is to offer a critique of the 2017 monolingual language of record policy directive. Moreover, we aim to identify the linguistic challenges plaguing the monolingual English legal system, as these hinder access to justice for litigants who are not mother tongue English speakers. Furthermore, we seek to advance the importance of legislating African language requirements for LLB students, legal practitioners and judicial officers to ensure that a linguistically competent legal profession will enable African languages to be used as languages of record.

The relationship between law and language in South Africa is pivotal in ensuring that constitutional rights, obligations, values and principles are implemented across society through the assistance of the legal system. What has recently emerged from litigation concerning university language policies is the judiciary's endorsement of monolingualism under the guise that English enables access for all to universities and to the legal system. Given that we ourselves are African languages and LLB graduates, we value the importance of graduating linguistically competent law graduates; and we understand the importance of language as facilitating and enhancing access to justice. It was this that motivated us to undertake the research as part of an auto-ethnographic approach. Specifically, our interest is in forensic linguistics and the relationship between law and language, including the role of language policies and legislation in ensuring that the constitutional provisions are realised, and that language rights are conferred equally upon all persons.

In pursuing the primary goal of critiquing the directive for the language of record for courts, the constitutional provisions are analysed to provide the foreground for this research. These constitutional provisions establishing language rights create a false impression, namely that the interpretation and application thereof is unambiguous. The cases with which this research engages will illustrate this point, where the fundamentality of language rights has been questioned. This constitutional framework, in turn, affects the contents of statutes and policies tasked with the implementation and realisation of constitutional rights. With regard to the legislation, the criteria used by the Magistrates Commission (MCom) and the Judicial Service Commission (JSC) in appointing judicial officers, in accordance with Section 174 of the Constitution, will be consulted. Relevant court cases which have been heard and recorded in an African language will be analysed.

This research examines the relationship between the language planning processes of universities and the legal system in giving meaning to the language provisions of Sections 6 and 29(2) of the Constitution. The role which university language policies play in affecting the linguistic competencies of legal practitioners will be assessed and how this impacts the realisation of Section 35(3) (k) of the Constitution and the development and elevation of the status of African languages. Other cases concern the litigation surrounding the constitutionality of the monolingual university language of teaching and learning policies of the Universities of the Free State (UFS), Pretoria (UP) and Stellenbosch (SU).

Research area: forensic linguistics or language and law

This research is interdisciplinary as it critiques the language of record policy for South African courts. Secondary to this critique is investigating the extent to which, through usage and development, African languages are recognised in the South African legal system. More specifically, the research pertains to language policy and planning in the contexts of both the South African legal system and universities. It is thus sociolinguistic in nature, located within the humanities. Sociolinguistics is the study of languages in relation to society (Webb & Kembo-Sure, 2000:84). Sociolinguistics combines sociological and linguistic concepts and techniques to study the role and function of language in society. It is relevant to the discussions at hand, given that one of the goals of this research is to investigate the status and use of African languages in the South African legal system; moreover, how language can play the role of enhancing access to justice for the broader society. These points are discussed in further detail in this chapter, with reference to the goals of the research.

The legal aspect refers to the constitutional and legislative frameworks, as well as case law discussed in forthcoming chapters. In almost all instances, academic texts (as evidenced in the references refer to this interdisciplinary research as law and language, or language and law. What has recently come to the fore, following the dissemination of research across countries, is the emergence of a network of what is termed 'forensic linguists' in the field of forensic linguistics. The use of the term 'forensic linguistics' first emerged in 1968 when Professor of linguistics, Jan Svartvik, recorded its first mention in the context of linguistically analysing a set of legal statements which were made by accused persons and provided to police. Svartvik specifically analysed phrases from the statements such as "I then observed" (Olsson, 2008:5). This became known as 'police register' and continues to be an area of research within forensic linguistics (Olsson, 2008:5).

The question arises as to what forensic linguistics is. Olsson (2008) explains that there are many definitions of forensic linguistics. It is simply the application of linguistics to legal questions and issues. Olsson (2008:3), who looks at the term through an applied linguistics lens, narrows down this broad definition. According to Olsson (2008:3), "…it is the application of linguistic knowledge to a particular social setting, namely the legal forum (from which the word forensic is derived)". The following excerpt by Olsson (2008:3) provides an in-depth understanding of forensic linguistics:

> In its broadest sense we may say that forensic linguistics is the interface between languages, crime, law, where law includes law enforcement, judicial matters, legislation, disputes or proceedings in law, and even disputes which only potentially involve some infraction of the law or some necessity to seek legal remedy.

Grant (2017) provided a brief, all-inclusive definition which, to an extent, summarises the definition by Olsson (2008), explaining that forensic linguistics is an attempt to improve the delivery of justice. It furthermore involves linguistic analysis of legal texts, contexts and processes. In applying the definitions to the nature of the research at hand, it is clear that this research can be positioned within the forensic linguistics context, where the role of language is assessed in legislation, policies and case law.

As evidenced by the numerous publications on the matter (e.g., Coulthard & Johnson, 2007; Gibbons, 2003), forensic linguistics is a developed research area in Europe and Australasia. Forensic linguists are called as expert witnesses in court cases to provide linguistic analysis of legal documents or the parameters of language rights when these are being infringed upon (Grant, 2017). According to Olsson (2004:4), there are eight disciplines of forensic linguistics, namely:

1. Authorship identification/mode identification
2. Legal interpreting and translation
3. Transcribing verbal statements
4. The language and discourse of court rooms
5. Language rights
6. Statement analysis
7. Forensic phonetics
8. Textual status

These eight disciplines are not static in nature; and, with the constant evolving nature of forensic linguistics, further disciplines may well be developed. At this stage of the research, disciplines 4 and 5 are classified as the study of 'language and law', a term which has now been used interchangeably with forensic linguistics, particularly in Southern Africa where it is a relatively new research field.

To date in South Africa, there has been a focus on interpretation and translation in courts. This research is subsumed under language and law, given that it focuses on the language of record and language policies of universities, as well as legislation that influence the language of record policy. Discipline 4 comprises a study of the relationship between courtroom participants and the language they use — issues of power, prejudice, culture clashes, and so forth. In addition, discipline 5 includes these: the language rights of minority groups in cultures dominated by other languages, or dialects of the same language; the linguistic rights of those without language; and the oppressiveness of bureaucratic language. In applying discipline 4, it will be evident from the discussions in the chapters of this book that language, class and power are evident in South African courtrooms. The current issues are threefold: firstly, the current language of record decision elevates English to a super official status; secondly, the language of record is unfair from the point of view of litigants being disadvantaged, given that the language of record is English only; and thirdly, the research involves creating a transformative legal system in which language is not a barrier to accessing justice. The centrality of this research in the area of forensic linguistics will become more apparent as the discussions are advanced.

Study area

With regard to the legal system, the study area comprises both lower and higher courts. We specifically refer to 'higher' and 'lower' courts, given that South African courts are structured hierarchically in accordance with Chapter 8 of the Constitution, specifically Section 165 to Section 180 and the various statutes governing each court structure. Section 8(1) prescribes that the courts are bound by the rights in Chapter 2 of the Constitution, namely the BOR. The courts are obliged by subsection (3) to give effect to these rights (Theophilopoulos,

Van Heerden & Boraine, 2012:8). Section 165 provides the hierarchical structure of the courts: The Constitutional Court (CC); the Supreme Court of Appeal (SCA); High Courts, including all High Courts of appeal, which may be established through an Act of Parliament hearing appeals from High Courts; Magistrates' Courts; and any other court which may be established through an Act of Parliament, resembling the status of a Magistrates' Court or a High Court.

The language of record policy directive applies to High Courts only; however, due to the hierarchical structure of the courts in South Africa and the appeal and review processes, the lower courts are directly affected. The issue is therefore threefold. Firstly, being the lower courts, the Magistrates' Courts will in effect be obliged to hear cases in English for the purposes of review and appeal in the High Courts where the language of record is English. Furthermore, the Magistrates' Courts are bound by the judgments of the High Courts through the doctrine of *stare decisis*, commonly referred to as 'the doctrine of precedent'. The doctrine of precedent is applicable to the courts' structure, where the lower courts are bound by decisions of higher courts on similar matters and thus where a precedent has been set. Furthermore, the doctrine of precedent can be understood in terms of the appeal and review processes where a higher court, hearing the case previously heard in a court *a quo* (lower court), sets aside a judgment and order of the lower court. The doctrine of precedent will become more apparent in Chapter Seven where case law is advanced and critically discussed.

The third reason relates to legal practitioners. The legal profession and hierarchal courts are structured similarly. The judiciary comprises judges and magistrates who are assigned to the various courts to hear cases. The governance of the judiciary is in terms of the Judicial Service Commission Act 9 of 1994 and the Magistrates' Court Act 32 of 1944. In addition, given the independence of the judiciary from the legislative and executive branches of government, in accordance with the doctrine of Separation of Powers (SOP), the judiciary is subject only to the Constitution and the Rule of Law (ROL) (Currie & De Waal, 2013:18). They are expected to execute their duties without fear, favour or prejudice, ensuring that the rights in the BOR, including language rights, are realised.

Apart from the judiciary, there is a divide between private and state for both the attorney and advocate professions. The state hierarchical structure comprises prosecutors in both the Magistrates' Courts and state advocates for the High Courts. The National Prosecuting Authority (NPA), in terms of Section 179 of the Constitution, regulates the state attorneys and advocates. Non-state Attorneys are affiliated to the Side Bar, while non-state advocates who are specialist litigators are affiliated to the Bar. Attorneys and advocates are affiliated to one of four law societies and bar councils, depending on their geographical position. The law societies and bar councils' rules are advanced and critiqued with specific reference to language in forthcoming chapters of this book. Furthermore, a point of discussion which emerges in Chapters 5 and 6 is the geographical argument, where the language demographics per province are advanced and discussed in relation to the geographical position of practising attorneys and advocates.

Selected universities will be utilised as case studies, namely the Universities of Cape Town (UCT), KwaZulu-Natal (UKZN), Rhodes University (RU), and the University of South Africa (UNISA), as well as UFS, UP, SU. These universities have been selected, given the recent language policy developments at each institution. UFS has enacted an English-only policy, which was found to be constitutionally sound by the CC. Similarly, UP opted to adopt an English-only language policy after previously having a bilingual language policy. The trend of moving from a bilingual to a monolingual language policy was also opted for at SU, with judicial approval of a monolingual language policy. UCT is included as an example of a liberal English institution of higher learning, where the demographics of the university are assessed in relation to the language policy of the university, in accordance with UCT's transformational mandate. Both RU and the UKZN serve as examples where African languages, namely isiXhosa and isiZulu, are taught as vocation-specific courses to law students; and to identify issues concerning vocational-specific courses and their effects on the linguistic competencies of law students.

In essence, the legal system has moved from a bilingual language of record policy to a monolingual English-only policy in the name of transformation, ironically. This complexity is explored further in Chapter 2 of this book. The monolingual English only policy, in effect, is supported by the removal of all language requirements for attorneys and advocates and the non-inclusion of African language requirements in both the Constitution and amended statutes regulating the admission of legal practitioners to the Side Bar and Bar. The situation is exacerbated by the adoption of English-only language policies for universities. What is needed is a legal system that is linguistically competent to render justice in the languages spoken by most people in South Africa. This, in turn, requires universities to graduate linguistically competent law graduates. A legislative and policy framework, premised on the need for a multilingual and inclusive legal system, is needed.

Research problem

The research problem that this book will address concerns the monolingual language of record policy for South African courts. The language of record is "… the language(s) used in an official capacity in court proceedings … and for the delivering of judgments by presiding officers" (Malan, 2009:141); the language of record is discussed further in Chapter 4. As part of critiquing this policy, the legislation and case law are discussed in illustrating the need for universities to graduate linguistically competent legal practitioners, given that the language demographics for each of the nine provinces has a majority of African language mother tongue speakers.

The Attorneys Amendment Act 115 of 1993 and the Admission of Advocates Amendment Act 55 of 1994, both governing the admission of attorneys and advocates to the legal profession, saw the removal of the Afrikaans, English and Latin language requirements at university level. However, no reference is made to the insertion of African language requirements, which is not in line with the constitutional mandate. Section 6 obligates that the African languages, which were marginalised during Apartheid, be advanced through practical and positive measures. Further to this, Section 174 of the Constitution, which regulates the appointment of judicial officers, provides only racial and gender imperatives to the exclusion of language (Moerane, 2003). The situation has been exacerbated by the slew of litigation concerning university language policies. The proposed revised language policies favour English monolingualism over bilingualism and multilingualism, with the judiciary having endorsed a monolingual approach to learning and teaching and where the focus for graduates is on English only.

With no legislative authority conferred on the importance and need for linguistically qualified legal practitioners and judicial officers in a multilingual setting such as that of South Africa, the question then is: What is the authoritative position concerning the use of language in courts? To this end, the legislative and policy frameworks resemble the frameworks governing the admission of legal practitioners. Simply put, the exclusionary legislative position concerning the language(s) of record in South Africa during Apartheid was adopted post-democracy, where the language(s) of record remained English and Afrikaans. The Superior Courts Act 10 of 2013, as well as the Magistrates' Courts Act 32 of 1944 evidence this. In addition, the Uniform Rules of Court (2013), which regulates the proceedings in the higher courts, reiterates the exclusionary position of English and Afrikaans only.

In April 2017, the position concerning the language of record worsened with an announcement in the national *Sunday Times* newspaper (Nombembe, 2017) wherein it was reported that the language of record for High Courts in South Africa would be English only with immediate effect. CJ Mogoeng Mogoeng made the communiqué. An open letter was written in this regard as a response from concerned academics and legal practitioners (Docrat, Kaschula, Lourens, Bailey, De Vries & Ralarala, 2017b). To date, no reply has been received. The reasons cited by the CJ were premised on the need for transformation in and of the legal system. The removal of Afrikaans as a language of record was reported as marking an achievement towards reversing past discrimination. The decision, according to Docrat et al. (2017b), was contrary to the constitutional provisions of Section 6. In addition, it weakens the prospect of ensuring language equality for all languages and speakers thereof. In effect, the result is the elevation of English to a super official language, a position which needs to be guarded against.

Following the critique of the decision, the Judge President (JP) of the Western Cape High Court Division, Hlophe JP, released a directive. The directive applies to the jurisdictional area of the Western Cape High Court division and reaffirms the English-only language of record decision and that it be implemented with immediate effect.

Docrat et al. (2017b) argued that there is no legislative authority conferred upon the CJ in determining the language(s) of record; and, furthermore, that the determination of the language(s) of record is to be undertaken by the Minister of the Department of Justice and Constitutional Development (DOJCD) in consultation with the judiciary, following a public participation, consultative initiative. This is in accordance with the bottom-up approach advocated for by the late Neville Alexander (1992) when drafting language policies. Pretorius (2013), writing on the importance of public participation in the legislative drafting process, holds that the exclusion of meaningful public participation will, in effect, weaken the effectiveness of a statute or policy during the implementation stage.

A further problem contributing the language of record policy is the Language Policy of the DOJCD (2019). The policy was drafted by the Department as was required through the primary legislation of the Use of Official Languages Act, 12 of 2012. Section 9.1 of the policy provides no clarity or directive on the determination or regulation of the language(s) of record. The policy refers to the Rules of Court and the enabling legislation, such as the Magistrates' Courts Act, 32 of 1944 and the Superior Courts Act 10 of 2013.

The most recent legislative development concerning the transformation of the legal system, in alignment with the constitutional vision, is the Legal Practice Act, 28 of 2014 (2014). This Act does not refer to the use of language in courts, nor does the statute provide any legislative directive on the language of record. Furthermore, there is no mention of language requirements for legal practitioners as per the constitutional mandate of Section 6. Based on this, the primary problem at the heart of this book is the exclusionary monolingual language of record policy. The monolingual language of record correlates with the exclusionary legislative framework regulating the admission of legal practitioners to the South African legal system. There is no acknowledgement of the relationship between law and language. What is needed is a thorough investigation of the language of record decision. Moreover, there is a need to discuss the linkage between the need for linguistically-qualified LLB graduates to affect positively a future language of record policy, one that is legally sound and linguistically inclusive.

Goals of the research

This research seeks to advance that the language of record policy directive is unconstitutional and that there is a need for legislating African language requirements for LLB students, legal practitioners and judicial officers in order to change the language of record. This will include critiquing the language of record policy directive against the backdrop of the constitutional provisions and the legislation regulating the admission of attorneys and advocates.

Furthermore, the criteria used by the MCom and the JSC in appointing judicial officers, in accordance with Section 174 of the Constitution, will be consulted. This research will examine the relationship between the language planning processes of universities and the legal system. The nature of the role which university language policies play in determining the linguistic competencies of legal practitioners will be assessed and how this affects the realisation of the constitutional language right in Section 35(3) (k) and the development and elevation of the status of African languages, in accordance with Section 6 of the Constitution. Relevant court cases, which have been heard and recorded in an African language, are analysed. Other cases concern the litigation surrounding the constitutionality of the monolingual university language of teaching and learning policies of UFS, UP and SU. This research will assess the impact that the language of record has on the concept of access to justice. More specifically, the purpose of this research is to pursue the following interrelated goals:

- To critique the language of record decision by the Heads of Courts, and critically engage with the reasoning underpinning this decision; and, in doing so, to determine if there should be a distinction drawn between the language of record and language of justice;
- To examine court cases where African languages have been used in conducting trials in their entirety to illustrate that African languages can be used as languages of record;
- To analyse critically the legislation, amended legislation and policies regulating the admission of attorneys, advocates, magistrates and judicial officers to the Side Bar, Bar and judiciary in light of Sections 6, 9, 29, 35 and 174 of the Constitution;
- To engage critically with the proposal by the Parliamentary Justice and Corrections Oversight Committee in relation to the language policies of the selected universities in the next point;
- To critique the language of learning and teaching of selected universities, namely UFS, UP, UCT, UKZN, SU, RJ and UNISA, to determine whether their language policies promote the development of African languages and produce LLB graduates who are linguistically competent in one or more African language. Furthermore, these policies are relevant to case law where the judiciary has endorsed monolingualism. These universities have been selected for the stated reasons: UKZN has a bilingual model where isiZulu is taught alongside English; UFS, UP and SU offered parallel mediums of instruction; RU and UCT are included as liberal English institutions which are beginning to implement vocation-specific courses; and UNISA is included for reasons pertaining to a bilingually written judgment in which the court found an English only language policy to be in violation of Section 29(2) of the Constitution;

- To advance the linguistic and constitutional implications emanating from the recent judgments concerning the monolingual language policies of the UFS, UP, SU and UNISA (Kaschula & Maseko, 2012);
- To engage in an African and international comparative model, focusing on these multilingual countries: Kenya, Morocco, Nigeria, Australia, Belgium, Canada and India; and
- To propose legal reform to ensure that effective legislation and policies are drafted and successfully implemented.

These goals will be pursued using a methodology comprised of a jurisprudential analysis, as well as a close reading and critique of the legislation, policies, case law, case studies and texts.

Conclusion

This chapter has provided introductory discussions on the nature of the research, the research problem and the goals of the research against a contextualised setting, all of which are discussed in greater depth in the proceeding chapters of this book. The chapter that follows comprises African case studies of Kenya, Nigeria and Morocco to provide a holistic overview of the use of language in courts on the African continent.

THE LANGUAGE OF PROCEEDINGS IN COURTS ON THE AFRICAN CONTINENT

Kenya, Nigeria and Morocco

This chapter comprises a comparative African case study. Kenya, Nigeria and Morocco were selected based on their geographical position in Africa: in the east, west and north, in comparison to South Africa positioned in the south. Beyond the geographical position are the similarities between the legal systems of each country, specifically the history of the legal system of each of the African countries. Each country has a colonial history, so colonial languages were imposed on its indigenous people. This chapter explicates that, post-independence, colonial languages such as English and French were conferred with official status, this at the expense of promoting, developing and using the indigenous languages of each country in high status domains, such as the legal system, where they would serve as languages of record in courts of law.

This chapter foregrounds the forthcoming discussions concerning the use of languages (particularly the official African languages) in South African courts and the legal system more broadly. In relation to Chapter 3, which serves a similar function to this chapter, the African case studies in Chapter 2 are used to highlight the language problems, language rights and language resources on the African continent, with a specific focus on the legal system. This comparison lays bare the fact that, as a discipline, forensic linguistics is yet to be recognised and developed on the African continent. Although there are pockets of academics and legal practitioners working in the discipline, such work exists in a vacuum; but, accumulatively, where language rights of indigenous language litigants are fully protected on paper and implemented in practice through collaborative and other efforts, the development of forensic linguistics could prove to be a recipe for success on the African continent.

International jurisprudence

The United Nations instruments (policies and treaties), where countries are signatories to agreements, guide Chapters 2, 3 and 4. Four international documents are of relevance: The Universal Declaration of Human Rights (1948); the Universal Declaration of Linguistic Rights (1998); the International Covenant on Civil and Political Rights (1996); and the Framework Conventions for the Protection of National Minorities (1995). The international framework must be complied with through national constitutions and legislative means where countries are signatories to these agreements.

The Universal Declaration of Human Rights (1948) is an overarching document that is underpinned by human dignity, equality and social justice. The preamble of the Universal Declaration of Human Rights (1948) reads similar to that of the Constitution of the Republic of South Africa (1996) (the Constitution). It has an aspirational tone to it, however. The prescripts prohibiting unfair discrimination and unfair treatment on grounds, including language, is clearly set out in Article 2.

The International Covenant on Civil and Political Rights (1996) provides further protection for development of language rights. The following provisions from Article 14 are of relevance to our discussions and the overall objectives of this book:

Article 14

(1) All persons shall be equal before the courts and tribunals. In the determination of any criminal charge against him, or of his rights and obligations in a suit at law, everyone shall be entitled to a fair and public hearing by a competent, independent and impartial tribunal established by law. The press and the public may be excluded from all or part of a trial for reasons of morals, public order (*ordre public*) or national security in a democratic society, or when the interest of the private lives of the parties so requires, or to the extent strictly necessary in the opinion of the court in special circumstances where publicity would prejudice the interests of justice; but any judgement rendered in a criminal case or in a suit at law shall be made public except where the interest of juvenile persons otherwise requires or the proceedings concern matrimonial disputes or the guardianship of children.

(2) Everyone charged with a criminal offence shall have the right to be presumed innocent until proved guilty according to law.

(3) In the determination of any criminal charge against him, everyone shall be entitled to the following minimum guarantees, in full equality:

   (a) To be informed promptly and in detail in a language which he understands of the nature and cause of the charge against him;

   (b) To have adequate time and facilities for the preparation of his defence and to communicate with counsel of his own choosing;

   (f) To have the free assistance of an interpreter if he cannot understand or speak the language used in court...

As with the preamble of the Universal Declaration of Human Rights (1948), these provisions of Article 14 of the International Covenant on Civil and Political Rights (1996) are reflected in the South African Constitution. This will be evident in Part One of Chapter 6, where the South African constitutional language provisions are advanced and discussed in their entirety. Suffice it to say at this stage of the discussion that the semblance between Article 14 of the International Covenant on Civil and Political Rights (1996) resonates with Section 35(3) and subsections (f), (g) and (k) and subsection (4) of the South African Constitution. These read as follows:

> (3) Every accused person has a right to a fair trial, which include the right —
>   (f) to choose, and to be represented by, a legal practitioner, and to be informed of this right promptly;
>   (g) to have a legal practitioner assigned to the accused person by the state and at state expense, if substantial injustice would otherwise result, and to be informed of this right promptly;
>   (k) to be tried in a language that the accused person understands or, if that is not practicable, to have the proceedings interpreted in that language;
> (4) Whenever this section requires information to be given to a person, that information must be given in a language that the person understands.

The Framework Convention for the Protection of National Minorities (1995) also protects the rights of linguistic minorities in the legal sphere, ensuring all persons' language rights are protected, regardless of whether they are speakers of a minority or majority spoken language. Article 10 subsection (3) is relevant and reads as follows:

> The Parties undertake to guarantee the right of every person belonging to a national minority to be informed promptly, in a language which he or she understands, of the reasons for his or her arrest, and of the nature and cause of any accusation against him or her, and to defend himself or herself in this language, if necessary with the free assistance of an interpreter.

This point will be of further relevance to the discussion in Part Two of Chapter 6, with reference to the demographics-based arguments relying on South Africa's language statistics as recorded in the National Census (2011).

The Universal Declaration of Human Rights (1948), The International Covenant on Civil and Political Rights (1996) and the Framework Convention for the Protection of National Minorities (1995) all give effective meaning to the Universal Declaration of Linguistic Rights (1998). The Universal Declaration of Linguistic Rights (1998) cements the linguistic rights of citizens of countries who are signatories to the agreement. The Universal Declaration of Linguistic Rights (1998) is a practical, all-inclusive document where signatories thereto are compelled to comply with the provisions. Failure to comply or infringe the provisions can result in a legal challenge being launched beyond the confines of the courts in the country. An example of this is the case of *Lourens* v *Speaker of the National Assembly and Others* (2015) which has now been taken to the United Nations International Human Rights

Committee under the case name of *Lourens v State Party: Republic of South Africa* (2018). The application is currently before the committee and both the Applicant and Respondent have filed heads of argument in the matter. The case is discussed in further detail in Chapter 7. We have, however, specifically referred to it at this stage of the discussion given the relevance of the international documents presently being discussed. Furthermore, the example illustrates that these international documents are relevant to South Africa given that the country is a signatory. Reverting to the applicability of the Universal Declaration of Linguistic Rights (1998), Article 20 subsections 1 and 2 are relevant and read as follows:

> Article 20
> (1) Everyone has the right to use the language historically spoken in a territory, both orally and in writing, in the Courts of Justice located within that territory. The Courts of Justice must use the language proper to the territory in their internal actions and, if on account of the legal system in force within the state, the proceedings continue elsewhere, the use of the original language must be maintained.
> (2) Everyone has the right, in all cases, to be tried in a language which he/she understands and can speak and to obtain the services of an interpreter free of charge.

Once again, the similarities between the provisions of the Universal Declaration of Human Rights (1948) and the South African Constitution are identifiable when taking account of Section 35(3) (f), (g), (k) and subsection (4) of the Constitution, as explicated earlier. On this note, it can be said that the international jurisprudential model is applicable to South Africa and the broader discussions in this book concerning the legal status of languages in courts.

What follows is a presentation and critical discussion of Kenya as a jurisprudential case study, followed by Nigeria and Morocco. The language of record and language in the legal system more broadly is discussed in relation to South Africa with reference to each country's constitutional and legislative frameworks, as well as the relevant case law.

Kenya's sociolinguistic landscape

As a signatory to the United Nations articles cited and discussed earlier, Kenya is obliged, at a political and moral level, to comply with the articles and to enforce them for enhanced democratic citizenship (Ogechi, 2003:277). Depending on the scholar's perspective, Kenya's linguistic landscape can be seen as complex or richly diverse, given that 42 languages are spoken there (Ogechi, 2003:279). There is a divide between the exoglossic and endoglossic languages. A further distinction is made between a national language and an official language. In Kenya, English is the official exoglossic language used in government for international business purposes and diplomacy, amongst other high status domains (Ogechi, 2003:279). The endoglossic language used as a national language in Kenya is Kiswahili (Ogechi, 2003:279). Kiswahili is also used for government purposes but not to the extent of English. Kiswahili is used more for casual governmental interactions and inter-ethnic communication. The remaining Kenyan languages are used in subordinated domains for intra-ethnic communication in homes and rural areas (Ogechi, 2003:279).

Ogechi (2003:279) explains that a large disparity exists between the languages. This disparity relates to the number of speakers per given language in Kenya. According to Ogechi (2003:279), there are languages such as Gikuya which have approximately 5.3 million mother tongue speakers, while languages such as Elmolo have a minimal number of mother tongue speakers. Ogechi (2003:279) refers to the 2003 UNESCO report on endangered languages which recorded that 16 Kenyan languages are threatened with extinction or death. Elaborating on the point of possible extinction or death, Ogechi (2003:279) claims that the languages in Kenya are not equal in status, given that there are majority and minority spoken languages. The number of speakers of a given language in Kenya appears to affect their status, which is conferred upon the language in terms of importance (and by importance, we mean the use of the language in high status domains).

Having said this, it is concerning to see that, in a multilingual country with approximately 42 languages, English triumphs as the official language for all government purposes and in high status domains. The unequal treatment of the Kenyan indigenous languages results in the hegemonic rise of English. English, as a single medium, supposedly has the potential of unifying the country though one common language – it is also an international language. On this basis, the state is able to convince the citizenry that the use of English in high status domains will result in the creation of employment opportunities and access to the market. This point relates to the work of Grin (2010) who shows that language is linked to the economy. The latter point is expanded upon in Chapters 8 and 9.

According to Ogechi (2003:279-281), the described language situation in Kenya provides the rationale for a need to argue for a case of language rights to be recognised and enforced for speakers of the various languages; and that these rights form part of their human rights.

The language rights situation is more complicated than conferring language rights on persons and enforcing them. The reason is that there is no violation of a language right where the concentration of a homogeneous speech community is sparse and the state chooses to use a language of wider communication, such as English (Ogechi, 2003:281). Kenya has chosen English as the language of wider communication, a language that has been imposed upon the people of Kenya since the British occupation. Following independence from Britain, the dominance of English rose and strengthened over time at the expense of the indigenous languages. The patterns of Kenya's history are similar to those of South Africa, as will be evidenced in Chapter 4.

The discussions that follow concerning Kenya highlight the constitutional and legislative developments entrenching the dominance of English. The discussion is somewhat focused on the constitutional and legislative developments concerning the legal system.

Kenya's constitutional and legislative frameworks

The constitutional and legislative frameworks of each country provide the blueprint on which language rights are protected. The Constitution of Kenya (2010) contains language provisions conferring language rights on Kenyan citizens. Section 7 is the linguistic blueprint of Kenya, conferring official status on languages. It reads as follows:

(1) The national language of the Republic is Kiswahili.
(2) The official languages of the Republic are Kiswahili and English.
(3) The State shall –
   (a) promote and protect the diversity of language of the people of Kenya; and
   (b) promote the development and use of indigenous languages, Kenyan Sign language, Braille and other communication formats and technologies accessible to persons with disabilities.

There is a distinct difference sought between the official and national languages, where Kiswahili is both the national and official language of Kenya. As with the South African Constitution, specifically Section 6, Section 7 of Kenya's Constitution (2010) is aspirational in nature and does create language rights. A critique of the South African constitutional provisions is advanced in Part One of Chapter 6. However, at this stage of the discussions, it can be noted that Section 6(1) accords all 11 languages official status, while Section 6(2) further elevates the nine indigenous African languages.

Section 7 of the Constitution of Kenya, on the other hand, does the complete opposite by conferring official status on only Kiswahili and English, even though Kenya has 42 spoken languages. Other than Kiswahili, the other indigenous languages are relegated to subsection 3(b) which speaks only to promoting the development and use of the indigenous languages. Although this may appear as a positive step towards inclusivity, it is by no means equality of status and use alongside the official languages. According to Lourens (2012) and the discussion by Docrat (2017b), when conferring official status on a language, the language, in turn, has to be used in high status domains and by government through all their formal communication channels. This point is discussed further as a point of contention regarding the theoretical South African constitutional provisions and what is happening in practice, as per Chapter 6, Parts One and Two.

A further point worth noting is the actual language used in Section 7 of the Constitution of Kenya (2010), specifically subsection (3), where the word "shall" is used. The term is discretionary and does not convey an obligation on the state; rather, the state has the discretion to do so. This further weakens the development and use of the indigenous languages. The word "shall" calls into question the intention of the drafters of the Constitution of Kenya (2010) and whether this discretionary term is inserted purposefully to ensure the dominance of a colonial language, English, at the expense of the indigenous languages.

As with Section 9 of the South African Constitution, Section 27 of the Constitution of Kenya (2010) includes provisions on the prohibition of direct and indirect discrimination against persons on various grounds, including language. Language, culture and the rights of linguistic communities are also protected by Section 44 of the Constitution of Kenya (2010), similar to Sections 30 and 31 of the South African Constitution.

The provisions in the Constitution of Kenya (2010) which are relevant to this book are Sections 49 and 50:

49. Rights of arrested persons
(1) An arrested person has the right –
   (a) to be informed promptly, in a language that the person understands, of –
      (i) the reason for the arrest;
      (ii) the right to remain silent; and
      (iii) the consequences of not remaining silent;

50. Fair hearing
(1) Every person has the right to have any dispute that can be resolved by the application of law decided in a fair and public hearing before a court or, if appropriate, another independent and impartial tribunal or body.
(2) Every accused person has the right to a fair trial, which includes the right –
   (a) to be presumed innocent until the contrary is proved;
   (b) to be informed of the charge, with sufficient detail to answer it;
   (c) to have adequate time and facilities to prepare a defence;
   (d) to a public trial before a court established under this Constitution;
   (e) to have the trial begin and conclude without unreasonable delay;
   (f) to be present when being tried, unless the conduct of the accused person makes it impossible for the trial to proceed;
   (g) to choose, and be represented by, an advocate, and to be informed of this right promptly;
   (h) to have an advocate assigned to the accused person by the State and at State expense, if substantial injustice would otherwise result, and to be informed of this right promptly;
   (i) to remain silent, and not to testify during the proceedings;
   (j) to be informed in advance of the evidence the prosecution intends to rely on, and to have reasonable access to that evidence;
   (k) to adduce and challenge evidence;
   (l) to refuse to give self-incriminating evidence;
   (m) to have the assistance of an interpreter without payment if the accused person cannot understand the language used at the trial.
(3) If this Article requires information to be given to a person, the information shall be given in a language that the person understands.

The quoted Articles 49 and 50 of the Constitution of Kenya (2010) comply with the international framework discussed in the preceding section of this chapter. In both articles, the use of language is made explicit where accused persons have the right to receive information in a language they understand. This is similar to the provisions of Section 35 of the South African Constitution, advanced and critiqued in Part One of Chapter 6. Suffice it to say at this point, the similarities are evident, where Article 40(1) (a) of the Constitution of Kenya (2010) refers to a language which the accused person understands, as does Section 35(3) (k) of the South African Constitution.

Article 50 provides no definition or further built-in test to determine what language the accused understands. This point must be stressed – as we discuss in Chapter 4 and Part One of Chapter 6 – there have been instances in which accused persons have had a basic understanding of English, the language of record, but their mother tongue is an African language. In these instances, the courts proceeded to communicate in English with the accused, regardless of their limited understanding of English. The case of *Mthethwa* v *De Bruin* (1998) is an example of this occurrence. Simply put, where no yardstick or a test exists, the discretion in determining whether the accused understands a language lies with the judicial officer, who simply asks the accused if he or she understands English.

The statistics that we present in the chapters concerning South Africa illustrate that there are varying degrees of understanding, reading, writing and speaking a language. The statistics also illustrate that legal practitioners acknowledge the need to communicate in their clients' mother tongue, however, their language competencies often do not enable this communication (De Vries, 2018). It has been noted that communication in English is easier for legal practitioners and saves time and money (De Vries & Docrat, 2019). This point can be linked to the role of forensic linguists in assisting the legal system in formulating a test to determine the linguistic competencies of accused persons or, as experts, to provide further meaning to the language rights provisions of litigants.

As we have explained in Chapter 5 with reference to the work of Botha (2004), Burger (2015), Du Plessis (2012) and Turi (1993, 2012), amongst others, legislation provides practical meaning to constitutional provisions. In the case of Kenya, three statutes are relevant to the discussions at hand: the Criminal Procedure Act 27 of 2008, the Criminal Procedure Code (2012) and the Judicature Act 16 of 1967 (1967). Chapter 20 of the Criminal Procedure Act is relevant to the book at hand. The following provisions serve the argument:

Part II Procedure Relating to Criminal Investigations

A. -Arrest, Escape and Recapture, Search Warrants and Seizure

(3) Any police officer making an investigation may, subject to the other provisions of this Part, examine orally any person supposed to be acquainted with the facts and circumstances of the case and shall reduce into writing any statement made by the person so examined. The whole of the statement, including any question in clarification asked by the police officer and the answer to it, shall be recorded in full in Kiswahili or in English or in any other language in which the person is examined, and the record shall be shown or read over to him or if he does not understand the language in which it is written it shall be interpreted to him in a language he understands and he shall be at liberty to explain or add to his statement. He shall then sign that statement immediately below the last line of the record of that statement and may call upon any person in attendance to sign as a witness to his signature. The police officer recording the statement shall append below each statement recorded by him the following certificate:

"I ...., hereby declare that I have faithfully and accurately recorded the statement of the above-named ....".

23.

(1) A person who arrests another person shall, at the time of the arrest, inform that other person of the offence for which he is arrested.

(2) A person who arrests another person shall be taken to have complied with subsection (1) if he informs the other person of the substance of the offence for which he is arrested; and it is not necessary for him to do so in a language of a precise or technical nature.

53. Where a person is under restraint, a police officer shall not ask him any questions, or ask him to do anything, for a purpose connected with the investigation of an offence, unless –

(b) the person has been informed by a police officer, in a language in which he is fluent, in writing and, if practicable, orally, of the fact that he is under restraint and of the offence in respect of which he is under restraint;

(c) the person has been cautioned by a police officer in the following manner, namely, by informing him, or causing him to be informed, in a language in which he is fluent, in writing in accordance with the prescribed form and, if practicable, orally –

(i) that he is not obliged to answer any question asked of him by a police officer, other than a question seeking particulars of his name and address; and

(ii) that, subject to this Act, he may communicate with a lawyer, relative or friend.

135. The following provisions of this section shall apply to all charges and information and, notwithstanding any rule of law or practice, a charge or an information shall, subject to the provisions of this Act, not be open to objection in respect of its form or contents if it is framed in accordance with the provisions of this section –

(ii) the statement of offence shall describe the offence shortly in ordinary language avoiding as far as possible the use of technical terms and without necessarily stating all the essential elements of the offence and, if the offence charged is one created by enactment, shall contain a reference to the section of the enactment creating the offence;

(iii) after the statement of the offence, particulars of such offence shall be set out in ordinary language, in which the use of technical terms shall not be necessary, save that where any rule of law limits the particulars of an offence which are required to be given in a charge or an information, nothing in this paragraph shall require any more particulars to be given than those so required...

(c) (i) the description of property in a charge or any information shall be in ordinary language and such as to indicate with reasonable clarity the property referred to, and, if the property is so described, it shall not be necessary (except when required for the purpose of describing an offence depending on any special ownership of property or special value of property) to name the person to whom the property belongs or the value of the property...

(f) subject to any other provision of this section, it shall be to describe any place, time, thing, matter, act or omission of any kind to which it is necessary to refer in any charge or information in ordinary language in such manner as to indicate with reasonable clarity the place, time, thing, matter, act or omission referred to...

C-Accelerated Trial and Disposal of Cases

192. -(3) At the conclusion of a preliminary hearing held under this section, the court shall prepare a memorandum of the matters agreed and the memorandum shall be read over and explained to the accused in a language that he understands, signed by the accused and his advocate (if any) and by the public prosecutor, and then filed.

C-Taking and Recording of Evidence

210. -(1) In trials, other than trials under section 213, by or before a magistrate, the evidence of the witnesses shall be recorded in the following manner –

(a) the evidence of each witness shall be taken down in writing in the language of the court by the Magistrate or in his presence and hearing and under his personal direction and superintendence and shall be signed by him and shall form part of the record...

211. (1) Whenever any evidence is given in a language not understood by the accused and he is present in person, it shall be interpreted to him in open court in a language understood by him.

(2) If he is represented by an advocate and the evidence is given in a language other than the language of the court, and not understood by the advocate, it shall be interpreted to such advocate in the language of the court.

237. Without prejudice to the generality of section 236, a subordinate court presided over by a resident Magistrate may, subject to the provisions of this section, for the purpose of assessing the proper sentence to be passed, take into consideration any other offence committed by the accused –

(a) if it has been explained by the court to the accused person in ordinary language that the sentence to be passed upon him for the offence of which he has been convicted in those proceedings may be greater if the other offence is taken into consideration;

312.-(1) Every judgment under the provisions of section 311 shall, except as otherwise expressly provided by this Act, be written by or reduced to writing under the personal direction and superintendence of the presiding Judge or Magistrate in the language of the court and shall contain the point or points for determination, the decision thereon and the reasons for the decision, and shall be dated and signed by the presiding officer as of the date on which it is pronounced in open court.

313. -(1) On the application of the accused person a copy of the judgment or, when he so desires, a translation in his own language, if practicable, shall be given to him without delay and free of cost.

321.-(1) Without prejudice to the generality of section 320 the High Court may subject to the provisions of this section, for the purpose of assessing the proper sentence to be passed, take into consideration any other offence committed by the accused person but of which he has not been convicted.
(2) The High Court shall not take any offence into consideration unless –
(a) it has been explained by the court to the accused person in ordinary language that the sentence to be passed upon him for the offence of which he has been convicted in those proceedings may be greater if the other offence is taken into consideration.

Prior to engaging with these quoted provisions of the Criminal Procedure Act, we advance the provisions of the Criminal Procedure Code. The provisions of the Criminal Procedure Code overlap to a certain degree with the above quoted provisions, and it is thus logical for purposes of discussion to advance and discuss these provisions simultaneously. The relevant provisions read as follows:

137E. Form of plea agreement
A plea agreement shall be in writing, and shall –
(a) be reviewed and accepted by the accused person, or explained to the accused person in a language that he understands;
(b) f the accused person has negotiated with the prosecutor through an interpreter, contain a certificate by the interpreter to the effect that the interpreter is proficient in that language and that he interpreted accurately during the negotiations and in respect of the contents of the agreement...

197. Manner of recording evidence before magistrate
(1) In trials by or before a magistrate, the evidence of the witnesses shall be recorded in the following manner –
(a) the evidence of each witness shall be taken down in writing or on a typewriter in the language of the court by the magistrate, or in his presence and hearing and under his personal direction and superintendence, and shall be signed by the magistrate, and shall form part of the record...

198. Interpretation of evidence to accused or his advocate
(1) Whenever any evidence is given in a language not understood by the accused, and he is present in person, it shall be interpreted to him in open court in a language which he understands.

(2) If he appears by advocate and the evidence is given in a language other than English and not understood by the advocate, it shall be interpreted to the advocate in English.
(3) When documents are put in for the purpose of formal proof, it shall be in the discretion of the court to interpret as much thereof as appears necessary.
(4) The language of the High Court shall be English, and the language of a subordinate court shall be English or Swahili.

Chapter 20 of the Criminal Procedure Act cited above includes extensive provisions on the use of language in Kenyan courts. There are several provisions providing for the use of plain language to be used during interaction with an accused person, in order for the latter to understand the charges and the terms of the plea agreement that they may enter into. The provisions are Sections 23, 135, 192, 237 and 321(2). This is important in the context of a multilingual country with 42 languages, where only English is the language of record in High Courts and English and Kiswahili in lower courts. Simply put, besides accused persons being disadvantaged by the language of record where they are not proficient in one of, or neither, English or Kiswahili, the problem is complicated further by the use of legalese and the technicality of the legal language of the legal systems.

From the onset of the legal process, emphasis is placed on ensuring an accused is provided with all relevant information in a language they understand. Section 53 of Chapter 20 of the Criminal Procedure Act (quoted earlier) holds that a police officer must inform the accused of the reason for their restraint in a language in which the accused is fluent. Section 53 (b) extends the meaning of "fluent" to include written and, "if practicable", oral communication. It is significant that 'fluency' is included, as opposed to the South African constitutional provisions which refer to a language which the accused 'understands'.

Section 53 furthermore includes written and oral fluency. The provision gives further meaning to the provisions in the Constitution of Kenya (2010). The role of the police is outlined further in Section 3, Chapter 20 of the Criminal Procedure Act (2008) where police statements are concerned. A statement can be provided in Kiswahili, English or any other language. The statement must then be read back to the accused, if it has been recorded in a language the accused does not understand, it is to be interpreted into a language the accused understands. Once again, these provisions are more extensive than the provisions in the Draft Language Policy of the South African Police Service (2015), discussed in full in Part Two of Chapter 6. Section 3 of Chapter 20, however progressive, does rely largely on interpretation and translation. There is no indication that interpreters and translators are employed to undertake this service; and, given that a statement is read back to the accused immediately after it has been written, a conclusion can be drawn that the police officer is actually acting as an interpreter and translator. The police officer would need to be proficient in the specific language and thus be linguistically competent and, presumably, bilingual. Theoretically, Section 3 provides an entirely new meaning to multilingualism in the workplace and the importance of language in high status domains where the implementation of peoples' language rights is at stake.

Progressing to the next stage in the course of a criminal case, if a plea agreement is entered into by the accused and recorded in writing, Section 137E (a) of the Criminal Procedure Act of Kenya provides that the contents of the plea agreement be explained to an accused in a language he understands. As opposed to Section 3 of the Kenyan Criminal Procedure Act, subsection (b) ensures the reliability of the interpretation. Simply put, subsection (b) provides that, if the plea is negotiated through an interpreter, the interpreter to the state must provide a certificate that he or she is proficient in that language and that the interpretation was accurate.

Both the Kenyan Criminal Procedure Act and Code include provisions on the use of language in the trial. Section 210(1) (a) of the Criminal Procedure Act and Section 197 of the Criminal Procedure Code mirror each other in stating that a Magistrate is to record the evidence of witnesses in the language of the court, as seen in the provisions quoted in full earlier. Once again, translation is in effect where a witness imparts evidence in a language other than the language of the court.

Further mirroring of provisions is evidenced from the sections quoted earlier, including Section 211(1) and (2) of the Criminal Procedure Act and Section 198 (1) and (2) of the Criminal Procedure Code. All these provisions call for evidence to be interpreted for the accused should the accused be present and not understand the language in which witnesses are giving evidence. Section 198 of the Kenyan Criminal Procedure Act, as opposed to the provisions in the South African constitutional and legislative frameworks (discussed in Chapter 5 and Part One of Chapter 6), makes specific reference to evidence being interpreted for the accused's advocate as well where necessary. The progressiveness of this provision is, however, limited by the fact that the threshold is English. The evidence will be interpreted for the advocate in English; thus, the advocate is to be fully conversant in English. The entire legal system is therefore premised on understanding English. This is reinforced by Section 198(4) of the Criminal Procedure Code that explicitly states that English is the language of the High Court and English or Kiswahili of subordinate courts. As is evidenced in Chapter 4, the language of record in South African courts is guided by policy and directive means and not through legislation.

In concluding the discussion on the legislative frameworks concerning language in Kenyan courts, it can be said that language is central in the process and the importance of the accused understanding proceedings is not hindered by language. Sentencing procedure is to be explained to an accused in a language he understands. Access to justice in Kenya is explicated further through the remaining provisions, quoted in full above. The judgment must be recorded by the judicial officer in the language of the court. Upon application by the accused, the judgment must be translated, free of cost and without delay, into the accused's own language, as per Section 313(1) of the Criminal Procedure Act. This is not provided for in South Africa. A similarity can be drawn with Canada and the language in which the judgment is provided. This will be more evident in Chapter 3 of this book.

Kenya's language of record and language usage in courts

Apart from the literature that we have referred to pertaining to Kenya's sociolinguistic landscape, Odhiambo, Kavulani and Matu (2013) have written extensively on language usage in Kenyan courts in a multilingual setting. The work of Odhaimbo, Kavulani and Matu (2013) offers further insight into the language situation in Kenyan courts with reference to the legislation quoted and discussed earlier. Regarding the language of record, it is noted that, as per the legislative provisions advanced above, English is the language of record in Kenyan High Courts, while English and Kiswahili are the languages of record in the lower courts. Odhaimbo, et al. (2013:911) state that, in lower courts, the use of Kiswahili as a language of record is not guaranteed, as is the case with English, as this is dependent on the linguistic competence of judicial officers. The courts assume a monolingual position, with English as the language of the courtroom (Odhaimbo et al., 2013:911). Monolingualism in Kenyan courts is reinforced by the fact that all training of advocates, magistrates and prosecutors takes place in English (Odhaimbo et al., 2013:911). This point must be borne in mind in Chapters 8 and 9 where we discuss the South African legislative position and the 2019 decision by the Legal Practice Council to make English the sole medium for communication and official purposes. Furthermore, it is important to bear this point in mind with reference to the university language polices and the LLB degree.

Litigants who do not speak English are thus placed at a disadvantage in Kenyan courts where they are reliant solely on an interpreter. The same applies to judicial officers. Odhaimbo et al. (2013:911) explain the difficulty faced by non-English speaking litigants: on the one hand, litigants face a foreign system which is intimidating and where they have limited or no knowledge of the legal system and its procedure or legal language; on the other hand, litigants do not understand English – and this applies to the majority of people in Kenya (Odhaimbo et al., 2013:911). The research conducted by Odhaimbo et al. (2013:915) saw an entire province in Kenya in courtroom discourse when litigants in that province said they preferred to use their regional mother tongue, Dhaluo. When participating through the medium of English, they cannot fully participate in their own trials; it also adversely affects complainants where language barriers are in place (Odhaimbo et al., 2013:911).

With the focus thus on interpretation in Kenyan courts, the linguistic competency and accuracy of interpretation comes to the fore. Interpreters need to be both bilingual and familiar with the legal terminology in use. Furthermore, where equivalents are not in existence in the language into which communication is being interpreted, the interpreter is to explain this (Odhaimbo et al., 2013:911). Odhaimbo et al. (2013:913) reported in their study that 80% of interpreters confirmed they had not been trained; 10% did not answer the question; and the remaining 10% who said they were trained indicated this was not court interpreter training but rather sign language training. Interpreters shed further light on the language dichotomy that exists between legal professionals, where interpreters explained that they communicated in English with judicial officers and advocates and in Kiswahili with the prosecutors (Odhaimbo et al., 2013:917).

What follows is a discussion concerning the second comparative country, namely Nigeria.

Nigeria's sociolinguistic landscape

Like South Africa and Kenya, Nigeria is a multilingual country. The history of English language usage in Nigeria dates back to the British colonial period. Nigeria became a British colony in the eighteenth century. It was initially the colony of Lagos, where the northern and southern protectorate became an entity called Nigeria (Olanrewaju, 2009:105). According to Olanrewaju (2009:154), Nigeria is a heterogeneous society in which multilingualism thrives. Geographically, Nigeria is divided into three major areas: north, west and east. Each division comprises majority spoken languages. In the north, it is Hausa; in the west, it is Yoruba; while in the east – Igbo (Olanrewaju, 2009:154). These three languages are spoken by most people. There are, however, a further 400 indigenous languages spoken in Nigeria. The indigenous languages are spoken among communities and linguistic cultural groups, but English remains the language used in high status domains such as the legal system.

The rise of English through Nigerian constitutional and legislative means

With English being the language of the coloniser, it was used historically as a language in high status domains. A number of constitutions marked the dominance of the colonial authority. In 1922, the Clifford Constitution followed the Constitution of the Colony and Protectorate of Nigeria in 1914 (Abioye, 2011:167). A further three constitutions were enacted prior to independence. The Macpherson Constitution of 1951 followed the Richards Constitution (Abioye, 2011:167). In 1954, the Federation was formed on the basis of the Lytleton Constitution. The 1957 and 1958 constitutional conferences resulted in the passing of the Independence Act of 1960 (Olanrewaju, 2009:154). The 1979 Constitution of the Federal Republic of Nigeria (1979) specifically Chapter V, Part B, Section 51, confers official status on three indigenous Nigerian languages, as well as English, namely Hausa, Igbo and Yoruba (Olanrewaju, 2009:155). Noteworthy is the inclusion of English as an official language post-independence. As indicated previously, English trumps the three African official languages in Nigeria in high status domains, bringing to the fore the disjuncture between theory and practice. Where, theoretically, African languages are conferred with official status, practical implementation of the statutes favours an English-only policy. In the next section, we advance the function of the courts and their geographical position in relation to the language demographics, as well as what the legal legislative framework includes on the use of language in courts.

The hierarchical legal system: Nigerian courts

Regarding the preceding discussion on Kenya, there was an evident divide between higher and lower courts where language was concerned. The High Courts used English as the sole official language of record while the lower courts use English and Kiswahili as languages of record, but in reality, English is also the only language of record in lower courts. The hierarchical structure of the courts in Nigeria is divided further by the fact that there are two parallel legal systems: a western and an Islamic system. This is similar to South Africa where a customary legal system exists. Olanrewaju (2009) provides an overview of the courts, explaining how courts are graded hierarchically according to the seriousness of the cases heard; and this is how jurisdiction is determined. Drawing on the text of Olanrewaju (2009:106), we have organised it in Figure 2.1 with brief explanations of each court's function.

The SC, being the highest court, has the mandate and jurisdiction to settle disputes between the federal and state government or between states. The SC's jurisdiction stretches further to appeals on matters concerning questions of law, the interpretation of constitutional provisions, as well as any breach of fundamental human rights, and cases concerning the death penalty emerging from the CA (Olanrewaju, 2009:106). The function and jurisdiction of the SC in Nigeria resembles that of the Constitutional Court in South Africa (Theophilopoulos, Van Heerden & Boraine, 2012). The CA, comprising 15 judges, is a court of appeal which hears appeals from all lower courts, whether state or federal, including the HC, CCA and SCA. The CA in Nigeria has a similar function to the Supreme Court (SCA) in South Africa. The judicial makeup of the CA differs from the SCA in South Africa, not only in numbers but also in expertise, where three judges are experts in Islamic law and a further three are experts in customary law (Olanrewaju, 2009:107). In the SCA in South Africa, there are no such requirements for judges, even though customary law is constitutionally recognised.

The above discussions refer to federal and state courts, but this divide exists at High Court level. According to Olanrewaju (2009:108), federal High Courts are headed by a chief judge, as there is only one federal court geographically positioned in the Nigerian capital, Abuja. The jurisdiction of the federal court extends to criminal and civil cases, as well as cases concerning the revenue of the federation government of Nigeria (Olanrewaju, 2009:108). The state High Court, as with the federal High Court, has a chief judge. There are, however, two differences between the two High Courts: the first is that the state High Court hears appeals of a civil and criminal nature, regardless of whether it concerns the federal or state government (Olanrewaju, 2009:108); and the second is that the state court has the jurisdiction to hear all appeals from the lower Magistrate courts (Olanrewaju, 2009:108).

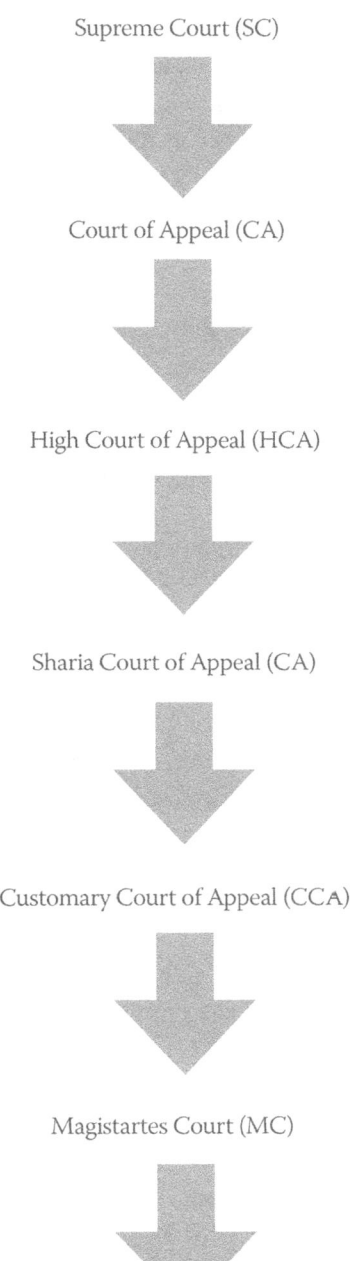

FIGURE 2.1 An overview of the Nigerian courts (based on Olanrewaju, 2009)

Parallel to the High Courts described is the Sharia Court which prescribes to the tenets of Islam (Olanrewaju, 2009:109). The court is situated in the north of Nigeria, given that 19 northern states have created Sharia Courts of Appeal (Sharia CA) (Olanrewaju, 2009:109). The CCA is different from the SCA as it is concerned with appeals of a customary nature concerning civil litigation (Olanrewaju, 2009:110). The difference between Sharia and customary law is not explained. However, it appears to be determined along religious lines where the SCA in Nigeria is concerned solely with Sharia law, hence the geographical position and confinement to north of Nigeria where the majority of citizens are Muslim. Customary law thus applies to disputes concerning customs, cultures and traditions outside of the realm of Sharia law. A north-south divide geographically determines the jurisdiction of the Nigerian Magistrates' Courts: in the south, Magistrates' Courts hear both civil and criminal cases (Olanrewaju, 2009:110); in the north, Magistrates' Courts are confined to hearing only criminal trials while civil cases need to be heard by the District Courts (DC) (Olanrewaju, 2009:110).

The DC only exist in the north for the primary purpose of hearing civil cases (Olanrewaju, 2009:111). The Area Courts (AC) in the north exist alongside the DC with the sole mandate of hearing criminal and civil cases of both Islamic Personal law and customary law (Olanrewaju, 2009:112). On the point of customary law, Customary Courts are established with precisely the same hierarchical status as Nigerian Magistrates' Courts. These are in existence in southern Nigeria and have a limited jurisdiction, focusing on customary law cases concerning inheritance of property according to customs, succession and marriage under customary law (Olanrewaju, 2009:112).

Nigeria's legal language legislative framework

With the hierarchical structure of the courts, as advanced above, the language rights of persons need to be carefully established so as to protect their rights to access justice and ensure they are treated fairly, regardless of their linguistic competencies. Those language rights in the Nigerian Constitution which are relevant to the legal system are housed in the following constitutional provisions:

Section 20

(2) Any person who is arrested or detained shall be promptly informed, in language that he understands, of the reasons for his arrest or detention.

(5) Every person who is charged with a criminal offence shall be entitled –

(a) to be informed promptly, in language that he understands and in detail, of the nature of the offence;

(e) to have without payment the assistance of an interpreter if he cannot understand the language used at the trial of the offence.

Prior to commentating on these provisions, we have advanced the relevant provisions emanating from the various statutes governing the legal processes and giving further meaning and practical implementation to the constitutional language rights. The Criminal Procedure Act of 1990 (Chapter 80, Laws of the Federation of Nigeria) (1990), advances the following provisions concerning language in legal proceedings:

Section 60

(4) Every such complaint shall be for one offence only but such complaint shall not be avoided by describing the offence or any material act relating thereto in alternative words according to the language of the enactment constituting such offence.

Section 152

(3) The particulars in the charge shall describe the offence shortly in ordinary language avoiding as far as possible the use of technical terms.

Section 154

(1) The description of property in a charge shall be in ordinary language and such as to indicate with reasonable clearness the property referred to and if the property is so described it shall not be necessary, except when required for the purpose of describing an offence depending on any special ownership of property or special value of property, to name the person to whom the property belongs or the value of the property.

(8) Subject to any other provisions of this Act, it shall be sufficient to describe any place, time, thing, matter, act, or omission whatsoever to which it is necessary to refer in any charge in ordinary language in such a manner as to indicate with reasonable clearness the place, time, thing, matter, act, or omission referred to.

Section 314

(1) If at the close of the evidence for the prosecution a prima facie case has in the opinion of the Magistrate been established against the accused, immediately after the last witness for the prosecution has been bound over to attend the trial, the Magistrate shall again read the charge or read the amended or substituted charge to the accused and explain the nature thereof to him in ordinary language and inform him that he has the right to call witnesses and, if he so desires, to give evidence on his own behalf.

Section 338

(1) Where an information is exhibited to the High Court under the provisions of this Act –
 (d) after the statement of offence, particulars of that offence shall be set out in ordinary language: Provided that where any written law limits the particulars of an offence which are required to be given in an information nothing in this paragraph shall require any more particulars to be given than those so required...

Section 441

Every male person, between the ages of twenty-one years and sixty years residing in Nigeria, who is able to speak the English language and understand the same shall be qualified to serve as an assessor: Provided that it shall not be an essential qualification for an assessor that he shall be able to speak the English language and understand the same when spoken.

As with the Kenyan hierarchical legislative framework evidenced above, the Nigerian Constitution and primary legislation in the form of the Criminal Procedure Act (1990) is given further meaning through the provisions of the Criminal Procedure Code (1960). The relevant provisions concerning the use of language in judicial proceedings read as follows:

> 232. No person of the Moslem faith shall be required to take an oath in any court unless –
> (c) the oath is taken upon a copy of the Holy Qur'an printed in the Arabic language.
>
> 233. The court shall prevent the putting of irrelevant questions to witnesses and shall protect them from any language, remarks or gestures likely to intimidate them; and it shall prevent the putting of any question of an indecent or offensive nature unless such question bears directly on facts which are materials to the proper appreciation of the facts of the case.
>
> 241. When any evidence is given in a language not understood by the accused and the accused is present in court, it shall be interpreted to him in a language understood by him.
>
> 268. (1) The judgment in every trial in a court shall be in writing and shall be pronounced, and the substance of it explained in a language understood by the accused in open court either on the day on which the hearing terminates or at some subsequent time of which due notice shall be given.
>
> 276. On the application of the accused a copy of the judgment, or when he so desires a translation in his own language if practicable, shall be given to him without delay and such copy shall be given free of cost.

As with the Kenyan model, prosecutors in Nigeria's courts are police officers and thus their linguistic competencies need to be aligned with the language of record in courts and the legal language. The Police Act 23 of 1979 includes numerous provisions on the language competencies and linguistic requirements of police officers. We have quoted these below, as per the statute:

> 46. Qualifications for appointment as Assistant Superintendent of Police (ASP)
> (1) The qualifications required of a candidate for a probationary appointment as an assistant superintendent of police (works) are –
> (b) education – must be in possession of the General Certificate of Education (Ordinary Level) with a pass in English language, plus advanced level passes in any two of the following subjects – History, Geography, Mathematics, Economics, British Constitution, British Economic History, any non-Nigerian language, or any science subject.
>
> 52. Qualifications for appointment as cadet sub-inspectors
> (1) The general qualifications required of a male or female candidate for appointment as a cadet sub-inspector of police are as follows –
> (b) education – must be in possession of –
> (i) a General Certificate of Education with passes at the Ordinary Level in at least four subjects including English language and mathematics; or
> (ii) the West African School Certificate, with credits in at least four subjects, including English language and mathematics.

75. Entrance examination syllabus
(1) The entrance examination shall consist of a written examination in the following subjects –
   (a) English;
   (b) Simple arithmetic;
   (c) Dictation; [and]
   (d) General knowledge.
(2) The entrance examination shall be conducted in the English Language.

110. Prescribed qualifications may be varied or dispensed with
(b) the Bureau of Investigation and Intelligence Branch or the Special Branch of the Force, if the candidate is especially qualified by a knowledge of languages, or other special knowledge relating to the work of the Bureau of Investigation and Intelligence Department or the Force Special Branch;

168. Accelerated promotion to the rank of corporal
A constable who has passed the West African School Certificate Examination or the General Certificate of Education Examination (Ordinary Level) in English and mathematics, and in not less than two additional subjects, shall be eligible for consideration for promotion to the rank of corporal after he shall have served for not less than two years from the date of appointment as a recruit constable.

333. Duties of the Charge Room Officer
(v) the causing the Station Writer to enter, in concise language, into the Station Crime and Incidents Diary, the details of every complaint made and incident reported.

384. Conduct of summary investigation
(23) Any evidence given in any language not understood by the defaulter shall be interpreted to him.

A member of the Force who commits any of the following acts or omissions shall be guilty of an offence against discipline –
   (l) INSUBORDINATE OR OPPRESSIVE CONDUCT, that is to say, if he –
      (iii) uses obscene, abusive or insulting language to a member of the Force; …

The starting point for the discussion pertaining to this extracted legislation is the Police Act 23 of 1979. The police are the first port of call when encountering the justice system (Docrat, 2017a). Both complainants and accused persons have their statements taken by police officers. Also, as explained above, the police officers in Nigeria have a further role to play in terms of prosecution. The provisions we have advanced are illustrative of two points. Firstly, appointments to the police service and promotions within the police service are guided by the linguistic competency of the individuals concerned. For example, Sections 46(1) (b), 52(1) (i) and 75(1) and subsection (2) expressly refer to a "sound knowledge of English for appointment and promotion". Section 46(1) (b), besides heightening the status of English by prescribing that an assistant superintendent must have a pass in English, requires that a non-Nigerian language be studied as well. This is concerning, given that the linguistic composition of the country favours a multilingual approach rather than a monolingual one, where the majority of the country cannot speak English, nor do they have access to the language. Secondly, the undermining and blatant exclusion of Nigerian African languages contributes to the exclusion of persons who are not fluent in English.

Section 75(1) (a) prescribes that one of the entrance examinations assesses the competency of police officers in the English language. Further to this, Section 75(2) prescribes that all entrance examinations will be conducted in English. English is, yet again, prioritised and used as a threshold to determine entrance to the police service. Subsection (2) illustrates that there is a need to be proficient in speaking, reading and writing English. This point is elaborated on, upon examination of Section 168, which prescribes that promotion from the rank of constable to that of corporal is dependent on passing the English examination.

Section 333(v) brings into question whether an English police officer is linguistically competent to record a statement provided by a non-English speaking complainant in compiling the record, as required in this provision. It is of further concern – given that the police officer will effectively have a limited linguistic competency in the African languages – that the officer will thus rely on interpretation in court where they act as prosecutors. This point can be cross-referenced with the case of *State* v *Sikhafungana* (2012). In critiquing the case, Docrat et al. (2017b) explained that the police are central to the success of a prosecution and that the chain of evidence commencing with them needs to be watertight. Docrat et al. (2017b) further explain that, as evidenced in the case of *Sikhafungana* (2012), language is central to the police service operating effectively and this requires the police to communicate directly with complainants in a language they fully understand. In turn, the recording of the statement in a language in which it was provided ensures no meaning is lost in translation. At a later stage, this further enables the police officer to be linguistically equipped to provide a statement with equivalence, where the literal meaning is captured and translated. We discuss the *Sikhafungana* (2012) case fully in Chapter 7.

Provision is made for information to be interpreted into a language understood by the "defaulter" through Section 384(23), but no mention is made of the need to communicate directly with complainants in any Nigerian African language. It is interesting to note that Section 110(b), dealing with prescribed qualifications, refers to persons who are "... especially qualified by a knowledge of languages". Although English is not referred to specifically, the only presumption that can be drawn is that English is implied, given the context and content of the Police Act (1979). It does, however, leave room for an argument to be made that referring to 'languages' in the plural implies the inclusion of African languages other than English.

The Police Act (1979), as with the Criminal Procedure Act and Criminal Procedure Code, are drafted within the framework of the Constitution. That said, the legislation needs to conform to the constitutional provisions and must not be contrary to the Constitution. As we explain in Chapter 5, primary legislation must give meaningful effect to the constitutional rights and provisions more broadly. Having said this, it can be questioned whether, in fact, English-only speaking police officers give meaning to Section 20(2) of the Nigerian Constitution as quoted above. Section 20(2) requires that every arrested or detained person be informed of his or her rights in a language they understand; it is the responsibility and the police mandate to undertake this function. However, the Police Act (1979), as we have explicated, promotes monolingual linguistic competency and thus has the potential of limiting detainees' constitutional language rights. Furthermore, through Section 20(5) (a), the Constitution requires that the arrested person be informed of the nature of the offence in sufficient detail in a language they understand; so again, this translates to the need to have multilingual police officers who can execute this constitutional mandate without limiting their rights.

As with all the legislation advanced thus far in this chapter, an emphasis is placed on interpretation. It is interesting to note that Section 20(5) (e) precludes the payment of interpreters if the accused does not understand the language used at the trial. The first point arising from this constitutional right is that, as with South Africa (this will be discussed in further detail in Chapter 6 with reference to Chapter 2 of this book), and Kenya, the language of record is monolingual (only English), thus the majority of litigants require interpretational services. Simply put, in our opinion, it is not an olive branch that the government of Nigeria is extending to litigants for free interpretational services. It is the complete opposite as a language right is being watered down where the majority of persons are not English-speaking and thus have an interpretational right. A second point arising concerns the absence of a standard built into the constitutional provisions with the phrase "a language the person understands", as no standard is inserted to determine the linguistic competency of litigants.

The Criminal Procedure Act (1990) provides no elucidation on the language for direct communication with litigants in the legal system. The provisions we have quoted earlier, namely Sections 60(4); 152; 154(1) and (8); 314(1); and Section 338, refer to the use of ordinary language, i.e., the preclusion of legalese or any technical language. No mention is made in either of these provisions of the use of language and a language other than English, such as an African language. Any recognition ensuring an African language is used and is the language of the accused, is absent from Section 152 that deals with the charge sheet. This will be cross-referenced to the Canadian case study in Chapter 3.

Section 441 is the sole section in the Criminal Procedure Act (1990) that refers to linguistic competency. Section 441, however, supports the English-only position, where the extent is far reaching to assessors who are appointed based on a criterion which includes being proficient in speaking and understanding English. This monolingual approach supports the sole use of English as the language of record.

The Criminal Procedure Code offers more protection for litigants in comparison to the Criminal Procedure Act (1990). Section 232(C) is the only provision thus far in the Nigerian legislative framework that includes a language other than English; given the court hierarchy we advanced earlier and the divide between the western and Islamic courts, where Muslims can take their oath in Arabic. The remaining provisions we have advanced from the Criminal Procedure Act focus on interpretation and translation and not on direct communication in a language which the accused understands. Simply put, English remains the language of record and the litigant is reliant on interpretation services.

The quoted Section 276 is of further relevance to the discussion at hand. Section 276, the translation of the judgment, free of charge, can be cross-referenced with the Canadian case study in Chapter 3. As we advance in that chapter concerning the Canadian discussion, Section 276, in making allowance for the translation of the judgment, permits the use of African languages as languages of record and an English translation where necessary. If the service is being offered in English, why can this not be done in a Nigerian African language where the majority of people speak an African language? There is no literature that we have found supporting this view in Nigeria. From the discussion we have advanced on Nigeria, it is evident that English consumes all literature and legislation.

The language of record in Nigerian courts

The Nigerian court structure advanced earlier illustrates the integral role of both customary and Sharia law. Simply put, the indigenous traditions of the country are recognised in the legal system. With customs recognised by law, it would follow that the indigenous languages are inherent in the legal system. The sociolinguistic landscape presented earlier suggests otherwise, showing that the indigenous languages are excluded from high status domains in Nigeria. The language of record in Nigerian courts is English. The selection of English as the language of record is justified on grounds of neutrality, so choosing English precludes the engenderment of ethnic hostility among the African languages. Olanrewaju (2009:116) explains that having English as the sole language of record ensures the peaceful co-existence of the indigenous languages in Nigeria and preserves linguistic diversity. This point can be countered through the works of Alexander (2013) and Crystal (2003). Alexander spoke to the point of language and ethnicity and how the use of an African language or languages does not result in tribalism or ethnic divisions. Crystal (2003) spoke to the point of English as a global language and how selecting English as the primary language of communication in multilingual countries, at the expense of the African languages, results in the eventual death and extinction of the indigenous languages. The point being espoused is that Nigeria, a multilingual country, is contributing to the rise of English as a global language and the further marginalisation and extinction of the indigenous languages by selecting English as the primary language of communication.

The legal system regulates the functioning of a country. It holds the government to account and ensures that a person's rights are enforced and protected. With this function, the legal system – and, in particular, the courts and all legal professionals – should be accessible to the public. Accessibility, in our opinion, is facilitated through language. The literature on Nigeria suggests that English is the chosen language of communication as it is said to be the key to success and to employment opportunities, given that it is the language of all three arms of the state (Olanrewaju, 2009:116). Defendants and witnesses are permitted to choose any of the three Nigerian official languages – Hausa, Yoruba or Igbo. This right is, however, qualified by the fact that English is the language of record, the law is written in English and all legal professionals are trained in English. Once again, only three of the African languages are recognised on paper. Practically, however, their status and use is diminished by the fact that English is the language of record, meaning that only evidence will be imparted in one of the three languages and then interpreted into English The interpretational system is thus still in effect with the threshold being English. Olanrewaju (2009:116) acknowledges that English, as the language of record, alienates the majority of the Nigerian populace. The complexity of the language of record is further complicated by the fact that English is used as a tool by many lawyers who exploit their knowledge of English to the detriment of witnesses who, in most instances, are illiterate and have no knowledge of either English or the legalese used in cross-examination (Olanrewaju, 2009:117).

English in the Nigerian legal system: legal education and training

With the legal system premised on English-only in reality and the fact that Olanrewaju (2009:117) makes no qualms about the exploitation of witnesses by lawyers through the medium of English, it follows that legal professionals need to be linguistically trained. The legal education of lawyers in Nigeria, as with the entire legal system, has been based on the legal training and the legal system of England. From a historical perspective, on completion of their law degree, graduates required further minimum qualifications for practice. This included either a call to the English, Irish or Scottish Bar, or a qualification as a solicitor in any of these three countries (Fabunmi & Popoola, 1990:34-37). Essentially, Nigerian lawyers were products of the English legal system and were actually foreigners in Nigeria upon their return; yet the majority of the country are African language speakers whose cultures and traditions are different to those of the western countries in which the lawyers have trained. There was no exposure to any form of Nigerian law to equip the lawyers to deal with issues of a legal nature in a non-western system (ibid, 37).

The legal education programme in Nigeria was in place until the enactment of the Legal Education Act 12 of 1962 which provided for the establishment of the Nigerian Law School (ibid, 38). The Nigerian Law School remains in operation for practical training following the completion of a university degree. An oversight body exists in regulating the legal education in Nigeria, namely the Council of Legal Education, which indirectly has the power to affect the legal education programming by rejecting a law degree from a university as a basic qualification for admission to the Nigerian Law School (ibid, 39). The Law School thus has an important role to play in monitoring law faculties' courses. From 1985 onwards, the Council of Legal Education established an Accreditation Panel to inspect the material used for teaching law students at universities (ibid).

Upon entering the Nigerian Law School, the second phase of training commences for prospective students. At the Nigerian Law School, the Council for Legal Education controls the programme for training students on the practicalities of the law. According to Fabunmi and Popoola (1990:39), the programme aims at providing practical training in the work of a barrister and of a solicitor. The main subjects are therefore concerned with practice and procedure and the preparation of legal documents, all to the end that the student acquires the necessary skills required in practice.

There are further gaps that can be identified at both university and practical training levels. As part of the law degree, students are required to complete non-legal courses which include other social science subjects, as well as English (ibid, 44). No African languages are listed among the subjects that law students are permitted to enrol for, but English is. The exclusion of African languages extends to the Law School training where no vocation-specific course is included. The training includes a range of other practical courses, such as legal drafting, conveyancing, civil and criminal procedure and professional training, but excludes all language-based practical training (ibid, 44-45).

In the legal system, there appears to be a lack of development of African languages concerning legal terminology. Furthermore, there is no recognition of the importance of language in the legal system and the need to ensure that lawyers and judicial officers are linguistically competent and equipped to grapple with the language barriers that exist in a multilingual country such as Nigeria. This deficiency may be attributed to the ongoing minimal amount of literature on the research area of language and law or forensic linguistics in Nigeria (Olanrewaju, 2009:118). According to Olanrewaju (2009:119-129), the problem in Nigeria is threefold: firstly, the absence of research in the area of forensic linguistics and language and the law is a result of the continued focus of research efforts on lexical and syntactic aspects; secondly, being based on the British system, the Nigerian legal system adopts a pro-English approach to communication in the courtroom, as well as to the language of record (ibid) and thirdly, the influence of the English legal system has unfortunately failed to result in the establishment of a forensic linguistics association in Nigeria that could contribute to the development of research in the field (ibid).

As with Kenya, English is prioritised in Nigeria across all domains, including the legal system. Theoretically, African languages are recognised, but practically, English is used.

What follows is a discussion of the third and final African case study, namely Morocco.

Morocco's sociolinguistic landscape

Morocco's sociolinguistic landscape has been influenced by its geographical position on the African continent while also bordering Europe and the Middle East (Marley, 2005:1487). As a result of this geographical positioning, Morocco has had a wide range of linguistic and cultural influencers (Marley, 2005:1487). Berber, Arabic and French are the dominant language groups in Morocco. Marely (2005:1488) explains that Berber is a European name given to the indigenous languages of Maghreb which are spoken in Morocco, Algeria, parts of Tunisia and adjoining sub-Saharan countries. The term 'Berber' refers to a number of mutually intelligible languages. In the case of Morocco, Berber speakers belong to three language groups, namely Tashelhit, Tamazight and Tarifit (ibid). The term 'Berber' is not used in Morocco where persons instead refer to 'Tamazight', the origins of which date back approximately 5 000 years to a time when the Berbers in Morocco embraced Islam which was brought to Morocco by the Arabs. Tamazight eventually became known as the language of the 'peasants' and, as a result, the status and use of the language diminished significantly (ibid). The fate of Arabic is not being threatened, as with Tamazight, it remains a language of prestige to the extent that an educated elite have developed a new dialect named 'intermediate' which is utilised in formal and semi-formal domains (ibid). Arabic remains a language used for official, educational and religious purposes.

French was introduced in Morocco during the Protectorate of the twentieth century between 1912 and 1956. During this period, French was associated with power and the elite of the country learnt the language as a sign of power and dominance. Many citizens began learning French, despite its lack of official status. Presently, French is widely spoken and used in certain domains such as commerce, finance, science, technology and the media (ibid). French is said to be a language of social and professional success that maintains a privileged position socially and professionally, as well as in the state education and the private sector of Morocco.

Morocco's linguistic make-up favours a multilingual, inclusive approach that needed to be pursued and reflected in legislation and policy frameworks. However, the complete opposite occurred instead. Moroccan independence saw the government pursuing a monolingual agenda with the purpose of achieving a linguistically united country (ibid). It was a policy of Arabisation similar to that in Algeria and Tunisia where English, the coloniser's language, was replaced with Arabic, a traditional language (ibid). Arabisation was not only a language change but, rather, a broader social and political change. The majority of Moroccans supported the move in the belief that it would create opportunities of employment and equality for all. The use of Arabic was not pivotal to the majority, as the elite minority were those who had access to French and English.

Linguistically, it was therefore an insignificant change in their lives. The hope was that everyone would speak the national language, Arabic, and all vernaculars would become obsolete, as was the case with the French. Arabisation resulted in a further polarisation where Arabic became the language associated with power and religion; and a religious Islamic state translated into a closer relationship with the Arab world. Berber language and culture became synonymous with inferiority and ignorance, relegated to a regional language rather than a national language (ibid). Arabisation was intended to restore Morocco's traditions and national identity. Linguistically, Arabisation favoured monolingualism, regardless of the multilingual reality of the country. From 1980 onward, changes were seen as a result of Arabisation. These changes are summarised in the following except from Marley (2005:1489):

> I will simply resume the situation until 2000 by saying that the government has put in place a legislative and operational framework to enable Arabisation to take place, and that by the end of the 1980s the state education system was completely arabized, as were large sections of the administration. Despite this, French continued to be used in many important domains, and the Tamazight speakers, although nearly all bilingual by now, were becoming increasingly vocal in their demands for linguistic rights. It was thus apparent that the goals of Arabisation were not being met, and a change was needed.

The Moroccan Constitution

The period of Arabisation saw significant changes in all domains of Moroccan society with a definitive need to change, as explicated in the quoted excerpt. A new era commenced with the enactment of *Morocco's Constitution of 2011.* There are several provisions in the Constitution (2011) that refer to language and that house language rights. These read as follows:

> Preamble
>> Founded on these values and these immutable principles, and strong in its firm will to reaffirm the bonds of fraternity, or cooperation, or solidarity and of constructive partnership with all other States, and to work for common progress, the Kingdom of Morocco, [a] united State, totally sovereign, belonging the Grand Maghreb, reaffirm that which follows and commits itself:
>> - To ban and combat all discrimination whenever it encounters it, for reason of sex, or colour, of beliefs, of culture, of social or regional origin, of language, of handicap or whatever personal circumstance that may be;

Article 5

> Arabic is the official language of the State.
>
> The State works for the protection and for the development of the Arabic language, as well as the promotion of its use.
>
> Likewise, Tamazight [Berber/Amazigh] constitutes an official language of the State, being common patrimony of all Moroccans without exception.
>
> An organic law defines the process of implementation of the official character of this language, as well as the modalities of its integration into teaching and into the priority domains of public life, so that it may be permitted in time to fulfil its function as an official language.
>
> The State works for the preservation of Hassani, as an integral component of the Moroccan cultural unity, as well as the protection of the speakers [of it] and of the practical cultural expression of Morocco. Likewise, it sees to the coherence of linguistic policy and national culture and to the learning and mastery of the foreign languages of greatest use in the world, as tools of communication, of integration and of interaction [by which] society [may] know, and to be open to different cultures and to contemporary civilizations.
>
> A National Council of Languages and of Moroccan Culture [*Conseil national des langues et de la culture marocaine*] is created, charged with, notably, the protection and the development of the Arabic and Tamazight languages and of the diverse Moroccan cultural expressions, which constitute one authentic patrimony and one source of contemporary inspiration. It brings together the institutions concerned in these domains. An organic law determines its attributions, composition and the modalities of [its] functioning.

Article 7

> The political parties may not be founded on a religious, linguistic, ethnic or regional basis, or, in a general manner, on any discriminatory basis or [basis] contrary to the Rights of Man.

Article 28

> The law establishes the rules of organization and of control of the means of public communication. It guarantees access to these means respecting the linguistic, cultural and political pluralism of the Moroccan society.

There are similarities and differences that can be drawn between the Moroccan constitutional provisions cited here and the South African constitutional provisions advanced fully in Part One of Chapter 6 of this book. The first similarity is between the Preamble of the Moroccan Constitution (2011) and Section 9 of the South African Constitution. The preamble precludes discrimination on a number of grounds, including language; and the South African Constitution does precisely the same, except for the fact that an entrenched right in the BOR exists and is not aspirational, as with the provisions of a Preamble. A full discussion of Section 9 of the South African Constitution can be found in Docrat (2017b) with reference to the case of *Lourens v Speaker of the National Assembly and Others* (2015).

Suffice it to say at this point in the discussion, the gravitas of language rights and provisions more broadly, although informed by the Constitution in theory, are only determined in practice when applied.

Article 5 confers official status on both Arabic and Tamazight. However, from the provisions, Arabic appears to be heightened in status where the state must protect, promote and develop Arabic. This protection is not accorded to Tamazight which, in our opinion, appears to be conferred with official status as an indigenous language inherent to the people of Morocco. Article 5, in our view, confers further protection to Tamazight through the second paragraph where it refers to "this" language that needs to be used for educational purposes and in high status domains. Equal protection is accorded to both Arabic and Tamazight through the establishment of a National Council of Languages and of Moroccan Culture, tasked with the development of both languages.

There are similarities between the provisions of Article 5 above and Section 6 of the South African Constitution where official status is conferred on all languages and, constitutionally, an established organisation is tasked with the protection, promotion and development of the official languages, as with Section 6(5) of the South African Constitution establishing the Pan South African Language Board (PanSALB) (1995). The provisions of Section 6(2) of the South African Constitution appear to provide further protection for the nine African languages on paper (see the discussion in Part One of Chapter 6, regarding the practical limitations when implementing Section 6).

The South African Constitution does not include insertions such as Articles 7 and 28 regarding political parties being founded, on amongst others, linguistic grounds. Thus, no one language can be used as a basis to form the party, ensuring equality. Article 28 can be cross-referenced to the quote by Reagan (1986:94) who defines pluralism as: "… the acceptance of the presence of linguistic diversity in the society and the commitment by the polity to allow for the maintenance and cultivation of the different languages on a reasonable and equitable basis". This indicates that, through Article 28, the Moroccan Constitution (2011) acknowledges the linguistic diversity of the country and permits the development and maintenance thereof.

History of language usage in Moroccan courts

We have differentiated between provisions in theory and the practical implementation thereof with reference to the South African constitutional provisions. This is discussed fully in Part One of Chapter 6. The same now applies to Morocco. Saadoun (2015) acknowledges that, although conferring official status on Tamazight theoretically, the Moroccan Constitution (2011) does not include practical implementation which is dependent on legislation. Moroccan legislation does not correlate with the constitutional provisions we have cited above: currently the legislative position permits only the use of Arabic for litigation in accordance with the Arabisation, Moroccorisation and Unification Law of 1965.

Prior to 1965 and Morocco's independence, French and Spanish, amongst other languages were used in courts. Until 1965, Arabic was limited in courts, confined mainly to the Islamic courts and the judiciary thereof who were Arabic speaking (Saadoun, 2015). There was ongoing activism for the inclusion of Tamazight in courts prior to and after 1965, with the basis of the argument being that more than half of the Moroccan population speak Tamazight (ibid). However, 1965 failed to herald a new era for the speakers of Amazigh. Instead, Arabic became the official language of litigation across all courts at all levels. One exception was made for French for contracts written in French and registered in court under the business record (ibid). The Arabisation, Moroccorisation and Unification Law of 1965 had the unwavering support of the then Minister of Justice who ensured the implementation of the Unification Law (1965).

Language of record as opposed to a language of interpretation

With Arabic being the sole official language of record in all Moroccan courts, interpretation plays an important role in ensuring that the right to a fair trial is not unfairly limited. There is, however, a professional difference between the level of interpretation for foreign language speakers and indigenous language speakers. The divide is evident where professional translation is available, with a cohort of competent translators holding a degree from institutes that have specialised in the field (Saadoun, 2015). A similar service to translate to and from Amazigh is not available as there are no sworn translators who have specialised in Amazigh (ibid). As more than half of the population speak Amazigh, this marginalises them from accessing the legal system and enjoying their right to a fair trial. Moroccan legal rights activists have argued for adequate legal requirements for translators and interpreters, as well as the adoption of Amazigh as a language of record for the benefit of litigants who can only speak this language (ibid). They have argued that the sole official language of record constitutes a flaw that adversely affects their right to a fair trial.

The use of language, specifically Amazigh, was inadvertently dealt with before a Court of Cassation. The court dealt with the question: "Are pleadings in a language incomprehensible by the litigant, a violation of defence?" (Saadoun, 2015). In answering the question, the court held the following (2010) primary point communicated in the judgment:

> With regard to the argument on violation of the defence's rights, given that the appellant speaks Amazigh, not Arabic, and the court did not enable them to get a lawyer, nor did it ask them whether they are proficient in Arabic or ask about the reason for their appeal, the decision may be challenged. However, since the appellant did not request a translator at any stage of the proceedings and did not seek a lawyer, and the court verified their identity, stated the charge, and discussed the case in which the appellant defended themselves, the argument is unfounded.

The courts' decision was thus based on a technicality. The first half of the courts' reasoning must be noted, where argument was made for the use of Amazigh in proceedings as part of the right to a fair trial. This would ensure the litigant's rights are not breached. This case can be cross-referenced to the South African case of *State* v *Pienaar* (2000) in which the court held that the right to legal representation includes the right to communicate directly with the legal representative in the accused's own language of choice; and that indirect communication may only occur indirectly through interpretation in exceptional cases. In this instance, the court in *State* v *Pienaar* (2000) found that the right in Section 35(3) (k) did not confer a default interpretational right, but rather a language right where the accused should be tried directly in his or her own language (De Vries & Docrat, 2019:7).

There have been instances where judges have communicated directly with litigants in Amazigh. There was one widely publicised case in Morocco, heard in the Southern Court, where a Judge permitted litigants to communicate in Amazigh (Saadoun, 2015). Trial proceedings were conducted in Amazigh and the Judge himself communicated directly in the litigants' mother tongue (ibid). The judge, being fluent in Amazigh, was able to communicate with the interpreter who was used in the case, for the remaining judicial officers were unable to speak Amazigh fluently (ibid). This would be possible if there were linguistically competent judicial officers in courts located in geographical positions where the majority of citizens speak Amazigh (ibid). Docrat (2017a) has advanced this argument for the South African legal system. Important for the discussion at hand is the need for linguistically competent judicial officers.

What remains in place in all Moroccan courts is an exclusionary monolingual language of record policy that excludes the majority of the population who speak Amazigh and have no, or a limited, understanding of Arabic. There is thus an inherent call for linguistically competent judicial officers that can positively affect the use of language in courts and, ultimately, the language of record so that it reflects the language demographics of the country, where the languages are equally represented.

Linguistic proficiency in Moroccan higher education

With the need to have linguistically competent judicial officers in Morocco, the focus of the discussion turns to language in higher education. Saadoun (2015) explains that the Minister of Justice observed a need for judges to be linguistically proficient in Amazigh. Having said this, the Minister explicated further that proficiency in Amazigh should be a criterion for the transference and appointment of new judges (ibid). To date, no implementation has resulted with the continued marginalisation of Amazigh, the indigenous language, and the rise of foreign languages such as English alongside French. The Moroccan education system has promoted the use of English as an international language in higher education.

El Kirat El Allame and Laaraj (2016:44) state that adopting English as the medium of instruction will improve the quality of higher education and simultaneously enhance students' employability and professional success.

Three sets of reform in 2003, 2007 and 2009 saw Moroccan education authorities grappling with the language question and the growing need to master foreign languages such as English (El Kirat El Allame & Laaraj, 2016:44). No decision was taken until the fourth reform in 2014, as a result of the need to have linguistically qualified teachers (ibid). In 2014, it was said that English was recognised for professional mobility and international research purposes (ibid, 45). The use of English in higher education was promoted, with documents, Ministerial notes and official speeches produced in English.

El Kirat El Allame and Laaraj (2016) reported that a survey conducted across state higher education institutions concluded that students wanted to learn English and increasing numbers of students were majoring in English with the view that English creates employment opportunities in formal sectors of Moroccan society (ibid, 54). What will emerge in Moroccan society is predicted to be a tussle between English and French, the latter being the language of science and technology and English being seen as an empowering international language.

The article by El Kirat El Allame and Laaraj (2016), forming the basis of discussions, presents an overwhelming view that English is growing in dominance, resulting in further marginalising of indigenous languages such as Amazigh. Furthermore, what emerges is the association between English language competency, employability and success. Juxtapose this with the Minister's observance that Amazigh be a requirement for judicial officers, it would render Amazigh irrelevant, and highlight the disjuncture between the language policies of the legal system and those of the higher education department. The language policy for higher education is thus contrary to the Moroccan constitutional (2011) provisions which were advanced earlier, promoting the development and usage of Arabic and Amazigh. It also brings into question the intentions of the Moroccan government in promoting monolingualism in a foreign language, namely English, as opposed to promoting, developing and using Amazigh and Arabic, thereby adopting a bilingual and multilingual approach that favours the linguistic diversity that should be celebrated and not seen as a problem that English can solve.

Conclusion

Each of the three case studies we have presented has common threads that influence the language of record policy in the courts of each of the three countries, Kenya, Nigeria and Morocco. Each country's sociolinguistic landscape was influenced by colonial rule, or, as in the case of Morocco, by the additional aspect of geographical positioning, with that country bordering Africa and Europe. The indigenous languages were synonymous with inferiority, compared to English and French. Although attempts have been made through constitutional and legislative means in each of the three countries, in practice, English emerges as the preferred language, bringing to the fore the failure to implement constitutional and legislative directives.

A monolingual position is preferred to a bilingual or multilingual position on the basis that English is a unifying language, one that creates access to opportunities, results in employability and economic access on an international stage. This reasoning of each country's government speaks to the social, political and economic aspects of language policies, finding resonance with the views of Cooper (1989) and Grin (2010). All three of these aspects can be subsumed under the discussion of opportunity planning with which we engage in forthcoming chapters, namely Chapters 4, 8 and 9.

There is a misconception that has been created in each of the three countries – Kenya, Nigeria and Morocco – that English has to be developed, promoted and used in high status domains to ensure employability. Each government has failed to take account of the need to develop a micro-economy before contributing to the macro-economy, as explicated by Kaschula (2004). It must be questioned whether each government is not pursuing an elitist agenda, disguising their quest for power behind the misconceived banner that English-only is the best way forward. These views find resonance with South Africa and the language policies determined during the Convention for A Democratic South Africa (CODESA) talks, where the African languages remained marginalised.

There is no reason why the indigenous languages of each of the three countries cannot be used as languages of record. A case in point was the use of Amazigh in Morocco where the entire trial was conducted in a language everyone spoke and understood. In all three countries, there are no more than three African languages that are spoken by the majority of the people. Furthermore, in Nigeria, the country is divided along linguistic lines, so it makes sense to use each of the three languages in the areas in which the majority speak the languages, thereby creating access to justice and inclusion for all.

Political independence might have been achieved; however, with regard to language, each of these countries is abandoning their mandate of equality for all. The entire system needs to be rethought, beginning with the legal education of each country. Nigeria is a case in point as it is still premised on the English legal system, whereas Morocco has failed to produce anything tangible on language requirements for legal practitioners, besides the Minister's sentiments that are tantamount to nothing in practice. This chapter has, however, advanced points from which South Africa could benefit and which we have explicated in this chapter. Many of these are discussed throughout the chapters of this book.

At the conclusion of this chapter, one is left with a feeling of despair for the future of African languages on the African continent and the need to motivate continuously for the inclusion of African languages in high status domains. The continued growth of English and the decline of African languages in the three countries is cause for concern and will, eventually, result in a larger gap between the rich and poor. What is needed is an economy that builds on the strength of an education system that educates people in their mother tongue and provides access to English and a legal system that upholds language rights and social justice. The structures are in place; what is needed is a change in mindset based on linguistic inclusion and equality of languages. The chapter that follows provides an international comparative perspective.

INSIGHTS FROM INTERNATIONAL CASE STUDIES ON LANGUAGE AND LAW

Australia, Belgium, Canada and India

This chapter mirrors Chapter 2 in a sense in that we present comparative case studies of language and law in four countries, though these are beyond the African continent. The purpose of this chapter is to provide an overview of the use of language in the legal systems of each of the four selected countries. We specifically focus on the language of record in courts of law for each country and examine the relationship between legal professionals and litigants. Furthermore, the purpose is to assess whether linkages can be drawn between the linguistic competencies of legal professionals and the language of record; and if this affects the litigant's right to a fair trial and their language rights. For each country discussed here, we have engaged with the constitutional, legislative and policy developments in relation to the sociolinguistic make up and how, on a broader level, the country functions socially, politically, economically and, most importantly for the book at hand, linguistically. We will draw parallels between the international countries presented in this chapter in relation to the main model of South Africa, the core focus of this book. Chapters 2 and 3 are intended to serve as jurisprudential case studies that South Africa, with regard to language and law, could emulate or steer clear of.

Australia's sociolinguistic landscape

Australia only became one country in 1900. Up until this point, it was just a group of unfederated states or colonies (Cooke, 2019). Cooke (2019) makes this point given that the sociolinguistic make-up of Australia was influenced by the geographical positioning of the country. For example, the indigenous languages of Australia are not limited to the Aboriginal languages but include the languages of the Torres Strait Islanders (ibid). The languages of the Torres Strait Islanders are included owing to their geographical positioning where they occupy a number of islands at the tip of Queensland (Cooke, 2019). The Australian Institute of Aboriginal and Torres Strait Islanders Studies (AIATSIS), as part of the 2019

International Year of Indigenous Languages, outlined the history of Aboriginal languages and the current plight of these languages. The AIATSIS reports that, at the time of the European settlement in 1788, more than 250 indigenous languages were spoken, and an additional 800 dialectal varieties existed. Although 100 of these indigenous languages are presently spoken, the languages are spoken only by elders in the communities and so risk extinction with the death of the elders (AIATSIS, 2019). The number of languages to be extinct is determined on the basis that a mere 13 indigenous languages are acquired by children (AIATSIS, 2019). That leaves the status of the remaining indigenous languages unknown and, in all probability, they also face extinction. Historically, the value of indigenous languages has been low with emphasis placed on English.

From the Federation in 1901 up until 1959, language was used as a tool by the Australian government to prohibit access to immigrants. This occurred in the form of the 'White Australian Policy' enforced through the Immigration Restriction Act of 1901. The purpose of this Act (1901) was to prohibit immigrants from entering Australia due to the fact that they were unsuitable as a result of being Asian or of non-European race (Robertson, Hohmann & Stewart, 2005:241). A key element of the Immigration Restriction Act (1901) was the dictation test (Robertson et al., 2005:241). The test administered to non-European immigrants was a test to examine their suitability to enter Australia (Robertson et al., 2005:242). Simply put, it was a racial test to prohibit non-White persons from entering. This racial test was administered in a language the aspiring immigrants did not understand to ensure the test was failed (Robertson et al., 2005:242). Section 3(a) of the Immigration Restriction Act (1901) defines a prohibited immigrant. In doing so, it highlights how language has been used to discriminate against people. Section 3(a) defines a prohibited immigrant as follows:

> Any person who when asked to do so by an officer fails to write out a dictation and sign in the presence of the officer a passage of fifty words in length in a European language directed by the officer.

According to Robertson et al. (2005), "a European language" referred to English. We have advanced this discussion pertaining to the racial test as an example of how language and, in this case, English, has been used to exclude persons. It also highlights the dominance of English with a parallel which can be drawn with Afrikaans in South Africa during Apartheid, followed by English under the liberation movement.

According to Meakins (2015), there is also a culture of obliviousness in Australia regarding the existence of Aboriginal languages. Meakins (2015) explains that she often asks her linguistics students to name an Australian indigenous language and is met mainly with silence – most cannot manage to name even one. In a few instances, she points out that the students would name Warlpiri, Yolngu Matha or Arrente. The point is that, of 250 indigenous languages, linguistics students are only able to identity three. Meakins (2015) further states that, if she were to ask the students about indigenous American languages, they were able to identify these with ease, given their visibility through media forums. The same can be said of South Africa where a sense of economic and social utopia is created around the prospects of learning and speaking English as opposed to the African languages.

Crystal (2003:20) explained that introducing English or, in the case of Australia, a simpler version (pidgin), was not intended as a means to communicate with the indigenous people but as a means of conquest and assimilation. This had disastrous effects on the use and development of indigenous languages over time. According to Meakins (2015), there are presently initiatives in place to revitalise the indigenous languages through organisations and universities: Adelaide University has been tasked specifically with the revitalisation of Kaurna Warra Pintyanthi while the Victorian Aboriginal Corporation is tasked with revitalising the languages in Melbourne including signage in cities, the media and movies.

While we attended the 14th Biennial Conference of the International Association of Forensic Linguists in July 2019, the NAIDOC week 2019 was taking place. NAIDOC stands for the National Aborigines and Islanders Day Observance Committee which celebrates the history, culture and achievements of Aboriginal and Torres Strait Islander people. The week-long festivities are held annually in July across Australia. In 2019 we observed that there was a distinct emphasis placed on using indigenous languages in public spaces in Australia.

Language of record: Australian English

According to Cooke (2019), there is no specific constitutional or legislative provision that states what the language of record is in Australian courts. Regardless of the fact that there are state courts in each territory, the language of record across all courts is English. Bush courts also exist in Australia. These are circuit courts operating in remote areas to which magistrates from major centres travel to hear cases. We discuss three issues: firstly, we review what Australian English is and how it is used in courts of law; and, in doing so, we outline the advantages and disadvantages of using Australian English. Secondly, we discuss the disadvantage before the law for Aboriginal litigants and the system of interpretation for Aboriginal litigants. Thirdly, we discuss the Bush courts and the linguistic difficulties experienced therein.

Cooke (2009:27) advances that an Aboriginal learner's English differs from Standard Australian English and that this difference contributes to miscommunication. Aboriginal learners' first language heavily influences their acquiring of English. The differences in language are in pronunciation, grammar, semantics and pragmatics (ibid). Communication confusion is more prevalent with temporal reference, distance and other quantitative matters (ibid). This can be disastrous for a complainant, witness or accused, as time, facts and distance can be central to proving or disproving a charge. Cooke (2009:27) provides numerous extracts of examination in chief and cross-examination where the witness is an Aboriginal speaker of Australian English and miscommunication results, as per this example:

> Counsel: None of those men were searching for him on the Thursday, were they?
> Witness: Yes.
> Counsel: They weren't, were they?
> Coroner: He says none of them were.
> Counsel: And none of them were searching for him on the Friday either, were they?
> Witness: Yes.
> Counsel: And none of them were searching for him on the Saturday, were they?
> Witness: Yes.

Cooke (2009:27) explains the excerpt as follows:

> The witness here is responding to the proposition ("none of them were searching") rather than the tag ("were they?"). This is what he would do in his language. This was well into the case and the coroner had become accustomed to this feature of Aboriginal Learner's English, but counsel had not.

Most indigenous people from communities in remote areas of northern Australia do not speak English as their mother tongue (Cooke, 2009:26). A few indigenous people have a full command of English and many possess a minimal level of proficiency for basic communication skills in social settings (ibid). This is important to note for the proceeding sections of this discussion on Australia where Aboriginal speakers are disadvantaged by a legal system with an English language of record policy. This is also important to note in relation to Chapter 6 which comprises language surveys on the English language proficiencies of both litigants and attorneys in South Africa (De Vries & Docrat, 2019).

The differences between Aboriginal English and Standard Australian English have been investigated for a number of years. Eades (1994) discusses these differences in English in the Australian legal system and makes several points that correlate with the work by Cooke (2009) presented above. Eades (1994:237) defines Aboriginal English as a name given to varieties of English spoken by Aboriginal people. The difference is not solely linguistic, but more sociocultural (Eades, 1994:240). Aboriginal people are not direct in their communication: through their indirectness, they avoid prying or asking direct, personal questions. Thus, their social and cultural patterns influence how they ask and answer questions. As Eades (1994:234) points out, this is disastrous in the legal setting. She provides a simple example similar to Cooke's (2009:27) one: An Aboriginal speaker would ask a question in this way: "You were at the pub", as opposed to, "Were you at the pub?" In Aboriginal English, an Aboriginal speaker's linguistic form is usually a statement with a rising intonation (Eades, 1994:240).

Aboriginal English makes no gender distinction in the third-person pronoun; therefore, him is used to mean he or she (Eades, 1994:204). The same applies with isiXhosa in South Africa where there is no distinction between 'he' and 'she'; and isiXhosa mother tongue speakers who have limited English language competency often refer to the incorrect gender. This can have serious consequences in the legal setting, commencing with the police statement recording and then in court when providing evidence. Furthermore, Eades (1994) points out that, with Aboriginal English speakers' quantitative questions, such as 'when', 'where', 'who', 'how' and 'what', time is not responded to directly. If asked how many people were present, names will be provided rather than numbers. For example, 'What time did you witness the crime taking place?' may result in different answers. 'Before dark' can be any time in the afternoon (Eades, 1994).

Eades (1994) makes the important point that every person who does not have a legal background or some familiarity with the legal system (and specifically police interviews and courtroom questioning) are disadvantaged before the law. For speakers of Aboriginal English, this disadvantage is even greater, as language is a barrier and miscommunication is present in most instances. The work of Eades (1994) and Cooke (2009) will be drawn upon in Chapters 6 and 7, within the South African context, specifically drawing parallels with the language survey by Legal Aid South Africa (2017) and the language survey conducted with attorneys in South Africa on their communication with clients (De Vries & Docrat, 2019).

What can be deduced from the discussion thus far is the disadvantage that exists in the legal system and how the indigenous people are placed at a disadvantage due to their limited English language competency: everything is measured according to Standard English which was essentially a foreign language before the colonisers arrived. This situation speaks to the relationship between language, law and power, to which our focus now turns.

Disadvantage before the law: language and power

The previous section of this chapter comprising the discussion on the language of record brings into focus the disadvantages faced by Aboriginal people in the Australian legal system. Language can be a barrier to accessing justice; and language can be used as a powerful tool to exclude people. Gibbons (1994:196) makes this profound assertion:

> Simply providing the same treatment for everyone within the legal system may not ensure true justice, particularly if that treatment has emerged from the culture and interests of a power elite. Within the language sphere it may be important to recognise that there are people who are disadvantaged by their lack of mastery of the language through which the law is accessed and applied and/or by the discourse conventions of legal proceedings.

This is an important assertion that brings into focus the difference between equal treatment and 'true justice'. Gibbons (2003:201) points out that, in courtrooms, the power vests with legal professionals and that this power is linguistic in nature. Gibbons (2003:205) specifically mentions the Aboriginal people and acknowledges the academic contribution made by Eades on the subject in highlighting the plight of Aboriginal people. The injustices suffered by Aboriginal people in courts was acknowledged in the year 2000 when the Magistrates' Courts of Victoria made a public apology (Gibbons, 2003:205). The power relations embedded in language within the courtroom are also highlighted by Gibbons (2003:207), who explains that Aboriginal witnesses are more inclined to answer 'Yes' when asked a question. Aboriginal witnesses agree in an effort to halt the line of further questioning (Gibbons, 2003:208). This, in a legal context, disadvantages the witness and brings into question the witness's reliability and, in effect, the admissibility of the evidence. Gibbons (2003:227) holds that it is the way in which language is used that disadvantages people. This form of disadvantage is exacerbated where people are already less powerful or disadvantaged in other ways, such as ethnic groups including the indigenous people (Gibbons, 2003:227). Gibbons (2003: 227) succinctly summarises this in the following excerpt:

> These types of disadvantage, which have deep social roots, cannot be remedied only by linguistic means. However, there are measures that can be taken to improve the situation...just treatment does not mean the same treatment, but rather recognising difference, and developing measures to cope with these differences.

This excerpt must also be applied to the South African context where it is arguable that a monolingual language of record policy for courts does not address the disadvantages faced by African language speakers in South Africa, but rather attempts to apply a general Band-Aid that furthers the advantage of the English-speaking minority and socio-political elite. One measure which Gibbons (2003:221) recommends for Australia is "the additional resource – the interpreter and translator". Legal interpreting and translating for Aboriginal people in courts is the focus of the next part of this discussion.

History and development of interpretation in Australia

Thus far, the discussion on Australia has highlighted the issues of miscommunication in courts, where the problem is threefold. Firstly, there are the differences between Aboriginal English and Standard Australian English; secondly, social and cultural norms of Aboriginal people affect demeanour and, ultimately, the admissibility of evidence; and, lastly, there are the unequal power relations that favour persons' familiar with the legal context, specifically courtroom discourse, where language is used to exclude or mislead. These issues lead to one solution or possible way in which these issues can at least be minimised – legal interpretation. We are specifically using the term 'legal interpretation' as there is a general misconception that a mother tongue speaker of a language can act as an interpreter. In

Chapter 2 of this book, we advanced Article 14(3) of the International Covenant on Civil and Political Rights (1996) where persons are permitted:

> (f) To have the free assistance of an interpreter if he cannot understand or speak the language used in court.

Article 14(3) (f), according to Gibbons (2003:238), relates directly to court interpreting and states that this service be free of charge. The service is extended to include the translation of all documents for court proceedings (Gibbons, 2003:238). One aspect of Article 14(3) (f) leaves open, for determination on a case-by-case basis, the level of comprehension and speaking ability necessary for an interpreter to be used (Gibbons, 2003:238). Cooke (2009:29) argues that it is questionable whether a Judge or a Magistrate is qualified to determine reliably the witness's English proficiency and that guidance is needed from an appropriately qualified linguist.

According to Goldflam (2012:2), the first recorded case in which an interpreter was used was in 1885 in Queensland. The Judge dismissed the case in which four men were charged with murder. The case was dismissed as no interpreter could be found to enable them to hear and understand what they had been charged with (Goldflam, 2012:2). With this case, justice had not run its course, especially for the victim's family. Goldflam (2012:2) explains that Australia does not have legislation addressing the use of interpretation. However, the country is a signatory to the International Covenant on Civil and Political Rights (1996) and thus needs to comply with the provisions of Article 14, advanced above.

Gibbons (1994, 2003), Eades (1994) and Cooke (2009) have documented instances in which interpreters have not been supplied for Aboriginal witnesses and accused persons and this remains an ongoing problem. MacFarlane, Kurt, Heydon and Roh (2019:51) argue that the provision of interpreters in Australian courts remains inadequate in both quantity and quality. There are instances in which qualified interpreters are available but are not used. This non-use of interpreters is indicative of the ideology that privileges English monolingualism and supresses the language rights and preferences of indigenous minorities (MacFarlane et al., 2019:51).

There are instances in which legal representatives decline the use of an interpreter for their clients where a Judge suggests this (Cooke, 2009:29). This is done in some instances as a matter of strategy so that the Judge is unable to understand the witness or accused. If employed, it is a dangerous strategy and fails to work. This will be seen in forthcoming chapters concerning the South African case law. Again, this speaks to Gibbons's (2003) earlier point about understanding what 'true justice' is. Cooke (2009:29) engages with Goldflam's (1995) earlier work that brings into question how the client communicates with the lawyer if interpretational services are declined; and how the attorney receives instructions from the client if there is a communication barrier. Some lawyers argue that interpreters complicate matters and that judges are then able to understand the proceedings better without interpretation for witnesses (Cooke, 2009:30).

Aboriginal people are courteous and will answer questions posed by White people in the way in which the questioner wants. Even if people are not courteous, there is the same reaction when they are dealing with an authority figure such as a policeman. Some Aboriginal people find the standard caution quite bewildering; even if they understand that they do not have to answer questions, this is confusing as, if they do not have to answer questions, then why are the questions being asked?

The use of interpreters in judicial proceedings is not standard practice but is influenced by whether the court is seated in a Federal state in Australia or follows the Common Law. The Common Law doctrine does not guarantee the right to an interpreter. However, an interpreter may be provided at the discretion of the judicial officer (Gibbons, 2003:238). In Australia, at Federal level, the 1995 Federal Evidence Act is applicable. Although this statute does not entrench the right to an interpreter for second language speakers, the judicial officer is compelled to justify why an interpreter was not employed in the proceedings (ibid). The onus is thus reversed and no longer falls on the witness to prove the need for an interpreter (ibid). This is not necessarily advantageous as there can be an instance in which the judicial officer does not recognise the need for an interpreter on the basis that the witness can speak English. This relates to previous points in this discussion, where judicial officers fail to recognise the disadvantage that Aboriginal speakers experience when communicating in English.

In south Australia the right to an interpreter is conferred through the Evidence Act Amendment Act 1986, which states the following:

> 14(1) Where
> (a) the native language of a witness who is to give oral evidence in any proceeding is not English; and
> (b) the witness is not reasonably fluent in English, the witness is entitled to give that evidence through an interpreter.

Gibbons (2003:239) focuses on the word "entitled" in this provision. This form of language in the provision is obligatory and guarantees a second language English speaker the right to an interpreter. Gibbons (2003:239) also highlights the phrasing, "reasonably fluent in English" as problematic, as it is discretionary: the determination of fluency is undertaken by the judicial officer who, according to Gibbons (2003:239), is most likely to be a monolingual English speaker with minimal or no knowledge of second language comprehension problems. This speaks to the importance of having linguists who can assess the competency of witnesses and the need for a more linguistically transformed legal system, not only in Australia but also in South Africa.

Legal interpreting and translation in Australia

Our focus shifts to legal interpreting where parallels can be sought between the qualifications of interpreters. The following extract by Gibbons (2003:241) is of relevance and summarises the two issues of legal interpretation:

> There are two issues in the supply of interpreters/translators. First the availability of bilinguals who have the potential to act as courtroom interpreters. The second issue is the quality of translators/interpreters – adequate legal interpreting demands the following special knowledge and abilities: a high level of proficiency in both languages; knowledge of regional variants of these languages used in local communities; good general knowledge; and knowledge of the following: professional ethics; the legal process and legal language; and courtroom/police discourse conventions.

Legal translators have more time to find equivalents that best describe concepts that are not directly translatable from English into the Aboriginal languages. Legal translators are given the text beforehand and are able to grapple with and find solutions to language non-equivalence. Legal interpreters do not have this luxury in court, especially with cross-examination.

In courtroom interpreting, two forms of interpreting can be identified: consecutive interpreting and simultaneous interpreting. Consecutive interpreting is "…where the interpreter waits until the speaker has finished a stretch of speech, usually a small number of sentences, then during a silent period left by the speaker, the interpreting takes place" (Gibbons, 2003:245). Simultaneous interpreting "is a specialised skill in which the interpreter interprets at the same time as the speaker is speaking, usually producing an interpreted version a few words behind the speaker." (Gibbons, 2003:245).

Judge Belinda Hartle (Hartle, 2019) refers to issues of consecutive interpretation where interpreters, in her experience, tend to summarise what the judicial officer is saying. A further point picked up from McConnachie (2019) is the issue of dialect of a language in court interpreting (see also Mbangi, 2019).

The point of departure is the important function of interpreters and translators in the legal system, especially within courtrooms where the judicial officer weighs the admissibility of evidence and a discrepancy between a police statement and *viva voce* evidence. The consequences may be disastrous for either the accused or the complainant.

Interpreter qualifications in Australia

The previous section highlights the importance of quality interpretation by qualified legal interpreters. In civil cases in the State of Queensland, the litigants are to engage an interpreter and pay for such services rendered. This is similar to South Africa where, in civil cases, regardless of the court's jurisdiction, litigants are to engage an interpreter and pay such costs (Hartle, 2019; Mbangi, 2019).

In many Aboriginal communities in Australia an urgent need exists for interpreters in the legal system. However, obstacles are encountered where bilingual proficiency is not of a high level and educational levels are below what is required by standard certification of interpreters and translators (Gibbons, 2003:242). Gibbons (2003:242) questions, then, what level of justice the legal system is rendering to Aboriginal people and notes that these indigenous people are once again disadvantaged before the law.

It is also important for the interpreters to have a sound knowledge of the two cultures through which the interpretation is taking place as cultural terms are often difficult to transport through interpretation into another language whose speakers have their own culture. It was therefore a positive step by the Aboriginal Legal Service in 1970 to offer a legal aid service specifically for Aboriginal people who were essentially field officers that were competent cross-cultural interpreters (Eades, 1994:249-250). These services were employed for communication between Aboriginal clients and their legal practitioners (ibid). A parallel can be drawn with South Africa in relation to the case of *State v Pienaar* (2000) where the court held that an interpreter must be provided for by the state when a client is relying on legal aid services and the legal professional cannot communicate directly with the accused.

A recommendation from the Commonwealth Attorney-General's Department report on access to interpreters in the Australian legal system (1991) was that a professional level of interpreter accreditation be a minimum standard for legal interpreters in any language (Cooke, 2009:32). The National Accreditation Authority mostly accredits indigenous language interpreters for Translators and Interpreters (NAATI) at the level of paraprofessional, which is described as:

- [Paraprofessional accreditation] represents a level of competence in interpreting for the purpose of general conversations, generally in the form of non-specialist dialogues.

Accreditation is achieved through individual testing where the pass mark is 70%. Cooke (2009:32), who identifies himself as having conducted these tests, explains that there is a quality difference between the interpreter who obtains the minimum threshold pass of 70% and the other interpreters who achieve a test mark of 85% and above. Cooke (2009:32-33) advances both sides of the coin, explaining that, in some instances, interpreters with a minimum pass mark, or those who have failed their accreditation, are used as legal interpreters in courts. The other side of the coin is that, in some instances, there are accredited interpreters who are exceptionally competent and highly proficient in both languages and are used as court interpreters (ibid). This links to an earlier argument by Gibbons (2003) in which he explained the need for skilled court interpreters who can interpret simultaneously and consecutively. Cooke (2009:33) goes on to explain that by the end of 2009, for the first time, three indigenous interpreters were accredited by NAATI as professional level interpreters. This is a positive sign that the primary service of interpretation is growing for high status domains such as the legal system.

There is again a difference of interpretation of accreditation in different Australian states. The Northern Territory Aboriginal Interpreter Service had 300 registered interpreters, one quarter of whom were accredited (Cooke, 2009:33). According to Cooke, (2009:33), accreditation through the Northern Territory Aboriginal Interpreter Service could have been obtained through the completion of a Diploma in Interpreting which comprises a course of 300 hours offered through Bachelor Institute. The majority, however, have passed by completing short test preparation workshops over the course of a few days or a week, followed by taking NAATI's oral test.

A new development by the Judicial Council on Cultural Diversity (JCCD) is the Recommended National Standards for Working with Interpreters in Courts and Tribunals, a 132 page document from which we have extracted relevant sections. Part of the preamble summarises the intention of the recommended standards (JCCD, 2017:iv):

> The interpreter's role is to remove the language barrier so that the party can be made linguistically present at the proceedings and thereby be placed in the same position as an English-speaking person. This means that a party is entitled to participate in the proceedings in their own language. As such, the work of interpreters is essential to ensuring access to justice and procedural fairness for people with limited or no English proficiency in Australia's courts. Further, in the case of criminal proceedings, if an accused is unable to afford an interpreter and an appropriate interpreter is not provided at the expense of the court or an agency of government, the trial cannot proceed unless and until an interpreter is provided.

This extract attempts to preclude any form of disadvantage before the law relating to language and prioritises the rights of indigenous people to ensure equal treatment as English speakers. There is also the commitment of providing interpretational services at the state's expense for criminal proceedings. Recommended standards for interpreters are clearly set out and are as follows:

> Standard 18 – Interpreters as officers of the court
> 18.1 Interpreters are officers of the court in the sense that they owe to the court paramount duties of accuracy and impartiality in the office of interpreter, which override any duty that person may have to any party to the proceedings, even if that person is engaged directly by that party.
>
> Standard 19 – Court Interpreters' Code of Conduct
> 19.1 Interpreters must ensure that they are familiar with, and comply with, the Court Interpreters' Code of Conduct.
>
> Standard 20 – Duties of interpreters
> 20.1 Interpreters must diligently and impartially interpret communications in connection with a court proceeding as accurately and completely as possible.
> 20.2 Interpreters must comply with any direction of the court.

20.3 Where the interpreter becomes aware that she or he may have a conflict of interest, the interpreter must alert the court to the possible conflict of interest immediately, and if necessary withdraw from the assignment or proceed as directed by the court.

20.4 Requests by the interpreter for repetition, clarification and explanation should be addressed to the judicial officer rather than to the questioning counsel, witness or party.

20.5 There may be occasions when the interpreter needs to correct a mistake. All corrections should be addressed to the judicial officer rather than to the questioning counsel, witness or party.

20.6 If the interpreter recognises a potential cross-cultural misunderstanding, or comprehension or cognitive difficulties on the part of the person for whom the interpreter is interpreting, the interpreter should seek leave from the judicial officer to raise the issue.

20.7 Interpreters must keep confidential all information acquired, in any form whatsoever, in the course of their engagement or appointment in the office of interpreter (including any communication subject to client legal privilege) unless:
   a. that information is or comes into the public domain; or
   b. the beneficiary of the client legal privilege has waived that privilege.

These provisions regulate the practice of interpreters in Australian courts with an emphasis placed on accurate interpretation, speaking to the issue of quality of interpretation. Section 18.1 is strengthened in Sections 20.1, 20.4 and 20.5 that speak to diligence and the ability of an interpreter to ask for repetition, clarification and explanation where necessary in order to avoid a mistake and correct where necessary. This is important in ensuring quality interpretation and procedural fairness for all parties concerned. With reference to procedural fairness, the interpreter is to be impartial; where there is a conflict of interest, this must be made known, and the interpreter removed where necessary. An interesting inclusion was Section 20.6 concerning cross-cultural communication and its effect on cognition and comprehension.

As is seen thus far with the Australian case study, there are dialectal differences that are embedded in cultural communities amongst the Aboriginal people, and a miscommunication could have disastrous effects. The Recommended National Standards for Working with Interpreters in Courts and Tribunals document is extensive in its mandate and is a positive step towards regulating the profession of interpreters in Australia. The Recommended National Standards for Working with Interpreters in Courts and Tribunals document will also be important in the context of South Africa. Such a comprehensive document is absent there, yet the Heads of Court, through the monolingual language of record policy, have directly elected to operate a legal system where the majority of litigants and witnesses cannot speak, understand, read or write English.

MacFarlane et al. (2019) have argued that, although attempts have been made to regulate interpretation services in Australia, it remains an unequal system through which Aboriginal people are subjected to either low levels of interpretation or non-availability of an interpreter. The former relates to the low levels of qualifications where no tertiary qualification is needed to be a legal interpreter (MacFarlane et al., 2019:56-57). The latter relates to the fact that there is no guaranteed right to an interpreter. This is compounded by the judicial view of the lack of importance of interpreters for Aboriginal people. MacFarlane et al. (ibid, 56) substantiate this point by drawing on a statement made by then Chief Minister, Dennis Burke, before the introduction of the Aboriginal Interpreter Service in the Northern Territory in 2000. He said: "Providing Aborigines with interpreters was like giving a wheelchair to someone who should be walking."

This harrowing statement lays bare the treatment of indigenous people by a justice system tasked with impartiality, procedural fairness and equality before the law. It must be questioned, in the South African context, if this is not also the thinking and reasoning behind a monolingual language of record policy that excludes the majority of people on grounds of language. We engage further with this point in the forthcoming chapters of this book.

An Aboriginal interpreter's perspective of language in the courts

An online news article, Joyner (2018) provides practical examples of the difficulties Aboriginal people face in the Australian legal system. The article focuses on the area of Kalgoorlie, where surrounding remote areas have magistrates flying in to the Bush courts. The level of justice is always questionable, given that a Magistrate can hear up to 100 cases in a day (Joyner, 2018). One can question how much, if any, interpreting takes place in these courts, where interpreting is often time-consuming. Joyner (2018) reports that interpreters have a difficult time with interpretation as accused persons are always frightened by the daunting legal processes and appear to agree with everything or speak in hushed tones.

This is the case, according to Stubbs who acts as a guide for Aboriginal people navigating their way through the system. Although Stubbs has no formal training as an interpreter, he has become accustomed to interpretation through his 30 years' experience working for the Aboriginal Legal Service in Kalgoorie, a Legal Aid organisation based in Perth and 14 surrounding towns (Joyner, 2018). Stubbs, who interprets for Wongatha Aboriginal speakers, does not charge Aboriginal people and is one of many offering this service free of charge (Joyner, 2018). Stubbs has assumed the title of court officer, comprising the roles of interpreter, advisor, negotiator and fixer given that interpretation in these areas is more than merely acting as a third-party communicator (Joyner, 2018). In the news article, Joyner (2018) alerts us to the actual plight of indigenous speakers and their marginalisation from Australia's courts in which linguistic discrimination is a daily occurrence. Deanne Lightfoot, the Chief Executive Officer of the Aboriginal Legal Service in Kalgoorlie, has reported that there is an Indigenous Interpreters Project underway in the Goldfields region of Australia to increase the numbers of interpreters and train them to deal effectively with these cases in ensuring equal access to justice and procedural fairness (Joyner, 2018).

Through the sociolinguistic discussion, it is clear that, as with South Africa, Australia has a rich language history of many indigenous languages. As is the case with many countries across the globe, these indigenous languages are dying and many more face extinction. The death of languages lies with the fact that languages are not used in high status domains and are therefore not developed by the state and used as languages of learning and teaching. Through the work of Meakins (2015), the Australian case study illustrates that younger generations are unable to speak or identify their indigenous languages. A culture has been created which Crystal (2003) describes in terms that reflect a sense of the global rise of English, along with the death of all other languages.

Language has served as a tool of politicisation, marginalisation and discrimination – commencing with the colonisers' arrival in Australia. This politicisation has resulted in a further distinction and growing inequality between Aboriginal people and White Australians through Standard Australian English and Aboriginal English. The theme of language and power is evident where Aboriginal people are seen as less powerful and are ultimately disadvantaged in courts as a result of language barriers.

Drawing on the works of Eades (1994) and Gibbons (1994, 2003), it is evident that the cross-cultural communication impasses are overlooked in many instances, resulting in innocent persons being found guilty and sentenced, or the guilty being acquitted. These cross-cultural communication problems are not unique to the courtroom, as the discussion shows, but commence with the police services. Cooke (2009) has presented the many issues facing interpretation in Australian courts. These are compounded by the fact that there is no guaranteed right to interpretation in those courts. In a multilingual country such as Australia where the language of record is English, it is problematic not to have interpretation services that are of high quality and readily available. The matter is further compounded by the fact that the 'legal system' does not inherently recognise the importance of interpretation. Through the work of Joyner (2018), the Australian case study also highlights that the problems are practical and that there are no effective policies and initiatives addressing the continued disadvantage and discrimination endured by Aboriginal persons in the legal system.

Belgium's sociolinguistic landscape

Belgian linguistic history has been influenced by cultural, nationalist, political and economic power battles between the Dutch and the French. Although the Dutch were the majority group in Belgium, they felt threatened by the French and the dominance of the French language. The Dutch thus opted to support legal provisions that constrained the use of language, rather than opting for freedom of language use (Wynants, 2001:43). This favoured the adoption of the principle of territoriality. With the principle of territoriality in Belgium, one language is only officially recognised within a given territory (Wynants, 2001:43).

In 1840, the Dutch realised that there was not exclusive use of Dutch, as had been anticipated with the principle of territoriality. A petition was launched to denounce language discrimination in Belgium (Wynants, 2001:45). In 1859, a Commission of Grievances took up the same protests and demands recorded in 1840 (Wynants, 2001:45). The Commission failed to recommend the exclusive use of Dutch in the Flemish provinces and ordered instead that official documents be translated and be made available in both languages (Wynants, 2001:45).

Belgium is divided into four language areas, namely the Dutch linguistic area, the French linguistic area, the German linguistic area, and the bilingual capital of Brussels (Boes & Deridder, 2001:49). Within each area, the regional language is the sole official language with the exception of Brussels where French and Dutch are equally treated as official languages (Boes & Deridder, 2001:49). When choosing between the principle of territoriality and personality, a sociopolitical consideration determines the outcome. Wynants (2001:47) explains that the principle of personality implies greater freedom of individual choice and is therefore considered democratically sound. The principle of territoriality constricts freedom and imposes constraint and forced assimilation (Wynants, 2001:47). Selecting between either of the two principles is determined by material and financial factors relevant to the country or the area in which the language policy is to be applied (Wynants, 2001:47).

The current Belgian sociolinguistic landscape has been influenced and regulated by a number of constitutional and legislative enactments. These developments are identified and discussed in the following sections of this chapter.

Constitutional and legislative language enactments

The Belgian Constitution provided that the use of the official languages in Belgium was optional and that only legislation could regulate the use of the official languages for public authorities and legal matters (Boes & Deridder, 2001:49). In accordance with this provision, the Law of June 15, 1935 was enacted. This Law was comprehensive in that it replaced a number of previous statutes governing the use of language in the judiciary from 1889 to 1908 (Wynants, 2001:46). The replaced legislation included, but was not limited to, the first language legislation in Belgium, namely the Law of August 17, 1873, *Moniteur Belge*, 43, 238 and the Law of August 26, 1873. The *Moniteur Belge*, 43, 238 legislation dealt with language use in the judiciary and conferred a right upon Flemish accused persons to use Dutch in criminal proceedings (Wynants, 2001:45). The *Moniteur Belge*, 43, 238 was a significant victory for the Flemish in Belgium given that, in 1860, Flemish workers had minimal knowledge of French. If they were subsequently tried in French for murder, they were found guilty and executed (Wynants, 2001:45). It later transpired that the Flemish workers were innocent, proving that language barriers were the cause of the execution

(Wynants, 2001:45). The Law of June 15, 1935 therefore needed to address the linguistic deficiencies in creating a more linguistically just and equal legal system. The purpose of the Law of June 15, 1935 was two-fold:

1. The law applies for judgments and procedural acts; and
2. The law sets out rules to determine the language used by the court, as well as before the court.

It is evident that the Law of June 15, 1935 regulates proceedings in terms of the language competencies of judges and the language(s) to be used in delivering judgments. Moreover, the Law of June 15, 1935 determines the language in which proceedings are to be conducted and the subsequent language of record. The use of language in court is determined through different criminal and civil procedures, as outlined by the Law of June 15, 1935. Boes and Deridder (2001:51) explain that, through the implementation of the provisions in the Law of June 15, 1935, there might be an implication of derogation from the territorial linguistic competence of courts.

Language of record in the Belgian criminal justice system

Criminal proceedings can only be initiated following the conclusion of a criminal investigation that commences with a charge or complaint laid with the police. Thus, the criminal investigation is an important process in capturing the relevant information and evidence needed to prosecute the accused person. Language is instrumental in this process where communication between the complainant and police officer provides the foreground to the investigation, as is the questioning of the arrested person by the police. The linguistic issues plaguing the South African Police Service (SAPS) and, in some cases, directly affecting the outcome of a criminal trial, have been discussed by Docrat et al. (2017b). The South African perspective is discussed further from Chapter 4 onwards. Reverting to the Belgian context, Article 12 of the Law of June 15, 1935 provides that "members of the Public Prosecutor's Department and the investigating officers must use the language of the court". With the territoriality principle implemented in Belgium, Dutch will be used in a Dutch-speaking area and French will be used in a French-speaking area. In Brussels, either French or Dutch can be used, depending on the language of the suspect.

Article 12 clearly states that the police officer must record the complainant's statement in the language of the said complainant or witness where the police officer has sufficient knowledge of this language. Where the police officer has insufficient knowledge, an interpreter has to be called to record the statement. Article 12 ensures complainants and suspects have access to linguistically competent police officers who can record their statements without any issues of linguistic barriers; if there are such barriers present, interpreters are available to assist. This point will be juxtaposed with the South African context in Chapter 5 where the SAPS draft language policy (2015) is advanced and critiqued with practical examples are provided. What is significant about Article 12 is that the importance of language is outlined from the beginning; and that professional interpreters are available for both the police and Public Prosecutor's Department.

At trial stage, it must be noted that only in exceptional cases will the language law assign a case to a specific court. Nonetheless, according to Boes and Deridder (2001:52), in criminal proceedings, territorial competence of criminal courts is determined through the following criteria:

- the location where the crime was perpetrated;
- the usual residence of the accused, if he or she is a natural person; and
- the present location of the accused.

These three factors resemble those of the South African model when determining jurisdiction for prosecution.

In criminal courts of the first instance, trials are conducted in Dutch, French or German, depending on the area in which the court is seated. The judgment is then also written and delivered in the language in which the trial was conducted.

Article 23 of the Law of June 15, 1935 holds that, where an accused person can only express him- or herself in one of the three languages, and as such does not understand the language of the court, he or she can request to be tried in the nearest court in a language of his or her preference (Boes & Deridder, 2001:53). The Judge can refuse the request if of the view that the accused has sufficient linguistic competency, or it would be harmful to the proceedings. In instances of refusal, an interpreter will be provided for the accused (Boes & Deridder, 2001:53). Article 23 will be compared to Section 35(3) (k) of the South African Constitution. As evidenced in Part One of Chapter 6, South African accused persons will be solely reliant on an interpreter where they do not understand or speak English. There is no recourse for a request for another court to hear the trial, as all courts have an English-only language of record policy in place.

Language of record in the Belgian civil system

The civil system mirrors the criminal justice system with regard to language and so similarities are evident. Commencing civil litigation requires a summons to be filed and served on the defendant. According to Articles 7 and 38 of the Law of June 15, 1935, the writ of summons has to be drawn up in the language of the area (Boes & Deridder, 2001:54). There is no alternative to these provisions where the defendant is not able to ask for the writ of summons to be produced in another language. In the bilingual case of Brussels, the writ of summons can be drawn up in either Dutch or French, with the plaintiff choosing between the two.

The defendant has the option of requesting that the language of proceedings be changed where he or she has insufficient knowledge of the language (Boes & Deridder, 2001:54). There is also the option of both parties to litigation changing the language of proceedings through common agreement (Boes & Deridder, 2001:54). Individuals appearing before a judicial officer are not restricted to using one of the three national languages as an interpreter can be provided (Boes & Deridder, 2001:54). Judicial officers and lawyers are, however, bound to the language of the proceedings (Boes & Deridder, 2001:54).

As with criminal cases, civil cases are assigned on the basis of territorial competence which is determined according to Article 624 of the Code of Civil Procedure. The court is chosen by the plaintiff from among the following four possibilities (Boes & Deridder, 2001:54):

- the court in the municipal area of the residence of the defendant or one of the defendants;
- the court where the legal obligations arose or were executed;
- the court mentioned in the contract; and
- the court where the bailiff met the defendant in person if the defendant has no residence in Belgium.

The Belgian Court of Appeal and SC conduct proceedings in the same language used in the court of first instance. In Chapter 5, we advance the relevant provisions of the Magistrates' Courts Act (1944) and Superior Courts Act (2013). Suffice to say, at this stage of the discussion in relation to Belgium, South African legislation fails to confer language rights or any language protection on civil litigants; by default, all proceedings must be conducted in English. Furthermore, unlike the Belgian model, civil litigants in South Africa have to draw up the summons in English and cannot collectively decide to change the language of proceedings. Belgium goes as far as providing interpreters for those who do not have sufficient knowledge of the language of proceedings. In South Africa, in civil cases, the state provides no such service at their expense. Private interpreters can be hired and the costs be borne by the litigant or witness.

Language competency of Belgian judicial officers

By adopting the territorial principle there would need to be courts and public offices in each area fully functional in one of the three national languages. This, in turn, would require persons who are linguistically competent in the language(s) to staff these offices and courts. There was a need to establish Dutch universities to heed the requirement of having courts operating through the medium of Dutch (Wynants, 2001:46). Lawyers, magistrates and judges all received their education in French and therefore had minimal knowledge of Dutch in legal matters (Wynants, 2001:46). The problem was deep-rooted in that there was no professional literature in Dutch, nor was there any jurisprudence, textbooks, codes, law commentaries or teaching material in Dutch.

Dutch terminology and other relevant material were available from the Netherlands, however, there remained the problem of staffing the Dutch universities (Wynants, 2001:46). A few Flemish lawyers and private individuals began with translation, interpretation and teaching on a part-time basis. In 1923, the Belgian government established an official commission tasked with translation. The first Dutch-speaking university was established in Ghent in 1930 along with the establishment of training schools for translators and interpreters (Wynants, 2001:47). The Belgium model follows the principle that the basic priority of a judiciary must be equality between all parties to litigation (Wynants, 2001:47). What is important is that each party to court must at least be able to understand the judges and magistrates and to be understood by them as far as possible with the support of translators and interpreters (Wynants, 2001:47).

Following the inherent principles of understanding, judicial officers and being understood by judicial officers is now regulated by appointments to the bench. Simply put, a person cannot be appointed to the bench as a Judge in a specific language area if he or she does not have sufficient knowledge of the language in the area (Boes & Deridder, 2001:54). This knowledge is determined by the language of the candidate's law degree independent of their mother tongue (Boes & Deridder, 2001:54). For example, if a candidate is a French mother tongue speaker but obtained their law degree in Dutch (Boes & Deridder, 2001:54), they will be appointed to a court in a Dutch-speaking area, or in Brussels, since it has bilingual provision. The candidate thus has the requisite legal and academic proficiency in the language in which they graduated. A university degree in a specific language is not the requirement to attest to knowledge in that language but rather an additional examination to test their linguistic knowledge (Boes & Deridder, 2001:55). This is especially the case for German mother tongue speakers as there is no German university in Belgium and therefore proficiency is tested through an examination (Boes & Deridder, 2001:54). In Brussels, judgeships are allotted to French- and Dutch-speaking judges according to the various caseloads in the courts. There are minimum requirements for the composition of the bench in Brussels comprising the following: one-third of the bench must hold a diploma in Dutch; one-third must hold a diploma in French; and two-thirds of the bench must have a proven knowledge of their second language (Boes & Deridder, 2001:55). In the court of Cassation, an equal 50/50 representation between Dutch and French-speaking judges is required, with all having a knowledge of German as a requirement (Boes & Deridder, 2001:55).

The Belgian model illustrates the inherent emphasis placed on language and the human and financial support garnered towards the attainment of linguistic equality for all in Belgium. It is interesting to note the language requirements conferred on judges prior to their being appointed to the bench. This will be contrasted with the legislation relevant to attorneys, advocates, magistrates and judges in South Africa, advanced in Chapters 5 and 8 where, in South Africa, judges and legal practitioners have argued that judges cannot be 'shopped for' on the basis of language (Thulare AJ in *State* v *Gordon*, 2018) as this amounts to unfair discrimination. The foregoing discussion on Belgium also brings to the fore the important role that universities have in educating legal professionals, not only in the sense of their acquiring legal knowledge, but also the language in which this knowledge is acquired with separate linguistic communicative skills in a language that may not necessarily be the students' mother tongue. This speaks to the bilingual proficiency with which students graduate from Belgian universities and will be juxtaposed with, firstly, the growing trend of South African universities to adopt English-only language policies and, secondly, the endorsement by the South African judiciary that monolingual language policies are transformative and all-inclusive.

The Belgian model illustrates that, with human investment, commitment and financial capital, a system can be transformed to ensure an inclusive legal system that provides meaningful effect to litigants' language rights. From the onset of accessing the criminal justice system with reference to the police, both a complainant and accused are not disadvantaged by language. The Belgian model also importantly illustrates the role of universities in giving effective meaning to courts' language policies. It is interesting to note how universities and individuals are committed to the lexical development of each of the three languages in Belgium to ensure that academic texts are produced, and that translation of documents and sources of law are available in all three languages. This point will be juxtaposed with the South African context in Chapters 8 and 9 with reference to the work of Murray (2019) who advocates for universities to teach all content in English and only offer degrees through the medium of English; and where acquiring a second language, namely an African language, is seen as time wasted.

The recognition conferred on language and understanding of proceedings in the civil system is one that can be emulated and will be discussed in Chapters 6 and 7 with reference to the South African model.

The territoriality approach in Belgium is not without its problems, as outlined in the historical sociolinguistic perspective. However, the model is inclusive and does not problematise language in the legal system, instead viewing it as a right and a resource for dealing with practical problems as they arise.

What follows in the next section of this chapter is a discussion of Canada's model and the use of language therein.

Canadian sociolinguistic landscape

As established through the Founding Constitution Act of 1867, Canada represents itself as a bilingual state comprising French and English speakers. However, it has been noted that many citizens are monolingual and can only speak one of the two languages. Williams (2012:47) states that these monolingual citizens are primarily French speakers. From a historical perspective, the Canadian State's Founding Constitution Act of 1867 conferred upon all persons the right to "... use English and or French in courts and Legislative Assemblies of the Federal government and the province of Quebec". Doucet (2012:162) explained that Section 133 of the Constitution Act of 1867 was the only provision therein which dealt exclusively with language rights. Doucet (2012:162) states further that Section 133 was never intended to establish two official languages in Canada but rather to create what he termed an "... embryonic form of official bilingualism ..."

A parallel can be drawn with the South African model, discussed in Part One of Chapter 6 of this book, where Lourens (2012) refers to Section 6(4) of the Constitution as the "unborn" language legislation and the effects of a "delayed" birth. French assumed a subordinate position in government and parliamentary processes.

In the 1960s, Prime Minister Trudeau established a Royal Commission on Bilingualism and Biculturalism. The Commission's report in 1969 included a 'blueprint' for a bilingual language policy. The central theme of the report and, more specifically, the policy, was the "strengthening" and reaffirmation of bilingualism (Williams, 2012:47). It housed the objectives and principles upon which the Official Languages Act of 1968 was drafted and later enacted in 1969 (Williams, 2012:47).

The Belgian commission established in 1923 was tasked with translation of texts, legislation and other sources into Dutch. Although the Belgian and Canadian commissions had different objectives, they both illustrate the investment which these countries made into the development of their languages and for citizens to access a legal system in their mother tongue. This can be counterposed with the South African historical perspective which we will outline in the forthcoming chapters on South Africa where, following the CODESA talks, there was no government initiative to establish and follow through with the development of the nine African languages, nor the commitment of resources for the translation of important texts and legislation. This remains a contentious issue in South Africa, given the ongoing litigation (*Lourens* v *Speaker of the National Assembly and Others*, 2015; *Lourens* v *State Party: Republic of South Africa*, 2018) in which parliament has inherently argued that the Constitution does not compel that all legislation be translated into all 11 official languages.

The Canadian Official Languages Act of 1969 took significant linguistic strides providing for the establishment of language rights for both official languages (Williams, 2012:47). The relationship between citizens and the state more broadly was explicated with pronouncements on rights and duties of both the citizens exercising their language rights and the state, as well as state institutions in responding to these (Williams, 2012:47). The

Canadian Official Languages Act of 1969 must be borne in mind in Chapter 5 of this book where we have advanced the objectives of the South African Use of Official Languages Act (2012) and commented on the provisions thereof. The Languages Act 2012, unlike the Canadian Official Languages Act of 1969, provides no further interpretation or protection of rights beyond the skeletal framework of Section 6 of the Constitution. In reality, however, the provisions of the Canadian Official Languages Act of 1969 were not implemented; and the languages and speakers thereof were not treated equally. Williams (2012:48) advanced that clarification needed to be sought on the parameters of the language rights; and, in establishing these parameters, the obligation of the state was to be outlined in ensuring the realisation of the language rights.

There was a proclamation of the Canadian Charter of Rights and Freedoms in 1982 heeding this call (published online as 'Constitution Act, 1982'). The Canadian Charter of Rights and Freedoms (1982) is the reaffirmation of the core principle of linguistic duality (Williams, 2012:48). Linguistic duality refers to the equal status and treatment of the languages. This again can be counterposed with the provisions in Section 6 of the South African Constitution. The term 'linguistic duality' is absent; instead, Section 6(2) calls for the elevation of the nine African languages. Although Section 6(2) is qualified through Section 6(3), obligating the state to use at least two languages, the minimum standard built in does not guarantee the elevation of the African languages.

There are many sections in the Canadian Charter of Rights and Freedoms (1982) dealing primarily with language:

16. (1) English and French are the official languages of Canada and equality of status and equal rights and privileges as to their use in all institutions of the Parliament and government of Canada.
(2) English and French are the official languages of New Brunswick and have equality of status and equal rights and privileges as to their use in all institutions of the legislature and government n New Brunswick.
(3) Nothing in this Charter limits the authority of Parliament or a legislature to advance the equality of status or use of English and French.
16.1 (1) The English linguistic community and the French linguistic community in New Brunswick have equality of status and equal rights and privileges, including the right to distinct educational institutions and such distinct cultural institutions as are necessary for the preservation and promotion of those communities.
(2) The role of the legislature and government of New Brunswick to preserve and promote the status, rights and privileges referred to in subsection (1) is reaffirmed.
17. (1) Everyone has the right to use English or French in any debates and other proceedings of Parliament.
(2) Everyone has the right to use English or French in any debates and other proceedings of the legislature of New Brunswick.
18. (1) The statutes, records and journals of Parliament shall be printed and published in English and French and both language versions are equally authoritative.

(2) The statutes, records and journals of the legislature of New Brunswick shall be printed and published in English and French and both language versions are equally authoritative.

19. (1) Either English or French may be used by any person in, or in any pleading in or process issuing from, any court established by Parliament.

    (2) English or French may be used by any person in, or in any pleading in or process issuing from, any court of New Brunswick.

20. (1) Any member of the public in Canada has the right to communicate with, and to receive available services from, any head or central office of an institution of the Parliament or government of Canada in English or French, and has the same right with respect to any other office of any such institution where
    a. there is a significant demand for communications with the services from that office in such a language; or
    b. due to the nature of the office, it is reasonable that communications with and services from that office be available in both English and French.

    (2) Any member of the public in New Brunswick has the right to communicate with, and to receive available services from, any office of an institution of the legislature or government of New Brunswick in English or French.

21. Nothing in Sections 16 to 20 abrogates or derogates from any right, privilege or obligation with respect to the English and French languages, or either of them, that exists or is continued by virtue of any other provision of the Constitution of Canada.

22. Nothing in Sections 16 to 20 abrogates or derogates from any legal or customary right or privilege acquired or enjoyed either before or after the coming into force of this Charter with respect to any language that is not English or French.

As seen from these excerpts, the Canadian Charter of Rights and Freedoms (1982) is progressive and, according to Doucet (2012:162), heralded in a new era for the recognition of linguistic constitutional rights. Section 16(1) speaks to the principle of linguistic duality by stating that both French and English enjoy equality of status and equal rights and privileges. This speaks to the earlier point we made with reference to the case of *Lourens v Speaker of the National Assembly and Others* (2015) where Parliament argued that the South African constitutional provisions do not explicitly state nor imply that the languages enjoy equality, but should rather be treated equitably and used where practicable. Thus, Section 18(1) of the Canadian Charter of Rights and Freedoms (1982), advanced above, by stating that statutes and other relevant texts be made available in both languages is foreign to the mindset in South Africa where this is seen as impractical. Section 18(1) resembles the Belgian model, presented earlier in this chapter, where all statutes and texts were translated to ensure all speakers of the national languages have equal access. A further similarity with the Belgian model can be found in Section 16.1(1) where speakers of both French and English have the right to their own distinct universities: in Belgium, universities were established and law degrees are offered through the medium of one of the national languages. Again, this is different to South Africa: in Chapters 1 to 9, we advance the language policies of universities and the relevant litigation reaffirming English-only policies of teaching and learning (*AfriForum and Another v University of the Free State*, 2018).

One point of critique, though, is that the Canadian Charter of Rights and Freedoms (1982) focuses on the Province of New Brunswick, a focus that will also be apparent in the legislation advanced below. Simply put, the other Canadian provinces are not as advanced, from a language rights perspective. Canada still has to ensure implementation takes place across all its provinces.

Legislation: Official Languages Act of Canada

As with any constitutional framework, legislation is required to provide elucidation and practical effect to the constitutional provisions. The Official Languages Act of Canada, (1988) is the primary language legislation of Canada. According to Williams (2012:48), the Official Languages Act of Canada (1988) reaffirms the importance of linguistic duality; and in doing so, emphasises the importance of language equality. Linguistic equality is thus entrenched through the Official Languages Act of Canada (1988) in "… Parliament; within the government of Canada; the federal administration and all institutions subject to the Act" (Williams, 2012:48).

The Official Languages Act of Canada (1988) provides that both English- and French-speaking citizens can access all government services in a national language of their choice. According to Williams (2012:50), the Official Languages Act of Canada (1988) comprises three main objectives:

1. The equality of English and French in Parliament within the government of Canada, the Federal administration and institutions subject to the Act;
2. The preservation and development of official language communities in Canada; and
3. The equality of English and French in Canadian society.

It is our opinion that the Official Languages Act of Canada (1988) gives practical meaning to the Canadian Charter of Rights and Freedoms by obligating government and all state entities to provide services to citizens in the national language of their choice. By doing so, the languages are treated and used equally.

Thus far, the Canadian constitutional and legislative frameworks have not made mention of the legal system. To this end, what follows is a presentation of the New Brunswick Official Languages Act, (2002) regulating the use of language in the legal system and the language of record.

Language of record in Canadian courts: The New Brunswick Official Languages Act

The New Brunswick Official Languages Act (2002), focusing specifically on the legal system, was enacted in accordance with the provisions of the Canadian Charter of Rights and

Freedoms (1982). This is evident from the Preamble. Sections 16 to 26 of the New Brunswick Official Languages Act (2002) comprise provisions dealing with the language of record and, more generally, language use in courts. These provisions read as follows:

16. English and French are the official languages of the courts.
17. Every person has the right to use the official language of his or her choice in any matter before the courts, including all proceedings, or in any pleading or process issuing from a court.
18. No person shall be placed at a disadvantage by reason of the choice made under section 17.
19. (1) A court before which a matter is pending must understand, without the assistance of an interpreter or any process of simultaneous translation or consecutive interpretation, the official language chosen under section 17 by a party to the matter.
    (2) A court before which a matter is pending must understand both official languages, without the assistance of an interpreter or any process of simultaneous translation or consecutive interpretation, if both English and French are the languages chosen by the parties to the proceedings.
20. (1) A person who has alleged to have committed an offence under an Act or a regulation of the Province or under a municipal by-law has the right to have the proceedings conducted in the language of his or her choice and shall be informed of that right by the presiding Judge before entering a plea.
    (2) A person who is alleged to have committed an offence within the meaning of subsection (1), has the right to be understood by the court, without the assistance of an interpreter or any process of simultaneous translation or consecutive interpretation, in the official language chosen by the person.
21. Every court has the duty to ensure that any witness appearing before it can be heard in the official language of his/her choice and upon the request of one of the parties or the witness, the court has the duty to ensure that services of simultaneous translation or consecutive interpretation are available to the person who made the request.
22. Where Her Majesty in her right of the Province or institution is a party to civil proceedings before a court, Her Majesty or the institution concerned shall use, in any oral or written pleadings or any process issuing from a court, the official language chosen by the other party.
23. Where the parties to civil proceedings, other than Her Majesty in right of the Province or any institution, do not choose or fail to agree on the official language to be used in proceedings, Her Majesty or the institution concerned shall use such official language as is reasonable, having regard to the circumstances.
24. (1) Any final decision, order or judgment of any court, including any reasons given therefore and summaries, shall be published in both official languages where:
    (a) it determines a question of law of interest or importance to the general public, or
    (b) the proceedings leading to its issuance were conducted in whole or in part in both official languages.
    (2) Where a final decision, order or judgment is required to be published under subsection (1), but is determined that to do so would result in a delay or injustice or hardship to a party to the proceedings, the decision, order or judgment, including any reasons given, shall be published in the first instance in one official language and, thereafter, at the earliest possible time, in the other official language.

25 All decisions of the Court of Appeal are deemed to fall within the scope of Section 24.
26 Sections 24 and 25 shall not be construed so as to prevent the pronouncement of a judgment, in either official language and in such a case, the judgment is not invalid by reason only that it was pronounced in one official language.

Section 16 pronounces both English and French as the languages of record in Brunswick courts. From the onset, it is clear that the languages of record for courts is in line with the Canadian official languages. Thus, for practical purposes, both languages are treated equally. Section 17 of the New Brunswick Official Languages Act (2002) is more advanced than Section 35(3) (k) of the South African Constitution in that litigants have a language right of choice in any matter (see Part One of Chapter 6 for a full discussion of the South African context). In the provision, emphasis is on the language used, referring to a "language of choice" as opposed to the South African context where the phrase "a language the accused understands" is used. This is extended to civil cases as well, where Section 22 provides that Her Majesty (the state) use the language chosen by the other party when communicating in any oral or written pleadings. Where parties excluding Her Majesty (the state) are parties to litigation and cannot agree on the language of record, Her Majesty (the state) will determine the language taking into account what is reasonable in the circumstances. These provisions are profound and afford language rights to civil litigants, as opposed to the situation with the South African model where Judge Hartle (2019) explained that proceedings are in English and interpretational services are not provided at the state's expense. These costs, Judge Hartle (2019) explains, may be too high as there is no quantum of costs legislated for interpretational services in civil cases.

According to Section 19(2), the court must understand the language used without the assistance of an interpreter. This is reinforced through Sections 20(1) and (2), providing that, in having a language of choice right, the court must understand the litigant without any form of interpretation. Section 19(2) precludes the possible complication where both languages are used in proceedings, obligating the court to understand both languages. Two languages may be used, for instance, where a witness to a case provides evidence in a language other than the language in which the proceedings are conducted. According to Section 21, interpretation is permitted where a witness or any party before court requests the services of an interpreter and such services must be made available on request. Sections 16 to 23 are inclusive and ensure all litigants and witnesses are treated equally and have equal access to courts, where language is not a barrier. Section 18, in fact, entrenches the guarantee that there be no disadvantage before the law.

The language of record is often a contentious point of discussion with reference to the judgment and precedent-setting judgments to be published in the law reports. Section 24(1) of the New Brunswick Official Languages Act (2002) deals with these issues where there is a bilingual language of record policy and is illustrative of linguistic inclusivity in

New Brunswick. The objective of practical interpretation of the equality of two official languages is evident. Judgments must be made available in both languages where:
- (a) it determines a question of law of interest or importance to the general public, or
- (b) the proceedings leading to its issuance were conducted in whole or in part in both official languages.

The insertion of subsection (2) also addressed the potential time delays that may arise from the publication of a judgment in both official languages. The provision bears testament to the unwavering commitment of equality of status of both official languages. Of greater significance was the manner in which the legislature drafted the New Brunswick Official Languages Act (2002): instead of viewing time delays as a result of bilingual publication of judgments, the legislature skilfully drafted subsection (2) without limiting the right of litigants and other citizens in accessing judgments. This is the act of balancing rights without limiting either of the rights.

The legislative position in New Brunswick in the form of the New Brunswick Official Languages Act (2002) is said to be exemplary in nature in that New Brunswick is the only Canadian Province to be officially bilingual, both theoretically and practically, in all disciplines across society (Doucet, 2012: 59). Given the extensiveness of the New Brunswick Official Languages Act (2002), Doucet (2012) advances a theoretical discussion in an attempt to explain why a state would not just opt for the simplest solution of adopting the official language of the majority as the official language for use across all disciplines. In engaging with this paradox, it was stated that a state has two options in the process of language planning, namely the territorial or personal approach.

Doucet (2012:160) states that the adoption of a territorial-based approach will result in unilingualism in the specifically defined geographical area. Doucet (2012:160) advances further that this was a common human phenomenon where persons of the same linguistic community are positioned geographically. In the case of Canada, the personal approach may be ideal in the circumstances as there are only two official languages. Therefore, it is our opinion that the type of approach will be dependent on the nature of the linguistic framework of each country. Docuet (2012:161) also acknowledges the fact that a multilingual state faces greater concerns of linguistic choice in disciplines, such as the legislative process, national institutions, government services, administration of justice and education.

Judicial interpretation and application of a bilingual language of record: case law

Once again, the practicalities surrounding a bilingual language of record need to be assessed through relevant case law. The case law advanced in the proceeding paragraphs deals *inter alia* with the court's interpretation of litigants' language rights and the language of record. A further purpose of advancing Canadian case law is to illustrate the jurisprudential development in the courts' reasoning and interpretation of the provisions of the language rights. The cases are assessed with the aim of determining whether both the constitutional and legislative frameworks have been interpreted restrictively or purposively. Discussions below pertain to the selected cases in accordance with the doctrine of precedent.

Foucher (2012:333) explains that the Canadian courts ought to adopt a balance in interpreting the language provisions between an individual's human rights, the collective language rights and the constitutional framework giving effect to the national minority. Language rights are not to be interpreted narrowly, as opposed to other constitutionally enshrined rights. In avoiding narrow interpretation of language rights, the parameters and objectives of the language rights must be clarified by the courts (Foucher, 2012:234). The latter two points will be discussed in Chapter 7 with reference to the cases of *AfriForum and Another* v *University of the Free State* (2018); and *Gelyke Kanse and Others* v *Chairman of the Senate of the Stellenbosch University and Others* (2019), both South African CC judgments dealing with the parameters of language rights.

The interpretation of language rights was dealt with in the cases of *Jones* v *A.G. of New Brunswick* (1975) and *Ford* v *Quebec (Attorney General)* (1988). In both cases, the respective courts held that, although language rights were fully established rights, they were not absolute in nature and may therefore be limited where such limitations were reasonable in the circumstances (Foucher, 2012:234). The limitation of language rights in the South African context is discussed fully in Part One of Chapter 6. We engage with the limitations analysis of Section 36 of the Constitution, as well as the language-specific limitations analysis, namely the sliding scale formula (Currie & De Waal, 2005:632) which takes into account the context in which the right is being limited.

The case of *Reference re: Manitoba Language Rights* (1985) was heard by the Supreme Court of Canada (SCC) following the enactment of the Charter of Rights and Freedoms (1982). The SCC in *Manitoba* (1985) contextualised the importance of language more broadly within society across disciplines. What is important for the purposes of the judgment was the court's statement that all rights contained in the Canadian Charter of Rights and Freedoms (1982), including language rights, be interpreted fully, where the SCC would follow a "… broad liberal and dynamic approach…" (Doucet, 2012:162).

It was thought that the case of *Reference re: Manitoba Language Rights* (1985) would provide for further purposive interpretation of language rights; however, this was not to be, with the trilogy of cases that followed (Doucet, 2012:162). The trilogy comprised the following cases: *Bilodeau* v *Manitoba (Attorney General)* (1986); *MacDonald* v *Montreal (City)* (1986); and *Societe des Acadiens du Nouveau Brunswick* v *Association of Parents for Fairness in Education* (1986).

In the case of *MacDonald* v *Montreal (City)* (1986), the facts briefly before the SCC on appeal from the Court of Appeal for Quebec were that the Appellant was initially charged and convicted in the court *a quo* of contravening a municipal by-law. The summons served on the English Appellant was in French only (1986:460). The Appellant alleged, in both the court *a quo* and before the Court of Appeal for Quebec, that the French-only summons violated his fundamental right espoused in Section 133 of the Constitution Act of 1867. In both instances, the Appellant was unsuccessful. The SCC held from the onset that the Appellant had no right to be summonsed in his own language as the provisions provide that the summons can be in either of the official languages; and, as such, there is no "obligation nor a duty" to use the other official language (1986:462). Reasoning further, the SCC (1986:462) stated that Section 133 of the Constitution Act of 1867, which established a language right, protected "…litigants, counsel, witnesses, judges and other judicial officers…" This right was not extended to the writers or issuers of pleadings nor those who were the recipients of summonses (1986:462).

In the same restrictive breath, the SCC (1986:462) noted that, although it may be "… desirable or fair for summonses to be bilingual to ensure comprehension by the recipient…", there was specific reference to this in the provisions of Section 133 of the Constitution Act of 1867. The SCC (1986:462), in validating the narrow approach, held that it was not the court's responsibility "…under the guise of interpretation, to improve upon, supplement or amend this historical constitutional promise". The SCC (1986:463) held further that, in fact, language rights during judicial proceedings were not rights *per se*, but rather a consequential part of the right to a fair trial. In this instance, the court would be under an obligation to ensure that proceedings are understood by the accused with the aid of translation services (1986:463). The appeal was subsequently dismissed.

The *MacDonald* v *Montreal (City)* (1986) case highlighted that, although the Canadian Charter of Rights and Freedoms was progressive, this remained in theory and not in practice; and where the court was required to apply the provisions in a positive, practical manner, they opted instead for a limiting, restrictive interpretive approach. Similar to the majority judgment in the case of *AfriForum and Another* v *University of the Free State* (2018), the court's reasoning brought into question the role of the judiciary in safeguarding the constitutional and legislative ideals in the best interests of the citizens.

The dissenting judgment of Wilson J in *MacDonald* v *Montreal (City)* (1986) was in stark contrast to the majority judgment. Wilson J held that the litigant, namely the Appellant in the matter at hand, had a right to use his own language, as espoused in Section 133 of the Constitution Act of 1867. Wilson J (1986:463) recognised that a language right was in existence, and further explained the parameters of the right by interpreting that a correlative duty is imposed on the state during judicial proceedings to accommodate the right. In terms of what was meant by "accommodate", Wilson J (*MacDonald* v *Montreal (City)* 1986:463) explained that the use of the words "may" and "either" in the provisions of Section 133 of the Constitution Act of 1867 were not inserted with the purpose of conferring a discretionary choice on the state to choose the official language of their choice to communicate with the litigant, but instead to confer such an option on the litigant.

As a minimum requirement of Section 133 of the Constitution Act of 1867, all documents emanating from and initiating court processes should be in an official language which the recipient thereof understands. If the recipient's language of choice is not known, the state is obliged to advise that a translation of the documents in the official language of his choice is available upon application (Wilson J, *MacDonald* v *Montreal (City)* 1986:464). This reasoning, according to Wilson J (1986:463), gives practical meaning to the constitutional and legislative provisions that the official languages are equal in status and should be treated as such in judicial proceedings.

The dissenting judgment in *MacDonald* v *Montreal (City)* (1986) provides for the parameters of the right to be interpreted in favour of the litigant upon whom the right is conferred. The interpretation by Wilson J in *MacDonald* (1986) is important for the discussion pertaining to South Africa in the forthcoming chapters, specifically with regard to the interpretation of the constitutional provisions and the incessant inclusion of words such as "may" and "either". It is also important in drawing parallels with the dissenting judgment of Froneman J in the case of *AfriForum and Another v University of the Free State* (2018).

In the case of *Bilodeau* v *Manitoba (Attorney General)* (1986), the appeal concerned the conviction of an English accused for the contravention of a Highway Traffic Act. The summons was issued in French only. The Appellant alleged that the French summons was a violation of Section 23 of the Manitoba Act of 1870 (1986:449). Section 23 of the Manitoba Act (1870) prescribes that the printing of all legislation must be done in both English and French. To this effect, the majority judgment held that it was not mandatory, but rather directory in nature (1986:452-454). In substantiating this viewpoint, the majority adopted the precise reasoning of the majority in the *MacDonald* v *Montreal (City)* case (1986). In doing so, the court explained that, in this instance, the legislation was only in French as the prescribed period for translation into both English and French had not yet elapsed, hence the fact that the legislation from which the summons was issued was valid and did not contravene Section 23 of the Manitoba Act (1870). The appeal was subsequently dismissed.

Wilson J in *Bilodeau* v *Manitoba (Attorney General)* (1986) wrote a minority judgment. Wilson J (1986:458) therefore concurred with the majority in dismissing the appeal. However, his reasons for the dismissal differed significantly. Wilson J (1986:458) held that Section 23 of the Manitoba Act (1870) was mandatory and not directory. As such, the

Appellant's language rights entrenched under Section 23 of the Manitoba Act (1870) were in fact contravened. The only reason why Wilson J dismissed the appeal was that, if not, it would have opened the floodgates to litigation.

The third case in the trilogy, namely *Societe des Acadiens du Nouveau* v *Association of Parents for Fairness in Education* (1986), concerned an appeal from the Court of Appeal for New Brunswick regarding the Official Languages Act of New Brunswick (2002). The primary issue on appeal was the interpretation of the parameters of Section 13(1) of the Official Languages of New Brunswick Act (2002) which states that a party to court has the right to be heard in a language of their choice by the members of the court in both the oral proceedings and written pleadings.

Engaging with the provision above, the court explained that it was best to trace the sources of legislation which gave effect to the enactment of the New Brunswick Official Languages Act (2002), namely Section 19 of the Canadian Charter of Rights and Freedoms (1982), as well as Section 133 of the Constitution Act (1867). The court held that both Section 133 of the Constitution Act (1867) and Section 19 of the Canadian Charter of Rights and Freedoms (1988) did not guarantee that a litigant had a right to be heard in a language of choice or to be understood in that language of choice (*Societe des Acadiens du Nouveau v Association of Parents for Fairness in Education*, 1986:552). The court held further that it must be noted that language rights are separate to the requirements of natural justice (*Societe des Acadiens du Nouveau v Association of Parents for Fairness in Education*, 1986:552). Simply put, the court did not see language rights as a possible catalyst determining or influencing whether or not substantive justice or any form of justice is achieved. The court held that courts should "...pause before they decide to act as instruments of change, with respect to language rights" (*Societe des Acadiens du Nouveau v Association of Parents for Fairness in Education*, 1986:552). Moreover, the courts were cautioned to "...approach them with more restraint than they would in construing legal rights" (*Societe des Acadiens du Nouveau v Association of Parents for Fairness in Education*, 1986:552). The court ordered that the appeal be dismissed.

The trilogy of cases illustrated the adoption of a restrictive interpretative approach of the various language rights, as evidenced above. The court in *R* v *Beaulac* (1999) rejected the restrictive approach adopted in the *Societe* case (1986), reasoning that, regardless of the facts before a court, where language rights are concerned, such language provisions must be interpreted purposively.

Purposive interpretation must be guided by the need to ensure the "preservation" and "development" of official language communities in Canada (1999:770). The court held that, in criminal cases, courts were obligated to ensure that they were bilingually functional. This would allow for equal use of both official languages of Canada, in accordance with the core principle of linguistic duality. This, the court said, reaffirmed the language right as a substantive right and not a procedural right (1999:770). The court dismissed the reasoning that language rights were part of the right to a fair trial. Instead, the court held that the right of the accused to be heard in a language of their choice was in place to ensure the accused gained equal access to a public service, one that was linguistically competent to respond fully to the right (1999:772).

The purposive approach adopted in *R v Beaulac* (1999) was adopted in the case of *R v Pooran* (2011) – a case on appeal. Briefly, the facts dealt with the interpretation of Section 4(1) of the Alberta Languages Act of 2000 which states:

> Any person may use English or French in oral communication in proceedings before the following courts.

The Appellant argued that Section 4(1) inferred that English and French were the official languages of the Provincial Court proceedings, thus a French-speaking accused was entitled to a French-speaking prosecutor (*R v Pooran*, 2011:78). In a civil trial, the French-speaking litigant has a right to be understood in French, without interpretation services being employed. In both instances, a judicial officer must be linguistically equipped in the language of choice (*R v Beaulac*, 1999:78).

The Crown, acting as the Respondent in *R v Pooran* (2011), argued that Section 4(1) entitled the accused to have proceedings interpreted in French but not to have the entire trial conducted in French (2011:78). Brown J, in delivering judgment in *R v Pooran* (2011), imparted the reasoning in the *R v Beaulac* case (1999). Brown J (2011) accordingly held that the appeal succeeds, as Section 4(1) did entitle the accused to a French trial without the employ of interpretation. In Brown J's judgment, it was clearly stated that liberal and purposive interpretation was required in all instances concerning language rights (*R v Pooran*, 2011:79).

The Canadian case law provides an overview of the development the court has undergone in purposively interpreting language rights and the parameters thereof. The case law also illustrates how the courts have implemented the provisions that both English and French are languages of record and that the accused in criminal cases has the right to have the trial conducted in either of these languages based on his choice. Regardless of which language is chosen the court must be linguistically competent in both official languages.

The discussion on Canada has provided an overview of the Canadian constitutional and legislative language developments which have culminated in the entrenchment of language rights in recognising the official bilingualism of the country. The Canadian model illustrates that language has a significant role to play in the legal system for both litigants and legal professionals. This is evidenced in the New Brunswick Official Languages Act (2002).

More pertinently, the model is illustrative of the ability that more than one language can be employed successfully in judicial processes at all levels without the aid of translation and interpretation services and without causing unnecessary delay in the delivering of judgments and the consequent administration of justice.

As with the legislative developments, the courts, specifically the SCC, appeared hesitant (if not steadfast) in not giving effect to language rights, both in the employ of court proceedings and in the broader legal system. There was a definite divorce between language and law which the judiciary created, both directly and indirectly, through the trilogy of cases. The mere fact that the judiciary turned their backs on the restrictive approach to language rights and the limited role of language it recognised in the legal system, illustrates that, for litigants, legal professionals and the Canadian society, it is important that language assumes a rightful place in the legal system. Moreover, the case law following the trilogy of cases upheld the constitutional and legislative frameworks and the ideals of official bilingualism. The case law further provided an example of how skilful purposive interpretation should be undertaken where language rights were said to be substantive and not procedural in nature. The Canadian model is proof that, regardless of the restrictive constitutional and legislative frameworks, as well as the narrow approach of the judiciary in the trilogy of cases and prior to that, a determined resolve for linguistic equality can be achieved in a legal system where the important role of language is recognised.

India's sociolinguistic landscape

The Indian sociolinguistic landscape is characterised by the political influences that ultimately determined the language question. Crystal (2003) highlights the political events that led to the growth and dominance of English in India. The first English influences lie with the establishment of the British East India Company in 1600 (Crystal, 2003:47). In 1612, the British East India Company began its first trading station in Surat and later in Madras, Bombay and Calcutta. These cities are important to note for the forthcoming discussions concerning the dominance of English and the subsequent language divide across the north and south of India. British power was consolidated from 1784 to 1858 when the India Act of 1858 established a Board of Control that required direct reporting to the British Parliament (Crystal, 2003:47). The use of English was strengthened during the period of British sovereignty (1765-1947) during which time English was the medium of administration and education throughout the subcontinent (Crystal, 2003:47). The language question gained momentum in the early nineteenth century with the debating of an educational policy of learning and teaching English (Crystal, 2003:47). The establishment of the Universities of Bombay, Calcutta and Madras in 1857 saw English become the primary medium of instruction, cementing its development (Crystal, 2003:48). Again, this point is important for the forthcoming discussions where legal education is discussed in relation to the use of language in the courts. In the 1960s, a language war broke out in India between the supporters of English, Hindi and other regionally spoken languages in the south of India. This resulted in the 'three language formula' where English was introduced as the primary alternative to the local state language (Crystal, 2003:48).

Parallels can be drawn with South Africa where the historical influence of colonialism and the growth of a language, in this instance English, was due to political and economic interests; and how, as a result thereof, the colonial language was seen as a language of unification. This speaks to the global dominance of English and how, through political and economic means, English as a language has been able to grow in both use and popularity in countries where the status and use of indigenous languages have been undermined. Furthermore, this point relates to the relationship between language and power, as explicated in this chapter with reference to Australia. Linguistic transformation lies in the hands of those who are powerful; and if the majority do challenge the English status quo, it results in intra-language battles or the adoption of English to fight for the African languages, as seen in South Africa.

Regarding majority, it is interesting to note that with the Indian population exceeding one billion, the number of English speakers rises as well, contributing to the growth of English as a second language, rather than the use and development of indigenous languages. What follows is a presentation of the language demographics in India emanating from the Census.

Indian language demographics

In 2011, India released its Census results. As will be evident from Part Two of Chapter 6, the language Census (2011) of India differs from that of South Africa, given that the Indian Constitution recognises 22 official languages. The Indian Census (2011:8) records 121 languages are spoken in India. The Census (2011) provides this table which records the language demographics pertaining to the 22 official languages.

Table 3.1 illustrates that Hindi is the most commonly spoken language in India. The Indian Census (2011:10) recorded 259,678 people who reported that English was their mother tongue. If one were to place English alongside the scheduled languages in Table 3.1, it would be sequenced after Punjabi language. This would amount to approximately 2% of the population; yet it is such a dominant language across society and in high status domains such as the legal system and higher education.

TABLE 3.1 Constitutionally scheduled languages arranged in descending order of use

Language	Persons who returned the language as their mother tongue	Percentage to total population
Hindi	52,83,47,193	43.63
Bengali	9,72,37,669	8.03
Marathi	8,30,26,680	6.86
Telugu	8,11,27,740	6.70
Tamil	6,90,26,881	5.70
Gujarati	5,54,92,554	4.58
Urdu	5,07,72,631	4.19
Kannada	4,37,06,512	3.61
Odia	3,75,21,324	3.10
Malayalam	3,48,38,819	2.88
Punjabi	3,31,24,726	2.74
Assamese	1,53,11,351	1.26
Maithili	1,35,83,464	1.12
Santali	73,68,192	0.61
Kashmiri	67,97,587	0.56
Nepali	29,26,168	0.24
Sindhi	27,72,264	0.23
Dogri	25,96,767	0.21
Konkani	22,56,502	0.19
Manipuri	17,61,079	0.15
Bodo	14,82,929	0.12
Sanskrit	24,821	Negligible

Indian constitutional framework

The discussions above have referred to the Constitution of India, with specific reference to the fact that official status is conferred on 22 languages, as listed in Table 3.1. The following extracted provisions are relevant to our discussions:

> Cultural and Educational Rights
>
> **29.** (1) Any section of the citizens residing in the territory of India or any part thereof having a distinct language, script or culture of its own shall have the right to conserve the same.

(2) No citizen shall be denied admission into any educational institution maintained by the State or receiving aid out of State funds on grounds only of religion, race, caste, language or any of them.

30. (1) All minorities, whether based on religion or language, shall have the right to establish and administer educational institutions of their choice.

(2) The State shall not, in granting aid to educational institutions, discriminate against any educational institution on the ground that it is under the management of a minority, whether based on religion or language.

Chapter I — Language of the Union

343. (1) The official language of the Union shall be Hindi in Devanagari script.

The form of numerals to be used for the official purposes of the Union shall be the international form of Indian numerals.

(2) Notwithstanding anything in clause (1), for a period of fifteen years from the commencement of this Constitution, the English language shall continue to be used for all the official purposes of the Union for which it was being used immediately before such commencement:

Provided that the President may, during the said period, by order authorise the use of the Hindi language in addition to the English language and of the Devanagari form of numerals in addition to the international form of Indian numerals for any of the official purposes of the Union.

(3) Notwithstanding anything in this article, Parliament may by law provide for the use, after the said period of fifteen years, of —
   (a) the English language, or
   (b) the Devanagari form of numerals, for such purposes as may be specified in the law.

344. (1) The President shall, at the expiration of five years from the commencement of this Constitution and thereafter at the expiration of ten years from such commencement, by order constitute a Commission which shall consist of a Chairman and such other members representing the different languages specified in the Eighth Schedule as the President may appoint, and the order shall define the procedure to be followed by the Commission.

(2) It shall be the duty of the Commission to make recommendations to the President as to —
   (a) the progressive use of the Hindi language for the official purposes of the Union;
   (b) restrictions on the use of the English language for all or any of the official purposes of the Union;
   (c) the language to be used for all or any of the purposes mentioned in article 348;
   (d) the form of numerals to be used for any one or more specified purposes of the Union;
   (e) any other matter referred to the Commission by the President as regards the official language of the Union and the language for communication between the Union and a State or between one State and another and their use.

(3) In making their recommendations under clause (2), the Commission shall have due regard to the industrial, cultural and scientific advancement of India, and the just claims and the interests of persons belonging to the non-Hindi speaking areas in regard to the public services.

(4) There shall be constituted a Committee consisting of thirty members, of whom twenty shall be members of the House of the People and ten shall be members of the Council of States to be elected respectively by the members of the House of the People and the members of the Council of States in accordance with the system of proportional representation by means of the single transferable vote.

(5) It shall be the duty of the Committee to examine the recommendations of the Commission constituted under clause (1) and to report to the President their opinion thereon.

(6) Notwithstanding anything in article 343, the President may, after consideration of the report referred to in clause (5), issue directions in accordance with the whole or any part of that report.

Chapter II – Regional Languages

345. Subject to the provisions of articles 346 and 347, the Legislature of a State may by law adopt any one or more of the languages in use in the State or Hindi as the language or languages to be used for all or any of the official purposes of that State: Provided that, until the Legislature of the State otherwise provides by law, the English language shall continue to be used for those official purposes within the State for which it was being used immediately before the commencement of this Constitution.

346. The language for the time being authorised for use in the Union for official purposes shall be the official language for communication between one State and another State and between a State and the Union: Provided that if two or more States agree that the Hindi language should be the official language for communication between such States, that language may be used for such communication.

347. On a demand being made in that behalf the President may, if he is satisfied that a substantial proportion of the population of a State desire the use of any language spoken by them to be recognised by that State, direct that such language shall also be officially recognised throughout that State or any part thereof for such purpose as he may specify.

Chapter III – Language of the Supreme Court, High Courts, etc.

348. (1) Notwithstanding anything in the foregoing provisions of this Part, until Parliament by law otherwise provides –
(a) all proceedings in the Supreme Court and in every High Court,
(b) the authoritative texts –
  (i) of all Bills to be introduced or amendments thereto to be moved in either House of Parliament or in the House or either House of the Legislature of a State,
  (ii) of all Acts passed by Parliament or the Legislature of a State and of all Ordinances promulgated by the President or the Governor of a State, and
  (iii) of all orders, rules, regulations and bye-laws issued under this Constitution or under any law made by Parliament or the Legislature of a State, shall be in the English language.

(2) Notwithstanding anything in sub-clause (a) of clause (1), the Governor of a State may, with the previous consent of the President, authorise the use of the Hindi language, or any other language used for any official purposes of the State, in proceedings in in the High Court having its principal seat in that State: Provided that nothing in this clause shall apply to any judgment, decree or order passed or made by such High Court.

(3) Notwithstanding anything in sub-clause (b) of clause (1), where the Legislature of a State has prescribed any language other than the English language for use in Bills introduced n, or Acts passed by, the Legislature of the State or in Ordinances promulgated by the Governor of the State or in any order, rule, regulation or bye-law referred to in paragraph (iii) of that sub-clause, a translation of the same in the English language published under the authority of the Governor of the State in the Official Gazette of that State shall be deemed to be the authoritative text thereof in the English language under this article.

349. During the period of fifteen years from the commencement of this Constitution, no Bill or amendment making provision for the language to be used for any of the purposes mentioned in clause (1) of article 348 shall be introduced or moved in either House of Parliament without the previous sanction of the President, and the President shall not give his sanction to the introduction of any such Bill or the moving of any such amendment except after he has taken into consideration the recommendations of the Commission constituted under clause (1) of article 344 and the report of the Committee constituted under clause (4) of that article.

These constitutional provisions quoted in full above are extensive in their mandate. However, a point of critique is that the majority of these provisions are qualified, or have internal qualifications built into them that secure the use of English. To an extent, the provisions are extensive and do reflect progress in that they include Hindi, specifically in high status domains. Simply put, though, whether one views these provisions from a positive or negative perspective depends on the type of interpretation employed, i.e., restrictive interpretation or purposive interpretation.

There are important points to note emanating from these provisions, the first of which is found in Article 29(2) above, providing that an individual may not be turned away from an educational institution based on, amongst other factors, language. This can be cross-referenced to the discussion on Indian legal education and how universities in India are battling to grapple with the language question that is resulting in a language divide that is also geographical, i.e., between the north and south. This also relates to the point of language and power in India. One must be conscious of the underlying discrimination and the classist society in India which is based on the caste system in which language is inherent. This, despite the fact that the Indian constitutional provisions exclude discrimination based on language and caste.

Article 29(2) of the Constitution of India is similar to the language in educational rights in Section 29(2) of the South African Constitution, advanced in Part One of Chapter 6. We mentioned that the provisions quoted earlier place Hindi alongside English, as per Article 343. The dominance of English in India can be seen from the provisions that attempt to place Hindi on an equal footing. Article 343 resembles the provisions of Section 6 of the South African Constitution that elevates the status and use of the nine African languages that were previously marginalised. In supporting Article 343, the Constitution of India provided for a Commission to be established 15 years following the enactment of the Constitution. Based on the provisions of the Indian Constitution, it appears that the Commission's purpose was similar to that of the Language Task Plan Group (LANGTAG) (1996) concerning South Africa. This will be discussed in forthcoming paragraphs. Furthermore, the provisions of Article 343 somewhat overlap with the mandate of PanSALB in South Africa, as per Section 6(5) of the South African Constitution.

Cognisant of Article 345, there is a divide between language use for the union (country) and state (regional and provincial) purposes. This distinction is important where, in the states, a regional language can be used for official purposes, such as in the courts. We discuss the point more fully in the paragraphs below.

What is of most significance about the provisions quoted above, for the purposes of this research, is the inclusion of Article 348 regulating the use of language in the SC and all High Courts. There is no such provision in the South African Constitution nor in the Superior Courts Act 10 of 2013. Article 348, however, falls short of being progressive, in our opinion, as it prescribes that English be used and ultimately be the language of record. This provision does not correlate with the language demographics provided in the Indian Census (2011) represented in Table 3.1, given that English is spoken by a mere 2% of the population. Furthermore, Article 348 provides that all legislation and all laws be enacted in English. A parallel can be drawn between the case of *Lourens* v *State Party: Republic of South Africa* (2018) and also with the discussion below: that having legislation and other primary texts in English only means that the large majority cannot access the law, neither can universities teach law students in a language other than English, resulting in an English-only language of record policy. There is a thin, positive aspect provided in subsection (3) that permits the use of Hindi in these courts, but this is discretional. The relationship between language and power and language and politics comes to the fore with this discretion, where the litigants do not have this power that directly affects their level of access to justice and procedural fairness.

Language of record and proceedings in Indian courtrooms

The constitutional provisions above are clear on the language of record in the SC and all High Courts, but not for the lower courts; this is where the majority of literature and contention has been based. As with any debate concerning the use of language in a legal system, there will be opposing views. India is no different. The language question in courts and the country more broadly is continuously debated, with no end in sight. One of the primary reasons cited for the ongoing debate is the linguistic diversity of India which, in most instances, is not viewed as a rich resource but rather as a dividing problem. Before engaging in a thematic account of the developments and debates concerning the language of record and proceedings in Indian courts, the language of record in the SC must be dealt with.

Although constitutionally determined, the language of record in the SC of India has been criticised as eluding the majority of the people who cannot speak, read, write or understand English. According to the SC Registry, an increase in the number of litigants requesting the translation of judgments into the indigenous languages has been recorded (Nambiar, 2019). In responding to the numerous requests, the SC Registry reported that it would make its judgments available in regional languages on the court website (Nambiar, 2019). The judgments would be translated into Assamese, Hindi, Kannada, Marathi, Odia and Telegu (Nambiar, 2019). This development followed a previous rejection by the judiciary to make Hindi the official language of all courts in India (Sonewal, 2016). The rejected proposal concerning the SC and the 24 High Courts was based on the fact that Hindi was not the accepted language of communication in many parts of India (Sonewal, 2016). Another reason cited for the dismissal is that cases tend to have a delay of five months for translation purposes. In 2008, the Law Commission, in its 216th report, held that introducing Hindi as a compulsory language of record in the SC and all High Courts was not feasible and that the Constitution of India was clear on the matter of the language of record (Sonewal, 2016).

The situation in the lower courts in the states differs given the absence of constitutional and legislative directives on the language of record. As a result of this situation, lower courts use the regional (local) languages for court proceedings, thus the languages of record (Sonewal, 2016). This permits litigants the opportunity of understanding proceedings and filing documents in their mother tongue, so justice is seen to be done and access to justice is enhanced for ordinary citizens and not just a political English-speaking elite (Naidu, 2018).

Speaking on this topic of access to justice for all Indian citizens, Vice President Shri M Venkaiah Naidu (2018) stated that the language used in courts should be understood by the petitioners who are seeking justice. Naidu (2018) explained that, from a political perspective, he was of the view that language use in courts was grounded in the Constitution where the judiciary is a key pillar of the democratic polity. Naidu (2018) further explained the importance of the judiciary in upholding the principles of the Constitution and stated that to exclude litigants on grounds of language would be abandoning this duty. A parallel can be sought with the judgment by Froneman J in the case of *AfriForum and Another* v *University of the Free State* (2018) discussed in Chapter 7. Simply put, it can be questioned whether a monolingual language of record policy does not undermine the constitutional provisions and discriminate against the majority of the people on grounds of language.

The situation is complicated by the fact that the Constitution of India recognises 22 languages besides English. There are, however, regional languages that can be used in the lower courts and this can be regulated by a policy in which the regional language(s) are placed alongside English as is done in Canada and, to an extent, in Belgium as per the discussions earlier in this chapter. This would require the collective effort of the judiciary (including legal practitioners) and the state. As with any society, this support is subjective and speaks to the power relations and agendas pursued by these individuals who are tasked with affecting the rights of the majority.

Sonewal (2016), through an investigation of whether it would be feasible for Hindi to be used in all courts of India, recorded the views of legal practitioners. Vivek Sood, a Senior Advocate in the Delhi High Court, provided three reasons why English should be the sole official language of record for all courts. Firstly, English was an established legal language, having been used in Indian courts for a period exceeding one 150 years (Sonewal, 2016). Secondly, the introduction of Hindi into the courts will be a burden on the courts (Sonewal, 2016). The second point was substantiated through the third, with Sood explaining that there was already a huge backlog in cases, coupled with a shortage of judges, amongst other issues that needed to be addressed as a matter of urgency, rather than being fixated on the fact that English, a colonial language, was being used (Sonewal, 2016). Sood's views undermine the important function of language and the role it plays in facilitating access to justice in a multilingual country where the majority do not understand English. Furthermore, his position seems to reflect that the English-only agenda does not adversely affect him, so why change it? The importance of the language question is downplayed by what is perceived as more pressing.

Yatindra Chaudhary, an advocate in the SC, presents both sides of the coin, arguing that the introduction of Hindi will be of benefit to the litigants; that, in some instances, cases may proceed in a language other than English where the judicial officer is competent and comfortable to proceed in that language (Sonewal, 2016). Allahabad High Court permits the use of Hindi for court proceedings (Sonewal, 2016). Chaudhary believes the introduction of Hindi will assist lawyers who have a limited command of the English language (Sonewal, 2016). Chaudhary recognises the limitations, not of introducing indigenous languages, but rather Hindi only, as there is a language divide in India between the north and south and east and west (Sonewal, 2016). Simply put, not a one-size-fits-all policy but regionally-based language policies will be more effective.

Another advocate of the SC, Aishwarya Bhati, expressed similar views, providing more examples of courts which permitted the use of languages other than English, namely: Rajasthan courts use Hindi, while the courts in Gujarat permit the use of Gujarati language (Sonewal, 2016). There is consensus by some advocates for the use of languages other than English but also the acknowledgement of the difficulties in doing this, given the language diversity, the development of English as a legal language and its colonial history which ensured the dominance of English.

The discussion on the language of record in Indian courts points to the need to have the entire system transformed and in which attorneys and advocates enter the legal profession having sound linguistic competency in a regional language in which they practise, as is the case in Belgium and Canada.

The next section of this chapter advances a discussion on the legal education in India, with specific reference to the language question.

Indian legal education through the medium of English

Access to education in English from primary school is not standard, although this is on the rise given the status of English as a global language. Hindi is the majority spoken language in the north of India where a large number of law schools and universities are located (Getman, 1969:517). In the preceding paragraphs, we mentioned the language war in India and the underlying caste system. This dates back to the 1960s in the education system where there was an insurgence in the north to do away with English in favour of Hindi in all schools and courts (Getman, 1969:517). Violent protests broke out at universities and law colleges with Banaras Hindu University going to the extent of removing all traces of English, including signage. At Banaras Hindu University, as well as all other law colleges and universities in the north of India, with the exception of students in Delhi, students had a minimal understanding of English (Getman, 1969:517). Their limited English linguistic competency made it difficult to engage with the cases and other academic and legal texts written in English (Getman, 1969:517). As a result, the north was primarily educated in Hindi and the south educated in English. This sparked a further divide between students who could not be recruited to universities in the north, given the growing tensions (Getman, 1969:518).

There is a need to educate students in their mother tongue and this should not result in the exclusion of other students from at universities or law colleges. Getman (1969:519) notes that course material and legal and academic texts will have to be translated in order to graduate lawyers who have a sound accord of the language(s) and where these students themselves are not disadvantaged as the litigants are. Getman (1969:519) recommends that courses be taught bilingually to ensure representation across Indian states and to allow students to be in a position to express themselves in their mother tongue, while also acquiring the skill in English.

Conclusion

This chapter is similar to Chapter 2 in that there are common threads among the international case studies. The case studies of Belgium and Canada illustrate the inclusivity that is being achieved in their legal systems through the prioritisation of the language question. In both countries, language is seen as a resource in courts. This progressiveness is enabled and regulated through constitutional and legislative frameworks. Indeed, there is a history of language marginalisation or restrictive interpretation; both case studies have proven that this can be overcome where commitment is key among all relevant persons and sectors in society. Languages are viewed as equal in status and use and the speakers of these languages are treated equally. The regionally based language policies are effective and the language policies for the legal system are workable and give effective meaning to language rights. The language attitudes and practices in both these countries can be emulated by South Africa and other African countries.

Australia and India are similar to South Africa with regard to historical political influences, particularly in the form of English that was entrenched as a result of colonialism. The countries are also similar in that there is greater language diversity than the other international models. It can be argued from the discussions that language diversity can be a complication depending on which view is adopted. In these countries, the language question was problematised; language, power, politics and economics are closely related in advancing a specific agenda of a political, English-speaking elite. There is an inherent system of inferiority bestowed on Aboriginal people and their languages. This is evidenced from the establishment of Bush courts and the non-existence (or, in some areas, low levels) of interpretation services for Aboriginal litigants. The disregard by a political English-speaking elite in Australia is evidenced by the sentiments of the Chief Minister as captured by MacFarlane et al. (2019) who said that providing interpretation services equated to providing a wheelchair to able people.

South Africa must take note of the danger of having a monolingual language of record policy in a multilingual country and the effect this will have on the indigenous people and their languages. Furthermore, that when adopting a monolingual language of record policy, interpretation services need to be of the highest level and readily available at all times, at the state's expense.

The case study of India also presents as a complex model in which language in a multilingual country is further problematised by cultural differences inherent in the caste system. India, although making an effort in certain aspects of the legal system, is plagued by additional problems such as the attitude of legal practitioners towards the indigenous languages and divisive higher education language policies. This is particularly important for South Africa, given the recent judgments in the cases of *Gelyke Kanse and Others* v *Chairman of the Senate of the Stellenbosch University and Others* (2019) where universities are adopting English-only language policies on the basis of access and transformation.

As with Chapter 2, the international case studies have highlighted the global dominance of English which, although spoken by a minority, is advanced through power, politics and economics. When English is the sole official language of record and is used in proceedings to the exclusion of the indigenous languages, a country will not be inclusive and will be divided along lines of language. This must be avoided. Where language policies are drafted that counteract this form of discrimination and marginalisation, inclusivity is achieved, as in Belgium and Canada.

The preceding two chapters have shown that language usage and policies for courts remains a politically and economically motivated process. The African case studies in Chapter 2 have illustrated that language usage, in particular that of the indigenous languages, is under-resourced and these languages are not seen as worthy of use in high status domains. English remains the default option on the African continent. The international case studies of India and Australia prove likewise that English is used regardless of the fact that the indigenous people are marginalised and in fact discriminated against on grounds of language. Belgium and Canada do however prove that languages other than English can be used for a more inclusive legal system, one that enables access to justice through a litigant's mother tongue. The geographical language planning approach adopted in Belgium and New Brunswick in Canada have proven to be both practical and inclusive. Nevertheless, in the chapter that follows, we begin to unpack the complexities of using the indigenous languages in South African courts and the resultant hegemonic power of the English-speaking elite in pursuing a monolingual language of record policy.

THE MONOLINGUAL LANGUAGE OF RECORD IN SOUTH AFRICAN COURTS

The complications of court interpretation and the introduction of administrative law

Defining the language of record

From the outset it must be noted that, currently, the language of record in South African courts is solely English. The discussion that follows refers to a bilingual language of record policy given that the monolingual language policy is being contested on a constitutional basis. Further discussion of the monolingual language of record directive is covered in sections that follow in this chapter.

According to Malan (2009:141), there is an official and unofficial use of language in South African courts. Language used in an official capacity concerns the language of record. In this instance, the language of record is the language in which the court proceedings are recorded and in which the judgment is written and delivered by presiding officers (ibid). The unofficial use of language refers to the language(s) used by accused persons, litigants and witnesses (ibid). Official and unofficial usage are related to each other. If there is a monolingual language of record policy in place – for example, if an accused person is isiXhosa speaking with no proficiency in English – they are then solely reliant on an interpreter and will not understand the proceedings presented in English. Gibbons (2003:202) expresses this point in the following excerpt:

> A second language speaker who does not speak the language of the court, and who is provided with interpreting services may receive the same treatment as native speakers, but such a process is clearly unjust, in that s/he can neither understand the proceedings, nor make a case.

This quotation highlights the important role of the language of record and the effect it can have on the administration of justice, involving the Section 35(3) constitutional right to a fair trial, part of which is reinforced by an accused person's right to be tried in a language they fully understand. This part of the discussion pertaining to language rights of accused persons is housed in Part One of Chapter 6. At this stage of the discussion, the question arises as to the determination of which of the two official languages of record to use in criminal proceedings. Malan (2001:144) identified two factors used in determining which of the two (English or Afrikaans) languages of record would be used in criminal cases:

(1) If the accused were a mother tongue speaker of either of the two languages of record, the case would be recorded in the language of the accused. The preference of the Magistrate or Judge ordinarily did not play a substantive role in exercising a choice between English and Afrikaans. In line with this, Judge presidents of the High Courts also assigned cases in accordance with the relative language proficiency of the judges of the court concerned. Afrikaans cases, i.e., cases where the accused was Afrikaans speaking, were not assigned to judges with a poor mastery of Afrikaans but to judges who were proficient in Afrikaans. In principle, the same applied in English cases (where the accused was English speaking).

(2) If the accused was a mother tongue speaker of an African language, the language of record was to a greater or lesser extent determined by the preferences and language proficiency of the presiding Judge or magistrate. If the Magistrate was English speaking and less fluent in Afrikaans, the proceedings would ordinarily have been in English, while the presence of Afrikaans speaking presiding officers usually meant that the proceedings were recorded in Afrikaans. The linguistic trends in the area in which courts were situated also exerted an influence in this regard, however. Criminal cases in the Eastern Cape and KwaZulu-Natal, where English (aside from the African languages concerned) has always been dominant, were therefore conducted in English rather than Afrikaans regardless of the personal preferences of the presiding officer. The same held true for Afrikaans in, for example, the Free State and various other provinces.

In applying the criteria above, mother tongue speakers of English and Afrikaans were, and are, placed at an advantage in the legal system given that the language of record policy in which to conduct proceedings was English and Afrikaans. Speakers of the nine official African languages have then been placed at a disadvantage in comparison to English and Afrikaans mother tongue speakers who had a choice of language in which to proceed.

There are four points of discussion arising from the quoted excerpt. These include but are not limited to, firstly, a determination of whether an English only language of record policy constitutes fair or unfair discrimination against persons on grounds of language, as protected by Section 9 of the Constitution, in addition to the Promotion of Equality and Prevention of Unfair Discrimination Act 4 of 2000. Secondly, there is the question of whether an accused person's Section 35(3) (k) constitutional right to be tried in a language they fully understand is unfairly limited through the application of the limitations analysis in Section 36 of the Constitution and the sliding scale formula (Currie & De Waal, 2005). Thirdly, there is a need to discuss the use of language demographics in formulating practical language policies for the courts; and, fourthly, to engage with the language requirements for legal practitioners to ensure linguistic competency in the official languages. This fourth point is linked to the university language policies, language requirements and vocation-specific courses for LLB students. These points are discussed fully in Chapters 6 to 9. For current purposes, the language of record can be understood to be the language in which the court records the proceedings and delivers judgment. The following section of this chapter traces the history of the language of record.

History of the language(s) of record in South African courts of law

A brief historical account of the role of use of language(s) in the legal system is important in understanding the conceptual linguistic issues currently plaguing the democratic legal system. Historically, the language(s) of record policy was influenced politically where the position of those in power was exploited in entrenching a language on the people of South Africa. Evidence of this can be traced back to the arrival of Jan van Riebeeck in the Cape (Van Niekerk, 2015:373). During the Dutch occupation, the Dutch language was imposed on the local population and the language of the courts was Dutch. English was introduced during the British occupation in the eighteenth and early nineteenth century. There was an insistent move to ensure that English became the sole official language for use in courts. Arguably, what is happening today is merely a re-enactment of the nineteenth century colonial, or now neo-colonial, sentiments.

In 1813, Governor Sir John Cradock published his sentiments about the importance of English and the need for all government employees to acquire good English skills (Van Niekerk, 2015:377). On 5 July 1822, a proclamation was issued whereby English was adopted as the "exclusive official and judicial language" (ibid, 382). The proclamation applied to all judicial proceedings of the lower and higher courts. The move to have English as the sole official language for legal proceedings was justified on the basis that it would unite "local inhabitants" and those of British origin (ibid, 383). Van Niekerk (2015:383) questions what he calls the "curious notion that a single language would lead to unity". This point must be borne in mind, specifically with regard to the proceeding discussion on the reasoning behind the recent monolingual language of record decision.

The dominance of English as the language of record was cemented further through the Royal Charters of Justice (ibid). In 1827, the first Charter of Justice determined that the language medium would be English-only in both the SC and circuit courts. The Second Royal Charter, in effect from 1834, identical to the First Royal Charter, reaffirmed the English-only language of record decision. Section 2 of the Constitution Ordinance Amendment Act 1 of 1882 reintroduced Dutch as an official language and it was awarded equal status alongside English. The Dutch Language Judicial Use Act 21 of 1884 permitted the use of Dutch to be used as a language of record, where the parties in court could chose Dutch to be heard in as their language of choice.

The South Africa Act of 1909 (Union of South Africa, 1909) recognised English as an official language in addition to Dutch. With the South Africa Act of 1909 resulting in the establishment of the Union, Section 137 cemented the dual official language status of Dutch and English. The definition of Dutch was extended to include Afrikaans in the Union Act 8 of 1925 (Union of South Africa, 1925). Through Act 8 of 1927, Afrikaans replaced Dutch as an official language alongside English. With the onset of Apartheid in 1948, the legislative formulations constantly reaffirmed the position of English and Afrikaans as the official languages. The Republic of South Africa Constitution Act 110 of 1983, specifically Section 89(1), entrenched the position of English and Afrikaans as official languages.

It is evident that legislative recognition of African languages in the form of official, developmental status or use, was always absent; hence, the entrenchment of English and Afrikaans and the marginalisation of African languages from mainstream society. It can be argued that the usage of African languages was recognised in Act 110 of 1986 in the form of an African language being utilised within the self-governing territories or homelands. In effect, African languages were being developed in the self-governing territories through the schooling system, where linguistic segregation was utilised to achieve racial segregation (Bambust, Kruger & Kruger, 2012).

Mirroring the legislative language position in South Africa advanced above, the legal system adopted English and Afrikaans as the mediums for court use. Bambust et al. (2012:221) state that the current legislative position regarding the use of language in court was inherited wholly into the democratic dispensation. This resulted in the use of English and Afrikaans as official mediums in lower courts as prescribed by Section 6 of the Magistrates' Courts Act 32 of 1944. The English and Afrikaans language requirements were legislated for attorneys and advocates in the Attorneys Act 53 of 1979 and the Admission of Advocates Act 74 of 1964. These statutes, in conforming to the official languages at the time of enactment, prescribed that English and Afrikaans, in addition to Latin at university level, were requirements for admission to the Side Bar and Bar. In an amendment, the Latin, English and Afrikaans requirements were removed; however, there was no insertion of African language requirements. According to De Vos (2008), the perpetuation of this linguistic discrimination fails to recognise the demographics of South Africa while, in turn, it undermines the constitutional framework supporting the transformation process of the legal system.

The current language dispensation of the legal system mirrors the historical position of African languages, which Van Niekerk (2015:375) succinctly summarises here:

> Indigenous African cultural institutions, including languages, have notoriously been ignored in the history of early South Africa. Thus, the needs of the indigenous population played no role in any decisions relating to judicial language during both the Dutch and the English administrations of the Cape, later in the territories beyond the borders of the Cape.

Historical legislative and policy developments of the language of record in South African courts

This section provides a thorough discussion of the legislative and policy enactments concerning the language of record. The language of record was determined by the political dispensation at the time. Evidence of this dates back to the arrival in South Africa of missionaries who imposed their language on the indigenous persons of South Africa. Dutch as a language was imposed in all facets of society upon the arrival of Jan van Riebeeck in the Cape, an official of the Dutch-East India Company (Van Niekerk, 2015:373). At that stage, deep legal pluralism, together with multilingualism, was introduced into the territory (ibid). The Dutch rule of the Cape saw Dutch being implemented in the courts. This language decision was reinforced through the Dutch East India Company's instruction, on 16 April 1657, that the language of court would be Dutch only (ibid).

The political influence on the language of record continued with the insurgence of the British occupation in the late eighteenth century and early nineteenth century with English introduced alongside Dutch. According to Van Niekerk (2015:373-375) there are several questions arising as to why English was introduced as a legal language. It is argued that it was not introduced for practical reasons but for political purposes and that of power. During the introduction of both Dutch and English as legal languages, the South African people had no power in determining the legal language. In fact, there was a blatant disregard of the "indigenous African cultural institutions, including languages..." (ibid, 375). This was the case not only for the Cape, but for all provinces across South Africa during this period.

On 24 July 1797, a Proclamation was issued establishing a CA for civil cases. The proclamation prescribed that all appellants and respondents were to translate their documentation into English. During the period of 1803 to 1806, Dutch was, once again, the language of record in courts and the return to English-only occurred in 1806. The 1797 Proclamation was repeated to entrench the position of English for all documentation in the court proceedings for litigants (Van Niekerk, 2015:375).

An important development in the history of the language of record took place in 1811 with the establishment of circuit courts. These were not only founded on the English legal model, but saw officers being appointed on a preferential basis if they were conversant in English (Van Niekerk, 2015:377). English proficiency for presiding officers became a benchmark requirement. To this end, the Governor at the time, Sir John Cradock, publicised his sentiments concerning the importance of English in the legal system and for presiding officers (ibid). He stated his reasons were underpinned by the practical need to be conversant in English:

> ...commerce had suffered because of the lack of proper translators and because the use of translators was an imperfect and limited way of communicating and contrary to the spirit and effect of government (Van Niekerk, 2015:377).

Sir John Cradock's sentiments on the importance of English proficiency for presiding officers must be borne in mind when we discuss the 2017 monolingual language of record of directive further on in this chapter. Furthermore, this point is of relevance to the discussion concerning the language requirements for legal practitioners and presiding officers. This point is explicated in Chapter 8 with reference to the relevant legislation regulating the admission of legal practitioners to the profession, as well as the language policies of universities with regard to the language competencies of LLB graduates. The history and power of English in the legal system must also be noted as the discussion progresses in this book.

Reverting to the discussion at hand, in 1820, the Colonial Office approved a decision to use English exclusively in judicial proceedings (Van Niekerk, 2015:382). In 1822, the Colonial Office Secretary instructed the governor at the time, Lord Charles Somerset, to issue a Proclamation on 5 July 1822 for the adoption of English as the exclusive official and judicial language. The 1822 Proclamation was said to have been adopted as a single language that would unite all South Africans with the British occupants (ibid). This point is important to bear in mind with regard to the reasons provided by Mogoeng Mogoeng CJ to make English the sole official language of record in courts on the basis of unifying all South Africans in the present transformational era. In this book, we argue that such unity through English-only remains a misconception. This misconception exists in most African countries, including Nigeria and Zimbabwe, where English-only has not necessarily led to national unity. The reasoning by the CJ is discussed fully as this chapter progresses.

The language question in the legal system was once again in question during the time of Acting Governor Richard Bourke from 1826 to 1828. During this period, Bourke held off on implementing the 1822 Proclamation and permitted the use of Dutch where it was practicable in the circumstances to use the language. In 1827, however, Bourke issued an Ordinance for the creation of the office of the Resident Magistrates (Van Niekerk, 2015:385). Section 7 of this ordinance prescribed that all sentences, judgments and summons had to be in English; and 1827 marked the first Royal Charter of Justice which officially came into effect on 1 January 1828. The Royal Charter of Justice had a significant effect on the use of language in the legal system. The Charter prescribed that English would be the sole language used in the SC and circuit courts (presently Magistrates' Courts). The Charter also saw the appointment of Sir John Wylde as CJ along with several judges being appointed to the SC, all of whom were British (ibid). This point is important in illustrating the dominance of the British and their positioning in domains such as the legal system where the indigenous people of South Africa failed to feature in authoritative positions. The appointment of British presiding officers meant the dominance of English in the legal system.

The English-only position was strengthened further through the Second Royal Charter of Justice, dated 4 May 1832, which came into effect on 1 March 1834. Section 32 stated that English would be the sole medium through which sentences, judgments and orders were to be made. The use of English-only in courts continued until the enactment of the Dutch Language Judicial Use Act, 21 of 1884 (Dutch Act). The Dutch Act (1884) stated the following:

> ...it was expedient to afford facilities for the use of the Dutch language equally with the English in courts of justice and in legal proceedings... when requested to do so by any of the parties (Van Niekerk, 2015:388).

The next legislative enactment concerning the use of language in the legal system was with Section 137 of the South African Act of 1909 which declared English and Dutch as the official languages of the Union of South Africa (Van Niekerk, 2015:390). The South African Act (1909) unequivocally prescribed that both languages be treated equally. The point concerning equality of languages in both status and use is important to note concerning the discussion of the constitutional provisions in Parts One and Two of Chapter 6. The Union Act 8 of 1925 extended the definition of Dutch to include Afrikaans. In 1961 and 1983 the Republican Constitutions saw Afrikaans replace Dutch as an official language alongside English (Van Niekerk, 2015:390).

The discussions in this chapter thus far have illustrated the historical development of the language of record in South African courts. Evident from this discussion is that the use of language in courts was politically determined, given who was in power at the time. Significant to note is the power of English as a language of record, how it was imposed upon the indigenous people at the time and how it established its dominance. A further point to note is that the language of record was determined through legislative means where acts, ordinances and proclamations were enacted. These types of statutes and laws are described in this chapter in the sections that follow. What follows here is a discussion on the language of record during Apartheid and up to the period of the Interim Constitution of 1993.

The language of record in the interim phase to democracy

Building on the discussion in the preceding section, the languages of record in South African courts during Apartheid were English and Afrikaans. Earlier, we advanced the criteria used to determine what the language of record should be. This, according to Malan (2009), was a choice of either English or Afrikaans, the only official languages during Apartheid. If an accused person or witness had no understanding of either of the two official languages, an interpreter would have been provided for purposes of evidence only and not for interpreting the remaining proceedings. The accused would thus not understand the proceedings. The language of record was therefore instructive and decisive in affecting the administration of justice and even access to justice.

The language of record was considered once again during the political transitional period. The South African Interim Constitution (1993) dealt extensively with the language of record and language usage in the course of judicial proceedings more broadly. Chapter 1: Constituent and Formal Provisions, specifically Section 3, comprises the provisions concerning language in the Interim Constitution (1993) and the relevant provisions read as follows:

(1) Afrikaans, English, isiNdebele, Sesotho sa Leboa, Sesotho, siSwati, Xitsonga, Setswana, Tshivenda, isiXhosa and isiZulu shall be the official South African languages at national level, and conditions shall be created for their development and for the promotion of their equal use and enjoyment.

(2) Rights relating to language and the status of languages existing at the commencement of this Constitution shall not be diminished, and provision shall be made by an Act of Parliament for rights relating to language and the status of languages existing only at regional level, to be extended nationally in accordance with the principles set in subsection (9).

(3) Wherever practicable, a person shall have the right to use and to be addressed in his or her dealings with any public administration at the national level of government in any official South African language of his or her choice.

(4) Regional differentiation in relation to language policy and practice shall be permissible.

(5) A provincial legislature may, by a resolution adopted by a majority of at least two thirds of all its members, declare any language referred to in subsection (1) to be an official language for the whole or any part of the province and for any or all powers and functions within the competence of that legislature, save that neither the rights relating to language nor the status of an official language as existing in any area or in relation to any function at the time of the commencement of this Constitution, shall be diminished.

(6) Wherever practicable, a person shall have the right to use and to be addressed in his or her dealings with any public administration at the provincial level of government in any one of the official languages of his or her choice as contemplated in subsection (5).

(7) A member of Parliament may address Parliament in the official South African language of his or her choice.

(8) Parliament and any provincial legislature may, subject to this section, make provision by legislation for the use of official languages.

(9) Legislation, as well as official policy and practice, in relation to the use of languages at any level of government shall be subject to and based on the provisions of this section and the following principles:
   (a) the creation of conditions for the development and for the promotion of the equal use and enjoyment of all official South African languages;
   (b) the extension of those rights relating to language and the status of languages which at the commencement of this Constitution are restricted to certain regions;
   (c) the prevention of the use of any language for the purposes of exploitation, domination or division;
   (d) the promotion of multilingualism and the provision of translation facilities;
   (f) the non-diminution of rights relating to language and the status of languages existing at the commencement of this Constitution.

The 'general' language provision, as quoted in the excerpt, is clear, unambiguous and authoritative. By "authoritative", we mean the provisions are not littered with discretionary words such as "may", "if", "when" and so forth. We acknowledge that subsection (3) includes the word "practicable" and that this can be seen as an internal limitation or modifier. However, read in the context as a whole, ss (3) provides no alternative to the effect that an interpreter will be provided as with the final Constitution. The use and phrasing of this language in subsection (3) is illustrative of the clear mandate the drafters of the Interim Constitution had at the time. There is a resolute undertaking to confer language rights upon all speakers of the official languages.

The provisions are not watered down but are qualified in each subsection. These provisions of the Interim Constitution are important to keep in mind when Section 6 of the final Constitution is advanced in Part One of Chapter 6 and juxtaposed with Section 3 of the Interim Constitution (1993), as advanced in part one of Chapter 6 of this book. As will become clear there, Section 3 of the 1993 Interim Constitution, as with Section 6 of the final Constitution, informs the other specific provisions on language rights. Section 3 of the Interim Constitution informs Section 107 (languages) of Chapter 7, comprising the provisions of judicial authority and the administration of justice, which reads accordingly:

(1) A party to litigation, an accused person and a witness may, during proceedings of a court, use the South African language of his or her choice, and may require such proceedings of a court in which he or she is involved to be interpreted in a language understood by him or her.
(2) The record of the proceedings of a court shall, subject to section 3 be kept in any official language: Provided that the relevant right relating to language and the status of languages in this regard existing at the commencement of this Constitution shall not be diminished.

Section 107(1) of the Interim Constitution (1993b), as opposed to the final Constitution discussed in Part One of Chapter 6, refers specifically to the language usage by witnesses, litigants and accused persons. This is important in that a distinction is drawn between the parties before court. A witness can be defined as a person providing evidence; a litigant can be defined as a person litigating in court, primarily in civil cases, and which could include an appellant or respondent; and an accused person is a person charged with committing a criminal offence. The language rights of these individuals are thus recognised and protected through Section 107(1) of the Interim Constitution (1993b).

Cassim (2003:25) explains that language rights in the judicial system, discussed in Part One of Chapter 6, has direct implications for the determination of the choice of the language for purposes of the proceedings and the right to address the court in the official language of one's choice. It must be borne in mind that the language in which the court proceedings are conducted is the language of record. Thus, there is an inextricable linkage between an accused's language right and the language of record. Cassim (2003:25) further states that there is a fundamental distinction that needs to be drawn between the right of a party, litigant or witness to obtain the services of an interpreter which flows from the principles of fundamental justice; while there is the right of everyone appearing before a court to use the official language of his or her choice. The language of the accused in a criminal matter would then be the language of record for that case. This was how the language of record was determined during Apartheid, given that only two languages were official and considered languages of record, as per the criteria and explanation by Malan (2009) quoted earlier.

According to Cassim (2003:25), it is a fundamental principle that persons not only have access to the courts and law more broadly, but also to understand it. With specific reference to accused persons, Cassim (2003:25) holds that such persons must understand the language of the proceedings and be able to communicate in the language. These sentiments imparted by Cassim (2003) are essential as theoretical underpinnings for the discussion on the case law in Chapter 7, as well as the discussion on the parameters of the Section 35 language rights for any accused, arrested and detained persons, thereby determining the yardstick for linguistic proficiency. The latter point expressed by Cassim (2003:25) would entail that the language of the accused person determines the language of record, where such language is an official language as per the constitutional provisions of Section 6 of the Constitution. Cassim (2003:25) encapsulates this in the following excerpt:

> ...proceedings must be conducted in a language that he or she (accused person) understands and that it must fall within the scope of his or her ability to comprehend the proceedings.

The Interim Constitution (1993b) is therefore significant given the specific mention of the language of record. Cassim (2003:26), however, notes that Section 107(2) of the Interim Constitution was subject to two qualifications: the first pertains to Section 3(8) of the 1993 Interim Constitution, quoted in full above, where parliament could designate which official language should be used on the basis of usage, practicality and expense; the second qualification is in accordance with Section 3 which prescribed that, by designating the official languages, the status and use of English and Afrikaans as official languages of record could not be diminished.

Selecting an official language as a language of record will be determined by taking into account "... usage, practicality, expense, regional circumstances and the needs and preferences of the population in a particular province" (Cassim, 2003:26). When determining practicability, it would follow that, where the language the accused understands is not one of the official languages of record, it would not be practicable to do so (ibid, 28).

This section of this chapter is illustrative of the developments of the language of record in South African courts during the political transitional period prior to the adoption of the final Constitution. The developments are positive in that the language of record is included in the Interim Constitution (1993). The qualifications in determining the language of record in each province are aligned with a practical approach taking into account the number of speakers in a given area. This point is discussed in greater depth in this chapter and with reference to the language demographics of each province, as well as the criteria in the sliding scale formula when limiting a constitutional language right (in Part One of Chapter 6).

The provisions of the 1993 Interim Constitution are instructive on the role of the legislature in determining the language of record. The overarching point of departure emanating from the Interim Constitution (1993b) is that the language of record must be the language that the accused person understands. The process of ensuring that the accused person's language be used as a language of record, where such language is an official language, has been explored through the African and international comparative case studies in Chapters 2 and 3. Having proceedings conducted in a language that the accused understands is a fundamental principle of access to justice for all persons. What follows is the advancement of historical developments from 1996 onwards.

The language of record in South African courts: 1996 onwards

The final Constitution was enacted and replaced the 1993 Interim Constitution as discussed previously. For purposes of the discussion at hand, the constitutional provisions of the final Constitution are explicated and critically engaged with in Part One of Chapter 6. The Language Task Plan Group (LANGTAG) was established to provide an extensive report on, and recommendations to, the Minister of Arts, Culture, Science and Technology (as it was then) on language usage in South Africa. This is a broad explanation of LANGTAG (1996).

At the current stage of our discussions, it must be noted that the 1996 LANGTAG report conceded that language in all domains could not have been discussed in producing the report; and one omission was the legal system. As a result, the LANGTAG report (1996:9) recommended that a special study be undertaken to address the use of language in this domain.

Du Plessis (2001) documented the developments concerning the language of record in South African courts from 1996 onwards. Use of language in South African courts, including the language of record, was discussed and debated at an internal meeting of the Department of Justice (as it was then) on 10 November 1997 (Du Plessis, 2001:101). The next development took place a year later when the JSC was tasked by the Minister of Justice to investigate the possibility of having English as the sole official language of record. The paper, released in 1999, proposed that it might be cost efficient to have one official language of record, English. It appears from the developments documented by Du Plessis (2001) and which were traced back to newspaper articles that appeared in *Die Volksblad*, an Afrikaans newspaper, that the Afrikaans community was most disgruntled by the announcement of removing Afrikaans as a language of record. In fact, the Department of Justice stated that it was merely an intimation and a final decision had not been taken on the matter. Despite saying this, the Minister of Justice forged ahead and organised a roundtable discussion to include the JSC, (MCom), as well as the National Director of Public Prosecutions (NDPP) (Du Plessis, 2001:101). The discussions were seen as a façade intended to create the impression that public participation on the issue of the language of record had been ensured.

In February 2000, the Department of Justice announced the conclusion of its round of consultations at the roundtable discussions and was, consequently, preparing a report for the Minister of Justice. On 6 February 2000, the *Rapport* newspaper reported that the roundtable report recommended English as the sole official language of record. On 7 February 2000, *Die Burger* newspaper subsequently reported that the English-only position would be implemented by June 2000. The Minister of Justice seemed to have done a complete turnaround when he announced on 18 February 2000, at a gathering of the legal fraternity in Johannesburg, that his department had presented to him the above recommendation.

The turnaround came when he explained that, despite the recommendation, a monolingual language of record would be unconstitutional and he would prefer a situation where all 11 official languages could be used on an equal basis (Du Plessis, 2001:102). There was strong resistance from the officials at the Department of Justice, with the Minister's views contradicted. In fact, on 22 March 2000, *Die Volksblad* newspaper reported that a representative of the Department of Justice had argued that the then current bilingual language of record was unconstitutional; furthermore, that it would be impractical to use all 11 official languages. Thus, in his opinion, the only practical solution to the problem was to have English as the sole official language of record.

On 30 March 2000, *Die Volksblad* reported on the Second Language Indaba which was held on 29 March 2000 in Durban. At this Indaba, the Minister of Arts, Culture, Science and Technologies', Chairman of the Advisory Panel on Language Policy and Language Planning, further criticised the English-only language of record proposal (Du Plessis, 2001:102). It remains a concern that, in May 2000, the Minister of Arts, Culture, Science and Technology sent a letter to the then Minister of Justice saying the following:

> Looking at all the implications... I am inclined to say that one should seriously consider introducing one official language of record in our courts. This view is supported by the role South Africa is to play in not only Africa but also the broader international world. To play this role, proceedings need to be recorded in a language which can be understood by everyone, locally, nationally and internationally. Practice therefore, it seems to me, dictates that English needs to be the language of record in our courts (Strydom, 2001:108).

The discussion on the developments of the language of record following the immediate conception and enactment of the Constitution is marred by an agenda to drive an English-only legal system. Once again, there is a clear element of politicking by an elite for a legal system that serves a minority in South Africa, and without any informed background knowledge of the linguistic implications of multilingualism as a transformative agent. This discussion happened as soon as a constitutional democratic state was established, without involving (forensic) linguists. During Apartheid, persons were marginalised and excluded on grounds of race, ethnicity and language. The language of record developments from 1996 to 2000 see the entrenchment of monolingualism through a language, English, which has a long colonial history of oppression. Simply put, Afrikaans and English were pitted against each other, contrary to the constitutional provisions of Section 6 which calls for all languages to be treated equitably. On the point of the Constitution, Section 6(2) instructively calls for the elevation of the nine African languages in status and usage, given the past marginalisation of such languages. The complete opposite was taking place: The African languages were only mentioned twice where it was said that it would be impractical to use these languages as languages of record, the common assumption being that English-only would solve the 'problem' of multilingualism.

The only consistent dissenting voice was that of the Afrikaans-speaking community who protested in the strongest terms against the removal of Afrikaans as a language of record. Such criticism undoubtedly influenced the decision to hold off on removing Afrikaans as a language of record. There were important developments from the Afrikaans perspective that were, in our opinion, never brought to the fore or considered. One such development was the conference organised by the *Federasie van Afrikaanse Kultuurvereniginge* (Federation of Afrikaans Cultural Organisation [FAK]) which took place on 21 March 2000 to discuss language in the judiciary (Du Plessis, 2001:101-102).

Dissenting voices need to be vocal; and they need to be given a space to be heard and their views considered before dismissing them or paying lip service to speakers of languages other than English. There remains a silence by African language associations and speakers on advocating for the use of African languages as languages of record in South African courts.

An important point to take cognisance of is the fact that the Department of Arts, Culture, Science and Technology (DACST) and the Department of Justice were at the forefront of proposing the changes to the language of record. In the letter by the Minister of DACST to the Minister of Justice, English was proposed as a sole official language of record for international accessibility. This reasoning will be juxtaposed against the reasons given by Mogoeng Mogoeng CJ in the 2017 language of record directive, premised on English as enabling and fostering transformation. The concurrent point, throughout the historical developments and post the enactment of the Constitution, is that the language of record appears to be determined by the executive. The executive is enabled to make the decision through the legislative arm of the state, while the third arm, the judiciary, merely plays a consultative role in informing the eventual language of record policy for courts.

What follows is a discussion on administrative law and how decisions taken can be reviewed and set aside. This is important to engage with prior to advancing the recent monolingual language of record directive and our critique thereof. The administrative law discussion also informs our discussions from Chapter 5 onwards, in particular Chapter 7, comprising the case law. We explain these points in greater depth in the next section.

Administrative law as an enabling framework

The constitutional language rights presented and critiqued in Part One of Chapter 6 are to be applied practically and given meaning to through policy and legislative means. The application of rights is dealt with in Section 8 of the Constitution which states the following:

(1) The Bill of Rights applies to all law, and binds the legislature, the executive, the judiciary and all organs of state.
(2) A provision of the Bill of Rights binds a natural or a juristic person if, and to the extent that, it is applicable, taking into account the nature of the right and the nature of any duty imposed by the right.
(3) When applying a provision of the Bill of Rights to a natural or juristic person in terms of subsection (2), a court –
   (a) in order to give effect to a right in the Bill, must apply, or if necessary, develop, the common law to the extent that legislation does not give effect to that right; and
   (b) may develop rules of the common law to limit the right provided that the limitation is in accordance with Section 36(1).

Subsection (3) (a) speaks to the role of both the legislation in giving meaning to the language rights, as well as the court in developing the language rights where such interpretation and development exceeds the ambit of the legislation. This will become clearer in Part One of Chapter 6. Subsection (3) (b) speaks to the limitation of rights in accordance with the limitations clause in Section 36 of the Constitution. The limitation of rights is advanced in Part One of Chapter 6 with an illustration of the practical application thereof in the case law discussion, housed in Chapter 7.

What we are concerned with, at the current stage of the discussions, is subsection (1), specifically the fact that the rights bind organs of state. An organ of state is defined in the definitions, Section 239 of the Constitution:

> Organ of state means –
> (a) any department of state or administration in the national, provincial or local sphere of government; or
> (b) any other functionary or institution –
> (i) exercising a power or performing a function in terms of the Constitution or a provincial constitution; or
> (ii) exercising a public power or performing a public function in terms of any legislation, but does not include a court or a judicial officer; …

The relevance of defining an organ of state is for the purposes of discussing the mandate that flows from legislation that enables organs of states to perform functions and powers. This is relevant to universities who are mandated through, for example, the Higher Education Act 101 of 1997, discussed in Chapters 5 and 8, which enables universities to draft language policies. In this instance, the university would be exercising a power or performing a public function in terms of legislation. Whether a university is an organ of state in terms of satisfying the definition in Section 239 of the Constitution, for purposes of drafting language policies, has been subject to much debate and varying viewpoints and has resulted in litigation and the courts having the final say on the matter. This is evident from the case law concerning language policies at UFS, UP and SU as discussed in Chapter 7.

The relevance of administrative law can be found through Hoexter's (2012:2) current seminal work on administrative law, stating that it is concerned with "…regulating the activities of bodies that exercise public powers or perform public functions, irrespective of whether those bodies are public in a strict sense". From this understanding of administrative law, one is able to see the linkage with the definition of an organ of state. Administrative law, in its broadest sense, is "…a branch of public law that regulates the legal relations of public authorities whether with private individuals, organisations or with other public authorities" (ibid).

Organs of state do not self-generate administrative power; law confers the power. Hoexter (2012:30) explains that every administrative act performed by the organ of state "…must be justified by reference to some lawful authority for the act". The sources of administrative authority are also sources of constraint, given that the limitations of what administrators may do is included. Hoexter (2012:31) explains that legislation is the most important source of administrative power in that most of the administrative power is derived from legislation. There are varying types of administrative power. Conversely, a distinction is to be made between powers and duties. Hoexter (2012:43) explains:

> ...powers enable things to be done, duties require them to be done. If an official has a duty, she is obliged to perform it. Where she has a power, a measure of discretion or choice is implied...public powers are always accompanied by duties of some kind, whether express or implied.

The nature of the power and the determination of whether there is a duty or obligation to perform a function will be evident from the language used in the legislation. Whether it be obligatory (mandatory) will be dependent on instructive language, such as the inclusion of the word 'must'; and whether it be discretionary will be evident through words such as 'may' and 'should'. Express powers would therefore use obligatory language, while implied powers may be ancillary to express powers; however, they may exist as a necessary result of the express power.

The determination and review of administrative action no longer takes place in terms of the common law but rather through the Promotion of Administrative Justice Act 3 of 2000 (PAJA) which flows from Section 33 of the Constitution on just administrative action and reads as follows:

> (1) Everyone has the right to administrative action that is lawful, reasonable and procedurally fair.
> (2) Everyone whose rights have been adversely affected by administrative action has the right to be given written reasons.
> (3) National legislation must be enacted to give effect to these rights, and must –
>   (a) provide for the review of administrative action by a court or where appropriate, an independent and impartial tribunal;
>   (b) impose a duty on the state to give effect to the rights in subsection (1) and (2); and promote an efficient administration.
>   (c) promote an efficient administration.

The PAJA (2000b) is thus enacted in terms of subsection (3). Subsections (1) and (2) must be borne in mind with the discussion concerning the language policy cases advanced in Chapter 7. The determination of administrative action through the PAJA (2000b) and not via the common law was confirmed by O'Regan J in the case of *Bato Star Fishing (Pty) Ltd v Minister of Environmental Affairs and Others* (2004: para. 22), who stated the following:

> The Courts' power to review administrative action no longer flows directly from the common law but from PAJA (2000) and the Constitution itself. The grundnorm of administrative law is now to be found in the first place not in the doctrine of *ultra vires*, nor in the doctrine of parliamentary sovereignty, nor in the common law itself, but in the principles of our Constitution. The common law informs the provisions of the PAJA (2000) and the Constitution, and derives its force from the latter. The extent to which the common law remains relevant to administrative law review will have to be developed on a case-by-case basis as the Courts interpret and apply the provisions of the PAJA (2000) and the Constitution.

With the excerpt illustrating the instructive authority of the PAJA (2000b), the focus turns to the provisions thereof. Section 1 of the PAJA (2000b) unpacks how administrative action will be determined and reads accordingly:

1. In this Act, unless the context indicates otherwise –
   (i) Administrative action means any decision taken, or any failure to take decision, by –
      (a) an organ of state, when
         (i) exercising a power in terms of the Constitution or a provincial constitution or
         (ii) exercising a public power or performing a public function in terms of any legislation or
      (b) a natural or juristic person, other than an organ of state, when exercising a public power or performing a public function in terms of an empowering provision, which adversely affects the rights of any person and which has a direct, external legal effect, but does not include –
         (aa) the executive powers or functions of the National Executive…
         (bb) the executive powers or functions of the Provincial Executive…
         (cc) the executive powers or functions of a municipal council;
         (dd) the legislative functions of Parliament, a provincial legislature or a municipal council;
         (ee) the judicial functions of a judicial officer of a court referred to in section 166 of the Constitution or of a Special Tribunal established under section 2 of the Special Investigating Units and Special Tribunals Act, 1996 (Act no. 74 of 1996), and the judicial functions of a traditional leader under customary law or any other law;
         (ff) a decision to institute or continue a prosecution;
         (gg) a decision relating to any aspect regarding the appointment of a judicial officer, by the Judicial Service Commission;
         (hh) any decision taken, or failure to take a decision, in terms of any provision of the Promotion of Access to Information Act, 2000; or
   (ii) any decision taken, or failure to take a decision, in terms of section 4(1);…

The latter half of the extracts from the PAJA (2000b) lists the exclusions, which are important in noting which decisions cannot be reviewed in terms of administrative law. Section 1(a) to (b) lists the requirements which can be divided into seven elements. The elements tend to overlap to a certain extent (Hoexter, 2012:197). Furthermore, the elements alone cannot determine whether administrative action was taken; the application of the facts in each case will give meaning to each of the elements in guiding the court in its determination (Hoexter, 2012:197). The seven elements are:

1. A decision
2. by an organ of state (or a natural or juristic person)
3. exercising a public power or performing a public function
4. in terms of any legislation (or in terms of an empowering provision)
5. that adversely affects rights
6. that has a direct, external legal effect
7. and that does not fall under any of the listed exclusions.

These seven elements are applied to the case law, specifically the cases of *AfriForum and Another* v *University of the Free State* (2018); *AfriForum and Another* v *Chairperson of the Council of the University of Pretoria and Others* (2017); and *Gelyke Kanse and Another* v *The President of the Convocation of the Stellenbosch University* (2017), advanced in Chapter 7 and critiqued in Chapter 8. Chapter 7 also includes a full application and analysis of the cases from both a constitutional and administrative perspective where we apply the seven elements in proposing a counter argument in critiquing the majority judgment by Mogoeng Mogoeng CJ in the case of *AfriForum and Another* v *University of the Free State* (2018), as well as the judgment by Kollapen J in the case of *AfriForum and Another* v *Chairperson of the Council of the University of Pretoria and Others* (2017). The relevance of administrative law to the book at hand is now visibly relevant in that it applies to the legislation empowering the drafting of language policies and the nature of the language policies, when taken on review, in deciding whether an administrative decision should be reviewed and set aside. This discussion on administrative law forms the basis upon which the monolingual language of record decision is critiqued below.

Language of record directive

With the historical context of the language of record advanced in much depth in preceding discussions in this chapter, as well as the administrative law discussions, our focus turns to the 'recent' monolingual language of record directive. On 16 April 2019, the *Sunday Times* newspaper reported that the Heads of Court, acting under the leadership of the CJ, had elected to make English the sole official language of record in all High Courts (Nombembe, 2017). The newspaper quoted the CJ as validating the decision on grounds of transformation, greater access to justice and reversing the discrimination of the past.

It must be questioned how resorting to a monolingual language of record can be regarded as a change for the better and for fostering greater access to justice. The case studies in Chapters 2 and 3 prove otherwise, highlighting the disastrous effects of having a monolingual language of record and how this adversely affects the indigenous people of either the country or vulnerable minority groups of people. It is questionable how reversing the discrimination of the past is associated with Afrikaans as a language. Afrikaans is not only spoken by White South Africans but also by Coloured South Africans. This involves a racialised view of our languages and an 'othering' in a sense; yet English, a non-South African language, is seen as a unifying neutral language, regardless of its history, as outlined in Chapters 1 and 2. There is a fine line of double standards within the elitist voice that needs to be critiqued.

Following the announcement in April 2017, a series of communication was sent to the CJ by language activist and practising attorney at law, Cerneels Lourens, resident in the North West province of South Africa and Afrikaans mother tongue speaker. According to Lourens, no response was received from the CJ. On 17 September 2019, in a national South African Sunday newspaper, *City Press*, a group of academics, legal practitioners and language activists, ourselves included, joined in writing an open letter to the CJ (Docrat et al., 2017b). The group voiced their concern about a monolingual language of record policy and questioned whether this had been correctly reported, given that the decision had not been published in the *Government Gazette* and thus was not legal.

On 28 February 2018, JP of the Western Cape High Court Division, Justice John Hlophe, released the following directive concerning the language of record:

OFFICE OF THE JUDGE PRESIDENT
WESTERN CAPE HIGH COURT

PRIVATE BAG X9020
CAPE TOWN
8000

Telephone number: +27 21 480 2564
Fax number: 086 6424753
Email: lpotgieter@judiciary.org.za

TO : THE LEGAL PROFESSION AND OTHER STAKEHOLDERS

FROM : HLOPHE, JP

SUBJECT : OFFICIAL LANGUAGE OF RECORD OF THE COURT

IMPLEMENTATION DATE : 28 FEBRUARY 2018

DIRECTIVE

OFFICIAL LANGUAGE OF RECORD IN ALL COURTS WITHIN THE WESTERN CAPE

WHEREAS on 31 March 2017, the Heads of Courts Forum resolved that English must be the official language of record in all courts in the Republic of South;

AND WHEREAS no national directive has been issued by the Office of the Chief Justice as to the application of this resolution;

ACKNOWLEDGING that the dynamics of each Division of the High Court/ Region differ in as far as it relates to predominant languages spoken and therefore the way the different stakeholders are currently applying the relevant directive of English being the official language of record in all courts;

AND WHEREAS the commitment by all the role players to ensure adherence to the national resolution applicable to both criminal and civil cases in all courts, will result in speedier and more efficient adjudication and finalisation of ALL cases.

THE ROLE PLAYERS ARE THEREFORE, HEREBY, DIRECTED TO ADHERE TO THE FOLLOWING:

COURT DOCUMENTS:

ALL court documents submitted to courts in both criminal and civil cases and which will form part of the eventual court record **SHALL** be submitted in English.

The only limited exception permitted to the said directive will be the submission of witness statements in a language other than English and only if the witness is not sufficiently conversant in English.

COURT PROCEEDINGS:

Court proceedings should as far as possible be conducted in English.

In order to comply, the presiding officer should ideally at pre-trial stage or if not possible, after the witness has been sworn in at trial stage, enquire as follows:

"IN TERMS OF A NATIONAL DIRECTIVE BY THE HEADS OF COURTS, THE OFFICIAL LANGUAGE OF RECORD IS ENGLISH. ARE YOU CONVERSANT IN ENGLISH? DO YOU HAVE ANY OBJECTION TO THE COURT PROCEEDINGS CONTINUING IN ENGLISH?"

Should the witness not have an objection to the evidence being led in English, the court should continue as such. Should the witness not be conversant in English the **leading of evidence only** may be conducted in any other language. In such cases an interpreter should as far as possible be utilised to interpret the evidence into English.

It is advisable that this enquiry be conducted at pre-trial stage before a matter is certified trial ready. This will enable the administration at the court to make adequate arrangements for interpretation services, if needed, to avoid unnecessary postponements.

In such cases where there is no interpreter available and there is an indication that the matter is to proceed to appeal or review, the presiding officer should, for the purposes of the court record to be in English, order the Administration of the Office of the Chief Justice and/ or the Department of Justice and Constitutional Development to have the portions of the evidence led in any other language **simultaneously translated into English whilst it is being transcribed**. The translated version of the evidence will form part of the court record.

The order should read as follows:

"IN TERMS OF THE HEADS OF COURTS RESOLUTION DATED 31 MARCH 2017 RELATING TO THE OFFICIAL LANGUAGE OF RECORD BEING ENGLISH, THE COURT HEREBY ORDERS THE ADMINISTRATION OF THE OFFICE OF THE CHIEF JUSTICE AND /OR DEPARTMENT OF JUSTICE TO HAVE THE EVIDENCE LED IN ANOTHER LANGUAGE TRANSLATED INTO ENGLISH, SIMULTANEOUSLY TO IT BEING TRANSCRIBED."

> Although evidence may have been led in a language other than in English, the Presiding Officer should render all verdicts/ outcomes/ sentences in English. An interpreter should be utilised for the translation into another language should the parties /accused not be conversant in English.
>
> **SUBMISSION OF COURT RECORDS TO THE HIGH COURT:**
>
> All records whether criminal or civil submitted to the High Court either by means of an appeal or review, from any lower court will only constitute the English record.
>
> *JUDGE PRESIDENT HLOPHE*

This directive cemented the decision by the Heads of Court that English be the sole official language of record. Making English the sole official language of record means that the court proceedings are conducted in English and the judgment is delivered in English. This decision has been taken, despite the language demographics which overwhelmingly illustrate that the majority of people speak an African language and not English as their mother tongue.

The first issue arising from the extracted provisions is that this directive reaffirmed the Heads of Court directive, even though this was not published in the *Government Gazette*. This directive fails to provide details of the authority under which they acted, or the empowering legislation from which the Heads of Court derived the power to determine the language of record in all High Courts.

The second issue concerns the statement that English as a sole language of record "… will result in speedier and more efficient adjudication and finalisation of ALL cases". These questions can be posed in response: How can interpretation result in speedier case finalisation? Also, how is it efficient to provide for English-speaking litigants to proceed in their mother tongue and African language- and Afrikaans-speaking litigants to be wholly reliant on an interpreter? A parallel can be drawn with the Indian case study in Chapter 3, particularly the views of legal practitioners, one of whom said that English is more practical as it is speedier to continue with one language. One must question whether this is more important than access to justice and the level of justice received.

The third issue, applicable to both criminal and civil cases, affects the constitutional language rights in Section 35 of the Constitution; it also adversely affects the Section 29(2) language in education right. What would be the purpose of graduating with a bilingual LLB, or being proficient in a language at university level, when entering a profession that is premised on English only? This is in stark contrast to the Higher Education Act 101 of 1997 and the Draft Language Policy of the Department of Higher Education (2018).

Furthermore, there are the financial implications for civil litigants who bear the costs of interpretation (Hartle, 2019). With the submission of documents in English only, there is no indication who will bear the costs for this in criminal cases. It would be ironic if the state bore the costs, yet they make a costs argument on the grounds of the use of other languages as languages of record. Double standards, perhaps, or a misunderstanding of the language question in a legal system, both bearing the same consequences.

The fourth issue, one of grave significance in our opinion, is this statement:
> "IN TERMS OF A NATIONAL DIRECTIVE BY THE HEADS OF COURTS, THE OFFICIAL LANGUAGE OF RECORD IS ENGLISH. ARE YOU CONVERSANT IN ENGLISH? DO YOU HAVE ANY OBJECTION TO THE COURT PROCEEDINGS CONTINUING IN ENGLISH?"

Posing these questions to a litigant or accused person raises several issues. In what language is the question being asked? A layperson is inclined to answer affirmatively where they have minimal English language competency. The use of the word "conversant" is problematic, as evidenced in the Australian case study set out in Chapter 3. 'Conversant', to our minds, is having a conversation in a social or informal context where minimal linguistic skills are required and not an advanced vocabulary. This is not true of the legal system in court where cross-examination, or even examination in chief, may raise complex issues and in some instances legal practitioners may use their linguistic skills to confuse a witness. The point is that there are varying degrees of speaking, understanding, reading and writing a language, as recorded in the language surveys presented below. The situation is further complicated by courtroom discourse, including the use of legalese; and witness demeanour and credibility affect the admissibility of evidence.

Would a litigant of a lower social and economic standard feel comfortable with objecting to the proceedings continuing in English? It is highly improbable, given the power relations at play and that the litigant might think that, by objecting, they would be disadvantaged in some way. This is not unrealistic, given the case studies presented in Chapters 2 and Three, especially in those case studies dealing with indigenous people in an English or western legal system. If the litigant or witness objects, an interpreter is provided. This is problematic, as interpretation in South Africa is not regulated, there is a shortage of interpreters, and interpreters are under-skilled (Mbangi, 2019).

The legality of the language of record directive

One important question is whether the monolingual language of record directive is in fact law. By 'law', we mean, 'Is it legal?' If not, then why are these arguments being put forward, and how can the directive be legally challenged on constitutional grounds? Besides the media report in the Sunday national newspaper, *Sunday Times*, no tangible policy was gazetted stating that the language of record in courts would be English only. The monolingual language of record directive by Hlophe confirms that the decision was taken by the Heads of Court to make English the sole official language of record in all courts.

The starting point is to trace back to the empowering legislation to assess if the Heads of Courts, under the Chairmanship of Mogoeng Mogoeng CJ, had the authority to change the language of record for all courts. Of relevance is Chapter 3, Governance and Administration of all Courts, of the Superior Courts Act (2013), specifically Section 8 therefore, concerning, judicial management of judicial functions. This reads:

(1) For the purpose of any consultation regarding any matter referred to in this section, the Chief justice may convene any forum of judicial officers that he or she deems appropriate.
(2) The Chief Justice, as the head of the judiciary as contemplated in section 165 (6) of the Constitution, exercises responsibility over the establishment and monitoring of norms and standards for the exercise of the judicial functions of all courts.
(3) The Chief Justice may, subject to subsection (5), issue written protocols or directives, or give guidance or advice, to judicial officers –
  (a) in respect of norms and standards for the performance of the judicial functions as contemplated in subsection (6); and
  (b) regarding any matter affecting the dignity, accessibility, effectiveness, efficiency or functioning of the courts.
(4) (a) Any function or any power in terms of this section, vesting in the Chief Justice or any other head of court, may be delegated to any other judicial officer of the court in question.
  (b) The management of the judicial functions of each court is the responsibility of the head of that court.
  (c) Subject to subsections (2) and (3), the Judge President of a Division is also responsible for the co-ordination of the judicial functions of all Magistrates' Courts falling within the jurisdiction of that division.
(5) Any protocol or directive in terms of subsection (3) –
  (a) may only be issued by the Chief Justice if it enjoys the majority support of the heads of those courts on which it would be applicable; and
  (b) must be published in the *Gazette*.
(6) The judicial functions referred to in subsection (2) and subsection (4) (b) include the –
  (a) determination of settings of the specific courts;
  (b) assignment of judicial officers to sittings;
  (c) assignment of cases and other judicial duties to judicial officers;
  (d) determination of the sitting schedules and places of sittings for judicial officers;
  (e) management of procedures to be adhered to in respect of –
    (i) case flow management;
    (ii) the finalisation of any matter before a judicial officer, including any outstanding judgment, decision or order; and
    (iii) recesses of Superior Courts.

As quoted, Chapter 3, Section 8 of the Superior Courts Act (2013) is the legislation from which the argument stems: that the language of record for courts cannot be determined by the CJ together with the Heads of Court. Our reasoning follows: subsection (1) provides the authority for the Heads of Court forum who, under the leadership of the CJ, took the decision to make English the sole official language of record. Subsection (3) provides that the CJ may issue directives; and the language of record decision was recorded as a directive. Subsection (3) (a) and (b), however, make no direct mention of the language of record. Subsection (3) (b) refers to "accessibility" and "efficiency". This is interesting to note in the context of the language of record directive; the fact remains that such a reasoning would be far-fetched and there is no direct mention. Besides, subsection (3) is to be read with subsection (5), where (a) clearly states that the directive by the CJ must enjoy majority support, which was the case. Subsection (5) (b), however, requires that it be published in the *Gazette*, which had not happened.

Hlophe JP has exercised his delegated power in issuing the directive in terms of subsection (4). Subsection (4) (c) explains the far-reaching powers of a JP in his or her jurisdiction, where their decisions apply to both the High and Magistrates' Courts in their division. The fact remains that a decision concerning the language of record could not be taken by any JP, nor the CJ.

It appears from these discussions that the decision concerning the language of record for courts can be reviewed and set aside in terms of administrative action, as explained earlier in this chapter. Having said this, we maintain that the argument is not solely of a constitutional nature. It is our opinion, based on our reasoning above, that Section 8 of the Superior Courts Act (2013) does not enable or confer the authority on the CJ or the Heads of Court to determine the language of record policy for courts. The decision or directive by the CJ and Heads of Court on the language of record can be brought in terms of administrative law. Section 239 of the Constitution excludes a judgment by a judicial officer, but not administrative decisions, in the definition of an organ of state. Furthermore, according to Section 1 of PAJA (2000b) administrative action, taking or failing to take a decision must be done by an organ of state to fall within the ambit of administrative law. That being said, the point remains that the language of record in courts is a policy or legislative matter that needs to be stated explicitly where the legislature has failed to deal with the matter, as evidenced in Chapter 5 with specific reference to the Language Policy of the Department of Justice and Constitutional Development (2019).

Interpretational rights and the failures of social justice

Those not opposing the English-only language of record directive argue that accused persons can still exercise their right in Section 35(3) (k) and use their language, as an interpreter is provided at the state's expense in criminal cases. We disagree with these views as the current system of interpretation in South African courtrooms is not of a high quality and is inconsistent. Secondly, there is a shortage of interpreters. Thirdly, interpretation as a profession in the legal system does not require any formal degree qualification as a prerequisite. Fourthly, there is an overarching distinction between interpretation *per se* and legal interpretation. These are the issues we will flesh out in relation to the case law advanced in Chapter 7.

Leung (2019:213) states that quality interpretation is problematic in many jurisdictions where local and foreign speakers of non-official languages enter the court system. In South Africa, the system is complex when it comes to speakers of official languages trying to access justice, such as where accused persons are speakers of African languages or Afrikaans. Leung (2019:214) reminds us that interpretational rights are protected by the International Covenant on Civil and Political Rights (1996), as discussed in Chapters 2 and 3. Simply put, if the Heads of Court are intent on pursuing a monolingual language of record policy for courts, interpretation services that are of the highest quality and readily available at all stages of criminal investigation and prosecution must be available; this applies to civil cases as well.

Leung (2019:216) makes an important point regarding bilingual or multilingual accused persons who may be more comfortable and proficient in their mother tongue than the language of court. The court will assess the standard of linguistic competency of the accused to speak the language of the court. This was evidenced in the case law, in *Mthethwa* v *De Bruin No and Another* (1998): the accused understood English, regardless of the extent to which the accused could speak English. This reaffirms the point that, if you appear to speak English or say so when asked, the trial proceeds in English, as you are assumed to be competent in English.

Importance is not to be placed solely on the right to speak in your mother tongue but also the right to be understood by the court in your mother tongue. Leung (2019:217) encapsulates this point:

> How often does the right to speak in an official language (by a litigant/defendant) translate into the right to be understood (directly, not via an interpreter) in that language? The right to argue a case in one's own language is of strategic value in adversarial trials, where the rhetorical resources may be crucial in legal argumentation but may be lost in translation.

This excerpt highlights the many permutations arising from the right in Section 35(3) (k) of the Constitution while also highlighting the complexities of interpretation. Even though this is in a legal domain, the issues are linguistic. This point alludes to the conclusions and recommendations in Chapter 10 in relation to forensic linguists in South African courts and the importance of legal practitioners and judicial officers being either linguistically competent and undergoing necessary training on language matters in courts, or calling forensic linguists as experts. Conversely, three important questions central to this book and objectives outlined in Chapter 1 are captured by Leung (2019:217):

> Can a defendant demand that a particular official language be used as the medium of trial proceedings, or that a Judge who can understand a particular official language presides over his or her trial? Should the approval of such an application be conditioned upon the defendant's language proficiency? How might this proficiency be measured, and by whom?

The first question emanating from the excerpt has been directly dealt with and disposed of in the *Mthethwa* case (1998). The second question, too, has been dealt with in a number of the cases presented in Chapter 7 of this book, specifically in these cases: *State* v *Damani* (2016); *State* v *Damoyi* (2004); *State* v *Gordon* (2018); and *State* v *Matomela* (1998). The third question has been raised in relation to the language of record directive by Hlophe, which we have discussed earlier. It is our opinion that this has been intentionally overlooked in the South African context given that the language question has never been afforded the space to be discussed and assessed with experts in the field. We can substantiate our point by referring to the language of record directive by Hlophe JP in which the litigants are merely asked at pre-trial stage whether they can speak English.

According to Leung (2019:218), with official status conferred on language(s), there is an expectation that, as a citizen, you are free to use the official language of your choice and be heard directly in that language in courts. We have also relied on Canada as a case study, which satisfies all four questions above, Leung (2019:218) similarly credits Canada with their progressive interpretation and application of the language rights in both criminal and civil courts. Leung (2019:218) also speaks about the trilogy of cases and how the courts developed the law from a narrowed interpretation of language rights to one of purposive interpretation, where accused persons have the inherent right to be heard by a Judge in a language of their choice, and where that language is official. Although we have discussed the Canadian case of *R* v *Beaulac* (1999), Leung (2019:218) advances further insights, stating the following that is relevant to our discussions:

> The court granted the accused a new trial before a Judge and jury who speak both official languages, and established that this right is not derived from the right to a fair trial, but rather from the country's guarantee of equality between the two official languages. It is absolute and substantive. The defendant's native language and ability to speak the other official language are irrelevant, because the accused should be able to freely and subjectively assert either official language as part of his/her cultural identity.

Again, the Canadian case study, as with the Belgian, proves to be a leading example which can be emulated in bilingual and multilingual legal orders. Moreover, the emphasis is placed on the right as substantive rather than procedural. The important linkage between language and culture is overlooked in the African case studies, specifically in Nigeria and Kenya, while

Australia ignores cultural behaviour of indigenous people in trials. India discriminately maintains the caste system which creeps into and influences court proceedings and legal education. Morocco also, in a sense, classifies different cultures along linguistic and classist lines. Simply put, although Canada is only a bilingual jurisdiction, their model is inclusive and premised on equality rather than reasonability conveyed through equitability. We refer to 'equality' as opposed to 'equitability' in the South African context, about which Leung (2019:222) says, "…fair trial instead of linguistic equality is the overriding consideration". Leung (2019:222) made these comments in relation to the cases of the *Mthethwa* v *De Bruin NO and Another* (1998) and *State* v *Damoyi* (2003), which we have advanced in Chapter 7.

This part of the discussion has confirmed that Section 35(3) (k) of the Constitution does not confer a language right but rather affords persons the right to use and be understood in a language they fully understand through interpretation. This is true, for African language- and Afrikaans-speaking accused persons. We maintain that this gross omission provides a lesser standard of justice on linguistic grounds and that this is contrary to the prescripts of Section 6 of the Constitution. To apply the work of Leung (2019), South Africa as a multilingual order, does not marginalise the minority (English language speakers), but rather does so to the majority of people (African language- and Afrikaans-speaking people).

The problem with interpretation: quality versus efficacy

The next step is to explain why we are of the opinion that, as a long-term language plan, the courts in South Africa cannot focus solely on interpretation and have a monolingual language of record policy, rather than adopting bilingual and multilingual language policies to regulate the language question for court proceedings and record purposes. Throughout this research, we have alluded to – and directly referred to – quality of interpretation. In this book, through the African case studies in Chapter 2, as well as the international case studies in Chapter 3, we have highlighted the various inconsistencies resulting from the use of interpreters in courts and how this affects access to justice. In this part of the discussion, we focus on the qualifications for interpreters and the quality of interpretation in South Africa.

In South Africa, with a monolingual language of record policy, the quality of interpretation is central to ensuring the attainment of justice for all and that the right to a fair trial is protected. According to Namakula (2019:230), as part of the deliverables of Section 35(3) (k) of the Constitution, only competent interpreters can produce quality interpretation. As noted in the case of *State* v *Ndala* (1996:221), discussed in Chapter 7, the court explained that competent interpreters are those who are "able to give a true and correct interpretation of the evidence". With the competence of the interpreter determined at the onset of the trial, the following criteria are applied, as identified by Namakula (2019:230):

(1) proficiency in both the source and target languages, (2) a basic understanding of the legal process at the least, (3) impartiality and (4) professional conduct including operating within the boundaries of neutrality.

The limitation to these determining criteria is that an assessment of the competence of the interpreter is based on their track record. This is problematic as all cases are different and present different challenges, and the level of interpretation required varies. Simply put, it is not a precise science and thus non-regulatory. Given the non-regulation of interpreters for courts through legislative and policy means, this results in instances where interpreters "…ask their own questions, omit certain information, and add information that was not conveyed by the original speaker" (Namakula, 2019:230). Speaking from a point of practice, Judge Hartle (2019) bore testament to instances such as these. Judge Hartle (2019) shared an experience in which an isiXhosa-speaking accused was before her and she was postponing the matter.

During this time, Judge Hartle said she provided detailed reasons for the postponement, which took her a "while" to read. The interpreter before court interpreted the reasoning into isiXhosa. What was startling and of grave concern for Judge Hartle was the fact that the interpreter was able to interpret her lengthy reasoning within approximately two minutes. Given that Judge Hartle is bilingual (fully proficient in English and Afrikaans, but not isiXhosa), she enquired from the interpreter whether in fact everything she had said had been interpreted, given the brevity of interpretation, to which the interpreter responded along the lines of, "I took it upon myself to summarise your reasoning", when interpreting for the accused. Instances such as these alert one to the practical issues concerning competent interpretation in South Africa.

The aspect of competence relates to quality of interpretation where, according to Namakula (2019:228), "interpreting of good quality is correct and comprehensible; it is simultaneous and conducted by a competent and sworn interpreter". There are three points of departure from this quotation, namely: correctness, consistency and sworn evidence, each of which Namakula (2019:228-229) addresses. Namakula (2019:228) advances that correctness is embedded in the Section 35(3) (k) right and requires the interpreter to interpret the proceedings properly and intelligently. Whatever the interpreter interprets is recorded in the record; this will be in a high number of cases where there is an English-only language of record policy. Therefore, if it is interpreted incorrectly, the record will reflect as such (Namakula, 2019:229). In Chapter 7, we will provide one such example through the case of *State* v *Manzini* (2007) in which, during sentencing, an isiZulu accused alleged that his evidence had not been properly interpreted. The magistrate, after receiving confirmation from the chief interpreter that there were numerous errors and the interpretation was alarmingly poor, proceeded with sentencing on the grounds that it did not affect the materiality of the facts. The dictum on appeal, as quoted in Chapter 7 of this book, is relevant at this stage of the discussion and we quote it in advance:

> Tshiqi J and Schwatzman J (2007) concurring held if incorrect interpretation had occurred, the Magistrate would not be in a position to determine the credibility of the witness imparting evidence in isiZulu. This would adversely affect the Magistrate's ability to evaluate such evidence, and obstruct the legal representatives from preparing arguments in mitigation and aggravation of sentence (2007:107). This would also affect the outcome of the case, particularly whether or not to convict the accused. The Magistrate failed to recognise the importance of language as part of the right to a fair trial. The court held that Section 35(3) (k) of the Constitution had been adversely affected, and ordered that the appeal succeed and conviction and sentence be set aside (2007:110).

This proves the point about the importance of correctness in interpretation and the effects thereof in affecting the outcome of a trial for both accused and complainant. On the point of a witness's credibility, language is central, as noted in the Australian case study in Chapter 3. Where interpretation is employed, the credibility of a witness's evidence will be determined through the correctness of interpretation.

With regard to the consistency of interpretation, where an interpreter is called to interpret for an accused, that interpreter is required to interpret all proceedings, not only parts of the trial (Namakula, 2019:229). Partial interpreting will result in a procedural irregularity that will adversely affect the outcome of the trial proceedings and limit the Section 35(3) (k) constitutional right to a fair trial. This overlaps with sworn evidence and the irregularities arising where interpreters have not been sworn in, as evidenced in the cases of *State* v *Ndala* (1996) and *State* v *Siyotula* (2003). Although a procedural irregularity, it is of grave consequence for a complainant where, for instance, the trial is to commence *de novo*.

Namakula (2019:231) also points out that judicial officers are tasked with determining the accuracy of interpretation but are unable to do so as they lack the necessary language skills. Simply put, the point that must be conveyed is that interpretation "…is time-consuming. It may lead to loss or distortion of evidence, and to misunderstandings, and it may dilute the effect of cross-examination" (Namakula, 2019:231). Further shortcomings include the inability to determine demeanour, "…voice intonations, and useful projections of paralinguistic forms of expression" (ibid). From a practical perspective, this can be substantiated by considering the case studies in Chapters 2 and 3, with the Australian case study proving this point.

Our intention is not to discredit the important profession of interpretation but merely to lay bare the challenges that currently present in courts of law in South Africa; and also to recognise that these problems are not inherent to South Africa only but are seen throughout Africa and internationally, as far away as India and Australia. We have advanced varying opinions, highlighting the challenges. The next point of discussion advances the 'other side of the story', the views of an interpreter.

There are interpreters who have displayed their skill, quality and accuracy. McConnachie (2019) shared these views, but also noted that an interpreter's skill, quality and accuracy depended on the interpreter and his or her ability and was thus unpredictable. Yoliswa Mbangi (2019), a senior interpreter in the Bhisho High Court in the Eastern Cape Province of South Africa, explained how she became an interpreter. The interview with Mbangi (2019) confirmed that a university degree in interpretation or translation studies is not a prerequisite for appointment as an interpreter in either the Magistrates' or High Courts. Initially employed in an administrative clerkship position, Mbangi, together with fellow colleagues, were appointed as interpreters on the basis of their matric marks for their language subjects.

According to Mbangi (2019), an interpreter will commence at the MC at what is referred to as 'Entry level 5'. Mbangi (2019) explained the levels:

> Senior court interpreter, level 7; Principal interpreter, level 8; Cluster manager, level 9; and Provincial manager, level 10.

Mbangi (2019) stated further that the requirements from Principal level upwards is a diploma or degree in legal interpreting, or equivalent qualification. It is gravely concerning, as stated by Mbangi (2019), that the current requirements for entry-level interpreters is a matric qualification. These entry-level interpreters will then be assigned to the MC(s) where the majority of cases heard are criminal and the assignment of these interpreters affect the application of the right in Section 35(3) (k) of the Constitution. There are prerequisite qualifications in place and this framework can be built upon and strengthened through legislative and policy developments. This must occur if English is to be the sole official language of record.

From a theoretical perspective, relying on the discussions advanced previously in this section, we have outlined what is required of an interpreter. Mbangi (2019) was asked what the role of interpreters was and to describe her role as a senior interpreter. She responded as follows:

> ...senior interpreter, supervising other interpreters. It is to communicate effectively, the message from source language to target language. Place those who understand the source language on an equal footing with those who understand the target language by conserving every element of information contained in the source language communication when it is rendered in the target language. Interpret accurately without altering, omitting or adding anything to what is stated and without explanation, unless permission for explanation has been given by the Presiding officer.

There are indeed parallels with what Mbangi (2019) says in this excerpt and the theory advanced earlier. The last point in the excerpt, that interpreters are not permitted to deviate from what is being said, is important in the context of what Judge Hartle (2019) said concerning the interpreter who summarised her reasoning. Having said this, Mbangi (2019) also listed three areas of difficulty she experienced with interpreting:

> Inability to hear the speaker: when he speaks very soft and I have to plead with him for several times. Cultural differences: I have the responsibility to not only understand and to fluently speak the target language, I must also have a deep-rooted sense of cultural awareness, regional slang and idioms. Social evolution provides new words and phrases on a continuous basis. So an interpreter should be able to deliver any given word or phrase accurately. No pre-prep or sight interpretation materials: very long judgment delivered without seeing it first or given to look while interpreting.

We have dealt with the first two challenges above. The last challenge points to a lack of understanding of the language question by judicial officers and the difficulty of interpreting legal language emanating from judgments. This also points to the need to have interpreters who possess a diploma or degree in legal interpreting and who have specialised in both the source and target languages. There are clear roles for universities, together with the legal system, in ensuring these qualifications are offered at tertiary level and warranted for practice through legislative and policy requirements.

Conclusion

This chapter began with the definitional elements of the language of record prior to engaging in a thorough discussion of the historical position concerning the language(s) of record in South African courts. A theme was detected, one of racial, political and economic policy influences. Political influence was traced to post-1994 where the language of record was seen to be a political compromise. This compromise, however, failed to favour the African languages; instead, one dominant language, Afrikaans, was merely replaced with another politically-dominant language, English. The African languages have thus been relegated a lesser status, even though litigants and witnesses who are African language speakers are solely reliant on interpretation.

In this chapter, we have illustrated the problematic system of legal interpretation in courts from the perspectives of both theory and practice. There are also, however, frameworks that we have identified by drawing parallels from African and international case studies in Chapters 2 and 3. These frameworks can be developed through collective efforts in policy and legislative developments. The primary purpose of these developments would be to have a regulated court interpretation system which would be needed if the 2017 monolingual language of record policy directive is implemented.

This chapter has questioned the legality of the language of record directive through the Superior Court Act (2013). Discussions were advanced in terms of administrative law which proves to be pivotal in enforcing persons' rights – in these instances, language rights – through the review of administrative action guided by the PAJA (2000b). By challenging the administrative authority of an organ of state, the people have the right to hold accountable those enabled through legislative or other means, to perform a function or exercise a public power and review such decisions. The administrative law discussions have highlighted the interdisciplinarity of this research and the need for a language of record policy for courts to be determined through a review process informed by consolidated research and expert opinions.

Against the backdrop of the issues highlighted in this chapter, the following chapter advances the theoretical underpinnings to legislative and policy drafting in the South African context.

THE LANGUAGE QUESTION IN LEGISLATIVE AND POLICY INSTRUMENTS

A forensic linguistics approach to language planning and legislative drafting

In Chapter 4, we constantly referred to legislation and policies, not only in relation to the language of record directive, but also in terms of administrative law. The continuous reference to empowering legislative provisions and the need for a language policy for courts to guide the language of proceedings and record requires the theoretical underpinnings of legislative drafting and language planning to be explained. This chapter therefore engages with the various stages of both legislative drafting and the language planning process. These theoretical discussions, which may be advanced from a global perspective for language planning, are applied to the South African context, given the focus of this book.

With the theory advanced, we present the practical developments that have taken place concerning primary language legislation and the various language policies that regulate the use of language in the South African legal system.

The chapter engages with authors' works concerning the development of language policy in South Africa where the relationship between language and law is discussed. This chapter identifies four types of language planning, with the fourth tier of opportunity planning (Antia, 2017) linked to the research area of forensic linguistics. This, in itself, reinforces the point that forensic linguistics is a branch of applied linguistics and is related to African sociolinguistics.

The chapter is consolidated through the application of the theory to the relevant legislation and policies where we advance the relevant provisions and offer a critique. The critique is advanced from the perspective of favouring a bilingual and multilingual language of record policy for courts, rather than the current monolingual status quo.

The relationship between forensic linguistics and applied language studies

In Chapter 1, the introductory chapter of this book, we advanced definitions of forensic linguistics and categories thereof with reference to the work by Olsson (2008). As per the discussion in Chapter 1, disciplines 4 and 5 are classified by Olsson (2004) as the study of law and language. In this section of Chapter 5, the presented discussions build on the definition and introductory aspects of forensic linguistics with the aim of locating the language planning and legislative drafting processes for courts and the higher education system in South Africa.

The language of record, as discussed in Chapter 4, is concerned with the use of language in which an accused person's case is heard. It is the language used to record proceedings and deliver judgment. Thus, the language of record can be subsumed within discipline 4 of forensic linguistics (Olsson, 2004:4), the language and discourse of court rooms, given that it concerns the use of language within the proceedings of a courtroom. It is also relevant to discipline 5 (Olsson, 2004:4), language rights, as an accused would be exercising his or her Section 35(3) (k) constitutional language right to provide evidence in a language he or she fully understands. This is a broad theoretical application of forensic linguistics as a discipline to the language of record in courts.

Both Olsson (2008) and Gibbons (1994) advance that forensic linguistics is an intricate research area, although it covers a broad spectrum of sub-disciplines. By understanding precisely what forensic linguistics is, one has to ask what type of texts forensic linguists examine (Olsson, 2008:1). In answering this question, Olsson (2008:1) explains that, where a text is implicated in a legal or criminal context, then it is classified as a forensic text. This is one instance in which forensic linguistics is applied. Another way of determining what forensic linguistics is, is to consider the application of linguistics to legal questions and issues. Forensic linguistics is the application of linguistic knowledge to a particular social setting, in this instance, the legal forum, hence the derivation of the word 'forensic' (ibid, 3). Again, the application of linguistic methods to legal questions is only one sense in which forensic linguistics is an application of a science, as linguistic theories may be applied in analysing language samples, either in written or oral form (ibid). Olsson (2008:4) summarises these points in the following excerpt:

> ...the forensic linguist applies linguistic knowledge and techniques to the language implicated in (i) legal cases or proceedings or (ii) private disputes between parties which may at a later stage result in legal action of some kind being taken.

Gibbons (1994) adopts a more practical approach to explaining what forensic linguistics is and how it can be used in courtroom discourse. The primary focus for Gibbons (1994:319) is the work of forensic linguists in the legal system, where forensic linguists provide expert

evidence in court. Forensic linguistic evidence, according to Gibbons (1994:320), can be categorised into two main classes:
1. There is evidence as to whether a specific person, persons or a class of people could comprehend certain language.
2. There is evidence as to whether a specific person, persons or class of people could produce certain language.

The first point Gibbons (1994:320) makes concerns persons understanding a specific language (for example, English) and understanding legal language. Thus, "certain language" has two meanings. This is also the case concerning the second point. These two points speak to the linguistic proficiency of accused persons, litigants and witnesses in court proceedings. Understanding proceedings is pivotal to ensuring justice and is a central principle underpinning the justice system, as espoused by Cassim (2003). Gibbons (1986) succinctly summarises the issue of proficiency:

> ... it is not possible for a low proficiency, or second language speaker to suddenly begin to speak like a native speaker.

As touched upon with reference to Cassim's (2003) work, proficiency is directly related to determining the language of record. One cannot expect a majority of African language speakers to be proficient in an English-only language of record, as is the current situation in South Africa. A double disadvantage exists in the legal system. The first is that there is a need to master the legal language. According to Gibbons (1994:196), there are people who are disadvantaged by their lack of mastery of the language through which the law is accessed and applied. The problem in courtrooms is spoken interaction, as there is an intrinsic difficulty in understanding legal language; and this is compounded by disparities of power in that context (ibid). Examples of this include cross-examination, which can be stressful and difficult for those on the receiving end – in this instance, an accused person (Gibbons, 1994:196-197).

The purpose of cross-examination is to discredit the version of the opposing party. This becomes increasingly easy when legal language is being used. A current example is the case of *Omotoso and Others* v *State* (2018) where the complainant testifying first, Cheryl Zondi, was badgered by counsel through cross-examination involving an onslaught of intricate questions loaded with legalese. The witness is not an English mother tongue speaker; she appears to be linguistically competent in English, given her understanding of the questions and her responses which she expresses directly in English without an interpreter. Simply put, one might question how the situation might differ if, for example, Zondi was solely reliant on an interpreter. Would the level of accuracy displayed by the interpreter be a mastery of legalese, or would the interpreter take it upon him- or herself to explain to the witnesses in their own terms? The latter could result in an unintended answer being provided, bringing into question the credibility of the witness and her testimony.

Gibbons (1994:197) summarises this point by stating that second language speakers are placed at a further disadvantage when trying to understand the legal language, even through an interpreter. Therefore, there is nothing simple about determining a language of record. If there is one which caters for one group of speakers only and marginalises the rest – this is not what justice is about, nor should it be. It must be about providing the same treatment for everyone within the legal system (Gibbons, 1994:196). The role of the language of record is pivotal in this instance, an important role that is downplayed. Gibbons (1994:197) summarises the language situation in courts by stating the following:

> The complex, power laden and adversarial language of the courtroom is archetypically male, middle class adult and high proficiency.

A linkage has thus been created between this part of the chapter and Chapter 4 in which the language of record was advanced, and which is now located within the area of forensic linguistics. This discussion has also illustrated that forensic linguistics is a broad field, one which is premised on ensuring that forensic linguists assist in ensuring that justice is accessible to and attainable for all.

Forensic linguistics is not only relevant in contextualising the language of record but also influences language policy and planning. This is evident from the discussion thus far where a language of record policy and other language policies regulating the use of language in courts and the legal system more broadly falls within the ambit of forensic linguistics. This point becomes clearer with the discussion on language planning and policy below. According to Wei (2013), language planning and forensic linguistics are common branches of applied linguistics. The International Association of Applied Linguistics (AILA) classifies forensic linguistics as part of applied linguistics where they state:

> Applied linguistics is an interdisciplinary field of research and practice dealing with practical problems of language and communication that can be identified, analysed or solved by applying available theories, methods or results of linguistics or by developing new theoretical and methodological frameworks in linguistics to work on these problems (Wei, 2013:2).

Given the relationship between forensic linguistics and applied linguistics, a language planning theoretical framework is advanced next.

Defining language planning

What follows is a discussion in which language planning is defined and discussed. This discussion is theoretical with the purpose of outlining what language planning is and how, when and where it is applied in practice. This includes reviewing what has been learnt thus far that needs to be altered in South Africa. Each of the four tiers of language planning are discussed in relation to the monolingual language of record policy directive for courts.

Engaging with the seminal work on language planning, Cooper (1989:3-28) begins with four examples of language planning that occurred at different periods, illustrating the historical development of language planning. Cooper (1989:29) uses these four examples of language planning to argue that there is no "single universally accepted definition of language planning". Cooper (1989:29) traces the history of a definition of language planning to Einar Haugen who, in 1965, stated that Uriel Weinreich used the term 'language planning' at a seminar. It was, however, Haugen (1965:188) that cited the term academically in 1965, and defined language planning as:

> ...the activity of preparing a normative orthography, grammar, and dictionary for the guidance of writers and speakers in a non-homogeneous speech community.

Cooper (1989:30) listed a further 12 definitions of language planning. Of this list, there are three definitions which, in our opinion, are understandable, descriptive and practical in the context of this research, namely:

1. Language planning is a deliberate language change; that is changes in the systems of language code or speaking or both that are planned by organisations that are established for such purposes or given a mandate to fulfil such purposes. As such, language planning is focussed on problem solving and is characterized by the formulation and evaluation of alternatives for solving language problems to find the best (or optimal, most efficient) decision;
2. We do not define language planning as an idealistic and exclusively linguistic activity but as a political and administrative activity for solving language problems in society; [and]
3. The term language planning refers to the organised pursuit of solutions to language problems, typically at the national level.

A common thread through these three definitions is that language planning is focused on solving language problems of some sort. Interestingly, the second and third definitions confine language planning to a political and administrative activity taking place at a national level. As the discussion progresses, this point must be borne in mind where Alexander's work (1993) is discussed and his argument for a bottom-up approach is put forward. It is not to say that language planning is undertaken by the people, but rather that language planners inform their planning and decision-making based on the opinions of the people that their planning process will affect. Language planning, therefore, has to be a careful process. Bamgbose (1999:17) makes this point, stating that the language planner probably sees him- or herself as merely formulating policy, the implications of which will not be of interest nor implication to the language planner.

Eastman (1992:96) defines language planning as "...efforts in a socio-political context to solve language problems, preferably on a language term basis..." Again, Eastman's (1992:96) definition classifies language planning as a political activity. Similarly, McLean (1992:151) argues that language planning and the end result of language policies contribute to sociopolitical and economic development. Baldauf (2004:1) also states that language planning is often undertaken on a large scale at national level, a function usually undertaken by government.

Busch, Busch and Press (2014:144) note that most definitions of language planning are associated with government control, action and implementation. All processes are carried out through the legislature and the executive. Busch et al. (2014:144) substantiate this point noting that government is central to language planning. The point is that Alexander (1993) has a valid argument that a bottom-up approach would give effective meaning to the actual problems which the language planning process is trying to solve. On this note, the definition which, in our opinion, is workable and relevant in the context of this research is by Kaplan and Baldauf (1997:3) which reads as follows:

> Language planning is a body of ideas, laws, regulations (language policy), change rules, beliefs, and practices intended to achieve a planned change in the language use in one or more communities.

This definition by Kaplan and Baldauf (1997:3) speaks to language use in communities. This, in our opinion, is what language planning should be aimed at: creating ways in which communities can access the legal system in a language they understand and where language acts as a tool that will enable access to justice. We are by no means stating that language planning does not and should not be a government-orientated process, but rather that, if this were the case, the language planning process be driven by the people affected by the planning.

This speaks to the process of meaningful engagement, as advanced in Chapter 10. Recent academic voices have echoed these sentiments of a more inclusive approach to language planning. Kamwendo and Ndimande-Hlongwa (2017:63) explain that language planning "…entails a systematic and theory-based attempt to address the country's linguistic communication challenges". More importantly, Kamwendo and Ndimande-Hlongwa (2017:63) speak to the need for taking into consideration the language demographics of the country as a whole where language policies following the language planning process are appropriately drafted for particular domains. This does not exclude the function of government in driving the language planning process, but it also allows for non-government institutions and individuals to serve as actors in language planning (ibid, 64).

Status planning

Having set out the definitions of language planning, our next logical step in the discussion is to explore the stages of language planning to comprehend better the process as a whole. There are four stages to language planning, namely, status, acquisition, corpus and opportunity planning. We explain each of the four with reference to the scope of our research.

Reverting to the language planning seminal work, Cooper (1989:99) defines status planning as "…deliberate efforts to influence the allocation of functions among a community's languages". Stewart (1968) advanced a list of language functions concerning national multilingualism, four of which are applicable to our discussions. Cooper (1989:100) explains the first: "The first is **official** function as a legally appropriate language for all politically and culturally representative purposes on a nationwide basis". Official function, according to Cooper (1989), is usually specified constitutionally where the languages are identified by a government as being official or declared so by law. A further distinction can be made where "official" can be a language which a government either uses for its day to day running, or as a medium of a symbolic nature (ibid. 100). In Part One of Chapter 6, this theoretical explanation of official status of languages will be applied to Section 6(1) of the Constitution, as well in the discussion concerning the implications when a language is conferred official status.

The second is **provincial** function "…where language(s) function as provincial or regional official languages" (ibid, 103). The application of a provincial language is not for the entire country but rather for a province or provinces. This speaks to the point put forward by Kamwendo and Ndimande-Hlongwa (2017:63) about taking into account language demographics. The point is also elaborated upon in Part One of Chapter 6 with specific reference to these: Section 6(3) (a) and (b) of the Constitution; the sliding scale formula, when limiting language rights (Currie & De Waal, 2013); and language statistics from the national census with reference to the work of Docrat (2017a).

The third is **wider communication** which, according to Stewart (1968), is a function of a linguistic system, other than the official or provincial functions, operating as a medium of communication across language boundaries within the country. Cooper argues that a language of wider communication may be an official language, depending on the country and the respective Constitution.

This function is contrasted to the fourth function, namely, **international**, which is for a medium of communication used internationally, for example "…diplomatic relations, foreign trade and tourism" (Cooper, 1989:106). The fourth function is of relevance to the language of record directive, in particular, the reasoning behind the directive, as discussed in Chapter 4. While defining status planning, Kamwendo and Ndimande-Hlongwa (2017:64) also mention functions as "…choices made in allocating functions or roles to a language".

Baldauf and Kaplan (1997:30) went into further depth, defining status planning as "…those aspects of language planning which reflect primarily social issues and concerns and hence are external to the languages being planned". According to Baldauf and Kaplan (1997:30), language selection and language implementation are the two status issues which make up the model. The second of these status issues is discussed with regard to the policy developments in the legal system, highlighting implementation, as well as implementation failures. Language selection (Baldauf & Kaplan, 1997:30-32), the first of the statuses, is similar to the four functions identified by Cooper (1989) and comprises the following five components:

1. [Language selection] involves the choice of a language by/for a society through its political leaders;
2. A state must have a language in which it can communicate with its citizens;
3. The state must recognise its need for a language of communication, and subsequently it must select one or more languages for official purposes;
4. Leaders of a polity should have basic social and linguistic information about the language situation in the polity to make language selection decisions; and
5. Language choice cannot be made in a vacuum, but rather needs to be made in light of linguistic information (Baldauf & Kaplan, 1997:30-32).

There is a correlation between Cooper's (1989) language functions and Baldauf and Kaplan's (1997) language selection where the latter identifies these: official language usage; language for wider communication; language for communication by the government with the people; and taking into account the language demographics before selecting a language.

The next step in the language-planning model is to discuss how to perform the functions. This takes place through corpus planning.

Corpus planning

Corpus planning is the second tier of language planning. Baldauf and Kaplan (1997:38) define corpus planning as "…those aspects of language planning which are primarily linguistic and hence internal to language". Kamwendo and Ndimande-Hlongwa (2017:64) elaborate further on the activities undertaken with corpus planning. These include, but are not limited to "…language standardisation, lexicography and terminology development". Although this book is not located within the area of language development, it is relevant to this research for two interrelated reasons. Developed languages need to be selected as languages of record and languages of tuition. For example, one cannot have a language that has a limited corpus base and expect to use this language in domains such as law. There needs to be sufficient terminology. The second is that, for terminology to be developed (and consequently the language), these languages need to be taught at university level; with this high-status function, terminology can be developed. This will be illustrated with reference to a discussion concerning language policies at universities, in addition to the discussion on the need to graduate linguistically competent LLB students from universities through vocation-specific courses, to be discussed in Chapters 8 and 9.

According to Cooper (1989:154), corpus planning is a "...delicate balancing act between the old and the new, traditionalism and rationality". This is applicable to language planners in determining the language of record policy in South African courts. There should be no knee-jerk reaction to a particular language in the case of South Africa; this is what has taken place and is continuously taking place with Afrikaans, given its historical development as a language of power and dominance in South Africa during Apartheid. This can be guarded against "where corpus planning requires sensitivity to what the target population will like, learn, and use" (ibid). Moreover, "the public must be told why what is being offered to it is desirable, admirable and exemplary" (ibid, 154-155). The latter is important in the context of our critique of the 2017 monolingual language of record policy directive advanced earlier in Chapter 4.

Acquisition planning

Acquisition planning is the third tier of language planning. This type of planning is evident from its name, 'acquisition'. Cooper (1989:159) explains that there are three types of acquisition goals:

> ...those designed primarily to create or to improve the opportunity to learn, those designed primarily to create or to improve the incentive to learn, and those designed to create or improve both opportunity and incentive simultaneously.

Acquisition planning is essentially part of a language policy as it speaks to achieving the goals set out in that language policy. Thus, a language planning process results in a language policy. The policy relates to language usage or acquiring a language. Important for the research at hand is the fact that acquisition planning encompasses opportunity and incentive. These are important components in ensuring that the people at whom the policy is directed implement the policy and comply with the provisions therein. Incentive and opportunity are therefore motivators for securing successful implementation of the language policy. This gives rise to the fourth tier of language planning, namely opportunity planning.

Opportunity planning

Opportunity planning, although a new addition to the three tiers of language planning, was initially termed and developed as an 'econo-language plan' by Kaschula (2004), building on the work of Grin (2010). The term was developed as a result of what Kaschula (2004) identified as constant language policy implementation failures. This chapter addresses these implementation failures. For the purposes of discussing econo-language planning, we provide a brief background here. Kaschula (2004:13-14) holds that the problem does not lie with a policy itself but rather with the implementation plan, which he describes as "...elaborate and ambitious, if not somewhat clumsy". Kaschula (2004:14) explains that language policies need to be drafted with a broader framework in mind, that of the country as a whole. Simply put, what difference or contribution will the language policy make to South Africa's economy? Kaschula (2004:14) explains that the macro-economic position, which is a global one, favours English in South Africa. However, this is at the expense of the micro-economy where employment is created (Kaschula, 2004:14). The micro-economy affects the macro-economy and vice versa. Employing language planning strategies and language policies in the micro-economy that could facilitate job creation through persons having access to education in their mother tongues would stimulate the economy as a whole (Kaschula, 2004:14). This would also make South Africa more economically viable – as a country where people are educated and skilled, South Africa would be more attractive to potential global investors.

Kaschula (2004:16) quotes Heugh (1995) who, in 1995 already, spoke to the point of language policies having an economic effect on a country as a whole. Heugh (1995:23) argued for the maintenance of African languages in South Africa where these languages are mastered by South Africans with the primary purpose of educating them; and then growing linguistic repertoires by acquiring languages spoken on the African content, such as Kiswahili and French, to strengthen economic ties with neighbouring countries. The point of extraction, however, is the important link between the economy and language.

The relationship between language and the economy is a well-established one according to Alexander (1992) who states: "…language policy and language practice can either stimulate or impede economic efficiency, labour productivity, economic growth and development". Alexander (1992) elaborates further, stating that communication is key to a labour force where linguistic markets are developed. Those who control the wealth production determine language practices in the workplace. These persons, according to Alexander (1992), are convinced that their 'tried-and-tested' language policies and practices are best suited to the workplace, without assessing the situation. This form of language planning is counterproductive and ill conceived. In the case of South Africa, Alexander (1992) argues that everything in the workplace is packaged in English and this excludes the majority of people who are integral participants in the economic development of our country.

Coulmas (1992) talks to the point of language and the economy in greater depth. He (1992) argues that language can be seen as a negative aspect of the economy with regard to implementing language policies. In this instance, the beneficiaries of the system argue that a change in language policy and practices will only benefit the micro-economy and that this is a cost waste as it has no benefit to the macro-economy (Coulmas, 1992:148-149). This line of thinking, according to Coulmas (1992:148-189), is counterproductive and again, misconceived. This point is important for the discussion that follows concerning the costs involved in having a multilingual language of record policy in South Africa. In South Africa's case, not including an African language remains a political choice: Alexander

(1999:3) said that, by including an African language, the political elite were of the opinion that it would "...unleash a separatist dynamic...", resulting in the destabilisation of the country. English was therefore seen as the best option; in their opinion, this choice would not cause disruption and discontinuity, resulting in a language of unity and liberation, as opposed to using the language of the oppressor (Alexander, 1999:7).

Building on Kaschula's (2004) econo-language planning model, Antia (2017:166) holds that issues of finance, the economy more broadly, infrastructure and support services are all subsumed under opportunity planning. As mentioned before, opportunity planning is a fourth component of language planning. It is primarily focused on the implementation failures of language policies and the need to rethink the implementation plan. Baker (2006), who instead used the terms "usage" and "opportunity" as part of the language planning process, did not directly refer to 'opportunity planning' as such. What is opportunity planning, then? In answering this question, Antia (2017:166) states the following:

> Opportunity planning is understood and offered as a framework that foregrounds implementation in language policy and planning. It engages with the requirements for the adoption of language policies.

Opportunity planning is dependent on the other three tiers of language planning. In saying so, opportunity planning goes a step further by addressing "sites of use, incentives, directives, infrastructure, training and values" (Antia, 2017:166). The relevance of opportunity planning to the research presented in this book is threefold. In the first instance, opportunity planning is of relevance in creating job opportunities for forensic linguists to be employed, not only to assist in the drafting of language policies for the legal system, but to act as experts in assisting the courts with interpreting the constitutional language provisions and determining the parameters of language rights. Secondly, opportunity planning can assist in ensuring that employment is created for LLB graduates who would be linguistically competent in an African language. This would be with the purpose of making these graduates more employable so that they, in turn, can communicate effectively with litigants in their mother tongue. This will enable access to justice and guard against linguistic oversights that have the potential to negatively affect a litigant's corresponding right, for example their Section 35(3) constitutional right, to a fair trial. Thirdly, opportunity planning creates employment for all persons, regardless of race, where such persons acquire an additional official language or languages. This, in itself, contributes to decolonisation at universities and transformation in the legal system.

Ideologies underpinning language planning in South Africa

The language planning process described thus far is premised on a three-tier system with the addition of opportunity planning as a fourth tier. McLean (1992), relying on the work of Reagan (1986), proposes that there are four ideologies underpinning language planning, namely: assimilation, pluralism, vernacularisation and internationalisation. Pluralism can be understood to entail "…the acceptance of the presence of linguistic diversity in the society and the commitment by the polity to allow for the maintenance and cultivation of the different languages on a reasonable and equitable basis" (ibid, 94). Applying this ideology to South Africa, it would be visible in the constitutional provisions, specifically Section 6(5) which calls for the promotion and creation of conditions for the development of all 11 official languages. Section 6(5) of the Constitution can be read together with Section 6(4) which calls for parity of esteem and the equitable treatment of all official languages. We discuss the constitutional language provisions in Part One of Chapter 6.

The second ideology, vernacularisation, is the "…centrality of an indigenous language in the language policies of a society and involves either the restoration or elaboration of an indigenous language" (ibid). Again, the focus in South Africa would be the constitutional provisions. In this instance, Sections 6(1) and (2) recognise the previously marginalised African languages as official languages and call for the elevation in status and use of these languages. As will become evident with the progression of discussions in this book, African languages do not assume centre stage in language policies. The historical discussion on the language of record for courts thus far shows how African languages have been marginalised from mainstream society.

The third ideology, internationalisation, is most applicable to what is happening presently with the language question in South Africa. It is defined by Reagan (1986:95) as the "…adoption of a non-indigenous language of wider communication". In South Africa's case, it would be English, except that English is being used as the sole official language in all domains and replacing the use of, and potential use of, African languages under the guise of it being a global language. This can be juxtaposed with the discussions concerning language and the economy and how, at a macro level, the economics benefit those driving the policy agenda. However, in the long run, the underdevelopment of skills in the micro-economy will negatively impact the global markets. This correlates with Docrat and Kaschula's (2015a) point about the need to be socially aware of the impact of language both in the workplace and its broader function.

The third ideology, internationalisation, is linked to the fourth ideology, assimilation, which presupposes "…that in a given society every person should be able to function effectively in the dominant language, regardless of individual language background" (Reagan, 1986:94).

In South Africa, this is the precise thinking of language planners. Indeed, it is important to communicate effectively, but in a language that you understand best while acquiring an international language such as English to ensure inclusion on an international scale. Balance is key in this regard.

In South Africa, assimilation is taking place with English as the dominant language. The four ideologies are all relatable to South Africa as a country. This point is expanded upon in Part One of Chapter 6 regarding constitutional provisions. The remaining two ideologies are indeed true of what is happening in South Africa, but this shows the dominance of English, a language with a colonial history, and not the use and development of any of the nine African languages.

Eastman (1992) argues that the success of the language planning process is dependent on the language attitudes of people within a given society. It is nonsensical to think that one could include the use of African languages in a language policy where the attitudes of the people affected by the policy are negative towards the use of the languages. The policy is then doomed to fail from the beginning. Eastman (1992:108) proposes 'bottom-up' language planning, targeting the people and their attitudes and employing awareness campaigns. This can be linked to opportunity planning, with language planners creating opportunities for people targeted by language policies that are beneficial to them. According to Docrat and Kaschula (2015a), a meaningful engagement process needs to be undertaken among all persons who are affected by the prospective policy, including language planners and, in the instance of the legal system, forensic linguists. This will facilitate an open dialogue where the best possible policies are drafted and reviewed to ensure practicality.

Language planning and policies from 1993 to 2004

This chapter has thus far advanced the pre-Apartheid and Apartheid language planning models in the legal system with specific reference to the language of record, as well as the various tiers of language planning. Building on these advancements, we find it is important to backtrack to the language planning developments before the Interim Constitution and after the final Constitution. From 1990 to the enacting of the final Constitution in 1996, South Africa was in a transitional political phase marked by the CODESA negotiations. During Apartheid, language was used as a decisive tool driven by what Heugh (2002:450) identified as a two-pronged logic: firstly, to counteract the hegemony of English; and, secondly, to pursue the principle of separate development (Heugh, 2002:450). To this end, it was expected that the language question would be fiercely debated during the negotiations. The exclusion of African languages from mainstream society during Apartheid should have been the primary factor to address during those negotiations.

Instead, what occurred was a persistent attempt by the National Party (NP) to ensure the maintenance of Afrikaans as an official language (Heugh, 2002:456). The African National Congress (ANC) lacked the intensity displayed by the NP, failing to reclaim the space owed to the African languages. There was no political will by the ANC to advocate for the African languages to be treated equally to Afrikaans. The ANC, instead of focusing on the language question, was more concerned with the neutralisation and removal of Apartheid-era symbols (Heugh, 2002:456). This missed opportunity to focus on the most important issue can be compared with the present-day protests carried out by university students under the banner of 'decolonisation'. Their protests have shown how language, once again, has failed to be at the forefront of decolonisation drives. Instead, students have opted to protest for the removal of colonial statues, such as that of Cecil John Rhodes at the University of Cape Town. The semblance of the past is present in the current situation, suggesting if one may dare, that it is possible that the ANC might have preferred an English-only approach since 1994, which may explain contemporary attitudes.

Orman (2014:63) argues that the lack of political will on the language question displayed by the ANC during the negotiations was a result of a political elitist agenda pursued at the expense of African languages. The NP walked out of the negotiations in the same favourable position in which they entered while the ANC walked out strengthening the position of English based on inclusion for all, not the elevation of the African languages. It was expected that the ANC would represent the views of African language speakers where clear statements would have been a commitment to multilingualism. Moreover, that they would have given meaning to the constitutional language provisions through a fully-fledged language policy with guidelines for national and provincial governments and parastatal institutions (Heugh, 2002:461). The resultant effect is a *laissez-faire* approach, omitting any policy guidelines and, in the process, neutralising language rights through the hegemony of English (ibid). The ANC's actions during the negotiations were contrary to the ANC's Reconstruction and Development Programme that proposed the development of all South African languages, particularly the African languages (Reagan, 1997:426).

Reagan (1997:426) explained that contradictory policy decisions can be guarded against when applying a three-step test formulated by Kerr (1976) which reads as follows:

1. The desirability test. Is the goal of the policy one that the community as a whole believes to be desirable?
2. The justness test. Is the policy just and fair? That is, does it treat all people in an equitable and appropriate manner?
3. The effectiveness test. Is the policy resource sensitive? Is it viable in the context in which it is to be effected?

Further to the tests, Reagan (1997:425) proposes that language policies in South Africa need to balanced, taking into account three factors: national and/or political concerns; programmatic and pedagogical concerns; and concerns of social justice. Moving from the language planning and language policy guidelines presented by the authors, the two language policy developments at national level have been LANGTAG and South Africa's National Language Policy. In 1995, the then Minister of Arts, Culture, Science and Technology (as it was known), Ben Ngubane, announced the establishment of the LANGTAG, to be chaired by Neville Alexander. The primary purpose of the establishment was to advise the Minister in preparation of devising the National Language Plan for South Africa. The Final LANGTAG Report (1996:7) summarises the rationale for the need to develop a Language Plan for South Africa in the following way:

> A National Language Plan, which would be a statement of South Africa's language related needs and priorities, should set out to achieve at least the following goals:
> (1) All South Africans should have access to all spheres of South African society by developing and maintaining a level of spoken and written language which is appropriate for a range of contexts in the official language(s) of their choice.
> (2) All South Africans should have access to the learning of languages other than their mother tongue.
> (3) The African languages, which have been disadvantaged by the linguistic policies of the past, should be developed and maintained.
> (4) Equitable and widespread language services should be established.

The recommendations comprised short- and long-term measures. Fifteen short-term measures are presented, including these: language awareness campaigns; the development of a language code of conduct for the public service; using African languages at prestigious occasions; pressuring the legislature to give all official languages equitable space where appropriate; the use of incentives to encourage employers and employees in the public and private sectors to learn additional languages; promote languages other than English and Afrikaans in high status domains; commission and support research in the African languages; review the curricula at educational institutions; creating a central language database; as well as establishing educational language pilots (ibid, 2-4). These are the short-term measures which are relevant to this book. The eight long-term measures relate mostly to government and the development of official language services at national level with the aim of promoting, developing and using the African languages at national and provincial level.

The ministry was set to implement these recommendations. What emerged was the National Language Policy Framework (2002) followed by the Language Policy Implementation Plan (2003). Kaschula (2004) provided an in-depth critique based on the failure of the implementation. Kaschula (2004:5) argued that the National Language Policy Framework (2002), yet again, highlights the Apartheid historical context. Indeed, there is a need to acknowledge the historical past; however, this must be done in a manner that paves the way to move forward and learn from the past, not dwell on it.

A further point of critique that Kaschula (2004:5) noted was that implementation of the policy was shifted to the structures that were created through the actual policy it created. With internal structures having to implement the policy, the continued infighting between the PanSALB and the Department of Arts and Culture at the time hindered the implementation of the policy with the blame game and whose responsibility it was to implement the policy at the forefront (Kaschula, 2004:7). The implementation measures needed to be revised in accordance with the failures. This would help to avoid repeating the same mistakes and, instead, to give meaningful effect to people's language rights by enabling South African citizens to access services in an official language they understand. This would be an effective and well-run system within a functioning, multilingual democracy that encourages and enables active participation and access to justice through high status domains, such as higher education institutions and the legal system.

Legislative drafting

In Chapter 4 we discussed administrative law which brought to the fore the importance of legislation in conferring authority on natural, juristic persons and organs of state to perform functions, which are critical to the effective practical application and implementation of constitutional provisions. What follows in this section is an explanation of the process of legislative drafting, followed by a discussion on the principles of drafting and enacting language legislation.

Legislation is a means through which government can invest itself in the rights and interests of the citizens (Burger, 2015:6). In our opinion, legislation regulates the rights of citizens and gives meaning to the constitutional provisions. No statute may be enacted that is contrary to the provisions of the Constitution. The legislative process commences with a Cabinet Minister, who is head of a portfolio, deciding that a new statute is needed. The process is initiated with a 'Green Paper', a discussion document housing proposals by government. Comments on the Green Paper are called for from interested parties and civil society who are to respond by a specified date. The comments are then taken into account in producing what is referred to a 'White Paper' which can be open for further comment. Once all the comments have been considered, the legislative drafters in the respective government department, together with the Minister, will produce a legislative proposal that will be introduced as a 'Bill' to the Cabinet. If they agree with the proposal, the Minister has the authority to send it to Parliament for consideration (Burger, 2015:7).

Parliament sends the Bill to a portfolio committee of the National Assembly; this committee then meets to discuss the Bill (ibid). The portfolio committee comprises members of various political parties as per the party representation in the National Assembly. The process is open to the public; public submissions will be invited where the Bill is one that has garnered media attention. The Bill is then sent to the National Assembly where it is debated and where a vote to pass the Bill is undertaken. If passed by the majority in the National Assembly, the Bill is sent to the National Council of Provinces (NCOP) (ibid). As with the first committee, the same procedure is followed with a committee established by the NCOP.

One of two things happens with the Bill at the NCOP: the first is dependent on the nature of the Bill. If, for example, it directly affects the provinces, it is to be tabled at each provincial legislature and then returned to the NCOP with comments. The second option arises where the Bill does not concern the provinces, as it will then proceed to a discussion by the NCOP's committee. If the NCOP is in agreement with the National Assembly, the Bill will be sent to the President (ibid, 8). When a Bill is signed by the President and subsequently published in the *Government Gazette*, it is then an 'Act' in that it has been enacted (ibid). The number and year attached to the full name of the Act is indicative of the number of the Act in relation to other Acts that have been passed in that given year. The point of publishing in the *Government Gazette* is to officialise the law coming into effect. This is important for purposes of our focus on the 2017 language of record directive regarding which we have advanced a critique in Chapter 4.

There are two broad types of legislation: primary and secondary. Primary legislation comprises Acts of Parliament. Secondary legislation, also referred to as 'subordinate', comprises four types. The first is provincial ordinances which, according to Burger (2015:13), have been published since 1985. The second is provincial proclamations which provide for the substitution or amendment of provincial ordinances by an administrator appointed by the President. The third is provincial acts, those published after 1993 by any of the nine provincial legislatures. The fourth category is municipal law, essentially by-laws that regulate the functioning of municipalities.

These types of legislation are not the only sources of law. Other sources of law include common law, customs and customary law, indigenous law, international law and foreign law. The primary focus of this discussion is on legislation as a source of law, given the previous discussion on administrative law. The Constitution, through Section 39(1), the interpretation of the Bill of Rights, states the following:

(1) When interpreting the Bill of Rights, a court, tribunal or forum –
   (a) must promote the values that underlie an open and democratic society based on human dignity, equality and freedom;
   (b) must consider international law; and
   (c) may consider foreign law.

The point of extraction is that foreign law can be considered and applied by a court when, for example, interpreting the Section 35(3) (k) constitutional language right conferred upon accused persons. This point relates to African and international comparative studies housed in Chapters 2 and 3 where foreign jurisdiction that can be applied to the South African context has been presented.

Reverting to the discussion under administrative law, building on the work of Hoexter (2012:197), we made the point that the nature of the power and whether or not there is a duty or an obligation to perform a function, emanates from legislation and, more specifically, the language of legislation. What follows are the specific principles and theoretical underpinnings of language legislation.

Language legislation

With the legislative drafting process advanced in the preceding section of this chapter, our focus turns to language legislation. Language legislation was described by Turi (1993:5-6) as legislation "…generally aimed at legally determining and establishing the status and use of designated languages by means of legal obligations and rights; in other words, legal regulations concerning language". Language legislation exists in two categories based on its application. There is language legislation that deals with official or public usage, as well as non-official or private usage (Turi, 2012:73). Official language legislation is legislation which designates one or more language(s) as official in specific domains of legislation, justice, public administration and education (ibid, 7). The application of official language legislation depends on the circumstances with regard to which one of the next two principles are to be applied. The first principle is linguistic territoriality which prescribes the use of one or more languages in a specific territory. The second principle is linguistic personality which amounts to the obligation or right to use one's own language or any other language of choice (ibid). Turi (1993:8), speaking to the point of designating languages as official, notes that this does not mean that there are legal consequences attached to the official status. Instead, official status is a psychological status, one which will have practical bearing if there is effective legal treatment, accorded to the official languages concerned.

A further distinction can be sought based on the function of the language legislation. There are four categories: official, institutionalising, standardising and liberal. Where legislation fulfils all these functions, it is regarded as exhaustive language legislation while other language legislation would be regarded as non-exhaustive (ibid, 73). With the official function the sentiments noted above are applied and it is, in a sense, necessary for the state to use the official languages or those which the citizens of a country have the right to use (ibid). Both these functions are dependent on the circumstances as well as the application, therefore applying either the principle of linguistic territoriality or linguistic personality (ibid). Turi (2012:73-74) explains that, in a multilingual state, the official language of a state is the most commonly spoken language in the country. This is, however, not the case in African or Asian states where the official language chosen for state purposes is, in all probability, one not spoken by the majority of citizens. Applying this to a country such as South Africa is evident with the language of record policy.

The second function, institutionalising linguistic legislation, aims to make one or more languages the designated, usual or common language(s) for usage in non-official domains such as labour, communications, culture, commerce and business (ibid, 74). The third function is standardising linguistic legislation, aimed at making one or more designated languages adhere to certain language standards in highly technical domains (ibid). The fourth and final function is liberal linguistic legislation which is legislation that enshrines legal recognition of language rights (ibid, 75). According to Du Plessis (2012:197), primary language legislation has the power to bring about a turning point in the language dispensation of a country. This, however, can only take place where the language act contains sanctions and penalisations which will ensure the implementation of the legislation (Shohamy, 2006:59-60). These sanctions and penalisations are important in ensuring that meaning is given to the language rights.

A language act does not inhibit the enacting of further primary language legislation in other domains, for example, in the legal system (Du Plessis, 2012:198). This language legislation cannot be in contradiction to the national primary language act. Du Plessis (2012:198) acknowledges that comparative language legislation is on the rise. There are three different disciplinary approaches to comparative language legislation: the legal, linguistic and sociolinguistic perspectives.

Maurais's (1991:117) sociolinguistic approach to comparative language legislation entails the identification of five principles that underpin language legislation:
1. The proclamation of an official language;
2. The issue of the language of cohesion;
3. The language of communication with customers and citizens;
4. The language of education; [and]
5. Linguistic aspects of immigration.

Applying this to the South African model, the first principle would be Section 6 of the Constitution which confers official status on 11 languages. Regarding the second principle, English in South Africa is seen as the language of cohesion despite its colonial past. This is the point that constantly comes to the fore and will be more evident as we unpack the judgments in the cases of *AfriForum and Another* v *University of the Free State* (2018) and *State* v *Gordon* (2018). The third principle is guided by Section 6(3) (a) and (b) of the Constitution, prescribing that national and provincial government must use at least two official languages while municipalities are to take into account the language usage and preferences of the residents within the municipality. The fourth principle applied in South Africa is English as the language of education. The fifth principle is accounted for in Section 6(5) of the Constitution, as well as in Section 30 and 31, recognising the need of persons to use languages other than the official languages for various purposes: for individual religious and cultural purposes, or as part of religious, cultural or linguistic communities.

The application of all these principles refers to the constitutional provisions and not to legislation. This does not mean that the primary language legislation in South Africa, the Languages Act (2012), does not address the principles. The Languages Act (2012) has, however, come under immense criticism for being an Act for government by government, and for failing to address the actual language issues and constitutional language provisions (Docrat & Kaschula, 2015). This discussion is presented in further depth as this chapter progresses.

Maurais (1991: 118) elaborated on his five principles with a further seven principles focusing on the context of language legislation. These are:

1. The necessity for prior sociolinguistic description;
2. The necessity for state intervention;
3. The need for visible change;
4. Domains of non-intervention;
5. Special status of bilingualism;
6. The need to build consensus; [and]
7. The role of the time factor in language planning.

These seven principles will become clearer with the critique of the Languages Act (2012) further on in this chapter.

Language legislation: Use of Official Languages Act

In the previous sections of this chapter we outlined the principles guiding the drafting of language legislation in a multilingual country and the importance of having primary language legislation. As will be evident in Part One of Chapter 6, Section 6(4) of the Constitution obligates government, at national and provincial level, to regulate and monitor their use of the official languages without detracting from the provisions of subsection (2). This entails a language act at national level that regulates and monitors the use of the official languages by prescribing that all languages be used 'equally' and how this will be achieved. We have placed the word 'equally' in inverted commas, given that the Constitution uses the word "equitable"; but in our opinion, languages can only be used reasonably where they are used equally.

We have, furthermore, discussed the LANGTAG (1996) which was supposed to be the groundwork upon which primary legislation was to be enacted. This did not happen; and South Africa accepted that language use and planning was a simple task that did not have to be guided through legislation and regulated by policies. There was a failure to comply with Section 6(4) of the Constitution. The failure to enact national primary language legislation was challenged by a legal practitioner in the North West Province of South Africa, Cerneels Lourens, who also has a distinct interest in language rights and the use of language in courts as a means to access justice. In the case of *Lourens v President of the Republic of South Africa and Another* (2013), the court held that government failed in its constitutional mandate of Section 6(4) to enact legislation and ordered government to do so with immediate effect. The judgment thus resulted in the drafting and enacting of the Use of Official Languages Act, 12 of 2012.

When the Languages Act (2012) was in Bill form, there were reports that no public participation had taken place, contrary to the legislative drafting principles that we advanced earlier. The lack of public participation results in the adoption of a top-down approach. This is contrary to Alexander's (1992) bottom-up approach which Pretorius (2013) argued was necessary to avoid, weakening the legislation and rendering it ineffective. The public participation process is an opportunity to engage with the very people that the statute will affect, be it positively or negatively. The public have an opportunity to provide their opinions, concerns and recommendations for the production of the final Bill sent to the President to sign into law. The public are less inclined to accept and comply with a statute that does not positively affect their situation, or one with which they are unfamiliar. Nonetheless, the Bill was signed into law and we have therefore extracted the provisions relevant from the Languages Act (2012). The objectives in Section 2 of Languages Act (2012) are:

(a) to regulate and monitor the use of official languages for government purposes by national government;
(b) to promote parity of esteem and equitable treatment of official languages of the Republic;
(c) to facilitate equitable access to services and information of national government; and
(d) to promote good language management by national government for efficient public service administration and to meet the needs of the public.

The objectives of the 2012 Languages Act are not elucidatory and instead resemble the provisions of Section 6 of the Constitution. There is no issue in resembling Section 6 of the Constitution. However, the Languages Act (2012) is supposed to provide a framework in which Section 6 of the Constitution can be implemented in practice, not repeat what is stated. The objectives of the 2012 Languages Act also include the word "equitable" and thus includes the reasonable and not 'equal' use of the official languages.

Section 3(1) of the Languages Act (2012) provides for the application of the Languages Act (2012) in the following contexts:

(a) national departments;
(b) national public entities; and
(c) national public enterprises.

The relevance and application of the Languages Act (2012) to the research at hand may be questioned in light of Section 3(1) where the judiciary is not included. This follows the terms of the doctrine of Separation of Powers (SOP). Although it does not apply to the judiciary, it applies to the Department of Justice and Constitutional Development which employs prosecutors and all other legal personnel, including interpreters. The 2012 Languages Act also applies to the South African Police Services (SAPS), the first port of call for complainants in criminal cases, including arrested, accused, and detained persons as per Section 35 of the Constitution. The 2012 Languages Act obligates each of the entities identified in Section 3(1) to draft a language policy that gives practical effect to the Act (2012), as well as the constitutional provisions. These directives are in Section 4 of the Languages Act (2012) and require that practical measures be taken in publicising the language policy for the broader citizenry. This point can be contrasted with the lack of public participation during the drafting stages of the Languages Act (2012). We are of the opinion that buy-in following the enactment of a statute will be increasingly difficult as citizens will be raising issues during implementation that should have been addressed at the drafting stage. According to Docrat and Kaschula (2015a), language planning in South Africa has had a high failure rate during the implementation stage, as the policy does not address the needs of the people and fails to address practical problems.

Language policies: Department of Justice and Constitutional Development and SAPS

Regardless of whether the Languages Act (2012) has been criticised as an Act for government by government, it is the primary language legislation. Given our history in South Africa and the failure to enact primary language legislation, it would be inane to challenge the constitutionality of the 2012 Languages Act. We would be back to square one with no legislation at all. Our point is that the focus should shift to the language policies, as per Section 4(1) of the Languages Act (2012) and the effectiveness thereof. The Language Policy of the Department of Justice and Constitutional Development was gazetted on 26 April 2019. At the onset, the note from the then Minister, Michael Masutha, provides a caveat: "…it is further made known that this Policy will be implemented incrementally with effect from 1 August 2019 taking into consideration the resource implications arising therefrom". It is realistic and reasonable to assume, then, that the Policy will be implemented incrementally although no time frame is provided. Furthermore, one cannot but question the intention behind "…resource implications…" This will need to be assessed in determining whether this policy is not being implemented as a result of a resource-based defence. The following provisions of the Policy are relevant to our discussions and are quoted verbatim:

4. Objectives of the Policy
    4.1 This Policy seeks to –
        4.1.7 redress the linguistic inequalities of the past, which resulted in the underdevelopment of indigenous African languages and discrimination against speakers of such languages.

5. Guiding Principles and Values

5.2 Recognition that English is understood across the country, and has become a general language of use nationally and internationally.

5.4 Acknowledgement that Afrikaans is an indigenous language that enjoys popularity in the country, except in the Mpumalanga and Limpopo provinces. It had official status in the past, is still an official language in terms of the Constitution, and is a second language in many communities.

7. Scope of the Policy

7.1 This Policy applies to all personnel of the Department and all services offered by the Department at its offices and service points.

8. Use of Official Languages for Government Purposes

8.1 The Department having considered the language demographics report published in Census 2011 by the Statistician-General in terms of the Statistics Act, 1999 (Act No. 6 of 1999), and taking into account the guiding principles and values in paragraph 5 above, as contemplated in section 4 of the Act, determines the use of official languages as indicated below, subject to the availability of resources.

8.2 It is determined that English is the language of record for the Department.

8.3 It is further determined that in the national office the following languages are selected for official use:
    8.3.1 English;
    8.3.2 Sesotho;
    8.3.3 Afrikaans; and
    8.3.4 isiZulu.

9. Use of Official Languages by the Department in the Various Provinces in Communicating with the Public

9.1 The official languages selected for use in the regional offices are indicated in the table below:

Use of official languages in provinces/regions [the table is summarised here]
    9.1.1 Eastern Cape: English, isiXhosa, Afrikaans and Sesotho
    9.1.2 Free State: English, Sesotho, Afrikaans and isiXhosa
    9.1.3 Gauteng: English, isiZulu, Afrikaans and Sesotho
    9.1.4 KwaZulu-Natal: English, isiZulu, isiXhosa and Afrikaans
    9.1.5 Mpumalanga: English, Siswati, Xitsonga and isiNdebele
    9.1.6 Northern Cape: English, Afrikaans, Setswana and isiXhosa
    9.1.7 Limpopo: English, Sepedi, Xitsonga and Tshivenda
    9.1.8 North West: English, Setswana, Afrikaans and Sesotho
    9.1.9 Western Cape: English, Afrikaans, isiXhosa and Sesotho

9.2 All public information signs and signage identifying facilities and services may be displayed/ published in line with the determinaton above.

9.3 The Department's reports, documents, records and transcripts may be published in line with the determination above.

10. Hearings and Other Official Proceedings

10.1 Hearings and other official proceedings may be conducted in English where a party to the hearing or proceedings does not understand any of the official languages selected for that area.

10.2 Where all parties understand any of the selected official languages, other than English, the hearing or proceedings may be conducted in that language.

10.3 Where all parties understand any of the official languages, other than those selected for that area, the hearing or proceedings may be conducted in that official language.

10.4 In the event of a review or appeal of the hearing or other official proceedings conducted in terms of paragraph 10.2 and 10.3 above, the Department shall make available the said record in English if required/necessary to do so.

14. Language of Court Proceedings

14.1 The use of official languages in court, including court interpretation services, court processes, court documents and recording of court proceedings, shall be regulated, consistent with section 171(3) of the Constitution, by the Rules of Court or any other applicable legislation.

Sections 4 and 5.4 are positive in that they correlate with Section 6 of the Constitution and go a step further by recognising Afrikaans as an indigenous language. The presence of Afrikaans as a language in South Africa is noted through the number of speakers as acknowledged in Section 5.4 of this policy. As with the constitutional language provisions, this policy detracts from the positive acknowledgements with the inclusion of sweeping, ill-informed statements, as per Section 5.2, that "English is understood across the country". This can only be seen to substantiate a monolingual language of record policy for courts. Section 5.2 also raises the question of what is meant by "understood". As evidenced in the Australian context, Gibbons (2003) explained that there is a difference between greetings and an informal discussion in a social setting and understanding a language in a courtroom or other formal sector. The scope of the policy, outlined in Section 7, relates directly to all employees of the Department of Justice and Constitutional Development and this would include prosecutors who, although performing their duties within the ambit of the public prosecutions office, are employees of the state.

There are two distinctive languages of record referred to in the policy. It can be argued that they are linked, given that the language of record referred to Section 8.2 for all documentation affects the language of record (proceedings) in courts. It is concerning to see that the policy supposedly takes cognisance of the 2011 Census language statistics, yet prescribes that English be the sole official language of record for all documentation. The remaining provisions of Sections 8 and 9 of the policy do allow for communication between officials and the broader public in the official languages of the province, including English.

Section 10 of the policy is advanced and provides practical meaning to Section 6 of the Constitution where all the official languages are treated equally in status and use. By providing for the use of an official language other than English where all the parties concerned are comfortable with the language – this is both practical and ensures language rights of all are implemented. It is thus disappointing to see that this practical and positive thinking was not extended to the language of record and language of proceedings in courts.

Section 14 of the policy fails to address the contentious issue of the language of record in courts. Instead, one is re-directed to the Rules of Court and "other relevant legislation" (none of the latter exist). Although the matter is not dealt with and continues to provide uncertainty, one thing which can be clarified is that the language of record for courts is not a judicial decision but must rather be determined by legislation.

The second and final language policy, enacted in accordance with the Languages Act (2012) and relevant to this research, is the Draft Language Policy of the South African Police Service (2015). This policy, however, is still in draft format and has not been signed into law. This policy is relevant to the research at hand, as accused persons and complainants access the justice system: this commences at the police station; or in the case of an arrested person, they are read their constitutional rights by a police officer as explained in Section 35 of the Constitution.

The SAPS Draft Language Policy (2015) deals primarily with internal communication within the service. It also adopts "Plain English as the main *working language of the Service*" in Section 7(1) (a), defined in Section 4 (r) as the "*official language(s)* chosen by the *Service* as the language(s) most practicable to use in a particular communication situation". The insertion of "practicable" is, again, vague; and the provision is discretionary. The provincial official languages are recognised as languages of communication, but this is subject to finances and availability of expertise of language practitioners and interpreters. It is distressing and a missed opportunity for the policy not to have addressed the language of statement-taking and communication between a police officer and a complainant, accused and witnesses. The SAPS Draft Language Policy (2015) is discussed in further detail in Chapter 7 of this book with reference to relevant case law.

A critique of the Use of Official Languages Act and its resultant language policies

With the Languages Act (2012) and the two language policies presented above, the discussion proceeds with a critique. As we pointed out, the Languages Act (2012) is broad and discretionary but nonetheless provides for the enactment of language policies by each government department and state entity to regulate their use of official languages. Although Lourens (*Lourens* v *President of the Republic of South Africa and Another*, 2013) litigated on the issue of language legislation and was successful, he also shared his opinions on the contents of the Languages Act (2012) when it was in Bill form. The overarching opinion was the need for enforcement mechanisms to be included with practical guidelines as to how the policy would be implemented and the associated time lines. Unfortunately, this was not included, as can be seen.

When the Languages Act (2012) was in Bill form, it came under much scrutiny and was publicly criticised for failing to set out how, precisely, the African languages would be used in each government department given that the purpose of primary language legislation was to provide for the practical implementation of Section 6(1) and (2) of the Constitution. The FW de Klerk Foundation (2011) also criticised the Languages Act (2012) on the basis that it adopted a top-down approach which was contrary to effective language planning, as pointed out by Alexander (1992) who advocated for a bottom-up approach. Although LANGTAG (1996) was drafted 16 years before the Languages Act (2012), extensive research, sound conclusions and recommendations were made that perhaps needed to be revised and updated but form the basis for the drafting of the Languages Act (2012). When one engages with the provisions of the Languages Act (2012), it is clear, to our minds, that this never happened. Pretorius (2013:310), having advanced a critique of the Languages Act (2012), also acknowledged that it does provide a shimmer of light, be it dim, where language policies are drafted to deal with the practicalities of using African languages in each domain.

An observation from the discussions on the Languages Act (2012) is that the critique emerged from the Afrikaans speaking community, whereas the African language speaking communities appeared to have been silent on issues directly concerning the status, use and promotion of their mother tongues. The commentary on the Languages Act (2012) from an African languages perspective emanated from Docrat and Kaschula (2015a). They wrote on the importance of language legislation, taking into account the language demographics of South Africans, in addition to the attitudes of people and their needs when accessing government services in their mother tongue.

Further, Docrat and Kaschula (2015a) highlighted the importance of the Languages Act (2012) in giving effective meaning to the language rights, an aspect in which the Languages Act (2012) falls short. The Afrikaans community should be commended for their constant promotion of their mother tongue post-Apartheid. As we noted in earlier discussions, during the CODESA talks, there was an unwavering commitment for Afrikaans as opposed to the African languages. This appears to be a continuous trend. It is concerning that, instead of promoting the African languages, the CJ and Heads of Court opted to vilify Afrikaans and select English. One can but question why you would not want to advance the use of your mother tongue which has been and is being marginalised. The same principle applies to the language legislation and policies: instead of finding ways in which to use the African languages in high status domains, the focus is on how to best avoid using African languages, usually on the basis of 'practicability' and costs.

The language policies of both the Department of Justice and Constitutional Development and the SAPS need to correlate with each other in terms of objectives. The policies should not have been drafted in isolation from each other. As we advanced earlier, the criminal justice system commences with the SAPS. In a police investigation, language is of critical importance as a tool of communication, both for an accused and a complainant. The process of statement taking is flawed where a complainant or accused is required to provide a statement to a police officer either in English when the police officer cannot speak their mother tongue, or through the medium of their mother tongue where the police officer then translates the statement into English as he is recording it in handwriting. In either instance, language may serve as a barrier to communication, resulting in the possibility of a statement being incorrectly recoded with the factual inaccuracies then forming part of the evidence that is to be gathered through examination in chief or cross-examination.

Ralarala (2019) highlighted the implications of these inaccuracies in many high-profile cases in South Africa during 2018 to 2019. In each instance, when a statement was put forward to the witness in court, there was a dispute of fact that brought into question the witness's credibility. Examples included the cases of *State* v *van Breda* (2018) and *Omotoso and Others* v *State* (2018) which will commence *de novo* as a result of the recusal of the judicial officer. In the latter instance, during cross-examination, the first witness was presented with her original statement that, according to the witness, was rewritten by the police officer in English and which she did not read in detail. The witness disputed facts emerging from the statement which placed the accused at the venues of the alleged crimes at the times recorded. In essence, the case highlighted the anomalies of police statement-taking and the importance of accurate language in this process.

The case of *State* v *Sikhafungana* (2012) highlighted the linguistic issues in the SAPS, specifically the issues concerning police statement-taking and the effects thereof on the outcome of the trial. The case concerned the alleged rape of a complainant by her neighbour in the rural area of Mount Frere in the Eastern Cape Province of South Africa (Docrat et al., 2017a). The accused was caught in the act of perpetrating the rape and a citizen's arrest was affected (Docrat et al., 2017a:289). The incident was reported immediately, but the police only arrived the next morning and failed to advise on the process that should be followed, namely that the complainant be taken to a medical facility to undergo the necessary medical examinations for evidence-capturing purposes. The accused was, instead, taken into custody, charged with sexual assault and house breaking and charged in the alternative with trespassing. At trial, the accused was acquitted on both charges and convicted in the alternative, then sentenced to three months' imprisonment or a fine of three thousand rand

(Docrat et al., 2017a:289-290). The issues arising from the case of *State* v *Sikhafungana* (2012) were compounded by the fact that the complainant in the case was deaf and her account of the incident was relayed from her (using gesticulation and sounds) to her sister (isiXhosa mother tongue speaker) to the isiXhosa speaking police officer who then hand recorded the statement in English.

Police officers are not linguists, and although it is expected that as part of their primary training language skills need to be addressed, the SAPS Draft Language Policy (2015) must address this issue. As seen earlier in this chapter, the SAPS Draft Language Policy (2015) permits the use of interpreters where there are communication barriers in police stations, but it is not guaranteed at all times whether interpreters are available at a police station. Instead, this service is subject to financial resources being available and other 'practicalities' noted earlier.

Specialised interpretation services must be made available where complainants and accused persons are not permitted to make their statements in their mother tongue, where that language is an official language and spoken as a language of majority in that particular province, and where that original statement forms part of the 'record'. We acknowledge that a multitude of subsequent issues need to be addressed, such as training programmes and the deployment of interpreters, whether permanently stationed at the police station or 'on call' in outlying areas, as well as the issue of statement-recording by hand (Ralarala, 2019).

The proposition of interpreters in police stations can be piloted while resources are sought to ensure interpreters are available in all police stations across the country, and time frames will need to be clearly documented to hold government to account. Earlier, we defined opportunity planning (Antia, 2017) as having developed from econo-language planning (Kaschula, 2004) and how language planning relates to the economy (Grin, 2010). This can be applied to the SAPS with the employment of interpreters. Not only will employment opportunities be created, but African languages will be promoted and used in accordance with both Section 6 of the Constitution and the Languages Act (2012). The latter would also affect the rights of arrested people, in Section 35 of the Constitution, as advanced in Part One of Chapter 6.

These points and critiques would be irrelevant in a legal system that was premised on an English-only language of record policy for courts. As with the SAPS Draft Language Policy (2015), the Department of Justice and Constitutional Development's Language Policy (2019) fail to directly enforce the mechanisms for the use of African languages without wholly qualifying the provisions, with the insertion of phrases such as "where practicable" and "resource dependent". In Chapter 4, we established that the choice of the language of record for courts requires an executive and not a judicial decision to be made. It was thus the ideal opportunity to exercise this authority and establish a policy on the language of record.

Instead, "Section 14: Language of Court Proceedings" was inserted into the Department of Justice and Constitutional Development's Language Policy (2019), but this fails to state what the position is and instead refers one to the Rules of Court and other applicable legislation. This was done knowing very well that the language of record was not dealt with at the time the policy was formulated and gazetted. This is the major shortcoming of the Department of Justice and Constitutional Development's Language Policy (2019). As a result, the uncertainty and non-regulation of the language of record policy for courts remains in place and the directive of the CJ and subsequently that of Hlophe JP remains in place, even though there was no authority to take this decision. The point is that the judiciary has no authority to determine the language of record policy, regardless of whether the executive has determined this policy though legislation and other policies.

The Superior Courts Act and Magistrates' Courts Act

The Language Policy of the Department of Justice and Constitutional Development (2019) deferred the question of the language of record in courts to relevant legislation. The legislation governing and regulating the High Courts and Magistrates' Courts is the Superior Courts Act 10 of 2013 and the Magistrates' Courts Act 32 of 1944.

The Superior Courts Act (2013) makes no pronouncement on the language of record. The next point of determination is the Uniform Rules of Court (2013) which are procedural rules regulating court processes, applicable to the High Courts. Rules 59 and 60(1) are applicable and read as follows:

> (1) Where evidence in any proceedings is given in any language with which the court or a party or his representative is not sufficiently conversant, such evidence shall be interpreted by a competent interpreter, sworn to interpret faithfully and to the best of his ability in the languages concerned.

The rules – besides being sexist by presuming that only males are interpreters, as indicated through the use of the personal pronoun "his" – focus on interpretation and thus reinforce the current status quo of the language of record, not recognising the nine African languages as languages of record. In fact, the Rules of Court (2013) makes no direct mention of the language of record.

The Rules of Court (2013) and Superior Courts Act (2013) are not alone in avoiding the language of record in courts; the Supreme Court of Appeal Rules of Court (2013) also makes no mention of the language of record. The CC, being the apex court in South Africa through the Constitutional Rules (2003) of Court, includes Rule 25 on the use of language, stating the following:

> Where any record or other document lodged with the Registrar contains material written in an official language that is not understood by all the judges, the Registrar

> shall have the portions of such record or document concerned translated by a sworn translator of the High Court into a language or languages that will be understood by such judges, and shall supply the parties with a copy of such translations.

Rule 25 thus permits the lodging of documents in a language other than English only, and it provides for professional translator services at the expense of the court. This is important in the context of having more than one language as a language of record where that language is not English.

The Magistrates' Courts Act (1944) includes provisions on the language of record through Section 6(1) and (2):

> (1) Either of the official languages may be used at any stage of the proceedings in any court and the evidence shall be recorded in the language so used.
> (2) If, in a criminal case, evidence is given in a language with which the accused is not in the opinion of the court sufficiently conversant, a competent interpreter shall be called by the court in order to translate such evidence into a language with which the accused professes or appears to the court to be sufficiently conversant, irrespective of whether the language in which the evidence is given, is one of the official languages or of whether the representative of the accused is conversant with the language used in the evidence or not.

Section 6(1) regulates the language of record and proceedings. By "either", the Act refers to English or Afrikaans which were the official languages of record. This will now have to be amended if the language of record directive by the Heads of Courts is, in fact, constitutionally sound and gazetted. The point is, however, that official languages other than English can be languages of record as a bilingual language of record was already in place for many years. It is therefore neither foreign nor impractical to propose a bilingual language of record.

Subsection (2) is problematic, specifically the phrase: "…the accused professes or appears to the court to be sufficiently conversant…" The first reason why we view it as problematic is based on our earlier discussion of the Australian model in Chapter 3. Firstly, indigenous language speaking witnesses are inclined to state that they do understand the language of record. Secondly, how would a court determine an accused's linguistic competency? We have made this point previously: there is no yardstick in law to determine the linguistic competency of an accused; and the magistrate, in all likelihood, will not have a linguistic background and so be in a position to determine this. These points of critique will be more apparent with the presentation of the South African case law in Chapter 7.

Conclusion

This chapter locates our research presented in this book, in the area of forensic linguistics and builds on the definitional elements thereof as outlined in Chapter 1. As a discipline, forensic linguistics highlights the interdisciplinary nature of this research; by doing so, it connects the language of record in courts to language planning and policies at universities (the latter will become more apparent in Chapters 8 and 9).

This chapter offers a significant addition to the traditional language planning model by introducing opportunity planning as a fourth tier. Opportunity planning serves as the linkage between the language of record and university language policies through focusing on the need to graduate linguistically competent LLB students (see Chapters 8 and 9).

The language planning and policy formulations of South Africa generally – and the specific language policy developments – are illustrative of the sources of power in drafting policies and the need for legislation to enable the enactment of language policies. The legislative drafting process is also initiated, developed and enacted through political channels.

This chapter has, furthermore, laid bare the legislative and policy gaps that allow for a monolingual language of record policy to be reaffirmed. Moreover, no direction is provided on a future language policy for the legal system. The current legislation and language policies shift the onus to other legislative instruments where, as is known by all, there is no clarity on the use of the language of proceedings or record. In the chapter that follows, the South African constitutional language rights and provisions, which are unfairly limited by the monolingual language of record directive, are discussed.

PART 1:
SOUTH AFRICA'S CONSTITUTIONAL LANGUAGE RIGHTS AND PROVISIONS

A language right or an interpretational right?

This chapter is divided into two parts: the first, comprising the constitutionally-based argument distinguishing between the different rights afforded to English mother tongue-speakers, as opposed to African language and Afrikaans mother tongue speaking litigants; and the second, focusing on the equality-based argument from both a constitutional and legislative perspective.

In Part One, we advance the constitutional language rights framework as informed by the founding provisions of Section 6 of the Constitution, the language blueprint. This chapter presents the relevant provisions, as well as a critique thereof. As the discussion develops, the provisions and rights are applied to the monolingual language of record discussion.

In Part Two we continue our critique of the monolingual language of record through an equality-based discussion: we discuss the importance of placing the languages and the speakers of the languages on an equal footing as espoused in Part One of the chapter. Furthermore, we present statistics to illustrate why the African languages and African language speaking litigants are unfairly discriminated against, despite being in the majority across provinces. The chapter concludes with a language survey conducted by Legal Aid South Africa, the findings of which cement the fact that African language speaking litigants are unfairly discriminated against and disadvantaged by an English-only language of record policy for courts.

South African constitutional framework

Given that South Africa is a signatory to the United Nations Articles, as cited in Chapter 2, the constitutional and legislative frameworks (presented in Chapter 5) are to comply with these provisions. Throughout our discussions thus far, we have referred to the Constitution, given its authoritative nature as the supreme law in the country. As per the discussions in Chapter 5, the Constitution was the final 'product' of the historic CODESA negotiations. This is important given that the objective of the Constitution is to ensure a non-racial, democratic South Africa premised on the rights to dignity, equality and freedom. In Chapter 3, we cited Gibbons (2003) who spoke to the importance of dignity for litigants and speakers of the indigenous languages in courts and how this affects the equality of status of the language and the speakers of the languages (advanced fully in Part Two of Chapter 6). In the South African context, this is important given the historical discrimination and marginalisation endured during Apartheid and, prior to that, during colonial rule.

Section 6 of the Constitution, the languages provision, must be viewed in light of the discussions in Chapters 4 and 5 where we advanced that the NP's intention was clear: that Afrikaans had to remain an official language under the new democratic dispensation. Section 6, in addition, thus conferred official status on the nine African languages, as reflected in Section 6(1):

> The official languages of the Republic are Sepedi, Sesotho, Setswana, siSwati, Tshivenda, Xitsonga, Afrikaans, English, isiNdebele, isiXhosa and isiZulu.

In Chapter 5, we argued that the ANC had no similar intention to that of the NP in defending the African languages, so it can be argued that subsection (2) was merely inserted for the purposes of illustrating that they, too, were interested in the promotion of the African languages. Subsection (2) states:

> Recognising the historically diminished use and status of the indigenous languages of our people, the state must take practical and positive measures to elevate the status and advance the use of these languages.

It appears that subsection (2) provides for the development of the nine African languages to equate those languages to English and Afrikaans. The implementation of Section 6(2) would entail the use of the nine African languages in high status domains, the public sector, and in higher education institutions as languages of learning and teaching. As will be evidenced from the forthcoming discussions in this chapter, this has not been the case, particularly in the legal system and in higher education, the areas in which this research is located. The lack of implementation is due to the 'opt-out' provision in Section 6(3) (a):

> The national government and provincial governments may use any particular official languages for the purposes of government, taking into account usage, practicality, expense, regional circumstances and the balance of the needs and preferences of the population as a whole or in the province concerned; but the national government and each provincial government must use at least two official languages.

There are several points of discussion emanating from subsection (3) (a). The first point is the discretionary language used in the construction of this provision as a whole through the use of words and phrases such as "may", "any particular" and "at least". As per the Canadian case law discussion in Chapter 3, the discretion is not limiting but rather provides for a minimum standard. The method of interpretation employed can result in restrictive or purposive interpretation. In the South African context, outlined in Chapters 4 and 5, there is an inherent failure to implement policies and legislation in a purposive manner. Therefore, discretionary provisions such as subsection (3) (a) provide for government, at both national and provincial levels, to opt for the English and Afrikaans default position. The default provision is then justified against the criteria of usage, practicality and expense, as it is cost-effective to continue using English and Afrikaans as most documentation in public service departments is available in these two languages. Even though subsection (3) (a) includes obligatory language through the insertion of the word "must" in the last line, this is qualified by a minimum standard by the phrase "at least two official languages".

Subsection (3) (a) is also important for policy and legislative purposes where government cannot adopt one language only. This point can be contrasted to the discussions on the Languages Act (2012) and the Department of Justice and Constitutional Development's Language Policy (2019), where the default English-only position has been adopted.

The drafting and enacting of the Languages Act (2012) were provided for through Section 6(4):

> The national government and provincial governments, by legislative and other measures, must regulate and monitor their use of official languages, without detracting from the provisions of subsection (2), all official languages must enjoy parity of esteem and must be treated equitably.

Amongst other measures, subsection 6(4) provides for the drafting and enacting of legislation and policies in regulating to the use of the official languages. In our opinion subsection 6(4), by including subsection (2), provides that the legislation and other measures must conform to the provisions of subsection (2) regarding the elevation, promotion and use of the nine African languages. The phrase "… all official languages must enjoy parity of esteem and must by treated equitably" again appears to be vague, given the inclusion of the phrases "parity of esteem" and "treated equitably" which are not defined. The use of phrases such as "treated equally" is excluded in favour of cryptic language that requires interpretation and thus is discretionary. Our reasoning is informed by the discussions in Chapter 3, specifically the Canadian case study that includes the term "linguistic duality" that equates the languages equally in both status and use.

The Constitution, through Section 6(5), provides for the monitoring and evaluation of the legislative means in creating conditions for the development and use of the official languages with the creation of PanSALB. According to subsection (5), the role of PanSALB is to:

(a) promote, and create conditions for, the development and use of –
  (i) all official languages;
  (ii) the Khoi, Nama and San languages; and
  (iii) sign language; and
(b) promote and ensure respect for –
  (i) all languages commonly used by communities in South Africa, including German, Greek, Gujarati, Hindi, Portuguese, Tamil, Telegu and Urdu; and
  (ii) Arabic, Hebrew, Sanskrit and other languages used for religious purposes in South Africa.

Subsection 5(a) (i) is important for the purposes of this research where the provision refers the promotion and development of all official languages, not just one or two official languages. This is important in the context of the discussions on the Languages Act (2012) and its objectives, in addition to the Language Policy of the Department of Justice and Constitutional Development (2019) and the language of record directive of 2018, advanced earlier.

Although we have made initial critiques and observations on Section 6 of the Constitution, a full critique and application can be found further on in this chapter. Suffice to say at this point of the discussion, holistically, Section 6 appears to be discretionary and depends on the viewpoint adopted, which can be either a positive or a negative aspect. In Cameron's (2013:15) opinion, the Constitution merely creates a framework that enables the people of South Africa, government, the leadership and all relevant stakeholders to implement this framework. Therefore, the discretionary element is needed to provide for implementation within practical spheres.

South African constitutional language rights

In Chapters 4, 5 and the beginning of this chapter, we have spoken about the importance of dignity and equality with reference to languages enjoying equal status and the speakers of these various languages being treated equally and thus with dignity. The equality-based discussions are advanced fully in Part Two of this chapter. This was also discussed more prominently with reference to Chapter 3 and the case study on Australia where we evidenced with the work of Cooke (2009), Eades (1994) and Gibbons (2003), the plight of Aboriginal people and the loss of their dignity due to continued marginalisation and discrimination on grounds of language. The themes of dignity and equality are threaded throughout this book and this chapter where we advance the language in equality rights in Section 9 of the

Constitution and the need to redress the past discrimination in the legal system, as outlined in Section 174 of the Constitution, in Part Two of this chapter.

In this section of Part One of Chapter 6, we advance the language rights applicable in the legal system and higher education. The language rights are housed in the BOR, Chapter 2 of the Constitution, as opposed to Section 6 located in the Founding Provisions of the Constitution. This distinction is important for the purposes of the legislative and policy frameworks, as well as the case law. Section 7 of the Constitution states:

> (1) This Bill of Rights is a cornerstone of democracy in South Africa. It enshrines the rights of all people in our country and affirms the democratic values of human dignity, equality and freedom.
> (2) The state must respect, protect, promote and fulfil the rights in the Bill of Rights.
> (3) The rights in the Bill of Rights are subject to the limitations contained or referred to in Section 36 of elsewhere in the Bill.

Section 7 reaffirms the values of human dignity and equality in relation to the implementation of the rights discussed below. Subsection (2) obligates the state to implement the rights and respect these rights. Subsection (2) can be contrasted to the abandonment of these rights through the language of record policy directive presented in Chapter 4. Subsection (3) provides for the limitation of rights in accordance with Section 36 of the Constitution. This will be discussed in depth in relation to the sliding scale formula (Currie & De Waal, 2005) when limiting language rights.

The right concerning language in the legal system is Section 35 of the Constitution which deals with the rights of arrested, detained and accused persons. We have extracted the following provisions which are relevant to the discussions:

> (1) Everyone who is arrested for allegedly committing an offence has the right –
>   (a) to remain silent;
>   (b) to be informed promptly –
>   (i) of the right to remain silent; and
>   (ii) of the consequences of not remaining silent;
>   (e) at the first court appearance after being arrested, to be charged or to be informed of the reason for the detention to continue, or to be released;
> (2) Everyone who is detained, including every sentenced prisoner, has the right –
>   (a) to be informed promptly of the reason for being detained;
>   (b) to choose, and to consult with, a legal practitioner, and to be informed of this right promptly;
>   (d) to challenge the lawfulness of the detention in person before a court and, if the detention is unlawful to be released;
> (3) Every accused has the right to a fair trial, which includes the right –
>   (a) to be informed of the charge in sufficient detail to answer it;
>   (f) to choose, and be represented by, a legal practitioner, and to be informed of this right promptly;

(g) to have a legal practitioner assigned to the accused person by the state and at state expense, if substantial injustice would otherwise result, and to be informed of this right promptly;

(k) to be tried in a language that the accused person understands or, if that is not practicable, to have the proceedings interpreted in that language;

(4) Whenever this section requires information to be given to a person, that information must be given in a language that the person understands.

The primary focus in research located in language and law in South Africa focuses on Section 35(3) (k) (Docrat, 2017a; Docrat & Kaschula, 2015; Kaschula & Ralarala, 2004; Lubbe, 2008; Ralarala, 2012). However, this research focuses more broadly on the language of record in courts of law. Having said this, we have extracted other provisions beyond the ambit of Section 35(3) (k) given their relevance. The language of record influences more than just proceedings in courts. To proceed in one language, all documents have to be available and produced in that specific language, i.e., in the South African context, English. In criminal cases, to begin with, the police arrest a person; the police, in terms of Section 35(1) (b)(i) and (ii), are to inform the arrested person of their right to remain silent. Reading Section 35(3) (1)(i) and (ii) with Section 35(4), the police would need to provide such information in an African language in cases where the arrested person does not understand English. This implies that the police officer is to be linguistically competent in that specific language. This point has previously been discussed in detail with reference to the SAPS Draft Language Policy (2015).

The next step in the process is that the arrested person be brought before a court to be formally charged as per Section 35(1) (e). These proceedings are in English given the language of record; so, where the arrested person has a limited (or no) understanding of English, he or she would then need to rely on an interpreter. If a charge is brought, a charge sheet will be drawn up in English accompanied by witness statements, the complainant's statement and the accused's warning statement if one was taken (depending on whether the right to remain silent was exercised). There is a contradiction, then, when reading subsection (3) (a) where the charge is to be supplied in sufficient detail to answer it. This conversely requires the accused to understand the charge in order to answer it. As will be evident from the case law discussed in this chapter, there is presently no case law which examines this area of law.

To draw on the case studies in Chapters 2 and 3, there was also the question of understanding the charge and presenting a case to that effect. In Chapter 2, similar issues arise in the African case studies where emphasis is not placed on language in the legal system. In the case study on Australia in Chapter 3 we highlighted the issues plaguing the legal system and how Aboriginal indigenous speakers are excluded and discriminated against on the basis of language and understanding. In the case study on Canada, also in Chapter 3, we advanced a discussion with reference to case law concerning the charge sheet (indictment) being available in a language of choice based on the two official languages. In these case studies these issues are fleshed out given the literature available on the area, something which is absent in South Africa.

On the point of 'understanding', this is another contentious issue that can be debated, taking into account subsection (4) quoted above. What is the definition of 'understand'? To our knowledge, there is no yardstick in law that determines or can test a person's understanding in a court of law. It must be questioned if a judicial officer has the requisite knowledge to test understanding. This is also important for the purposes of the language of record policy directive by Hlophe JP presented in Chapter 4: he uses the word "understanding" for the purposes of interpretation. This is also important in the discussion concerning Section 35(3) (k) of the Constitution where a language right is conferred upon accused persons. However, this right is limited, given that, where a person does not 'understand' the language of the proceedings, interpretation will be employed. Thus, the insertion of words such as "practicable" and "understands" is vague and limiting. We use the word 'limiting' as it is our opinion that, in most instances, given the statistics presented in Part Two of this chapter, the majority of South Africans do not speak English as their mother tongue. Thus, the vast majority are reliant on interpretation services; that, in our opinion, provides a different standard of justice to English mother tongue speakers, as well as African language and Afrikaans mother tongue speakers. English mother tongue speakers have a language right conferred and the indigenous speaking accused have an interpretational right conferred. We elucidate this point in further detail as the chapter unfolds.

Reverting to the discussion of 'understanding' in the context of Section 35(3) (k), Schwikkard and Van der Merwe (2010:800) explain that the right is not for a language of choice but rather a language the accused fully understands. Schwikkard and Van der Merwe (2010:800) explain that this language must be fully and not partially understood; therefore, minimal understanding of a language is not sufficient. Schwikkard and Van der Merwe (2010:800) also do not provide any elucidation of how a judicial officer determines if an accused fully understands a language. In the Australian and Indian case studies presented in Chapter 3, the dangers are seen with regard to accused persons stating that they do understand English as they are of the opinion that, by saying otherwise, they will be disadvantaged before the law. The latter point must be borne in mind with the discussion concerning the case law, in particular the case of the *State* v *Pienaar* (2000).

We have constantly referred to the language of record affecting the rights of litigants, the effect that the language of record has on access to justice and, if accessed, the level of justice obtained. All of these factors are influenced by people, in particular legal practitioners and judicial officers. Simply put, the language in law rights are influenced and, in our opinion, determined by the language in education right of Section 29(2) of the Constitution:

> (2) Everyone has the right to receive education in the official language or languages of their choice in public educational institutions where that education is reasonably practicable. In order to ensure the effective access to, and implementation of this right, the state must consider all reasonable educational alternatives, including single medium institutions, taking into account –
> (a) equity;
> (b) practicability; and
> (c) the need to redress the results of past racially discriminatory laws and practices.

Section 29(2) confers a language right on all persons in both basic and higher education public institutions. Similar to the constitutional provisions advanced above, the language right is internally qualified through the phrase "…where that education is reasonably practicable". The reasonability standard is assessed through objective criteria, premised on the facts of each case. The reasonability standard is often a subjective test where the court will apply the criteria to the facts before it. In Chapter 7 comprising case law we discuss this point in greater depth.

The language right is qualified further through these words, "…the state must consider all reasonable educational alternatives, including single medium institutions…" This resembles the provisions of Section 35(3) (k) through the limitation "…where practicable…" It is, to a certain extent, mitigated in the sense of ensuring the right is not limited unfairly through the application of the criteria in (a) to (c). The vagueness of the term "practicability" is once again included as a criterion. Criterion (c), however, correlates with Section 6(2) of the Constitution in taking cognisance of the historical marginalisation of the nine indigenous languages. Section 6 should, in our opinion, permeate all other correlating rights and provisions of the Constitution, including Section 174 of the Constitution which regulates and guides the appointment of professionals to public office that directly affects all citizens.

Section 174 is related to Sections 29(2) and 35 of the Constitution. In our opinion, it would be of benefit to litigants, witnesses and legal practitioners to recognise the linguistic competency of legal practitioners when affecting judicial appointments to the bench. Unfortunately, the provisions of Section 174 fall short of transforming the profession in an inclusive way, where access to justice is prioritised through the language question. Section 174(1) and (2) of the Constitution, regulating the appointment of judicial officers, is relevant to this research and states:

> (1) Any appropriately qualified woman or man who is a fit and proper person many be appointed as a judicial officer. Any person to be appointed to the Constitutional Court must also be a South African citizen.
> (2) The need for the judiciary to reflect broadly the racial and gender composition of South Africa must be considered when judicial officers are appointed.

There is no inclusion of language alongside race and gender in subsection (2). It is our opinion that subsection (1), referring to "an appropriately qualified woman or man", must include linguistic competence, especially given the multilingual context in which these legal professionals are appointed to the bench with the majority of persons not speaking English as their mother tongue. This is not a foreign idea given the African and international case studies we have advanced in Chapters 2 and 3 where judicial officers have to be linguistically competent before being appointed to the bench. In a multilingual country such as South Africa, this is key to enabling and enhancing access to justice. In Chapters 8 and 9, we also advance the importance of ensuring greater representation of legal practitioners. This relates to the language in education right, Section 29(2), and universities' obligations through language policies. Besides the examples of Belgium and Canada, which are successfully producing bilingual and multilingual LLB graduates, legal professionals in India have themselves stated the importance of this. The case of Nigeria in Chapter 2 proves the dangers of adopting an English-only, Western system to educate law students as, in practice, it isolates these professionals from giving effective meaning to the broader populace accessing the legal system.

In Chapter 5 we advanced opportunity planning (Antia, 2017) as the fourth tier of language planning and we considered how language can be used to create employment opportunities: the investment in the micro economy, through language in education policies, positively affects the macro economy, as explained by Kaschula (2004, 2019) and Grin (2010). This rights framework requires interpretation and application in practice given Cameron's (2013) views that the Constitution is just a framework that needs to be developed. The Constitution itself recognises the application of the provisions in courts of law, especially when the rights or provisions contained therein are to be determined by a court of law. Section 8 of the Constitution provides for the application and development of the rights in the BOR advanced earlier.

The enforceability of the constitutional language framework

In Chapters 4 and 5 we explicated the political negotiations that led to the drafting of the Interim Constitution (1993) followed by the final Constitution. In this chapter we have extracted the constitutional language provisions commencing with Section 6, the languages provision. As part of this discussion we limitedly outlined the discretionary nature of the provisions. Our focus turns to advancing a critique of Section 6 where we draw on relevant authors' work in determining whether or not this is a positive ideal; and, if not, what the implications are for a multilingual country such as South Africa, with an English-only legal system.

One point of critique that arises through the work of Perry (2004) is that the languages provision is housed in the Founding Provisions of the Constitution and not in the Bill of Rights and thus limits the enforceability of the provisions. Perry (2004:131) advances a statement made by retired CC Judge Albie Sachs who stated that the provisions of Section 6 were "… messy, inelegant and contradictory". Therefore, according to Perry (2004:131), the provisions of Section 6 amount to "symbolic gesturing" only. As discussed in this chapter, the discretionary insertion of terms, including "practicable" and "may", is dependent on interpretation in practical situations. Our point is that the relevant authority (the state) should not be looking at exploiting the 'gaps' but rather implementing these provisions in a manner that is consistent with the constitutional ideals, whereby the 'gaps' are filled. There are obligatory provisions in Section 6 which we have highlighted in this chapter.

The starting point and where the issue arises is through the conferring of official status on languages and what this requires the state to do in practice, especially given the obligatory onus on the state in subsection (2) "… to take practical and positive measures …" in elevating the status and use of the nine indigenous languages. According to Lourens (2012), by conferring official status on all 11 official languages, the state is obligated to use all these languages equally in all domains in society. There is a disjuncture then between theory and practice. Leung (2019:123) confirms this disjuncture: "Official languages seem to have, at least on paper, the strongest possible legal protection a state can afford … public institutions rarely live up to the expectations explicitly or implicitly communicated by the law."

Leung (2019:123) explains that the lack of implementation "… is a product of, among other things, the general lack of specificity in constitutional provisions". For Leung (2019:123) these issues hinge on what it means to confer official status on a language which she argues carries "no fixed legal meaning". This allows states such as South Africa, which have conferred official status on languages, to "… diverge in their understanding of the legal implications of status, their degree of commitment, and their corresponding institutional adaption" (Leung, 2019:123). Leung (2019:124) advances further that constitutions tend to be "… vague, directive, and aspirational"; also that there is no spelling out of what the legal significance is of 'official' languages and "… how a government may act constitutionally or unconstitutionally regarding an official language provision".

There is a sense that there are moral rather than legal commitments made through the constitutional provisions. One such example, according to Leung (2019:125), is South Africa and Section 6(2) and subsection (4) of the Constitution where subsection (2) "… does not specify how much state action is required", whereas subsection (4) is mysterious in how precisely to achieve parity of esteem and whether equitability "… can be interpreted as fairly but less than equally". Leung (2019:126) highlights the importance of PanSALB in ensuring the constitutional provisions are implemented. The PanSALB has an important function in ensuring the equal development and use of all indigenous languages, including the use of Afrikaans alongside English. The PanSALB, through the Pan South African Language Board Act 59 of 1995, have the inherent authority in terms of Section 3(a) to ensure the use of all official languages in high status domains where organs of state do not interfere with this authority. Two objectives from Section 3(a) of the PanSALB Act (1995) are relevant and read accordingly:

(i) The creation of conditions for the development and for the promotion of the equal use and enjoyment of all the official South African languages;

(iii) The prevention of the use of any language for the purposes of exploitation, domination or division;

The first objective speaks to "equal use" as opposed to the constitutional provisions that use the term "equitable" which, as Leung (2019) and Perry (2004) suggest, not only weakens the enforceability but creates uncertainty as to precisely what actions need to be taken by the state. This objective also speaks to all official South African languages and not English only. This speaks to the third objective where language may not be used for the purposes of "exploitation, domination or division". It is our opinion that using English only as the language of record and proceedings amounts to the increased supremacy of English, which will prove to be decisive in a multilingual country such as South Africa. The point we are conveying is that PanSALB must play an active role in guarding against the exclusive use of English in the legal system where this will be to the detriment of the use and development of African languages in this and other high-status domains.

The overarching point that must be made is that Section 6 must not be undermined by the state, nor must the discretionary provisions be interpreted in a manner which detracts from the purpose of the provisions, which is to confer official status on the nine African languages and, by doing so, situating the languages equally alongside English and Afrikaans. It is our opinion, further, that the built-in practicability and equitability standards should not be used as defences when failing to implement the provisions. It is about the intention and agenda of the state in implementing these provisions. Section 6 has that aspirational tone that provides the feeling that the obligations created therein can be deviated from on grounds of practicability and equitability. The costs to the languages, the rights of the speakers of the languages, as well as their other rights to contribute and participate in a constitutional democracy will be unfairly limited; their access to justice will become an elusive find for those who cannot speak, understand, read or write English – that is, the vast majority of our country. We will discuss the important role of the PanSALB in Chapter 10 as part of the recommendations.

Section 35 imposing language or interpretational rights

Throughout the discussions pertaining to the rights in Section 35, one must be consciously aware of the fact that Section 6 influences the interpretation and application of these rights. In other words, the interpretation and implementation of the rights in Section 35 must not be undertaken in a manner that is inconsistent with the provisions of Section 6, whereby the African languages are to be elevated in status. Leung (2019:211-212) draws a distinction between language rights flowing from fundamental human rights (this includes the right to a fair trial) and language rights that may also flow from legal rights which are not universal human rights. As we advanced earlier in this chapter, language rights in South African courts emanate from the right to a fair trial. This follows the fact that South Africa is a signatory to the Universal Declaration of Human Rights (1948), as discussed in Chapters 2 and 3.

Leung (2019:210) imparts an interesting argument that "courts in multilingual jurisdictions, have been trying to come up with persuasive principles that justify the derivation of language rights from official status". This is indeed true in the South African context, particularly with the monolingual language of record directive for courts where, unlike in the case of English, there is a clear abandonment of the official status conferred on the ten official languages. In Chapter 5 we explained that the language of record policy directive affects more than just the Section 35(3) (k) fundamental right to a fair trial. Reading the rights contained in Section 35 as whole, it is clear that, in almost every instance, language is needed to communicate in exercising these rights.

Take, for example, subsection (1) (a) where an arrested person must be informed of their right to remain silent. This has to be communicated through the medium of a language. A police officer will do this. Applying the contents of the SAPS Draft Language Policy (2015) to this right, the right is then limited where an arrested person has no command of English given that English is the working language of the SAPS. The SAPS Draft Language Policy (2015), as seen in Chapter 5, does recognise the provincial official languages as languages of communication, but only where practicable. It is improbable that an arresting officer will make use of an interpreter when reading the arrested person's rights to them. Non-availability of costs and interpreters are most likely to be cited as reasons for not providing an interpreter at these preliminary stages of a criminal investigation.

The language of record policy directive affects an arrested person at their first court appearance, where the arrested person would immediately be reliant on an interpreter if they are not able to understand English. Given the monolingual language of record policy directive, this would be the case, regardless of the fact if all parties to court were, for example, competent in an African language or Afrikaans.

The undertone of language in these rights is again made known in Section 35(2): a detained person is to be informed, firstly, of the reasons for their detainment; secondly, of their right to consult with a legal practitioner; and thirdly, of their right to challenge the lawfulness of the detention. These have to be done through a language; and with an English-only language of record policy directive, the detainee will have to rely on interpretation services where they cannot speak or understand English. In all instances thus far the arrested and detained persons are essentially conferred with an interpretational right and not language rights, when they cannot speak, read, write nor understand English.

The right to a fair trial is guaranteed in Section 35(3); and, as with subsections (1) and (2) above, language is of prime importance for an accused person in formulating his or her defence and disproving a charge. On the point of a charge, the charge sheet will be provided in English only. This again is problematic in the context of South Africa with the majority of persons in criminal trials not understanding English, as evidenced in the statistics housed in Part Two of Chapter 6. This innately affects the other rights as part of the overarching right to a fair trial, including, but not limited to, securing legal representation for consultation purposes and to present the case. The importance of this right was outlined in the case of *State* v *Pienaar* (2000). The court held that subsections (3)(f) and (g) are central to the right to a free trial where the legal practitioner provided by the state must be able to communicate directly with the accused, unless in exceptional circumstances (see discussion in Chapter 7).

The standard – or, rather, the 'opt out' clause – is somewhat heightened through the phrase "exceptional circumstances". Simply put, the state cannot, in every instance, then provide the excuse that there are not enough attorneys who can communicate directly with accused persons in the African languages. This would prove the point that there is a flaw in the justice system where emphasis needs to be placed on employing linguistically competent attorneys. Conversely, there is a need for universities to graduate these students and the legislature to legislate African language requirements for the attorneys and advocates for admission to the Side Bar and Bar. This point highlights the intersecting disciplines of law and higher education in relation to language facilitating access to justice.

In both academia and in practice, Section 35(3) (k) of the Constitution, as opposed to the other provisions above, has been engaged with at various levels. The latter is evidenced by case law which we will refer to in Chapter 7. Section 35(3) (k), in our opinion, confers a language right in the first part of the provision and an alternative interpretational right in the second part of the right. According to Schwikkard and Van der Merwe (2010:800), it is essential for an accused to be given information in a language they understand and to be tried in a language they understand. Schwikkard and Van der Merwe (2010) qualify this statement by stating that Section 35(3) (k) does not confer a right to be tried in a language of choice, but rather in a language which the accused understands and where it is not practicable to have the proceedings interpreted into that language.

It is our opinion that, by adopting this interpretation, and read together with the monolingual language of record directive, a standard is created where if, as an accused, you cannot speak and understand English, your language right falls away by default and you have an interpretational right only. It is our opinion, further, that this creates an unfair advantage for English-speaking accused persons, as opposed to the majority who speak an African language and Afrikaans. This is, then, contrary to the provisions of Section 6(2) of the Constitution. This systemic disadvantage is perpetuated through the numerous issues arising from interpretation in the courts.

In Part One of this chapter we outlined the complexities associated with the constitutional language provisions and rights. In Part Two that follows, we discuss the linguistic inequalities that persist in the legal system, despite the fact that the Constitution supports a linguistically inclusive legal system for all South Africans, the majority of whom speak an African language as their mother tongue.

PART 2:
LINGUISTIC (IN)EQUALITY IN SOUTH AFRICA'S LEGAL SYSTEM

Linguistic equaltiy for African language-speaking litigants

Language equality in the South African legal system

In Part One of Chapter 6 we discussed the importance of equality amongst languages and for speakers of the various languages in relation to the constitutional provisions. In each of the case studies in both Chapters 2 and 3 there were elements of linguistic inequality, some more prevalent than others. With the Canadian case study, we advanced the principle of linguistic duality, an absent principle in the South African context where the focus is on equitable treatment rather than equal treatment.

Section 9 of the Constitution comprises the right to equality:

(1) Everyone is equal before the law and has the right to equal protection and benefit of the law.
(2) Equality includes the full and equal enjoyment of all rights and freedoms. To promote the achievement of equality, legislative and other measures designed to protect or advance persons, or categories of persons, disadvantaged by unfair discrimination may be taken.
(3) The state may not unfairly discriminate directly or indirectly against anyone on one or more grounds including ... language ...
(4) No person may unfairly discriminate directly or indirectly against anyone on one or more grounds in terms of subsection (3). National legislation must be enacted to prevent or prohibit unfair discrimination.
(5) Discrimination on one or more of the grounds listed in subsection (3) is unfair unless it is established that the discrimination is fair.

In applying subsection (1) to the monolingual language of record directive for courts, how can everyone be equal before the law and have equal access to justice if African language and Afrikaans speaking litigants are solely reliant on interpretation? English speaking litigants are then 'more equal' before the law and have easier access to justice than their African language and Afrikaans speaking counterparts. This scenario entails the majority of South Africans not benefitting from the equal enjoyment of all rights, in this instance, the language rights espoused in Section 35 of the Constitution, thus limiting the right in Section 9(2) of the Constitution. This is contradictory given the second half – the right in Section 9(2) which calls for measures to be put in place to ensure the equal treatment of persons who have been disadvantaged by unfair discrimination. The irony lies in the fact that African language speakers have been marginalised during colonialism and Apartheid as discussed in Chapters 4 and 5, yet the monolingual language of record policy is a measure that appears to entrench this discrimination, even though unfair discrimination on grounds of language is precluded by Section 9(3) of the Constitution.

Section 9 of the Constitution refers to unfair discrimination and fair discrimination being permissible. Colloquially, discrimination in any form is considered unfair; legally, however, discrimination can be fair if proved. Simply put, all discrimination is presumed to be unfair unless proved otherwise as per subsection (5). In accordance with subsection (4), legislation was enacted in the form of the Promotion of Equality and Prevention of Unfair Discrimination Act 4 of 2000 (Equality Act). The Equality Act (2000a) is not a replacement of Section 9, rather an elucidation. When alleging discrimination on one or more grounds in Section 9(3), the allegation must be brought in terms of the Equality Act (2000a). Direct reliance on Section 9 will only take place in exceptional circumstances, where the alleged discrimination is beyond the scope of the Equality Act (2000a) and any other legislation.

Unfair discrimination is determined through the application of Section 14 of the Equality Act (2000a) to the facts of each case:

> (2) In determining whether the respondent has proved the discrimination is fair, the following must be taken into account:
>
> (a) The context;
>
> (b) The factors referred to in subsection (3);
>
> (c) Whether the discrimination reasonably and justifiably differentiates between persons according to objectively determinable criteria, intrinsic to the activity concerned.
>
> (3) The factors referred to in subsection (2)(b) include the following:
>
> (a) whether the discrimination impairs or is likely to impair human dignity;
>
> (b) the impact or ikely impact of the discrimination on the complainant;
>
> (c) the position cf the complainant in society and whether he or she suffers from patterns of disadvantage;
>
> (d) the nature and the extent of the discrimination;
>
> (e) whether the d scrimination is systemic in nature;

(f) whether the discrimination has a legitimate purpose;
(g) whether and to what extent the discrimination achieves its purpose;
(h) whether there are less restrictive and less disadvantageous means to achieve the purpose;
(i) whether and to what extent the respondent has taken such steps as being reasonable in the circumstance to –
   (i) address the disadvantage which arises from or is related to one or more of the prohibited grounds; or
   (ii) accommodate diversity.

According to Docrat (2017a:301), Section 14(2) limits the possibilities of alleged acts of unfair discrimination being termed fair. Furthermore, that if one of the listed criterions in Section 14 is not satisfied, the alleged discrimination must be declared unfair (Docrat, 2017a:301). Section 14(3) of the Equality Act (2000) and the provisions of Section 6 of the Constitution both make an intrinsic call for the furtherance of the right of those persons previously marginalised and discriminated against. The equality provisions of both the Constitution and the Equality Act (2000) are to be applied to the monolingual language of record directive. There are two interrelated points of discussion: the first concerns whether or not the language of record directive results in unfair discrimination in accordance with an equality-based argument; and the second is whether the limitation of rights by the language of record directive is constitutionally sound. The latter is discussed to an extent in the following section of this discussion.

Given the critique we have advanced in Chapter 4 of this book concerning the monolingual language of record directive, the underlying imperative of each point of critique is the inequality that is created. Based on the discussions pertaining to the right to equality and the Equality Act (2000), there is no doubt in our minds that a monolingual language of record policy unfairly discriminates against the majority of persons in South Africa. There is no possibility of justifying fair discrimination in terms of the Equality Act (2000), given that fair discrimination would entail reversing the effects of the past and be the most plausible option, where everyone is discriminated against equally. With the monolingual language of record policy, an English-speaking minority enjoys the rights in Section 35 and Section 9 of the Constitution with no linguistic limitations; yet the majority (African language and Afrikaans speaking citizens) are conferred with interpretational rights and, as a result, are treated unequally. The disadvantage that the monolingual language of record directive creates is systemic in nature.

Examining the cases of *State* v *Damani* (2016) and *State* v *Gordon* (2018), both concerning the language of record in courts, it is clear that there was a failure to engage in a constitutionally-based equality argument grounded on either Section 9 of the Constitution or PAJA (2000b). We are fully aware that, in both instances, the courts were not asked to determine if unfair discrimination had taken place. However, given the nature of the cases, one would have expected the court, at the very least, to have spoken about equality of languages and the speakers thereof. Instead, in both instances, the courts were preoccupied with illustrating why it is impractical to conduct cases in African languages.

The court in *State* v *Gordon* (2018) focused on defending the decision on the basis of practicality and 'cutting the cloth' accordingly. Yet the statistics we provide in this chapter will illustrate that the majority of South Africans do not speak English as their mother tongue and that this is problematic when they enter the courts with 'conversant' English and are deemed to 'understand' English. Furthermore, the majority accessing the courts are reliant on interpretational services.

In the *State* v *Damani* (2016) case, it was disappointing that the court failed to engage with the equality of languages, and rather chose the discretionary terminology that the languages be treated equitably. The issue of dialectal variations within a language was unnecessarily overemphasised during the pilot project. These dialectal differences are often minor and should not pose any difficulties for speakers in the region. The point is that, when limiting the right through Section 36 of the Constitution, a balancing act must take place, something which the courts, in most instances, failed to do, as reflected in the case law in Chapter 7 of this book. In the case of *State* v *Pienaar* (2004), the court took account of all the relevant factors in determining the parameters of the right in Section 35 of the Constitution. There is a difference between rights in theory and the application of rights in practice.

In both the *State* v *Damani* (2016) and *State* v *Gordon* (2018) cases, the courts reasoned that it was impractical to have trials conducted in official languages other than English, as judicial officers cannot be 'shopped for'. The rights of accused persons need to be balanced against the 'rights' of judicial officers. Simply put, in our opinion, it would not be unfair to appoint a Judge who is linguistically competent in one specific language, as opposed to another, to hear a trial. The argument put forward by Thulare AJ in the *State* v *Gordon* (2018) case racialises the official languages; the inference is that only Black judges will be competent in an African language and White judges will most likely be English mother tongue speakers with no competency in an African language. This line of thinking and reasoning must be rejected. Furthermore, it continues to create an 'othering' of African languages and the speakers of these languages. There must be no divide between 'my' language and 'your' language; for South Africans as a collective, the official languages are 'our' languages. This is what true unity in diversity entails. There are many South African who are competent in multiple official languages and who possess mother tongue proficiency in these languages.

As Currie and De Waal (2013:154) suggest, when limiting the right and, ultimately, striking a balance with the rights and the needs of the other party, the reasonability and justifiability standards cannot be decided abstractly. This determination requires evidence in the form of sociological or statistical data, or both, in highlighting the impact that the limitation will have on society at large. We have presented the relevant statistics, including surveys and other language demographics, in this chapter and in Chapters 8 and 9. The most conflicting thereof are the views of attorneys on the language question in courts and the misunderstandings that legal practitioners have about the language question and, more specifically, the language competencies and preferences of their clients (De Vries & Docrat, 2019). From the case law presented in Chapter 7, the courts failed to engage with relevant statistics. For example, in the *State* v *Gordon* (2018) case, Thulare AJ, in referring to Docrat's Master of Arts thesis (Docrat, 2017a), failed to engage with any of the language demographics she had presented. This is illustrative of the failure to strike a balance; and, in failing to do so, failing to give effective meaning to the language rights of Section 35 of the Constitution.

Woolman (1998-2003:12-61) says that it amounts to how we wish the world to look, what kind of world we wish to live in. It is therefore a subjective interpretation of the law. Woolman (1998-2003) explains that, although *grundnorms* (legal norms/legal principles) are in existence in the theoretical underpinning of the limitations analysis, the implementation and application thereof in practical situations may differ, depending on a judicial officer's interpretation of the facts in relation to the law. We have spoken about balancing through the second of the two ways identified by Woolman (1998-2003:12-55), where balancing means 'striking a balance' between the competing rights or interests. The first instance in which balancing takes place, is with two competing rights, which we have touched upon earlier regarding the rights of an accused in Section 35(3) (k) and Section 9 of the Constitution for judicial officers in terms of being discriminated against on grounds of language.

The limitations analysis: sliding scale formula

We have previously referred to Section 36, the limitations analysis, and have made general reference to it throughout this book. What follows is a distinction between Sections 36 and 9 of the Constitution and when a right may be limited; and, if so, to what extent. Thus, there is an overlap with our earlier discussions about finding a balance when determining the parameters of rights.

Section 36 of the Constitution provides for the limitation of rights and this is referred to as 'the limitations analysis':

> (1) The rights in the Bill of Rights may be limited only in terms of law of general application to the extent that the limitation is reasonable and justifiable in an open and democratic society based on human dignity, equality and freedom, taking into account all the relevant factors, including –
> (a) the nature of the right;
> (b) the importance of the purpose of the limitation;

(c) the nature and extent of the limitation;
(d) the relation between the limitation and its purpose; and
(e) less restrictive means to achieve the purpose.
(2) Except as provided in subsection (1) or in any other provision of the Constitution, no law may limit any right entrenched in the Bill of Rights.

As with Section 14 of the Equality Act (2000a), the limitability of a right is minimal according to Section 36(1) and the criteria in (a) to (e). A two-stage approach is employed in limiting a right in the BOR. The first stage is where the court identifies the right in the BOR that has allegedly been infringed by either a person or the state. If the first stage is satisfied and a right has been infringed, the court proceeds to the second stage. In the second stage, the court will determine whether the infringement of the right can be justified as a permissible limitation of the right (Currie & De Waal, 2013:151-152). With the second stage, the court will apply the facts of the case to the criteria listed in Section 36(1) (a) to (e) of the Constitution in determining when the limitation is justifiable in an open and democratic society.

With Section 36 of the Constitution being a law of general application, Currie and De Waal (2005) drafted specific criteria for the limitation of language rights in the BOR. Currie and De Waal (2005) provide these criteria in the form of a sliding scale that the authors applied to the language in education right, Section 29(2). The sliding scale formula can, however, be applied to all language rights. Essentially, the sliding scale formula provides checks and balances to ensure that rights are not unfairly limited. This includes "…the number of speakers in a given area; their concentration; as well as the seriousness of the service involved" (Currie & De Waal, 2005:632). The sliding scale is important regarding the application of the monolingual language of record policy directive for courts that limits the language right in Section 35 of the Constitution.

The sliding scale formula checks and balances must be borne in mind in relation to the language demographics across provinces presented further on in this chapter. The seriousness of the service in the context of this research is access to justice. This is pivotal, especially in criminal cases, to ensure the accused is afforded a fair trial and language is not a hindrance in defending the charge; nor a hindrance for a complainant providing evidence, being cross-examined, or laying the charge in the initial stage of the investigation. Thus, the seriousness of the service has already been established at this stage our discussions.

South African language demographics: statistics

This chapter has constantly referred to language demographics, especially in light of the constitutional provisions and case law. Section 6 of the Constitution refers to the number of speakers, as well as the sliding scale formula (Currie & De Waal, 2005). The equality-based discussions also illustrate that statistical data be taken into account when determining when discrimination is to be deemed unfair. Furthermore, it strengthens our argument if there is a large contingent of people from a specific language group in a province where that language is an official language.

In this part of Chapter 6, we advance the relevant language statistics emanating from the last national census (2011) and the survey capturing the English language limitation of litigants. The language and racial demographics of the legal professionals in South Africa, as well as the language survey capturing the views of attorneys in South Africa on using official languages other than English in the legal system (De Vries & Docrat, 2019), are presented in Chapter 9 of this book.

Statistics South Africa, drawing on the work of the United Nations, defines a population census as:

> ...the total process of collecting, compiling, evaluating, analysing and publishing or otherwise disseminating demographic, economic and social data pertaining, at a specified time, to all persons in a country or a well-defined part of the country.

The last Census was conducted in 2011, with the next one expected in 2021, given the ten yearly review period. The Census is an extremely important process in South Africa. For languages, Lourens (2012:285) advanced that the census would be critically important in highlighting South Africa's linguistic demographics which could be used to assess whether these demographics are reflective across domains.

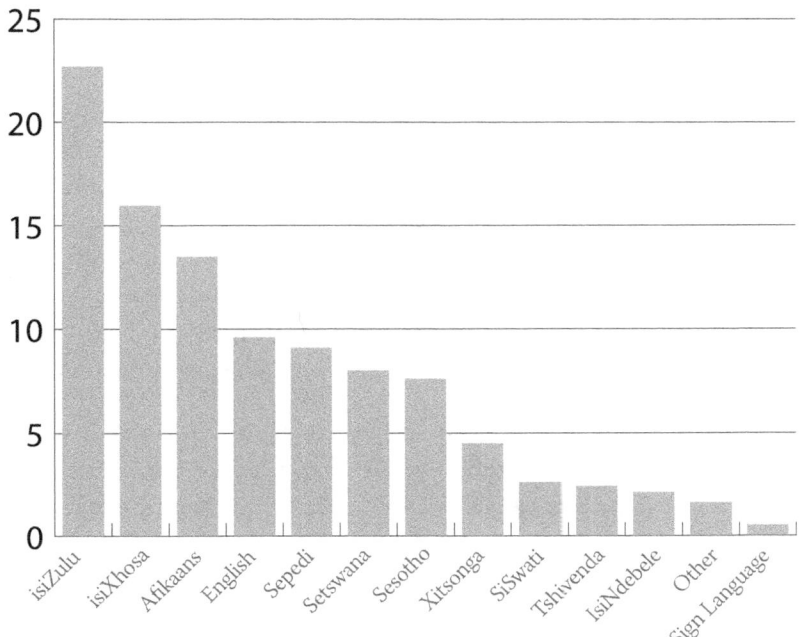

FIGURE 6.1 National language statistics (Census, 2011)

TABLE 6.1   National language demographics of South Africa (Census, 2011)

Language	EC	FS	GP	KZN	LP	MP	NC	NW	WC
Afrikaans	10.6	12.7	12.4	1.6	2.6	7.2	53.8	9.0	49.7
English	5.6	2.9	13.3	13.2	1.5	3.1	3.4	3.5	20.2
IsiNdebele	0.2	0.4	3.2	1.1	2.0	10.1	0.5	1.3	0.3
IsiXhosa	78.8	7.5	6.6	3.4	0.4	1.2	5.3	5.5	24.7
IsiZulu	0.5	4.4	19.8	77.8	1.2	24.1	0.8	2.5	0.4
Sepedi	0.2	0.3	10.6	0.2	52.9	9.3	0.2	2.4	0.1
Sesotho	2.5	64.2	11.6	0.8	1.5	3.5	1.3	5.8	1.1
Setswana	0.2	5.2	9.1	0.5	2.0	1.8	33.1	63.4	0.4
Sign Language	0.7	1.2	0.4	0.5	0.2	0.2	0.3	0.4	0.4
SiSwati	0.0	0.1	1.1	0.1	0.5	27.7	0.1	0.3	0.1
Tshivenda	0.1	0.1	2.3	0.0	16.7	0.3	0.1	0.5	0.1
Xitsonga	0.0	0.3	6.6	0.1	17.0	10.4	0.1	3.7	0.2
Other	0.6	0.6	3.1	0.8	1.6	1.0	1.1	1.8	2.2

Figure 6.1 represents the national percentage of speakers for each official language in addition to Sign Language. Nationally, it is recorded that only 9.6% of the population speaks English as their mother tongue; 13.5% speak Afrikaans as their mother tongue; this totals 23.1%, that is, less than one-quarter of the population. The number of African language speakers nationally amounts to 75% of the population. The national language statistics in Figure 6.1 provide a clear indication that the majority of persons in South Africa speak an African language as their mother tongue.

The argument here is for the adoption of provincially-determined language policies for courts, rather than the current national monolingual language of record policy directive. Table 6.1 represents the provincial language demographics. These figures are important in assessing whether there are majority spoken languages in South African provinces. More than 50% of persons in the Eastern Cape, Free State, KwaZulu-Natal, Limpopo and North West provinces speak an African language as their mother tongue as indicated in Table 6.1. A minority of speakers in these provinces speak English as their mother tongue.

In Gauteng there is no single language with an outright majority of mother tongue speakers, as apparent from Table 6.1. However, the number of mother tongue speakers of English and Afrikaans with recorded percentages of 12.4 and 13.3, when combined, equals a mere 25.7% of speakers in the province. By contrast, when percentages of the three dominant African languages in Gauteng are combined, namely, isiZulu with 19.8%, Sesotho with 11.6% and Sepedi with 10.6%, the total equals 42%. Therefore, as with the other provinces, the majority of speakers in Gauteng speak an African language as their mother tongue.

Similar to Gauteng's language demographics, Mpumalanga does not have a majority of persons in the province speaking one African language as their mother tongue. It is evident from Table 6.1 that there are two equally poised African languages, namely SiSwati with 27.7% and isiZulu with 24.1%. The total percentage of African language speakers outweighs the percentage of English speakers.

The Northern Cape and Western Cape provinces are two of nine provinces where the majority of persons do not speak an African language. In both provinces, the majority of persons speak Afrikaans as their mother tongue and not English; 33.1% speak Setswana and 24.7% speak isiXhosa. A further point to note is that the Western Cape Province has the largest percentage of English mother tongue speakers with 20.2% in comparison to the totals of the other eight provinces, as evident in Table 6.1.

These language demographics need to be considered against the constitutional provisions of Sections 6, and 35(3)(k), as well as the limitations analysis with specific reference to the sliding scale formula. These language statistics are also to be contrasted to the monolingual language of record policy directive. When applied, it makes no sense to have an English monolingual language of record policy for all courts across all nine provinces.

In the case of *State* v *Damani* (2016), the court also relied on the report by the Director of Public Prosecutions (DPP) in KwaZulu-Natal who explained that there were pilot courts in which African languages were being used and this had proved to be impractical on a number of grounds, listed earlier, including dialectal differences across districts. With the nine tables that follow here, relying on the Census (2011) results, we have presented the language demographics of each district for each of the nine provinces to assess whether there are vast language differences. We specifically focus on language differences, not dialectal differences, as a similar situation would exist within each district where people are able to communicate in that language variety. The argument is linked back to the thinking of Ruíz (1984) regarding language planning and how language planners or states see language as a problem, rather than a right or a resource.

What follows are tables, comprising the provincial language demographics per district municipality, of the Eastern Cape, Free State, KwaZulu-Natal and North West Provinces, which is followed by a discussion and analysis of these demographics.

TABLE 6.2 Eastern Cape Province language statistics per district municipality (Census, 2011)

Language	Cacadu	Amatole	Chris Hani	Joe Qgabi	O.R. Tambo	Alfred Nzo	Buffalo City	Nelson Mandela Bay
Afrikaans	43.6	2.0	6.0	5.8	0.5	0.8	7.0	28.9
English	6.2	2.2	2.6	1.6	2.7	2.3	10.7	13.3
IsiNdebele	0.2	0.2	0.2	0.2	0.2	0.3	0.2	0.3
IsiXhosa	43.9	91.6	87.4	69.8	93.1	84.0	76.9	53.2
IsiZulu	0.4	0.3	0.3	0.3	0.5	1.2	0.4	0.4
Sepedi	0.2	0.2	0.2	0.2	0.2	0.3	0.2	0.2
Sesotho	0.5	0.2	0.5	20.0	0.3	8.7	0.3	0.4
Setswana	0.3	0.1	0.2	0.1	0.1	0.2	0.2	0.3
Sign Language	0.3	0.6	0.7	0.6	0.8	0.9	0.7	0.4
SiSwati	0.0	0.0	0.0	0.0	0.0	0.0	0.0	0.0
Tshivenda	0.1	0.0	0.0	0.0	0.1	0.0	0.0	0.1
Xitsonga	0.1	0.0	0.0	0.0	0.0	0.0	0.1	0.1
Other	0.8	0.3	0.5	0.4	0.3	0.6	0.7	1.0

TABLE 6.3 Free State Province language statistics per district municipality (Census, 2011)

Language	Fezile Dabi	Lejweleputswa	Mangaung	Thabo Mofutsanyana	Xhariep
Afrikaans	13.8	11.3	16.2	6.0	31.6
English				2.0	
IsiNdebele					
IsiXhosa	6.0	12.2	9.9		15.8
IsiZulu	5.6			10.4	
Sepedi					
Sesotho	67.3	62.2	53.3	78.5	45.3
Setswana		5.9	12.6		3.5
Sign Language					
SiSwati					
Tshivenda					
Xitsonga					
Other					

Linguistic (in)equality in South Africa's legal system

TABLE 6.4 KwaZulu-Natal Province language statistics per metropolitan and district municipalities (Census, 2011)

Language	Amajuba District Municipality	eThekwini Metropolitan Municipality	iLembe District Municipality	Sisonke District Municipality	Ugu District Municipality	uMgungundlovu District Municipality	uMkhanyakude District Municipality	uMzinyathi District Municipality	uThukela District Municipality	uThungulu District Municipality
Afrikaans	3.1	1.7		1.3	2.1			1.0	1.2	2.3
English	5.2	26.8	9.6	3.2	8.3	15.3	1.7	3.1	4.7	5.1
IsiNdebele			1.2						1.1	1.3
IsiXhosa		3.9	3.3	28.6	4.3	1.9	1.2			
IsiZulu	87.5	62.8	82.2	62.7	82.7	76.4	94.6	91.0	90.5	89.1
Sepedi										
Sesotho						1.7		2.3		
Setswana										
Sign Language										
SiSwati										
Tshivenda										
Xitsonga										
Other										

TABLE 6.5 North West Province language statistics per district municipality (Census, 2011)

Language	Bojanala Platinum District Municipality	Dr Kenneth Kaunda District Municipality	Dr Ruth Segomotsi Mompati District Municipality	Ngaka Modiri Molema District Municipality
Afrikaans	7.2	18.4	7.6	5.0
English			1.9	3.2
IsiNdebele				
IsiXhosa	5.6	11.5		2.7
IsiZulu				
Sepedi				
Sesotho		15.3	1.8	
Setswana	55.3	44.8	83.6	81.8
Sign Language				
SiSwati				
Tshivenda				
Xitsonga	8.1			
Other				

Table 6.2 illustrates that isiXhosa is spoken by the majority of persons across the province. Table 6.3 provides similar statistics to those of the Eastern Cape, where Sesotho is spoken in every district of the province. The statistics pertaining to the district municipalities of KwaZulu-Natal in Table 6.4 illustrate that an overwhelming majority of persons in all districts speak isiZulu as their mother tongue. The statistics in Table 6.5 see Setswana mother tongue speakers outnumbering all other languages in each district.

Similar to the presentation above, what follows are tables, comprising the provincial language demographics per district municipality, of the remaining five provinces and the analysis of these language demographics.

TABLE 6.6 Northern Cape Province language statistics per district municipality (Census, 2011)

Language	Frances Baard District Municipality	John Taolo Gaetsewe District Municipality	Namakwa District Municipality	Pixley ka Seme District Municipality	ZF Mgcawu District Municipality
Afrikaans	38.6	16.5	93.9	76.8	76.4
English	6.2	2.6	1.2	1.6	1.8
IsiNdebele					

TABLE 6.6 Northern Cape Province language statistics per district municipality (Census, 2011) [continued]

Language	Frances Baard District Municipality	John Taolo Gaetsewe District Municipality	Namakwa District Municipality	Pixley ka Seme District Municipality	ZF Mgcawu District Municipality
IsiXhosa	4.9		1.5	17.5	2.7
IsiZulu					
Sepedi					
Sesotho					
Setswana	43.3	75.6	1.7	1.6	15.8
Sign Language					
SiSwati					
Tshivenda					
Xitsonga					
Other					

TABLE 6.7 Western Cape Province language statistics per metropolitan and district municipality (Census, 2011)

Language	Cape Winelands District Municipality	Central Karoo District Municipality	City of Cape Town Metropolitan Municipality	Eden District Municipality	Overberg District Municipality	West Coast District Municipality
Afrikaans	74.8	87.2	35.7	70.8	70.3	83.7
English	4.3	2.6	28.4	7.5	6.8	4.0
IsiNdebele						
IsiXhosa	16.6	7.8	29.8	18.3	17.9	8.6
IsiZulu						
Sepedi						
Sesotho	1.9				2.1	1.3
Setswana						
Sign Language						
SiSwati						
Tshivenda						
Xitsonga	0.1	0.0	0.0	0.0	0.0	0.0
Other	0.8	0.3	0.5	0.4	0.3	0.6

The district municipality language statistics of the Northern Cape and Western Cape provinces differ to those of Tables 6.2 to 6.5, as there is no overwhelming number of speakers of one particular African language. Table 6.6 represents the district language statistics of the Northern Cape, where the Frances Baard and John Taolo Gaetsewe district municipalities comprise the majority of persons speaking Setswana. In the remaining three district municipalities of Namakwa, Pixley ka Seme and ZF Mgcawu, Afrikaans is the majority spoken language. In the Northern Cape, Afrikaans and Setswana are almost equally poised in terms of the percentage of speakers.

Similarly, the districts and metropolitans in the Western Cape Province appear (Table 6.7) to have three dominant languages, namely Afrikaans, isiXhosa and English. These statistics must be juxtaposed with the reaffirming directive of Hlophe JP that English be the sole official language of all courts. This line of thinking precludes two-thirds of the people in Cape Town and relegates them to relying on interpretational services when implementing the Section 35(3) (k) constitutional right.

TABLE 6.8 Limpopo Province language statistics per district municipality (Census, 2011)

Language	Capricorn District Municipality	Mopani District Municipality	Sekhukhune District Municipality	Vhembe District Municipality	Waterberg District Municipality
Afrikaans	3.0	2.1		1.3	7.7
English	2.0				
IsiNdebele			4.4		
IsiXhosa					
IsiZulu			3.3		
Sepedi					
Sesotho	84.9	45.9	82.2	1.6	56.4
Setswana					11.5
Sign Language					
SiSwati					
Tshivenda				67.2	
Xitsonga	2.6	44.3	2.0	24.8	8.3
Other					

TABLE 6.9 Mpumalanga Province language statistics per district municipality (Census, 2011)

Language	Ehlanzeni District Municipality	Gert Sibande District Municipality	Nkangala District Municipality
Afrikaans	4.0	9.1	10.0
English			
IsiNdebele			28.4
IsiXhosa			

TABLE 6.9 Mpumalanga Province language statistics per district municipality (Census, 2011) [continued]

Language	Ehlanzeni District Municipality	Gert Sibande District Municipality	Nkangala District Municipality
IsiZulu		60.9	23.1
Sepedi			
Sesotho	10.3	4.2	14.7
Setswana			
Sign Language			
SiSwati	54.5	13.0	
Tshivenda			
Xitsonga	21.8		
Other			

In the Limpopo Province (Table 6.8), the language demographics of the district municipalities resemble those of the Western Cape and Northern Cape provinces, with no single language spoken by the majority of persons. The language policy in Limpopo would need to be carefully drafted to ensure that these language groups are all recognised; and this speaks to the argument of having linguistically competent legal practitioners and judicial officers servicing the lower courts. This approach, if adopted, could then be applied to the Mpumalanga Province language demographics of the district municipalities, as represented in Table 6.9, as well to those of the other provinces. Nonetheless, in both Limpopo and Mpumalanga, there is a majority spoken African language in each district. Moreover, it would be difficult to validate the use of English as a language of record in these two provinces where it is evident that there is a minimal number of English language speakers.

TABLE 6.10 Gauteng Province language statistics per metropolitan and district municipalities (Census, 2011)

Language	City of Johannesburg Metropolitan	City of Tshwane Metropolitan Municipality	Ekurhuleni Metropolitan Municipality	Sedibeng District Municipality	West Rand District Municipality
Afrikaans		18.8	11.9	15.2	16.9
English	20.1		12.0		
IsiNdebele					
IsiXhosa				7.1	14.9
IsiZulu	23.4		28.8	16.0	
Sepedi					
Sesotho	9.6	19.9	11.4	46.7	10.8
Setswana	7.7	15.0			27.3

TABLE 6.10 Gauteng Province language statistics per metropolitan and district municipalities (Census, 2011) [continued]

Language	City of Johannesburg Metropolitan	City of Tshwane Metropolitan Municipality	Ekurhuleni Metropolitan Municipality	Sedibeng District Municipality	West Rand District Municipality
Sign Language					
SiSwati					
Tshivenda					
Xitsonga		8.6			
Other					

In Table 6.10 three African languages are spoken by the majority of persons in the district municipalities, namely isiZulu, Sesotho and Setswana. In addition, Afrikaans is spoken in all the municipalities. Besides the Northern Cape and Western Cape Provinces, Afrikaans features prominently in all districts in Gauteng, thus it is questionable how the removal of Afrikaans as a language of record is justified on these statistical grounds. It is impossible to state that all Afrikaans speakers in these areas are White and not Coloured, by adopting the reasoning by the CJ and Hlophe JP on the monolingual language of record policy directive.

These language demographics support our critique of the monolingual language of record policy. The demographics are also important for Chapter 10 wherein we have proposed recommendations in the form of drafting and enacting language policies for the courts in each province, on the basis of these statistics.

English language limitations of South African litigants

The following step in the process is to assess the English language competency of litigants. It is expected that, when a decision is taken to make English the sole official language of record, a survey has already been conducted attesting to the high levels of English competency of litigants in the legal system. To our knowledge, this was not done by the Heads of Court nor the Department of Justice and Constitutional Developments prior to implementing the monolingual language of record policy directive.

To date, one such survey that has recently been made public was conducted by Legal Aid South Africa, a group that offers legal services to indigent persons and who are provided for by the state in terms of Section 35 of the Constitution. The results of the Legal Aid survey are presented in Table 6.11.

TABLE 6.11 Primary spoken language in criminal matters (Language Survey, Legal Aid South Africa, 2017:2)

Province	No. of Respondents	Zulu	Afrikaans	Xhosa	Sotho	Tswana	English	Pedi	Tsonga	Swati	Venda	Ndebele	Other
WC	9,302	0%	66%	26%	0%	0%	7%	0%	0%	0%	0%	0%	0%
KZN	7,031	85%	0%	3%	1%	0%	10%	0%	0%	0%	0%	0%	0%
GP	6,278	37%	8%	7%	15%	9%	7%	3%	5%	1%	2%	1%	0%
EC	5,392	0%	15%	82%	2%	0%	1%	0%	0%	0%	0%	0%	0%
FS	3,113	5%	5%	6%	74%	5%	3%	0%	0%	0%	0%	0%	0%
NW	2,631	4%	6%	7%	9%	69%	1%	2%	2%	0%	0%	0%	1%
MP	2,558	39%	3%	1%	4%	1%	1%	14%	3%	27%	0%	6%	1%
NC	2,065	2%	58%	6%	2%	31%	1%	0%	0%	0%	0%	0%	0%
LP	1,988	1%	1%	1%	9%	3%	0%	48%	20%	0%	15%	1%	1%
Grand Total	40,358	24%	22%	20%	10%	8%	5%	5%	2%	2%	1%	1%	0%

TABLE 6.12 Primary spoken language in civil matters (Language Survey, Legal Aid South Africa, 2017:3)

Province	No. of Respondents	Zulu	Afrikaans	Xhosa	English	Sotho	Tswana	Pedi	Tsonga	Venda	Ndebele	Swati	Other
KZN	1,083	68%	1%	1%	29%	0%	0%	0%	0%	0%	0%	0%	0%
GP	1,045	24%	12%	6%	11%	19%	9%	11%	4%	2%	1%	1%	1%
EC	797	0%	23%	67%	9%	1%	0%	0%	0%	0%	0%	0%	0%
WC	758	0%	63%	18%	18%	0%	0%	0%	0%	0%	0%	0%	1%
FS	480	1%	12%	8%	1%	70%	8%	0%	1%	0%	0%	0%	0%
NW	374	2%	20%	6%	3%	9%	58%	2%	1%	0%	0%	0%	0%
LP	318	1%	8%	1%	1%	3%	2%	44%	19%	21%	0%	0%	0%
MP	313	31%	8%	1%	5%	4%	0%	26%	2%	0%	12%	11%	1%

TABLE 6.12 Primary spoken language in civil matters (Language Survey, Legal Aid South Africa, 2017:3) [continued]

Province	No. of Respondents	Zulu	Afrikaans	Xhosa	English	Sotho	Tswana	Pedi	Tsonga	Venda	Ndebele	Swati	Other
NC	188	1%	59%	10%	5%	6%	20%	0%	0%	0%	0%	0%	0%
Grand Total	5,356	21%	20%	16%	12%	11%	7%	6%	2%	2%	1%	1%	0%

Tables 6.11 and 6.12 comprise the language statistics in criminal and civil matters for 2016. The statistics in Table 6.11 clearly indicate that the languages spoken by applicants varies across provinces. However, the table provides that, at national level, three languages are prominent across provincial borders, namely isiZulu at 24%, Afrikaans at 22 % and isiXhosa at 20%. Table 6.12 presents a similar pattern for litigants in civil cases, with the most widely spoken languages being isiZulu at 21%, Afrikaans at 20% and isiXhosa at 16%. What is most important for the research at hand is that, in criminal cases, a mere 5% spoke English as their mother tongue, while the total for civil cases was 11%. However, according to Mogoeng Mogoeng CJ, from his reasoning reported in the national *Sunday Times* newspaper (Nombembe, 2017) and Hlophe JP (from the language of record policy directive presented in Chapter 5), it is practicable to proceed in English only. In addition, one should note the large percentage of Afrikaans speakers and how, invariably, these statistics could not have been taken into account when removing Afrikaans as a language of record.

We have questioned how a court or Judge was in a position to determine linguistic competency in the context of the term "understand" in Section 35(3) (k) and in light of the African and international case studies in Chapters 2 and 3, where such understanding included speaking, reading and writing in a language at a high level. The case law presented in Chapter 7 also illustrates that judicial officers are of the view that they can determine when a witness understands proceedings – and how this actually adversely affected the outcome of a case. Legal Aid South Africa, therefore, as part of their language survey, included results on English proficiency for litigants in both criminal and civil cases. These statistics are encompassed in Tables 6.13 and 6.14.

TABLE 6.13 English proficiency in criminal cases (Language Survey, Legal Aid South Africa, 2017:4)

Province	Understand			Speak			Read/Write		
	Good	Satisfactory	Poor	Good	Satisfactory	Poor	Good	Satisfactory	Poor
EC	15.9%	27.7%	56.4%	14.2%	24.6%	61.2%	13.8%	23.6%	62.6%
FS	26.8%	39.7%	33.4%	24.0%	34.9%	41.1%	22.7%	33.1%	44.2%
GP	33.8%	41.7%	24.5%	30.7%	40.9%	28.4%	30.3%	38.5%	31.2%
KZN	21.9%	37.0%	41.0%	20.1%	33.4%	46.5%	18.8%	31.2%	50.0%
LP	27.2%	36.3%	36.6%	21.1%	35.4%	43.5%	21.5%	31.9%	46.6%
MP	25.4%	38.2%	36.4%	21.4%	36.7%	41.9%	21.5%	35.1%	43.4%
NW	28.3%	40.4%	31.3%	24.0%	39.3%	36.7%	24.6%	37.3%	38.0%
NC	15.0%	42.4%	42.6%	12.3%	37.9%	49.8%	11.9%	33.2%	54.9%
WC	24.4%	43.5%	32.2%	21.4%	40.6%	38.1%	19.4%	37.7%	42.9%
Grand Total	24.4%	38.7%	36.8%	21.5%	36.1%	42.4%	20.7%	33.8%	45.6%

TABLE 6.14 English proficiency in civil cases (Language Survey, Legal Aid South Africa, 2017:5)

Province	Understand			Speak			Read/Write		
	Good	Satisfactory	Poor	Good	Satisfactory	Poor	Good	Satisfactory	Poor
EC	44.8%	30.0%	25.2%	41.5%	30.4%	28.1%	43.4%	27.1%	29.5%
FS	46.9%	30.2%	22.9%	43.8%	32.1%	24.2%	44.2%	30.8%	25.0%
GP	52.6%	31.4%	16.0%	48.5%	34.4%	17.1%	49.6%	30.8%	19.6%
KZN	47.7%	29.8%	22.4%	44.1%	29.7%	26.1%	46.8%	25.5%	27.7%
LP	35.2%	40.9%	23.9%	33.0%	40.6%	26.4%	35.2%	36.8%	28.0%
MP	37.4%	30.7%	31.9%	36.4%	28.8%	34.8%	35.5%	27.8%	36.7%
NW	48.1%	28.3%	23.5%	43.6%	28.6%	27.8%	47.3%	25.4%	27.3%
NC	32.4%	33.0%	34.6%	31.9%	32.4%	35.6%	31.9%	27.7%	40.4%
WC	39.7%	40.4%	19.9%	37.7%	38.0%	24.3%	37.9%	36.0%	26.1%
Grand Total	45.2%	32.4%	22.4%	42.1%	32.7%	25.2%	43.5%	29.6%	26.9%

Table 6.13, illustrates that, at national level, in all three categories of understanding, speaking, and reading/writing, English was mainly 'poor' or 'satisfactory', with the 'good' percentage in each of the categories below 25%. Through further analysis, from a provincial perspective, the majority of litigants in the Eastern Cape do not understand English.

Exacerbating this is the fact that the overwhelming majority of litigants in the Eastern Cape cannot speak, read or write English. Litigants in KwaZulu-Natal also have poor proficiency in English, including understanding, speaking and reading/writing English.

Table 6.14, concerning civil cases, illustrates that, in comparison to litigants in criminal cases, the level of English proficiency across all nine provinces was in the 'satisfactory' range. Overall, English proficiency was higher in comparison to criminal cases, but remained below 50% in the 'good' category. These statistics lay bare the discrepancies in the reasoning and thinking of the Heads of Court in adopting a narrowed interpretation of language rights when formulating the monolingual language of record directive. These statistics by Legal Aid South Africa (2017) also illustrate the importance of a bottom-up approach to language planning, where empirical data, in the form of statistics emanating from surveys, are taken into account and provide policy direction.

Conclusion

This chapter has engaged with the constitutional language rights and general language provisions, while highlighting the internal limitations thereof created through vague and discretionary terms and phrases. Nevertheless, we have argued that the framework remained in place; and, applying the sentiments of Cameron (2013), that the Constitution is only a guide and requires further interpretation, as the rights established were to be applied in practice. Drawing on the work of Leung (2019) we acknowledge that, in a multilingual legal order such as exists in South Africa, interpretation and practical implementation are dependent on the intention of those implementing or interpreting. Applying the selected case law, this chapter has found that a narrowed interpretation was applied, with this creating an alternative right to interpretation in courts for African language speakers and Afrikaans speakers. This, in our opinion, created a 'lesser' standard of justice for those who cannot speak English.

The selected case law also brought to the fore the competing interests which judicial officers are balancing; and how the balancing act, through the limitations analysis and sliding scale formula, is misconstrued in favour of English (*State* v *Gordon*, 2018). How judicial officers are currently interpreting and applying the law is of grave concern, where compliance with the monolingual language of record directive is the primary goal (*State* v *Damani*, 2016; *State* v *Gordon*, 2018).

This chapter, through survey results presented in Part Two, has highlighted the inequality of African language speaking litigants in the legal system – this, while the majority of South Africans are African language speakers. The application of Section 9 of the Constitution, as well as of Section 14 of the Equality Act (2000a), to the monolingual language of record policy directive, illustrates that it unfairly discriminates and disadvantages African language and Afrikaans speaking litigants.

The chapter that follows presents the South African case law where the language question is discussed in relation to the language rights and limitations. The case law is illustrative of the judicial favouring of a monolingual language of record policy.

THE LANGUAGE QUESTION BEFORE COURTS

Selected South African case law

South African case law

Throughout our discussions thus far, we have referred to case law and, in some instances, we have briefly extracted and applied the relevant legal principles emanating from cases to our theoretical discussions. In this chapter of this book we unpack the judgments concerning language. Firstly, we discuss the case law directly addressing the language of record. Secondly, we advance the case law in which interpretation was an issue before court. Thirdly, the case law pertaining to university language policies is advanced. Although we discuss each category separately, all the case law and issues are linked, as will be evident throughout the discussions.

Language of record cases

The first case we discuss directly concerns the language of record. The case of *State* v *Damani* (2016) was before the KwaZulu-Natal High Court on automatic review from the MC, Mahlabathini in KwaZulu-Natal. The trial in the court *a quo* was conducted wholly in isiZulu, including the judgment and sentencing (2016:2). Upon review, Ndlovu J (2016:2) posed the following questions to the Magistrate:

> As an accused does not have a right to have his/her trial conducted in a language of his/her choice (*Mthethwa* v *De Bruin NO and Another* 1998(3) BCLR 336 (N)), was it the choice of the presiding Magistrate to have the entire proceedings conducted in isiZulu in this case? If so, did the Magistrate consider the logistical problems that could or would potentially arise when the manner was brought to the High Court for review? (see: *S* v *Matomela* (1998(3) BCLR 339 (Ck); *S* v *Damoyi* 2004(2) SA 564 (C)). In any event, was there no interpreter available to assist with the translation duties in court? As the accused was sentenced on 30 April 2014, why did it take nearly 3 months for the matter to be submitted to the Registrar, on 27 July 2014?

According to Ndlovu J (2016:2), the Magistrate responded by explaining that it was his decision to proceed wholly in isiZulu and that the translation of the record into English was available on 24 June 2014, so the delay was not caused by translation but rather the tardiness of the clerk of the court. The Magistrate cited the following reasons for conducting the trial in isiZulu:

> That the Mahlabathini district comprised mostly rural areas and 99.9 per cent of accused are Zulu speaking. That, in the present case, the presiding magistrate, the prosecutor, the complainant and the accused (who was not legally represented) were all Zulu speaking. That the Constitution called for recognition of the equality of all 11 official languages.

From this reasoning it is clear that the Magistrate adopted a practical approach, giving effective meaning to the constitutional provisions. The Magistrate also interpreted the constitutional provisions as providing for the "equality" of all languages rather than reasonable usage through the implication of the term "equitable". It was practical to proceed in isiZulu given that all parties before court were fully competent in the language. The Magistrate did not accord any delay to the translation of the record into English, as insinuated by Ndlovu J. For the remainder of the judgment, Ndlovu J appeared to have gone on an investigative mission to highlight the problems associated with conducting trials in languages other than English. Ndlovu J (2016:3) commenced with the legislative framework, Section 6(1) of the Magistrates' Courts Act (1944), being read with Section 6(1) of the Constitution, which provides for any of the 11 official languages to be used as languages of record in court proceedings. According to Ndlovu J (2016:3-4), this was "drastic" and, as such, Section 35(3) (k) of the Constitution needed to be engaged with for criminal trial purposes. Ndlovu J (2016:4-5) vehemently held that Section 35(3) (k) does not provide an accused with a right to choose a language but rather to have proceedings interpreted into a language they understand.

Ndlovu J (2016:5) held further that it is a 'constitutional ideal' to see all courts operating in the languages predominantly used in the region in which the court is seated. He however noted that this was elusive or impracticable, or both. The court *a quo* showed otherwise, in conducting the trial in isiZulu without any delays relating to language or any other practical issues.

Ndlovu J (2016:7) furthermore communicated with the DPP in KwaZulu-Natal who indicated that, during the period of October to November 2008, a campaign had been embarked upon through a pilot project to promote the use of indigenous languages in courts. The project was carried out in the KwaZulu-Natal districts of Msinga, Impendle, Nongoma and Hlabisa (this excluded Mahlabathini, from which this case emanates). Ndlovu J recorded the following difficulties (2016:7-8), as per the discussion with the DPP:

> Difficulty experienced by a presiding magistrate, prosecutor, defence attorney in articulating legal terminology in isiZulu, including quotation from statutes and legal precedents. Translation into isiZulu of court annexures, forms and statements in

police dockets. Difficulty for the transcribers in preparing court records for review or appeal purposes, hence undue delay caused in this regard. Different isiZulu dialects occasionally posed problems to court officials and litigants, despite all of them being, otherwise, Zulu speaking.

In 2011, the project ground to a halt with operational problems and lack of planning cited as reasons. As a side note, before we address the issues highlighted in the extracted text, no further information was ever reported on these pilot projects, thus a lack of planning may well be cited as the primary reason for the failure of the project. The dialectal and terminology problems could have been addressed inter alia with (forensic) linguists and illustrates the need for trained legal translators who are in a position to handle translation and interpretational challenges. These issues speak to the important role that universities have in affecting the language of record by ensuring that LLB graduates are linguistically competent, that legal terminology is produced and widely disseminated, and that degrees in legal translation and interpretation are offered. We discuss the latter points in Chapters 8 and 9. The point is that there is a breakdown in communication between academia and practice. The judiciary appears reluctant to engage forensic linguists and other experts on the matter of formulating sound language policies for courts, again bringing into question whether these pilot projects are doomed from commencement, and whether that was the plan.

On a somewhat positive note, the Chief Magistrates' Forum in 2014 concluded a report entitled, *Preliminary report on indigenous language courts.* The report was never publicly pronounced nor made available, but Ndlovu J extracts the contents thereof, which we quote here in full from the judgment (2016:8-9):

> That Executive Committee of the Chief Magistrates Forum must seek the guidance of the Chief Justice on the Language Policy as regards the MC(s). That the Executive Committee of the Chief Magistrates forum must establish, through the Office of the Chief Justice, as to whether the Department of Justice and Constitutional Development has ensured that there are proper structures to adequately, and timeously transcribe, and translate proceedings recorded in any of the nine indigenous languages into English. That the Chief Magistrates Forum in the meantime to do an audit of indigenous languages predominantly in use within Administrative Regions, in order to assist the National Department responsible for language policy in determining the most used languages within specific clusters and/or sub-clusters, for purposes of service level agreements with service providers of translation services. That the Chief Magistrates Forum must inform Mr Dawood that the Forum would not, for reasons specified in the report, support the use of indigenous languages in any courtroom for any proceedings, as long as it is practical to do so. That the Chief Magistrates Forum must inform Mr Dawood that the Forum would not, for reasons specified in the report, support the idea of 'indigenous language courts', but that it would take practical steps and positive measures to elevate the status and advance the of languages with historically diminished use and status in all the courts of the Republic of South Africa.

To date, implementation based on the above has been non-existent and it remains another report to add to the heap that provides no practical effect for the broader citizenry. It resembles, to an extent, the LANGTAG report (1996) where findings and recommendations were made, but implementation was lacking. As seen with the Language Policy of the Department of Justice and Constitutional Development (2019), the language of record issue is not dealt with and, instead, there is reference to legislation.

The second case was the criminal case of *State* v *Gordon* (2018), commencing with a District court sitting at a Periodical court seated in Darling, a small town in the Western Cape Province of South Africa. The case was transferred for sentencing to a Regional court seated in Malmesbury, another town in the Western Cape. The Regional court then referred the case to the Western Cape High Court on review, questioning whether the proceedings were in accordance with the administration of justice. The case was heard in Afrikaans in the court *a quo*.

According to Thulare AJ (2018:14), the Magistrate had a duty to ensure that his acts and the proceedings were captured and preserved for authority, truth, testimony and memory, especially for the possibility of review and appeal. Thulare AJ was referring to the importance of conducting the trial in a language used on appeal and review, namely English. This correlated with this comment to the magistrate:

> The proceedings were conducted in Afrikaans, against the backdrop of the direction of the Chief Justice that English is the language of record of all courts in the Republic of South Africa.

The Magistrate responded to this comment stating the following:

> I am aware of the directives of the Chief Justice and of the Honourable Judge President Hlophe dated 28 February 2018. The proceedings in this case had already started in Afrikaans on 11 July 2016 before another presiding officer. This trial was dealt with at the Periodical court of Darling. Because the accused decided to conduct his own defence and is also Afrikaans speaking, I decided to proceed in Afrikaans.

The Magistrate adopted a practical perspective while giving effective meaning to the language rights of an Afrikaans speaking accused in a province in which Afrikaans is the second most spoken language. Thulare AJ, however, did not stop following this response. Instead, what followed in the judgment was a series of contradictory statements. Thulare AJ (2018:28) acknowledged the understaffing of courts and the scarcity of interpreters and how these issues resulted in unnecessary delays. Thulare AJ, however, then proceeded to state the following:

> The expense and delay occasioned by both transcription and translation is immediately mitigated by the use of English.

A costs-based argument is again employed; yet the costs to the administration of justice, an accused's language rights, as well as the obligation in Section 6 of the Constitution to elevate the status of African language through practical and positive means, are simply overlooked. Thulare AJ (2018:35) misconstrues Section 6 and his mandate, validating his reason by stating the following:

> In the spirit of Section 6(3) (a) of the Constitution, the Heads of Courts elected English as the official language for purposes of litigation in our courts. In that way litigants from Khayelitsha cannot shop for their own Judge by constructively excluding Burns-Ward J from their matters through the use of isiXhosa in the same way that litigants from Langebaan cannot shop for their Judge by excluding Boqwana J by conducting the proceedings in Afrikaans, or litigants from the Cape Flats exclude Dolamo J by using the lingua franca.

This excerpt racialises the language question, where Black judges are associated with African languages and White judges with either English or Afrikaans. This line of thinking excludes the possibility of bilingual and multilingual judges and confines judges to the profile of being monolingual. According to Thulare AJ (2018:37), the onus rests with the Department of Justice and Constitutional Development to make available resources and systems to transcribe and translate expeditiously the court records of proceedings from other languages into English. Until such time, Thulare AJ (2018:37) stated that magistrates should heed the directive of the CJ and proceed with English as the sole official language of record. Thulare AJ (2018:34), in a sense, defended the directive by the Heads of Courts through the following statement:

> The leadership of the judiciary had the difficult task to trace the correct footing in balancing the needs and preferences of the population as a whole, considering the sometimes competing interest of, but free from, any misplaced allegiance of the masses, the intellectuals, economic, social and political influences in the spirit of one, sovereign, democratic state founded on our constitutional values. As the nation walks towards achieving the progressive realisation of an elevated status and advanced use of all official languages in our courts, the Heads of Courts could only cut the cloth to the size that fits the nation today.

This validation came on the back of Thulare AJ (2018:32) criticising, to a certain extent, Docrat's (2017a) Master of Arts degree research which deals broadly with the status of African languages in the South African legal system under the notion of transformation.

> Academics have the intellectual integrity and moral courage to argue about what the language of record should be in our courts. [*The Role of African Languages in the South African Legal System: Towards a Transformative Agenda;* A thesis submitted in fulfilment of the requirements for the degree of Master of Arts, Rhodes University by Zakeera Docrat, November 2017]. They can afford to argue about the law. Judges do not have the luxury to argue about what the law should be. They have a constitutional obligation to apply the law. The nation expects judges to resolve disputes expeditiously in a manner that is user-friendly, practical and cost-effective.

It is ill-conceived to defend a directive by stating that the judiciary had to cut its cloth to fit the nation today given that the majority of people in South Africa do not speak English as a mother tongue and many have limited, if any, English language skills. Furthermore, shifting the onus back to the Department of Justice and Constitutional Development, who shifted the onus to the legislature, is simply shifting the goal posts in favour of pursuing an English-only mandate, undermining the constitutional rights, values and principles.

The discussion – concerning the historical background and development of the language of record in South African courts and how political agendas were responsible for shaping these language policies and ultimately marginalising people on grounds of language – makes questionable the validation by Thulare AJ (2018) that a political, social and economic agenda is not being pursued. An English-only language of record does not serve the interests of the majority; there is no compromise, as such, the balancing act that Thulare AJ (2018) suggests has not happened. Our criticism can be substantiated through the application of the sliding scale formula (Currie & De Waal, 2005) advanced earlier, taking into account "…the number of speakers in a given area; their concentration; as well as the seriousness of the service involved" (Currie & De Waal, 2005:632).

Applying this to the *State* v *Gordon* case (2018), how can the Magistrate have been expected to heed the directive in an area where the majority of people are Afrikaans mother tongue speakers, in addition to the constitutional rights of an accused person to defend himself to the best of his ability and knowledge? It is thus contradictory for Thulare AJ (2018:38) to have stated the following in an attempt to validate the use of English and place an emphasis on interpretation, rather than proceeding directly in other languages used in these geographical areas of South Africa:

> Periodical courts are generally in far-flung areas away from the cities and towns. They are generally found in townships, villages and farms. These are generally settlement areas where the vast majority of the previously disadvantaged people are found. They are vulnerable because of levels of illiteracy. This matter showed that even the guardians sometimes need to be guarded. The provision of elementary resources like functionality literate Clerks of the Court, Court Machines and Court interpreters are very necessary at these courts. It cannot be, that justice is divisible and those from outside the cities find themselves in the island of miseries within the sea of a democratic and constitutional South Africa.

The case of *State* v *Gordon* (2018) also brings to the fore the far-reaching effects the directive has on the lower courts and thus does not just apply to the High Courts, as stated by both the CJ and Hlophe JP.

Interpretational cases

Our focus turns to the 'general' case law concerning language in court proceedings, where interpretational issues are highlighted. There is overlap with the language of record cases above, and this will be identified where necessary.

The case of *State* v *Lesaena* (1993) concerned a self-represented Afrikaans mother tongue speaking accused. The accused appealed both conviction and sentence on the grounds that his right to a fair trial was infringed upon (1993:264g) on the grounds that he was not permitted by the Magistrate in the court *a quo* to conduct his defence in a language of his choice, namely Afrikaans. The Magistrate stopped the accused from presenting his case in Afrikaans and cross-examining a witness in Afrikaans (1993:264-265). On appeal, the court held that the right to a fair trial was determined in relation to the language used. Mohamed J (1993:265) explained the importance of language within the right to a fair trial, stating that an accused must be:

> ...accorded the fairest and fullest opportunity to articulate his defence, to marshal his submissions and to present his evidence to the court with the most effective linguistic and intellectual resources at his command.

The court therefore held that, by denying the accused the right to present evidence in Afrikaans, a fundamental irregularity in the proceedings had occurred (1993:265). The court, in substantiating the fact that a procedural irregularity had occurred, advanced that any interference of the right, "...however laudable the motive..." (1993:265), resulted in a fundamental subversion of the right to a fair trial. With Van Dyk J concurring, Mohamed J found that the procedural irregularity resulted in a "fundamental injustice". The appeal was successful and both conviction and sentence were set aside (1993:265). The *State* v *Lesaena* (1993) judgment illustrates the importance of language use in courts and how it directly affects the right to a fair trial. In contrast to the case *State* v *Damani* (2016), a language of choice was entrenched, as opposed to a language understood by the accused.

The case of *State* v *Ndala* (1996) concerned a special review brought within the ambit of Section 25(3) (i) of the Interim Constitution (1993b), currently Section 35(3) (k) of the Constitution. The accused did not understand either English or Afrikaans – the official languages of record at the time – so an interpreter was provided. The accused testified in his defence and his evidence was followed by an adjournment. During the adjournment, the Magistrate was alerted to the fact that the interpreter had not been sworn in, as is required.

The court held that the accused's right to a fair trial included the right to be tried in a language they understand; and this included having the proceedings interpreted for the accused. It was the duty of the Magistrate to "ensure that the accused is sufficiently conversant with the language in which the evidence is being presented and to use a competent interpreter if necessary" (1996:219). The right to a competent interpreter is of prime importance, especially when the language the accused understands is not an official language of the court (1996:219). The Magistrate therefore failed in their duty to ensure a competent interpreter is before court, resulting in a gross procedural irregularity. The Court held further that interpretation after the fact is not permitted, as was done by the Magistrate in an attempt to remedy the issue. The *State* v *Ndala* case (1996) highlights the problematic nature of interpretation, the lack of linguistic training of judicial officers, and how both adversely affect the course of justice for both the complainant and accused persons.

The case of *State* v *Matomela* (1998) overlaps with the cases of *State* v *Damani* (2016) and *State* v *Gordon* (2018). The court *a quo* heard the entire case in isiXhosa. On automatic review, Tshabalala J (as he was then) posed the following questions to the Magistrate:

> Why was the evidence, conviction and sentence in the Xhosa language? Is this in terms of an instruction from the Department of Justice? Full reasons are required.

The response from the Senior Magistrate was recorded as follows:

> The fact that the evidence was recorded in Xhosa, is not in terms of an instruction from the Department of Justice, but due to the following reasons: (a) On the day that this matter came before Court, we had a shortage of interpreters. The matter would of necessity have to be postponed because of this. This would have caused the complainant in the matter further hardship. (b) When I was approached for assistance, I ascertained that the parties were all Xhosa speaking. The presiding officer is Xhosa and could thus communicate with the parties. I instructed the presiding officer to continue with the case in the language that the accused understood. The recording of the evidence was discussed between us. I advised that the recording be done in Xhosa. The reason for that was that I did not want the presiding officer to act as an interpreter. I believe and submit that this procedure at the time was the best we could do.

According to Hlophe (2000:692), further reasons for the use of isiXhosa as a language of record included the fact that isiXhosa is one of the 11 official languages and compliance is required with Section 6(1), read together with subsections (2) and (4) of the Constitution. Tshabalala J (1998) found the above reasons to be fair and reasonable under the circumstances. Tshabalala J (1998) discussed the practicalities of hearing cases in African languages and the limitations thereof imposed on an accused. As such, he stated:

> This is a matter that I consider should receive the urgent attention of the national legislature before injustices occur as a result of the present situation. An untenable situation would have arisen if the accused in this case were represented by a person who did not understand the Xhosa language. His case would not proceed and the complainant would be inconvenienced (1998:341-342).

Based on Tshabalala J's (1998) statements, it seemed that he was urging the legislature to draft legislation that would obligate legal practitioners and judicial officers to undergo vocation-specific language training. This was not, however, what Tshabalala J (1998:342) had in mind:

> In my judgment, the best solution is to have one official language for courts as stated above. All official languages must enjoy parity of esteem and be treated equitability but for practical reasons and for better administration of justice one official language of record will resolve the problem. Such a language should be one which can be understood by all court officials irrespective of their mother tongue.

The conflicting statements and reasoning supporting a monolingual language of record policy resembles the reasoning in the cases of *State v Damani* (2016) and *State v Gordon* (2018). Everything, including the reasoning, points to the need to have bilingual and multilingual language of record policies in courts; however, suddenly the judges opt for a monolingual language of record policy.

The case of *Mthethwa v De Bruin No and Another* (1998) dealt with the contents of Section 35(3) (k) of the Constitution and whether it conferred a language right of choice or a right to understand the proceedings. The accused was a mother tongue isiZulu speaker residing in Vryheid (KwaZulu-Natal). The accused applied for his trial to be conducted in isiZulu given that it was his mother tongue and an official language as per Section 6(1) of the Constitution. The application was dismissed, and it was ordered that the case be heard in English or Afrikaans, or both the official languages of record at the time.

Upon review, the Applicant argued that the failure to allow him to be tried in the official language of choice, isiZulu, was both unlawful and unconstitutional. The Applicant apparently understood English; however, the extent to which he understood English was not clear. Similar to the *State v Damani* (2016) case, the court on review, provided that, of 37 regional magistrates, only 4 had isiZulu as their mother tongue, 33 had English or Afrikaans, or both, as their mother tongue, with no proficiency in isiZulu. Of 256 prosecutors, only 81 were isiZulu speaking, while 135 were English or Afrikaans mother tongue speakers, or spoke both (Hlophe, 2000:691). Of 41 state advocates, 6 where able to speak isiZulu as their mother tongue; and 35 were either English or Afrikaans speakers (Hlophe, 2000:691). With these statistics made available, Howard JP (1998:338) held:

> Under these circumstances, as they obtain in this province [KwaZulu-Natal] at present, it is clearly not practicable for an accused person to demand to have the proceedings conducted in any language other than English or Afrikaans. Section 35(3) (k) does not give an accused person the right to have a trial conducted in the language of his choice. Its provisions are perfectly plain, namely, that he has a right to be tried in a language he understands or, if that is not practicable, to have proceedings interpreted in that language.

Although the statistics provided in the *Mthethwa v De Bruin NO and Another* (1998) case date back 19 years, the point remains that there is an intrinsic need to transform and create a more inclusive justice system that is representative of the country's language demographics. Howard JP (1998:338) was using English and Afrikaans as a yardstick; and if an accused could not comprehend English, interpretation services would be made available.

In the case of *State* v *Pienaar* (2000), the accused was an Afrikaans mother tongue speaker who was assigned an English mother tongue legal representative (through the state's legal aid services). Given the language barriers between the accused and his legal representative, the accused elected to represent himself. The accused informed the Magistrate of the language barrier and therefore the reasons why he was representing himself. An alternate legal representative was not assigned to the accused. The primary question on review was whether the accused had been prejudiced by the absence of legal representation. The court commenced by examining the content of the right to a fair trial and found that it included the right to legal representation, where the respective legal representative was able to communicate with the accused in his or her own language (2000:144). The court held that communication between the accused and legal representative must take place directly in the accused's mother tongue or, in exceptional circumstances, through an interpreter (ibid, 145). The presiding officer was obliged to inform and explain this right to the accused (ibid).

The second stage of the enquiry saw the court engage with how this right is implemented within the practical situation of a trial. The court explained that the implementation of the right was dependent on the obligation conferred upon government through Section 35(3)(k) of the Constitution. Specifically, the obligation vested in the Department of Justice (as it was then) to ensure that the languages in each province (namely, for the case at hand, the Northern Cape) which are used "overwhelmingly" be used and promoted to ensure the eventual attainment of equality and status, through equitable treatment (ibid). This line of implementation would be in accordance with Section 6 of the Constitution. The court said that the question for determination was whether the accused had this right when legal representation was provided for by the State (ibid).

The court engaged with the language demographics pertaining to courts situated in the Northern Cape found that Afrikaans was the language most used. Additionally, while Afrikaans was used in 72% of cases, English was used in only 1.4% of cases (ibid). The court stated that the English *status quo* was in fact a policy directive of the then Department of Justice (ibid) which was appointing English-speaking presiding officers and public defence attorneys (ibid). The court explained that the Department of Justice's English-only language of record policy would have "phenomenal cost and quality implications" (2000:145), with sole reliance placed on interpretation; furthermore, that the policy position would be in direct conflict with Section 6(4) of the Constitution (ibid).

The court stated that both Section 6 of the Magistrates' Courts Act (1944) and Section 6(1) of the Constitution conferred a right on the accused to be tried in Afrikaans. Therefore, no interpretation of Section 35(3)(k) of the Constitution "could restrict that right" (ibid); and their interpretation of the law was not impractical. The court validated their interpretation, explaining that the Department of Justice had to comply with Section 6 of the Constitution (ibid, 145-146). This, according to the court, entails the languages of the Northern Cape being promoted to enjoy equal status alongside English. In those cases – where it was not practical to try an Afrikaans speaking accused in Afrikaans, or to provide an accused with a legal representative who was competent in Afrikaans – this had come about through the failure of the Department of Justice and the Legal Aid Board to give effect to the provisions of the Constitution (ibid, 146). The Magistrate had an obligation but had failed to fulfil it, as the language right was not fully explained to the accused and this had resulted in the right to a fair trial being infringed, resulting in an irregularity in the proceedings (ibid).

The *State* v *Pienaar* case (2000) offers purposive interpretation of the language rights provisions in favour of accused persons who are disadvantaged by an English-only language of record policy. The judgment also places the onus upon the state, in particular the Department of Justice and Constitutional Development, to develop language policies that are practical and give meaning to the language demographics of each province while implementing the rights.

The case of *State* v *Siyotula* (2003) is similar to the case of *State* v *Ndala* (1996) in that it deals with interpretational irregularities. The accused was an isiXhosa mother tongue speaker who gave his evidence in isiXhosa, after which 18 witnesses gave their testimony. After all the evidence had been led, the court *a quo* found that the interpreter was not sworn in, as per Rules 68(3) and 68(5) of the Magistrates' Courts Rules.

On review, the primary question was whether there was an irregularity in the proceedings. The court explained that, where a trial is conducted in a language that the accused does not fully understand and that language is not interpreted correctly into the language of the accused, a 'proper' trial has not taken place (2003:157). The court held (2002:158) that "understand" in Section 35(3) (k) refers to full comprehension and not partial understanding, as held in the case of *State* v *Ngubane* (1995).

The primary question for determination in instances such as these should be whether the irregularity produced a "miscarriage of justice" (2003:157). Factually dependent and variable from case to case the court should be satisfied '...if the irregularity can be cured without prejudice to the parties" (2003:158). In the *State* v *Siyotula* case (2003), the adopted purposive interpretation focuses on ensuring the language rights of the accused are prioritised. This case, again, highlights the issues associated with interpretation with an English-only language of record policy.

The case of *State* v *Damoyi* (2004) concerned an isiXhosa mother tongue accused who, in the court *a quo*, appeared for trial on several occasions; however, the trial could not proceed as no interpreter was available. On a subsequent appearance of the accused, the interpreter remained absent. On this occasion, the Magistrate resolved to conduct the entire trial in isiXhosa as the magistrate, state prosecutor and accused were isiXhosa-speaking

(2004:122). The proceedings were recorded in isiXhosa (2004:123). The Magistrate detailed to the Review Judge the reasons why the record appeared in isiXhosa. These included: not unduly delaying the accused the right to a fair trial; the prosecutor and Magistrate spoke isiXhosa proficiently; isiXhosa was also one of the 11 official languages; and isiXhosa was one of the three official languages of the Western Cape, according to Section 5(3) of the Constitution of the Province of the Western Cape (2004:123).

Yekiso J (2004:122) noted that the language question had evaded the courts, and had not been resolved since the advent of democracy:

> If parity of the 11 official languages were to be adhered to in court proceedings it could result in a considerable strain on resources, which could, in turn, impact negatively on the quality of service delivery and efficiency in the administration of justice.

Yekiso J (2004:123) was satisfied that the facts of the case before him, the trial conducted in isiXhosa, was "in accordance with justice". The Review Judge's comments regarding the "tremendous problems" experienced in translating the isiXhosa record into English were noted with concern by Yekiso J. Yekiso J (2004:123) enquired of the DPP what the Department of Justice's language policy was regarding the use of an official language other than English or Afrikaans (or both) being used as a language of record. The DPP stated that no language policy existed, that the languages of record were English and Afrikaans. They supplied the following statistics from an audit in proficiency in official languages within the Directorate:

> ... [of] 262 prosecutors in the lower courts in the Western Cape, only 62 are African and proficient in an indigenous language and only 3 advocates out of 36 in the office of the Director of Public Prosecutions are able to speak one or more indigenous languages (2004:123).

Yekiso J (2004) held that this was contrary to the provisions of Section 6(2) and (4), read together with Section 35(3) (k) of the Constitution. Yekiso J (2004:125) held that the issue rests in the provisions of the Constitution, which 'falls short' of addressing the use of official languages in court proceedings. It must be noted that Yekiso J (2004) did not explicate the legislature's role in filling the 'gap' where the Constitution does not pronounce on the matter of the language of record in courts. We make this point in light of Cameron's (2013) statements advanced earlier that the Constitution is merely a framework that requires further interpretation through legislative and policy means.

In the case of *State* v *Manzini* (2007) the accused was an isiZulu speaker; his trial was, however, conducted in English with the assistance of an interpreter (2007:107). During sentencing, the accused alleged that his evidence was not interpreted correctly, prompting the Magistrate to refer the record to the chief interpreter to confirm whether this was, in fact, correct (2007:107). The chief interpreter found "numerous errors" in interpretation and concluded by stating that the interpretation was 'alarmingly poor' (2007:107). The

Magistrate concluded that the interpretational discrepancies did not affect the course of the trial, particularly the evidence imparted by the accused. As such, the verdict would be unchanged (2007:107), following which the court sentenced the accused (2007:107).

Tshiqi J and Schwatzman J (2007), concurring with each other, held that if incorrect interpretation had occurred, the Magistrate would not be in a position to determine the credibility of the witness imparting evidence in isiZulu. This would adversely affect the Magistrate's ability to evaluate such evidence and obstruct the legal representatives from preparing arguments in mitigation and aggravation of sentence (2007:107). This would also affect the outcome of the case, particularly whether or not to convict the accused. The Magistrate failed to recognise the importance of language as part of the right to a fair trial. The court held that Section 35(3) (k) of the Constitution had been adversely affected and ordered that the appeal succeed, and conviction and sentence be set aside (2007:110).

Language in education right cases

Although there are fewer cases concerning the language in education right for higher education, two of five cases are constitutional court judgments and thus precedent-setting. The first case concerned the 'new' language policy at UP, referred to in preceding chapters of this book.

The case of *AfriForum and Another* v *Chairperson of the Council of the University of Pretoria and Others* (2017) commenced with an application brought by Applicants: AfriForum and Solidarity, Afrikaans lobby rights groups against the Chairman of the Council of the UP, as well as the Minster of Higher Education, cited as a fourth Respondent.

The facts of the case were that the UP changed its language policy in 1993 to one which was bilingual (English and Afrikaans) and included Sepedi as a third language. English and Afrikaans were recognised as languages of instruction and communication, while Sepedi was recognised as a language of communication in the policy. The bilingual policy was reaffirmed by the relevant university structures in 2003. In 2016, the university, acting under the authority of Senate and Council, enacted a new policy which removed Afrikaans as a language of instruction and made English the sole official language of learning and teaching. The development of Afrikaans and Sepedi would be promoted. So, effectively, the 2016 policy, in addition to removing Afrikaans as a language of instruction and communication, also removed Sepedi as a language of communication. The Applicants therefore sought to review the decisions and have them set aside. A side point is necessary here; reviewing of decisions of an authoritative nature falls within the ambit of administrative law, as discussed in Chapter 5. The Applicants sought the review on three grounds of law:

1. The decision should be reviewed, as it is non-responsive to the language in education right, Section 29(2) of the Constitution.
2. The decision constitutes a denial of the right in Section 9 of the Constitution.
3. The decision constitutes a withdrawal of existing rights of current and future students.

The Respondents argued that the 2016 language policy did not violate the Section 29(2) right; and if the court found that the right was limited, it would be justifiable in accordance with Section 36(1) of the Constitution.

The first and overarching enquiry, according to Kollapen J (2017:13), was to determine whether the decision was reasonably practicable, taking into account relevant factors: equity, reasonable practicability and historical redress. With competing constitutional and administrative issues, a two-pronged approach must be adopted. The first stage of the approach concerns the identification of a right and whether it can be limited. The constitutional issue of Section 29(2) is that the right can be diminished with sound justification. Kollapen J (2017) therefore held that the right was limited and that it was justifiably limited in that all students were disadvantaged equally by the English-only language policy. Disposing swiftly of the constitutional enquiry, Kollapen J moved on to determine whether the decision was lawful and justifiable in the circumstances within the ambit of administrative law. Kollapen J adopted a narrowed view, stating that the function of the court was merely to ensure that decision makers, who were entrusted with performing the function, had done so. The UP had therefore taken the decision entrusted upon them through the empowering provisions of the Ministerial Policy and the HEA (1997).

The second stage of the two-pronged approach was determining the reasonability of the decision and that hinges on the fairness. Kollapen J turned to the *Bato Star Fishing (Pty) Ltd v Minister of Environmental Affairs and Others* case (2004) discussed in Chapter 5. In this instance, the case was used as a precedent in administrative law and the factors in determining the reasonability of the decision and the fairness of the process, namely:

> ...the nature of the decision; identity and expertise of the decision maker; range of factors relevant to the decision; reasons given for the decision; nature of competing interests; as well as the impact of the decision on the lives and well-being of those affected.

In applying these factors to the case at hand, Kollapen J held that the poll conducted in 2010 by the UP constituted a high level of engagement and thoroughness. The poll also illustrated that, in addition to research done by the UP, there was a steady decline in home language Afrikaans speakers, amounting to 25.1% of the student population. As a result of this reasoning, the application was accordingly dismissed.

The second case, *AfriForum and Another* v *Chairman of the Council of the University of the Free State and Others* (2016), involved an application being brought by AfriForum as the first Applicant against the chairman of the UFS Council and others. The application was brought as a result of a decision by the UFS to change the language of instruction to English only. Prior to this decision in 2016, a parallel medium of instruction language policy had been in place dating back to 1993 and reaffirmed in 2003. There were similar policy developments to the UP as evidenced above; and the policy removed Afrikaans from use for teacher education and theology courses. The Applicants' argument was based on three primary grounds with sub-allegations. We have extracted those relevant to our discussions at hand:

> In reaching the decision to adopt the new language policy of the UFS, the Council and Senate were unconcerned with:
> (i) considering whether it remain reasonably practicable for the UFS to offer Afrikaans as a medium of instruction, by having regard to the relevant factors to be brought into account in such an assessment;
> (ii) the legal implications of its election forthwith to deprive Afrikaans speaking students (current and prospective) of the opportunity to assert their Section 29(2) right at the UFS;
>   (a) the UFS Council and Senate were also unconcerned and did not take into account (or effectively so) the result of a poll conducted across all three campuses that demonstrated substantial support for parallel medium of instruction, with 3323 students in favour thereof compared to the 1107 that favoured English with tutorials in Afrikaans and Sesotho.
>   (b) The Language Committee tasked with preparing a report on the new language policy left it to the Council of the UFS to consider the legal and constitutional implications of its adoption. The UFS council took no internal or external legal advice on this issue. Both members of the UFS Senate and the members of the UFS Council making the decision were led to believe that no constitutional issue for consideration arose.

Against these issues, the Applicants attacked the decision, arguing that:

- relevant considerations were left out of account;
- account was taken of irrelevant considerations; and/or a material error of law influenced the adoption of the new language policy;
- no rational connection existed between the decision to adopt the new language policy and the purpose for doing so, the purpose of the empowering provision and/or the information available to the decision-maker; and
- the decision to adopt the new policy was otherwise unconstitutional or unlawful.

The Respondents argued that the language policy was adopted for transformational and academic reasons with the aim of achieving integration (2016:para. 48). Hendricks J was guided by the *dictum* in the case of *Head of Department: Mpumalanga Department of Education and Another* v *Hoërskool Ermelo and Another* (2010), where Moseneke DCJ stated the following:

> ...it is an injunction on the state to consider all reasonable educational alternatives which are not limited to, but include, single medium institutions. In resorting to an option, such as single or parallel/dual medium instruction, the state must take into account what is fair, feasible and satisfies the need to remedy the results of racially past discriminatory laws and practices. When a person already enjoys the benefit of being taught in an official language of choice, the state bears the negative duty not to take away or diminish the right without appropriate justification.

The point of reasonableness emanates from this excerpt; and Hendricks J reasoned that the UFS would have been required to adopt reasonable measures to fulfil current and prospective students' rights to receive education in both English and Afrikaans. Furthermore, for a single medium to be preferred to another reasonable practicable institutional arrangement, such as dual medium, it must be demonstrated that it is more likely to advance or satisfy the listed criteria of equity, practicability and historical redress. There are two parts in determining whether the decision was equitable. Following this line of reasoning, Hendricks J applied each of the three criteria in Section 29(2) (a)-(c), as advanced above, to the facts at hand.

Equity, according to Hendricks J, comprises two parts. The first part is an academic assessment in which case the vast majority of students (Black, mother tongue African language speakers) will not benefit from the new language policy, given that they are neither English nor Afrikaans mother tongue speakers. Secondly, the new language policy, by disposing of Afrikaans, violates Afrikaans speakers' right to be taught in their language of choice, as entrenched in Section 29(2) of the Constitution. The second criterion of practicability was disposed of with minimal engagement, given that Hendricks J was of the view that it was not impracticable to have a dual medium language of instruction policy. The redress criterion is inserted to ensure that language is not a barrier in accessing education, especially for Black, Indian and Coloured students. Applying this understanding to the facts before him, Hendricks J found that the new language policy does not favour "new over old". Hendricks J held that the 'old' policy favoured multilingualism, and that Afrikaans alone may be a barrier to many Black students, but that English may be a barrier to Coloured students.

Hendricks J held that, by abandoning the dual medium of English and Afrikaans, the decision to adopt the new language policy was inconsistent with the Ministerial Policy designed to promote multilingualism and enhance equity and access in Higher Education institutions through the retention and strengthening of Afrikaans as a language of scholarship and science. The belief of the decision-makers, that integration and transformation would justify their decision, without them taking into account factors universally accepted to form part of the reasonable practicability standard in Section 29(2) of the Constitution, constituted a material error of law. Hendricks J accordingly ordered that the decision be reviewed and set aside.

The decision was taken on appeal to the Supreme Court of Appeal (SCA) by the UFS, who were successful. Given that the appeal process did not end with the SCA appeal, the precedent-setting judgment of the CC is advanced. AfriForum applied to the CC for leave to appeal. Leave to appeal was not granted by the majority, with three judges dissenting.

Mogoeng CJ, writing the judgment of the majority, first considered whether the decision to formulate a language policy constituted an administrative action, in terms of administrative law. Mogoeng CJ (2018:17) explained that the requirements for an administrative action needed to be satisfied; and, in applying the facts thereto, the decision was not administrative in nature as it did not satisfy the listed grounds. It was not administrative action, according to Mogoeng CJ, as UFS's Council was not designated to make administrative decisions; and determining policy by nature is executive and not administrative. He therefore held that the appeal was grounded on legality. According to Mogoeng CJ (2018:17), the appeal gave rise to two key issues or questions to be determined:

1. Whether the UFS acted consistently with the provisions of Section 29(2) of the Constitution.
2. Did the UFS when adopting the new language policy, pay adequate attention to the Ministerial Language Policy concerning the language of instruction.

With regard to the language right in Section 29(2), the equity test emerging from the provision needed to be satisfied (Mogoeng, 2017:23). It would be equitable to maintain Afrikaans as a medium of instruction when the Section 29(2) right is exercised in a manner that is not inconsistent with any other provision and does not undermine any "constitutional aspiration or value". The exercise of the right to be taught in a language of choice must not "... pose a threat to racial harmony or inadvertently nurture racial supremacy" (ibid).

In applying this reasoning to the facts, Mogoeng CJ (2018:23) stated that the primary question arising is whether Afrikaans "had a comfortable co-existence with our collective aspiration to heal the divisions of the past or has it impeded the prospects of our unity in our diversity?". Mogoeng CJ consequently found that learning was racialised. White students were attending the lectures taught in Afrikaans, while Black students were attending lectures conducted in English.

Moving swiftly to the second issue concerning the Ministerial Language Policy framework, Mogoeng CJ held that the UFS had acted in accordance with the framework. Mogoeng CJ held that the UFS had ensured that a language of instruction (Afrikaans) not be employed where it creates racial segregation and does not heed the internal modifiers in the Section 29(2) right for equity, practicability and the need to redress the past discrimination. The majority thus held that the adoption of the language policy was lawful and valid and leave to appeal was accordingly denied (ibid, 79).

Although the majority ruled that leave to appeal was denied, Froneman J dissented, with Cameron J and Pretorius AJ concurring in the dissenting judgment. Commencing with the dissenting judgment, Froneman J (2018:para. 82) stated that it would have been in the interests of justice to have heard the matter *viva voce* and thus grant leave to appeal. It was explained that Mogoeng CJ, similarly to the SCA who had heard the case prior to this, had denied speakers of an official language (Afrikaans) the right to exercise their right in accessing education in their mother tongue. The "factual and normative" boundaries within which the Constitution permits the implementation of Section 29(2) must be explained; this, however, had not occurred (ibid, para. 83). The dissenting judgment advanced that one primary question arises for determination:

> …what circumstances would justify prevention of a person receiving education in a language of choice as prescribed in Section 29(2) of the Constitution?

This, according to Froneman J (2018:para. 85), is two-pronged, where a 'proper' interpretation of Section 29(2) of the Constitution should be advanced, as well as the role of the Ministerial Language Policy, in formulating language policies. With regard to the majority judgment, there was no engagement on the parameters of the right in Section 29(2) of the Constitution; instead, the judgment focused primarily on the use of Afrikaans as a racist tool, as was the case during Apartheid (Froneman, 2017:para. 91). What the main judgment failed to do is state that other official languages (African languages) should be imposed on Afrikaans and English speakers to ensure parity of esteem. To this effect, Mogoeng CJ made no reference to the state's obligation to advance the other official languages (ibid, para. 91).

Froneman J explained that it was "ironic" that the majority harped on the Afrikaans "historical oppression" bandwagon in favour of English, a language with a longer history of colonial oppression. Froneman J (2018:123) quoted Moseneke DCJ in the *Ermelo* case, who termed it "collateral irony" that learners and parents chose English, as opposed to their own African languages, as medium of instruction. Froneman J (2018:123) questioned whether discrimination would be found if an African language was used as a medium of instruction as the majority judgment states that the exercise of official languages, other than English, results in exclusion and discrimination – fostering segregation. Froneman J (2018:115-123) reasoned further that, by granting leave to appeal, students, affected persons and experts could have provided their input on Afrikaans and the other official languages as mediums of instruction.

With regard to the second issue of the Ministerial Language Policy, Froneman J (2018:115) held that there was no evidence presented to inform a decision by the majority, as noted in Mogoeng CJ's judgment advanced above, that students receiving instruction in a language of choice (Afrikaans, in this case) were guilty of racial discrimination. This did not justify the finding that the Section 29(2) right can be limited on grounds of entrenching racism and segregation. Furthermore, the Ministerial Language Policy stated that the current situation of English and Afrikaans as mediums of instruction should only be endured until the African languages have been developed to be used as mediums of instruction at higher education institutions. This, according to Froneman J (2018:94), was in concurrence with the objectives of the Ministerial Policy which recognises the constitutional imperative for African languages to be promoted and advanced in reversing the past historical marginalisation.

In conclusion, Froneman J (2018:127) held that the majority judgment's reasoning and order "... does not bode well for the establishment and nurturing of languages other than Afrikaans and English as languages of higher learning". The CC's constitutional duty is to create space for other official languages. That is what true unity in diversity entails. On this note, Froneman J (2018) held that he would have granted leave to appeal.

The third case concerning language policies is *Gelyke Kanse and Others v The Chairman of the Senate of the Stellenbosch University and Others* (2017). The case in the court *a quo* concerned an application brought against the chairman of SU. The Applicants asked the court to review and set aside decisions by Senate and Council to adopt a new monolingual English language policy in terms of Section 27(2) of the HEA (1997). The crux of the Applicant's argument was that the new language policy was contrary to Section 29(2) of the Constitution as it promoted and adopted the sole use of English to the exclusion of the other ten official languages.

Dlodlo J and Savage J, concurring with each other, held that the language policy conformed with the constitutional provisions, specifically Section 29(2). According to Dlodlo J, it was reasonably practicable in the circumstances to adopt the new language policy to ensure equity and equal access, while redressing the past discrimination. Language – and specifically Afrikaans – was once again associated with race and, in this instance, White, Afrikaans speaking people, to the exclusion of all Coloured Afrikaans speaking students. The role of African languages as official languages was not dealt with by the court. The application was subsequently dismissed with costs.

The case law examples are all linked having commenced with the cases dealing primarily with the question of the language of record. The preceding cases have highlighted the numerous issues concerning interpretation in courts and how the rights of both the accused and complainants were adversely affected. The cases have also illustrated that African languages could be used as languages of record where there were sufficient competent legal translators to translate the record for appeal and review processes. This would circumvent the numerous interpretational errors of both a procedural and substantive nature. The issue of legal language terminology development in relation to the university language policies, as raised in the case of *State* v *Damani* (2016), will be dealt with in the forthcoming chapters of this book. Suffice to say at this point in the discussion, terminology is being produced on a large scale, especially at UKZN. On the point of universities, the language policy cases highlight again the narrow approach adopted by the judges when interpreting language rights; and it is clear that English is seen as a unifying medium, not taking into account the barriers that English-only language of instruction policies create for African language and Afrikaans speaking students. Given the language situation and language complexities highlighted through the other case law, it proves more than pivotal to ensure graduates are bilingual or multilingual when leaving university. Instead, the mother tongue of students is undermined and underdeveloped.

The argument that English monolingual language policies discriminate equally against all is skewed as White English mother tongue students are not discriminated against. This reinforces the privileged position that has always been enjoyed by these speakers. The decision was taken on appeal and the CC heard the case and delivered judgment in the case of *Gelyke Kanse and Others* v *Chairperson of the Senate of the University of Stellenbosch and Others* (2019). A unanimous judgment was delivered by Cameron J, with Mogoeng CJ and Froneman J concurring, but with different reasons. The core challenge of this case was that the 2016 language policy violated Section 29(2), in addition to contravening other constitutional provisions, namely Sections 6(2) and 6(4) and the equality clause of Section 9, amongst others.

According to Cameron J (2019:para. 19), the question before the CC was "…whether the university has sufficiently justified the diminished role for Afrikaans in the 2016 Language Policy, as issued, and not as applied". We will not extract all the provisions concerning the contentions of each side, as there is considerable overlay with the CC's UFS judgment.

One argument put forward by *Gelyke Kanse* was to insist that SU implement parallel medium of instruction (English and Afrikaans), which was feasible but not practicable. In this instance, practicability was assessed based on costs. According to Cameron J (2019:para. 31), SU explained that, in total, it would cost 640 million rand for infrastructure, in addition to 70 million for personnel costs, which was not reasonably practicable. Cameron dismissed the appeal with an order to costs.

What is of direct relevance to this research, and interesting to note, given the CJ's view on Afrikaans as a language of record and his silence on the use of African languages as languages of record, was what Mogoeng CJ (2019:paras 61-63) stated at the end of his reasoning in the judgment after concurring with Cameron J:

[61] ... it needs to be said that Afrikaans is indeed an Afrikaans language, our historic pride to be treasured by all citizens. Its existence precedes colonialism. And its subsequent development with the appropriately enriching infusion of terms from Dutch or any other European language and the unjust attempt to impose it on others, do not at all affect its original African DNA.

[62] Our highly challenged fiscus has however, imposed a constraint on us to share all the acutely limited public resources among ourselves as generously as considerations of justice, equity and reconciliation, informed by reasonable practicability, permit us to. As a result, it is most fitting to appeal particularly to our corporate citizens' spirit of generosity, to help preserve Afrikaans, and develop other indigenous languages, as essential tools for knowledge impartation and comprehension. And that they can do by deploying resources to the establishment of private institutions of learning envisaged by section 29(3) of the Constitution, which would obviously not be driven by any sinister agenda to discriminate against others on any unconstitutional basis.

[63] ...Plans to enhance the status and promote the use of indigenous languages, in line with section 6 of our Constitution, must thus be developed and kept ready for implementation as soon as the contestation for our scarce resources, by key national priority areas, has ebbed out. Where immediate implementation is reasonably practicable it would arguably serve us well to act.

Paragraph 63 provides a glimmer of hope that the CJ may well be open to the idea of having bilingual and multilingual language of record policies for courts where such a plan is well thought out and resourced.

The final and most recent case of *AfriForum NPC v Chairperson of the Council of the University of South Africa and Others* (2020) was heard on appeal by the SCA. In the court *a quo*, AfriForum brought an application before the High Court seeking to review and set aside the decisions of both the Senate and Council of UNISA relating to the adoption of a new language policy where English was the sole Language of Learning and Teaching (LOLT) (*AfriForum NPC v Chairperson of the Council of the University of South Africa and Others,* 2020:para. 2).

In 2006, UNISA, through its language policy, provided an undertaking in which it would make tuition available in the South African official languages on the basis of functional multilingualism (ibid, para. 3). This undertaking was made against the backdrop that English and Afrikaans already had the developed capacity to be used as languages of teaching and learning in higher education. Part of UNISA's undertaking was proactively to support the development and use of the African languages with the view to them becoming mediums of instruction in higher education (ibid).

In 2013, UNISA began its review process of the language policy. The following parties were involved: Senate, Council; Senate Language Committee (SLC); UNISA management; and the Student Representative Council (SRC). The SRC supported the change to abandon Afrikaans as a LOLT in favour of an English-only LOLT policy (ibid, para. 8).

On 22 October 2014, a draft language policy, together with an implementation plan, was formulated and released. Members of Senate sought issue with having English as the only LOLT, following which the language policy was referred back to the SLC (2020:para. 9). The draft language policy was resubmitted on 26 August 2015 with further objections being raised, then remitted back to the SLC for further development to address the objections. Objections were once again raised on 21 October 2015 (ibid, para. 10). In 2016, following the reworking of the draft language policy and a presentation by the SLC to Senate, the language policy was recommended to Council for approval by Senate. Following this approval, Afriforum launched their application in the Gauteng Division of the High Court, Johannesburg, to review and set aside the decision (ibid, paras 12-13).

In their urgent application, AfriForum sought an order to suspend the implementation of the new language policy, pending the final decision of the application to review and set aside the decision. The relief in the main of the application was (ibid, para. 13):

1. That the respective resolutions of the Council and the Senate of the University of South Africa to approve a new language policy on 28 April and 30 March 2016 respectively be reviewed and set aside;
2. That the new language policy adopted by [UNISA] be set aside as being unconstitutional and unlawful;
3. That the new language policy be set aside as a whole; alternatively, be set aside insofar and to the extent that Afrikaans has been removed as language of learning and tuition at the University of South Africa;
4. That within 10 days from date of judgment, [UNISA] shall prominently publish on (a) its website and (b) in the three major Afrikaans newspapers in the country, (c) as well as by transmitting by email to all students a notice with the following content:
    4.1 A full list of the modules that had been on offer in Afrikaans as on 28 April 2016;
    4.2 Offering all prospective students for the next academic year admission in such modules as presented on first year level;
    4.3 Offering all existing students, if they were enrolled in any one of those courses or would have enrolled for the subsequent year course available in Afrikaans, but had perforce to follow the module in English, to re-enrol on the basis that they may follow the module in Afrikaans until completion of their studies;
    4.4 That all those modules will be presented in full in the following academic years until the language policy had been lawfully amended if at all; [and]
    4.5 That it shall, within 10 days after compliance with prayers 4, 4.1, 4.2 and 4.3 submit to this court proof that it has complied with the terms of the order.

AfriForum argued that the decision to adopt an English-only language policy violated the rights of approximately 30,000 existing and prospective Afrikaans speaking students to receive tuition in their mother tongue (*AfriForum NPC v Chairperson of the Council of the University of South Africa and Others*, 2020:para. 14). This number included White, Black and Coloured students from Afrikaans speaking communities (2020:para. 14). AfriForum argued that there was therefore a breach of Section 29(2) of the Constitution and no justification for the adoption of an English-only language policy (ibid). AfriForum's application was furthermore grounded on the fact that UNISA denied students their right, under Section 9 of the Constitution, not to be unfairly discriminated against and impaired their right to human dignity by removing Afrikaans, which was already a LOLT at UNISA (ibid).

UNISA denied its decisions were irrational and argued that the right was not abolished in any way (ibid, para. 20). UNISA argued that Afrikaans was placed on the same level as the African languages (ibid, para. 20). The court held that the new language policy did not violate Section 29(2) and that the decision to have English as the sole official LOLT was practical in the circumstances (ibid, para. 24).

AfriForum appealed the decision of the High Court. The issues on appeal before the SCA were whether (2020:para. 29):

(a) the impugned decisions contravened s (29)(2) of the Constitution;
(b) the Senate did not follow its rules, in breach of the principle of legality; and
(c) UNISA did not consult the persons most affected by the new language [policy], in breach of the principle of procedural rationality.

AfriForum contended that UNISA's review process and the new language policy fell short in respect of each of these aspects.

President of the SCA, Maya P (*AfriForum NPC* v *Chairperson of the Council of the University of South Africa and Others*, 2020:para. 29) advanced that Section 29(2) of the Constitution entails an enforceable right against the state to provide education in a language of choice where this is 'reasonably practicable'. Maya P (ibid) turned to the CC judgment in the case of *Head of Department: Mpumalanga Department of Education and Another* v *Hoërskool Ermelo and Another* (2010) which, among other issues, discussed the reasonable practicability standard, explaining that it was context-sensitive and would be determined through the application of the facts of the case. The CC in the *Ermelo* case (2010:para. 52) stated the following:

... when a learner already enjoys the benefit of being taught in an official language of choice the state bears the negative duty not to take away or diminish the right without appropriate justification.

Therefore, according to Maya P (*AfriForum NPC* v *Chairperson of the Council of the University of South Africa and Others*, 2020:para. 30), UNISA, having permitted students to elect to be taught in Afrikaans, bore the negative obligation of establishing appropriate justification for taking away their right. In establishing this justification, UNISA was to show that it was not reasonably practicable to sustain the dual medium (English and Afrikaans) tuition (ibid). UNISA, however, argued that, as opposed to the state, the institution was not liable to ensure effective access to and implementation of the Section 29(2) right (2020:para. 30). Maya P (2020:para. 34) held that UNISA's understanding of their responsibility conferred through Section 29(2) affected their decision and ultimately the validity thereof in drafting the new policy:

> Suffice it to say that UNISA's understanding of its responsibility under s 29(2) was fallacious. It ineluctably suggests that the institution did not properly comprehend the implications of the right to receive education in the official language of one's choice, the constitutional parameters within which its powers had to be exercised, and the precise ambit of responsibility which s 29(2) imposed upon it, when it reviewed its language policy and adopted a new one. This, of necessity, affects the validity of the decision to adopt the new policy.

In Part Two of Chapter 6, we discussed the importance of statistics and the application of the sliding scale formula when limiting a language right (Currie & De Waal, 2005:632). We have, furthermore, discussed the use of a costs-based argument as a defensive mechanism for adopting English-only language policies (Grin, 2010, Kaschula, 2004). All three are of relevance to the *UNISA* case (*AfriForum NPC v Chairperson of the Council of the University of South Africa and Others*, 2020) where the costs argument was used as a reason for opting for an English-only language policy. UNISA argued that it was not financially viable to print study guides in Afrikaans for those specific courses for a few students. AfriForum argued that UNISA did not print the study guides, but rather made them available online (ibid, paras 37-38):

> As AfriForum pointed out, UNISA never assessed the commercial viability of the approximately 300 modules offered in Afrikaans in comparison to the average commercial viability of about 2 300 modules offered in English. I agree that an equitable comparison would have been one comparing the commercial viability of the 300 Afrikaans modules to the 300 least profitable modules offered in English, as part of the exercise. This was not done.
>
> UNISA also did not explain why Afrikaans modules could not be cross-subsidised by English modules in terms of the common feature of university funding. AfriForum stated, without any challenge, that many university courses, such as philosophy, French and their ilk, are not commercially viable, as the cost of presenting them cannot be covered by the revenues they generate because of the low numbers of students who register for these courses. But they are still offered because they are of strategic and national importance, enhance the university's intellectual environment, and are cross-subsidised by the more popular courses which are highly profitable owing to the large student numbers who take them, and the attendant economies of scale. It is well to bear in mind that even if the removal of Afrikaans as a LOLT would result in a cost saving, that it would not necessarily render the decision to adopt the new language policy compliant with the test in s 29(2), which has a normative content that goes beyond the availability of resources. Nevertheless, UNISA failed to support its reliance on resource constraints because the figures it produced were not substantiated: there was no record showing any investigation or research with reference to proper data and the source of such data. It did not establish that it was not 'reasonably practicable' from a commercial standpoint to continue to offer tuition in Afrikaans.

With regard to the statistics, UNISA failed to disclose the source of their statistics, and went as far as arguing that it was not necessary to have provided Senate and Council with statistics that validated their argument for the removal of Afrikaans as a LOLT (ibid, paras 40-41). AfriForum disclosed their source of statistics, namely UNISA's Structured Query Language database system (ibid, para. 40):

> According to this data, in 2016 out of 1 881 267 module and year course registrations, 96 816 were offered in Afrikaans. This number translated to 15 per cent of the total modules offered at UNISA out of which 5,15 per cent were chosen by approximately 25 000 students, each taking an average of four modules. AfriForum contended that removing Afrikaans as a LOLT thus destroyed about 100 000 study opportunities in that language. Importantly, AfriForum highlighted that a single digit percentage was not indicative of a small number of students as, for example, 5 per cent could amount to as many as 600 students. So, whilst 25 000 students may be a negligible number in UNISA, which has massive student numbers, that number generally constituted the total student population in other major residential universities in South Africa and was far from insignificant.

The validity of the decision taken by UNISA hinged on the statistics; it was argued that Afrikaans was no longer commercially viable and that there was a large decrease in the enrolment of Afrikaans-speaking students. The lawfulness of the decision taken by UNISA was thus in question before the court, where Maya P (ibid, para. 41) had the following to say:

> It is incomprehensible why the SLC would see no need for the Senate and Council to have recourse to the hard numbers of the students who would be affected by its far-reaching decision, in determining whether it was reasonably practicable to retain Afrikaans as a LOLT. Its stance is entirely insupportable. The omission to place the statistics which founded the recommendation to remove Afrikaans as a LOLT before the Senate and Council breached s 29(2) and rendered the decision to adopt the new language policy unlawful.

In both the CC judgments in the cases of *AfriForum and Another* v *University of the Free State* (2018) and *Gelyke Kanse and Others v Chairperson of the Senate of the University of Stellenbosch and Others* (2019), the court dealt with the issue of language and racism and how the use of Afrikaans as a LOLT divided students in lectures according to race. In the UNISA case, Maya P (*AfriForum NPC* v *Chairperson of the Council of the University of South Africa and Others,* 2020) clearly stated that this was not an issue given that UNISA is a distance university. This was an important issue to dispose of, seeing that parties before court often racialize the language question, where such racialisation is skewed in favour of a specific agenda. We have noted with concern that Afrikaans is constantly associated with the historical context of Apartheid. However, the fact that Afrikaans is spoken by Coloured people and, in some communities, by Black and Indian people, is a fact which is often intentionally overlooked.

Based on the reasoning above, Maya P (2020:paras. 47-48) held:
> While the evidence suggests that there may have been a need for a revision of UNISA's language policy, it has not been established that the adoption of the new policy in 2016 was conducted in a constitutionally compliant manner, i.e. that the factual and normative 'reasonably practicable' requirement in s 29(2) of the Constitution was satisfied. UNISA failed to discharge the burden that it was not detracting from the right contained in s 29(2) of the Constitution without appropriate justification. This finding, in my view, is dispositive of and dispenses with the need to determine the other issues raised in the appeal.

The appeal accordingly succeeds and costs must follow the result. The following order is made:
1. The appeal is upheld with costs, including the costs of two counsel.
2. The order of the court a quo is set aside and replaced with the following:
   '(a) the resolutions of the Council and Senate of the University of South Africa to approve a new language policy on 28 April and 30 March 2016, respectively, are set aside;
   (b) the new language policy adopted by the University of South Africa is declared unconstitutional and unlawful and is set aside to the extent that Afrikaans has been removed as a language of learning and tuition;
   (c) the University of South Africa shall prominently publish on its website and in three major Afrikaans newspapers in South Africa and transmit by email to all its students a notice:
      (i) containing a full list of the modules that were on offer in Afrikaans as at 28 April 2016;
      (ii) offering all prospective students for the next academic year admission in such modules as presented on first year level;
      (iii) offering all existing students, if they were enrolled in any one of those courses or would have enrolled for the subsequent year course available in Afrikaans, but had perforce to follow the module in English, a choice to enrol on the basis that they may follow the module in Afrikaans until completion of their studies;
      (iv) all the modules mentioned above will be presented in full in the following academic years until the language policy has been lawfully amended, if at all.
   (d) the University of South Africa shall pay the costs of the application.'

Conclusion

The language of record cases illustrates the willingness of Magistrates to provide purposive interpretation of the rights contained in Section 35(3) (k) of the Constitution. The cases illustrate that the Magistrates in the courts *a quo* acknowledged the importance of proceeding in a language understood by all parties before court where that language was also an official language and spoken by the majority of the people in that area or province. This conforms with the provisions of Section 6 of the Constitution. It is unfortunate to have seen in both instances (*State* v *Damani*, 2016; and *State* v *Gordon*, 2018) the judges in the High Courts taking issue with this purposive approach. In both cases, the limitation of the rights through Section 36 of the Constitution and the application of the sliding scale formula were misconstrued to ensure compliance with the monolingual language of record directive. Both cases adopt an approach where interpretation is favoured, rather than proceeding in a language other than English.

The cases concerning interpretation highlight the issues plaguing court interpretation: whether this be a shortage of interpreters, procedural irregularities, or poor-quality interpretation, all adversely impact on the constitutional rights and access to justice for both the complainant and accused persons. The cases of *State* v *Matomela* (1998) and *State* v *Damoyi* (2004) illustrate that cases can be heard in an African language and that terminology is available to proceed in the African languages.

On the point of terminology development, universities are key to this process. It is thus concerning to see the legal system confirming the constitutionality of university language policies that adopt a monolingual English-only approach by foregoing the previously bilingual approach on the grounds of transformation, equity, equitable access and redress. The language policy cases illustrate the judiciary's narrow interpretative approach to the constitutional provisions in favour of English. As pointed out in the dissenting judgment of Froneman J in the case of *AfriForum and Another v University of the Free State* (2018), there is an inherent failure to engage with the African languages as languages of teaching and learning. This could change through a bilingual or multilingual approach. Instead, the African languages, including Afrikaans, are completely weakened and undermined as languages of scholarship by the adoption of English only. The UNISA judgment provided a glimmer of hope for the maintenance of a bilingual language policy, with the aim of developing the African languages to be used in a multilingual university setting as languages of learning, teaching and research.

The overall point of the case law is that an English-only approach is exclusionary, fails to redress the past marginalisation and discrimination, and thus undermines and unfairly limits the constitutional provisions and language rights. With the case law illustrating that judicial officers (with the exception of Maya P) and legal practitioners are more inclined to favour an English-only approach, the chapter that follows explores their qualifications and linguistic competencies.

SOUTH AFRICA'S LEGAL PRACTITIONERS AND JUDICIAL OFFICERS

Language qualifications and competencies

Legislative language requirements for legal practitioners

In the case law presented in Chapter 7 it was evident that African languages can be used as languages of record in the first instance and be translated for appeal and review processes. This was evident from cases of *State* v *Damoyi* (2004), *State* v *Matomela* (1998) and State v Damani (2016). For this to happen, legal practitioners and judicial officers would need to be linguistically competent in the languages of the province in which the court is seated. The same principle and line of reasoning applies for a bilingual or multilingual language of record policy to be existent in each of the provinces: there would need to be linguistically competent legal practitioners. By 'linguistically competent', we refer to LLB graduates who have also mastered, at university level, an official language other than, or in addition to, English. This line of reasoning is advanced from a point of practicality given that the majority of South Africans speak an African language or Afrikaans, or both as their mother tongue. Linguistic competency in a language other than English can readily be achieved where mother tongue African language and Afrikaans speaking students are able to learn their mother tongue at an intellectual university level. The same applies to second language speakers who already have a strong command of a second language and pursue this language at university level. The language competence required for the LLB curriculum is discussed in Chapter 9.

In Chapter 2, we advanced the fourth tier of language planning, namely opportunity planning (Antia, 2017); and how, through language planning, incentives must be created to implement the legislation and language policy successfully. University language policies thus have to relate to the broader legislative framework of disciplines, such as the legal system, where job creation is key.

In the introduction of Chapter 1 we noted that, during Apartheid, language requirements were legislated for attorneys in the Attorneys Act (1979). These language requirements were in accordance with the official languages at the time, namely English, Afrikaans and Latin. With the transition to a constitutional democracy, the legislation was amended in the form of the Attorneys Amendment Act 115 of 1993 (1993a). It was anticipated that the Attorneys Amendment Act (1993a) would be reflective of the then 'new' constitutional language provisions of Section 6 of the Constitution, which were already in existence in the Interim Constitution (1993). This was not the case, and no African language requirements were included.

Chapter 1, Sections 2 to 24 of the Attorneys Amendment Act (1993a), concerns the qualifications, admission and removal of attorneys from the roll. Language requirements for admission are absent from these provisions; specifically, Sections 4 and 15 solely concern admission to the attorneys' profession. Sections 13B and 14 concern the completion of training in legal practice management and practical examinations. Section 2 of the Attorneys Amendment Act (1993a) concerns the duration of service under articles. No listed provisions include language requirements or training of any sorts.

Similar to the Attorneys Amendment Act (1993a), the Admission of Advocates Act, 74 of 1964 was amended post-Apartheid, resulting in the Admission of Advocates Amendment Act, 55 of 1994 (1994b). The earlier Admission of Advocates Act (1964) recognised English, Afrikaans and Latin as language requirements at university level prior to admission to the Bar of Advocates. This changed with the amendment and the change was highlighted in the purpose of the Act (1994b):

> [To] Amend the Admission of Advocates Act (1964) to abolish the requirement that must be complied with by persons in respect of the Latin language in order to be admitted to practice as advocates; and to delete or substitute certain obsolete words and expressions; and to amend laws of the former Republics of Transkei, Bophuthatswana and Venda with regard to the admission of advocates; and to provide for matters connected therewith.

There was a clear abolishment of the Latin language requirement. However, no insertion of an African language requirement occurred. The English and Afrikaans language requirements were later also removed from the Act. Essentially, both the Attorneys Amendment Act (1993a) and the Admission of Advocates Amendment Act (1994b) failed to address the language question in the then 'new' dispensation. The legislature thought it neutral to removal all language requirements, but, by doing so, they maintained the status quo of the language of proceedings and record, namely English and Afrikaans. There was then no need or incentive for LLB graduates to acquire an African language before admission to the Side Bar or Bar. Thus, there was no onus upon universities to graduate bilingual or multilingual LLB students.

A transformed legal profession: Legal Practice Act

Thus far, we have established that the language of proceedings and record must be determined by the legislature through legislative and policy means, in accordance with the SOP doctrine. Having said that, courts are creatures of statute, and the legislature, in regulating the functioning of courts, must have due regard for the constitutional provisions. The legislation we have advanced thus far, pertaining to South Africa, is illustrative of the legislature's failure to incorporate African language requirements in accordance with Section 6 of the Constitution, and provide for the equal application of the rights in Section 35 of the Constitution. As Cowling (2007:94) points out, the legislature has a responsibility to amend and enact legislation, reversing the discrimination and marginalisation endured during Apartheid. This requires vigorous change with the aim of achieving inclusivity for all. In heeding this call, the legal system embarked on a new transformed path, with the incremental introduction of the Legal Practice Act 28 of 2014.

The Legal Practice Act (2014), unfortunately, makes no mention of language and the language question in courts. In substantiating this statement, we advance extracts from the Legal Practice Act (2014) to illustrate this absence where language, in our opinion, should have been included. The purpose of the Legal Practice Act (2014) is:

> To provide a legislative framework for the transformation and restructuring of the legal profession in line with constitutional imperatives to facilitate and enhance an independent legal profession that broadly reflects the diversity and demographics of the Republic...

From the extract, the phrases "...constitutional imperatives..." and "...reflects the diversity and demographics of the Republic..." refer to the inclusion of language, specifically the African languages. Section 3 of the Legal Practice outlines the purpose with more specificity:

> 3(a) provide a legislative framework for the transformation and restructuring of the legal profession that embraces the values underpinning the Constitution and ensures the rule of law is upheld;
>
> (b)(iii) measures that provide equal opportunities for all aspirant legal practitioners in order to have a legal profession that broadly reflects the demographics of the Republic;...

Subsection b(iii), in our opinion, should include language as a measure that would enable equal opportunities for legal practitioners, given that the majority of persons in South Africa speak an African language as their mother tongue. This is not the case, upon further examination of the provisions: this includes Section 24, regulating the admission and enrolment to the legal profession. Subsection (2)(a) refers to a duly qualified person, as set out in Section 26 of the Legal Practice Act (2014). Section 26, regulating the minimum qualifications and practical vocational training, prescribes no language requirements for attorneys, candidate attorneys, advocates, or pupils. Furthermore, Section 29 of the Legal

Practice Act (2014) governs community service, which will need to be undertaken for graduates to be admitted to the legal profession. Community service, to our understanding, would involve the small claims court or *pro bono* public interest law, and therefore involve communicating in some, if not most, instances with African language speakers. It is our opinion that these provisions should have included language requirements or language training programmes. This would have filled the language requirements gap in the Attorneys Amendment Act (1993a) and the Admission of Advocates Amendment Act (1994b).

Legal professionals: racial demographics

It is all well and good to propose provincial language policies for courts; however, it is meaningless if the legal professionals' language demographics do not correlate with language demographics of the country, presented in Part Two of Chapter 6. This again links to the role of university language policies (discussed in Chapter 9) and broader educational policies in shaping the linguistic trends of students at an early age prior to their entering the profession. Across the county, as far as we are aware, there has been no official or unofficial release of language competencies for legal professionals, including for judicial officers. In the case law presented in Chapter 7, we saw certain judges making enquiries with the relevant DPP authorities as to the linguistic proficiencies of state advocates (prosecutors). We elaborate upon this point in Chapter 10 as part of the conclusions and recommendations. That being said, the statistics at present pertain primarily to race and gender and, in a way, emulate the provisions of Section 174 of the Constitution in identifying only race and gender to the exclusion of language.

The reason that we have included these racial statistics of South Africa's legal professionals is that, in the *State* v *Damani* (2016), *State* v *Gordon* (2018), and *UFS* (2016; 2018) cases, amongst others, the judges have reverted to these statistics. There is a constant linkage in South Africa between race and language. This is not confined to South Africa, as we have seen in Australia, and in India where the caste system impacts the legal profession and access to justice. The thinking of racialising our languages must be excluded to build a united and inclusive society where languages are seen as the languages of all South Africans. The racial statistics pertaining to practising attorneys and advocates are housed in Tables 8.1 and 8.2. In Table 8.1, the Cape Law Society, the Free State Law Society and the Law Society of the Northern Provinces comprise a majority of White practising attorneys.

TABLE 8.1 Racial demographics of the practicing attorneys per law society from April 2014 to April 2015 (Law Society of South Africa, 2015:34-43)

Race	Cape Law Society	Free State Law Society	Law Society of The Northern Provinces	KwaZulu-Natal Law Society
African	919	214	3586	617
Coloured	1016	14	129	41
Indian/Asian	216	4	652	1257
White	4320	817	8381	1176
Unknown	39	6	312	1

TABLE 8.2 Racial demographics of the practicing advocates per Bar recoded in April 2014 (Law Society of South Africa, 2015:49)

Bars	African	Coloured	Indian/Asian	White
Cape	15	60	12	365
Port Elizabeth	6	6	2	54
Grahamstown	4	2	1	20
Free State	7	1	0	60
Northern Cape	2	0	1	8
Johannesburg	251	21	65	664
Pretoria	104	3	9	454
KwaZulu-Natal	49	5	97	157
North West	7	0	0	12
Transkei	26	1	0	1
Bisho	11	2	0	6

The KwaZulu-Natal Law Society is the only law society in which the majority of practising attorneys are not White – the overwhelming majority of practising attorneys across the various provinces are White. A similar situation exists for advocates, as captured in Table 8.2. There is an overwhelming majority of White advocates at each bar with the exception of the Transkei and Bhisho bars in the Eastern Cape. For purposes of drafting and enacting provincial language policies for courts, in line with the recommendations in Chapter 10, the Law Society and General Council of the Bar would need to assess, against these statistics, in what languages these legal professionals are able to speak, read and write and at what level. Table 8.3 pertains to the racial demographics of the judges per division in the various provinces.

TABLE 8.3 Racial demographics of High Court judges per division in each province, as at April 2015 (Law Society of South Africa, 2015:50)

Divisions	African	Coloured	Indian	White
Constitutional Court (Johannesburg)	7	0	0	3
Supreme Court of Appeal (Bloemfontein)	10	2	5	6
Northern Cape (Kimberley)	4	1	0	2
Eastern Cape (Grahamstown)	4	1	0	4
Eastern Cape Local Division (Port Elizabeth)	2	0	1	4
Eastern Cape Local Division (Bisho)	0	0	0	3
Eastern Cape Local Division (Mthatha)	4		1	2
Western Cape Division (Cape Town)	8	11	2	12
North West (Mafikeng)	3	1	1	1
Free State Division (Bloemfontein)	5	1		5
Gauteng Division (Pretoria)	27	2	2	19
Gauteng Division (Gauteng)	14	2	3	12
KwaZulu-Natal Division (Pietermaritzburg)	7	1	3	5
KwaZulu-Natal Local Division (Durban)	5	2	4	2
Labour Court	3			7

The demographics appears to be racially representative of the Republic's demographics. However, as we stated previously, in accordance with our recommendations in Chapter 10, a study will have to be undertaken to determine the linguistic competency of the judges, regardless of race, and ensure that this is representative of the language demographics across provinces. The racial statistics of magistrates in South Africa is presented in the table below.

TABLE 8.4 Racial statistics of magistrates in South Africa, as on April 2015 (Law Society of South Africa, 2015:2)

Magisterial Level	African	Coloured	Indian	White
Regional Court President	7	1	0	1
Regional Magistrate	147	23	32	132
Chief Magistrate	9	2	3	4
Senior Magistrate	37	6	4	31
Magistrate	464	113	126	447

The racial equitability among Magistrates in South Africa is evident from the statistics in Table 8.4. The linguistic competency of magistrates is ever more urgent and necessary given that the magistrates are presiding officers in the lower courts which are courts of first instance. The majority of these magistrates deal with criminal law cases that involve African language and Afrikaans speaking accused persons, who would not be in a position to fully realise their Section 35(3) (k) right if the Magistrate can only speak English. In almost all the cases we have advanced in Chapter 7, the magistrates grappled with the language of record, with interpretational errors and inconveniences that amounted to grave injustices for both the accused persons and complainants.

Attorneys' views on languages other than English

Although the legislature has the mandate of legislating language requirements for legal professionals, it is important to gauge the views of legal practitioners on multilingualism and the use of languages other than English in the legal system. This speaks to the point advanced earlier, where Alexander (1997) promoted a bottom-up, rather than a top-down, approach to language planning. The latter most often results in resistance during the policy implementation stage.

De Vries and Docrat (2019) conducted such a survey; however, they focused solely on the attorneys' profession. Participation in the survey was voluntary. This should possibly be revised when another survey is undertaken by the state or legislature, as participation should be mandatory. According to De Vries and Docrat (2019:96), approximately 25,900 attorneys are registered with the Law Society in South Africa. Of these, 2,157 completed a computerised self-administered survey that essentially investigated issues that were regarded as important. The first section of the questionnaire comprised biographical questions focusing on aspects such as gender, age, provincial location in South Africa, undergraduate legal qualification and institution(s) of study. Questions excluded race. In the second section, participants answered questions about language ability, their use of two official South African languages in which they were fluent, as well as the languages used most often, and then secondarily most often, in these contexts: at home; in their social circles; during written and oral communication with clients and during communication with colleagues.

Participants were also asked about these aspects: the language in which they mostly conducted their research; the language of documentation and correspondence with clients, courts and opponents; the language of legal training; the practitioner's competence in English; as well as their clients' competence in English (as evaluated by practitioners). The final section of the questionnaire included 18 Likert-scale questions on practitioners' language attitudes, needs and choices. There were four response options for the Likert-scale questions, where the value of 1 indicated that the participant strongly disagreed with the applicable statement, while a value of 4 indicated that the participant strongly supported the applicable statement.

TABLE 8.5 Clients' English proficiency: The legal practitioners' perspective (De Vries & Docrat, 2019:98)

Proficiency in reading and writing	100	N = 1 915
Measured average	2.16/3	
Reasonable	20.94	401
Good	41.83	801
Excellent	37.23	713
Proficiency in oral communication	100	N = 1 915
Measured average	2.15/3	
Reasonable	19.74	378
Good	45.43	870
Excellent	34.83	667
N = total number of participants answering this question		

TABLE 8.6 Survey results: Attorneys' language attitudes, needs and choices (De Vries & Docrat, 2019:100)

Legend:						
1=Strongly disagree; 2=Disagree; 3=Agree; 4=Strongly Agree						
The highlighted percentage under "Total" is a "measured mean".						
		1	2	3	4	Total
The general language of use in the legal profession should be English.	No.	443	196	320	821	1 780
	%	24.89	11.01	17.98	46.12	2.85

TABLE 8.6 Survey results: Attorneys' language attitudes, needs and choices (De Vries & Docrat, 2019:100) [continued]

Legend:

1=Strongly disagree; 2=Disagree; 3=Agree; 4=Strongly Agree

The highlighted percentage under "Total" is a "measured mean".

		1	2	3	4	Total
Transformation in the judicial system is fair.	No.	419	468	481	399	1 767
	%	23.71	26.49	27.22	22.58	2.49
Transformation in the judicial system takes place at a satisfactory rate.	No.	345	498	563	358	1 764
	%	19.56	28.23	31.92	20.29	2.53
The judicial system cannot transform adequately if multilingualism is sought	No.	684	397	324	367	1 772
	%	38.60	22.40	18.28	20.71	2.21
It is in the best interests of the client to consult with him/her in English.	No.	760	441	291	278	1 770
	%	42.94	24.92	16.44	15.71	2.05
It is in the best interests of the client to consult with him/her in his/her home language.	No.	180	257	365	970	1 772
	%	10.16	14.50	20.60	54.74	3.2
I have experienced communication problems with clients before because we did not properly understand each other's language.	No.	469	354	410	538	1 771
	%	26.48	19.99	23.15	30.38	2.57
I had to translate legal documents from another language into English before.	No.	798	221	256	490	1 765
	%	45.21	12.52	14.50	27.76	2.25
The translation of legal documents can influence the speed at which a case is settled.	No.	173	223	415	952	1 763
	%	9.81	12.65	23.54	54.00	3.22
Multilingualism can create confusion in the legal profession.	No.	365	270	344	787	1 766
	%	20.67	15.29	19.48	44.56	2.88
In a multilingual country, multilingualism in the courts should be a given.	No.	496	401	372	486	1 755
	%	28.26	22.85	21.20	27.69	2.48

TABLE 8.6 Survey results: Attorneys' language attitudes, needs and choices (De Vries & Docrat, 2019:100) [continued]

Legend:

1=Strongly disagree; 2=Disagree; 3=Agree; 4=Strongly Agree

The highlighted percentage under "Total" is a "measured mean".

		1	2	3	4	Total
It can be confusing to the client if an attorney does not litigate in his/her home language.	No.	378	367	463	558	1 766
	%	21.40	20.78	26.22	31.60	2.68
I regularly use language practitioners to translate legal documents.	No.	1 208	310	110	133	1 761
	%	68.60	17.60	6.25	7.55	1.53
I regularly use translators during court proceedings.	No.	650	344	325	422	1 741
	%	37.33	19.76	18.67	24.24	2.3
In a criminal case it is fair that a victim should pay for translation services himself if he/she cannot make a statement in English.	No.	1 279	188	96	185	1 748
	%	73.17	10.76	5.49	10.58	1.53
I have experienced before that interpreters' translations cause confusion during court proceedings.	No.	288	356	486	605	1 735
	%	16.60	20.52	28.01	34.87	2.81
In my profession I will benefit from learning another indigenous South African language.	No.	325	183	382	876	1 766
	%	18.40	10.36	21.63	49.60	3.02
During the translation process, I found that legal concepts could not be translated meaningfully and in context in other languages.	No.	252	390	494	596	1 732
	%	14.55	22.52	28.52	34.41	2.83

Table 8.5 illustrates that attorneys view the English language proficiency of clients as mainly 'good' and 'excellent'. This is contrary to the findings of the language survey by Legal Aid (2017); it also illustrates that some legal practitioners are somewhat oblivious to their clients' language difficulties. This was also the case in India, Morocco, Nigeria and Kenya, where the focus is on legal practitioners understanding the language, regardless of the client's language limitations. Table 8.6 presents mixed views on the importance of multilingualism and acknowledging this; responses show that there was disagreement among respondents about the importance of using other languages, with their cited reasons including difficulty in the translation process, time constraints involving translation, as well as costs for translation.

Conclusion

The discussions in this chapter illustrate that a transformational agenda is being implemented but, as with Section 174 of the Constitution, the Legal Practice Act (2014) excludes language as part of this agenda. That being said, the statistics in terms of racial demographics can be used in motivating for legislative language requirements for legal practitioners and judicial officers. However, as the discussions suggest, the starting point is with the education system and the LLB curriculum.

THE RELATIONSHIP BETWEEN SOUTH AFRICA'S LEGAL SYSTEM AND HIGHER EDUCATION INSTITUTIONS

A Policy-based approach

The previous chapters and discussions have clearly outlined the important relationship between higher education institutions and the legal system, not only in the South African context, but also in the selected African countries and international models. In Chapter 2, the African case studies, in particular Nigeria, illustrated that universities are trying to adopt multilingual approaches to teaching and learning with the aim of graduating bilingual students. In Chapter 3, the Indian case study illustrates language used as a tool to exclude students in higher education institutions; and that such a policy is propagated by cultural biases underpinned by the caste system. With the Australian case study, there is an indication that students are unaware of the indigenous languages that exist in the country given the emphasis placed on English.

This chapter focuses on South Africa, parallels can be drawn with each of the comparative case studies presented in Chapters 2 and 3, and this will become clearer as the discussion in this chapter develops. We argue that the Belgian and Canadian comparative case studies serve as models that can be emulated in South Africa where Belgium has adopted a geographical approach to language planning at universities and Canada has adopted a bilingual approach to court proceedings.

This chapter ultimately speaks to the transformational agenda of both the legal system and higher education where the important linkages between language planning in both systems need to be aligned. University language policies need to ensure that LLB graduates are linguistically competent to enter the profession, while the language policies and directives of the legal system need to incentivise linguistic competency in one or more of the African languages.

Language planning in higher education

The discussions thus far have provided theoretical overviews of language planning, the formulation of legislation, language legislation and policy formulation, as well as the policy developments in the broader South African landscape and the legal system more specifically. The administrative law discussion illustrated the importance of these theoretical frameworks which give meaning to language rights in practical situations through legislation that empowers a person or organ of state to perform a function or duty. Against the latter, we advance a discussion on language planning in the domain of higher education. This discussion forms the backdrop to the presentation of language policies of selected universities. Following the presentation of the selected language policies, we offer a legal-linguistic critique. The critique is aligned with the 2017 proposal by the Parliamentary Justice and Corrections Oversight Committee's former chairperson, Mathole Motshekga, to graduate linguistically competent LLB graduates.

Elaborating on the administrative law discussion, the enabling legislation empowering universities to draft language policies for their respective institutions is the Higher Education Act 101 of 1997. Section 27(2) of that Act empowers the drafting of language policies:

> Subject to the policy determined by the Minister, the council, with the concurrence of the senate, must determine the language policy of a public higher education institution and must publish and make it available on request.

Further to Section 27(2), an institution's language policy cannot be inconsistent with the Ministerial Policy. The institution's language policy must conform to the Language Policy for Higher Education (LPHE) (2002), read together with the National Language Policy Framework (2002). The National LPHE (2002) was informed by a special committee chaired by the late Neville Alexander. The National LPHE has since been amended and a new one drafted in 2017.

The initial LPHE (2002) was informed by a special committee chaired by Alexander, appointed by the then Minister of Higher Education, Kader Asmal. The special committee was established as a result of the failure by the National Commission on Higher Education (NCHE) to address the language question in higher education. Maseko (2014) and Kamwendo and Ndimande-Hlongwa (2017) provide an all-inclusive overview of the policy and ministerial committee developments concerning language in higher education. The LPHE (2002) makes allowance for the use of official languages other than English and Afrikaans. Maseko (2014:29-30) summarises the main points of the LPHE:

> (a) It acknowledges the current position of English and Afrikaans as languages of research and scholarship, but makes a point that it will be necessary to work within the confines of the status quo until such time as other South African languages have been developed to a level where they may be used in all higher education functions.

(b) It states that consideration should be given to the development of other South African languages for use in instruction, as part of a medium-to-long-term strategy to promote multilingualism.
(c) It recognises that the promotion of South African languages for use in higher education will require, among others, the development of multilingual dictionaries and other teaching and learning support materials.
(d) Language should not act as a barrier to equity of access and success. In this regard, the Ministry of Education encourages all higher education institutions to develop strategies for promoting proficiency in the designated language(s) of tuition, including the provision of language and academic literacy development programmes.

These four points, in our opinion, are in no way giving effective meaning to placing the nine official African languages on an equal footing alongside English and Afrikaans. Instead, the LPHE (2002) maintains the status quo of English and Afrikaans while paying nothing more than lip service to the African languages. Indeed, the African languages need to be developed as languages of science; however, the LPHE (2002) makes no attempt at providing practical ways in which universities are obligated to do this. This can be linked to opportunity planning; unfortunately, persons and institutions require incentives when dealing with language. If the system suits those empowered to make the changes, these changes will either be slow or not implemented at all. This also reaffirms the point of policies and legislation containing penalties and sanctions for those who fail to act. Thus, it can be questioned whether there is, in fact, a genuine intention by the Ministry, through the LPHE, to change the language situation, where 'inclusivity' means African languages being used as languages of teaching and learning.

In 2003, a ministerial committee presented a report titled: The Development of Indigenous African Languages as Mediums of Instruction in Higher Education (Kamwendo & Ndimande-Hlongwa, 2017). This report speaks to African languages as languages of instruction in higher education institutions. The recommendations in this report appear more tangible than the provisions of the LPHE (2002), which Maseko (2014:31-32) has summarised accordingly:

(a) Ensure the sustainability of all indigenous South African languages.
(b) Select, according to region, one or more indigenous languages to develop for use as medium of instruction in higher education, as well as short-, medium- and long-term implementation frameworks.
(c) Promote communicative competence of students in at least one indigenous language and encourage the labour market to make such competence an imperative, especially for civil service or state institutions.
(d) Promote partnerships between higher education institutions and the private sector in identifying and translating key texts into indigenous language/s selected for development by that institution.
(e) Ensure institutional collaborations, especially where languages selected are common, to ensure acceleration of work and non-replication of effort.

The recommendations correlate with Section 6(3) of the Constitution and apply a demographics-based argument in selecting a language. This will enable, at university level, the equal development of each of the nine African languages in the geographical area in which the language is most spoken. In turn, contributing to the graduation of students who are linguistically proficient in the language of the province. Another point of encouraging the labour market to make linguistic competence an imperative can be linked with opportunity planning and the 2017 proposal by the Parliamentary Justice and Corrections Oversight Committee's former chairperson, Mathole Motshekga, to graduate linguistically competent LLB graduates.

In 2008, a Ministerial Committee report was released on the need for social cohesion and the end of discrimination in higher education institutions. In 2015, a further report of a Ministerial Advisory Panel was presented on the use of African languages in higher education. This addressed four areas (Kamwendo & Ndimande-Hlongwa, 2017):

1. The language of instruction;
2. the future of South African languages as fields of the academic study and research;
3. the study of foreign languages; and
4. the promotion of multilingualism in the institutional policies and practices of higher education institutions.

The following development was the 2008 report by the Ministerial Committee on Transformation and Social Cohesion and the Elimination of Discrimination in Public Higher Education Institutions. The report fleetingly referred to the language question by acknowledging the history of South African higher education and how, during this period, the majority of persons were marginalised. This is a continued perpetuation which the report takes stock of in stating that students are not taught in a language they understand best, hindering their chances of success (Kamwendo & Ndimande-Hlongwa, 2017).

The final development that Kamwendo and Ndimande-Hlongwa (2017) note is the ministerial advisory panel on African languages in higher education (2015). Their purpose was to advise the minister on the development of African languages as languages of scholarship. Furthermore, the panel was tasked with assessing the existing national and institutional language policies and the implementation of those policies.

A common thread running through each of these ministerial task teams and panels is that constant reports have been produced and recommendations made, yet there is no sign of action and implementation to address the identified issues. A similarity can be sought with what Docrat and Kaschula (2015b:4) referred to as a "policy super highway": we continue to draft policies without stopping, taking a breath and assessing what the successes and failures are and how to address these.

Maseko (2014:28) states that the main goal of language policies in higher education is to promote linguistic and cultural diversity. This is contrary to the current move of entrenching monolingualism at higher institutions. An important point which Maseko (2014:28) makes concerns the important role that higher education institutions play in preparing students to participate fully in multilingual societies such as South Africa where "multilingual proficiency is critical". The Parliamentary Justice and Corrections Oversight Committee's former chairperson, Mathole Motshekga, stated in 2017 that all LLB students must pass one of the indigenous languages before being awarded a law degree, while the judgment by Mogoeng Mogoeng, in the case of *AfriForum and Another* v *University of the Free State* (2018), is contrary to this proposal.

The taken-for-granted notion of academics and higher education institutions that English is, and must be, the language of tuition, is ill conceived and needs to be rethought with the students' best interests in mind (Alexander, 2013:75). Alexander (2013:81) proposed a five-dimensional argument for the use of African languages in tertiary education. The five dimensions are:

> (bio-cultural) diversity; (economic) development, (political) democracy, (human) dignity and effective didactics.

The five-dimensional argument includes economic development which, McLean (1992) and Kaschula (2004) argue, must form part of language planning for it to be viable and positively affect the development of a society at both the micro and macro levels. Grin (2010) argued that higher education institutions are guided by economic factors in selecting the language of tuition. An increase in student registrations entails an increase in revenue for the institution. This is coupled with a three-pronged argument (Grin, 2010:11) in favour of selecting English as a language of tuition:

1. It is necessary to attract the best foreign students;
2. Others do it, so we must do it too;
3. A typical folk linguistics perception that English is the language of science.

The foreign student argument undermines the local students accessing higher education institutions; and, in a way, it prioritises the foreign student on the basis that the foreign student is likely to succeed while the local student will fail (Grin, 2010:12). This is contrary to what Kaschula (2004) spoke of: strengthening the micro economy to give effective meaning and growth to the macro economy of a country. The second argument is one pinned on the notion of conformity. This was evident in the case law where, one by one, universities which were previously bilingual are, instead of becoming multilingual, adopting English-only language policies. The third argument can be linked to earlier discussions concerning the LPHE (2002), in addition to the argument that African languages lack the necessary terminology to be used in high status domains such as science and law.

The discussions indicate that language planning at higher education institutions is guided by economic factors and conforms to the norm at the time. The many ministerial reports have largely repeated what the others say, and the overlap fails to address the vital question of using African languages for tuition purposes. *The Report of the Ministerial Committee on the Development of Indigenous African Languages as Mediums of Instruction in Higher Education* (2003), which addresses this, has not been fully implemented given the move by universities to make English the sole official language of tuition on grounds of access, equity, inclusivity and transformation. The actual language policies of the selected universities are presented in the next section. Thereafter is a discussion on language as part of transformation and decolonisation in the legal system and at universities.

Transformation and decolonisation

Transformation is relevant to our discussions on two grounds. The first is that the legal system is said to be undergoing a transformational period in which the profession as a whole is being overhauled in accordance with the Legal Practice Act 28 of 2014. A full discussion of the Legal Practice Act (2014) can be found in Docrat (2017a). Suffice to say for the discussion at hand that the Legal Practice Act (2014) is aimed at transforming the South African legal system in order for it to be more representative of the racial demographics in South Africa, where diversity is key, in accordance with the constitutional provisions. The second ground is transformation of university curricula and campuses. The point of curricula transformation has been couched under the banner of 'decolonisation' with the onset of the #FeesMustFall movement which commenced in 2015 at South African universities countrywide. For the purposes of the discussions in this book, we discuss transformation with reference to the legal system and decolonisation with reference to higher education institutions in South Africa. The reason for this is that the concepts of transformation and decolonisation have become synonymous with each of the two domains.

According to Wesson and Du Plessis (2008:2) transformation can be defined as "a change from a state of affairs that existed previously". De Vos (2010) explains that transformation, or the process thereof, is a "radical vision which has as yet not come to pass. It envisages a complete transformation of the legal system". There is no one definition of transformation and it is discipline-specific, so the context is important and affects the type and results of transformation. De Vos (2010) further explained that transformation has no definitive meaning, as it is now an overused concept which dominates political speeches. The overuse of the concept is not a positive sign as it rather indicates that either the government or the legal system (or both) is using the concept to try and legitimise their skewed understanding of what transformation actually is. This is a sweeping statement; however, it can be validated by examining the reasons given by the CJ and Heads of Court to make English the sole language of record on grounds of transformation, given that the removal of Afrikaans, in the view of the heads of court, is a reversal of past discrimination.

The point is that transformation as a concept can be skewed to suit a specific agenda and, in the process, conceal actual needed transformation, such as South Africans having access to justice in their mother tongue and not via an interpreter through the medium of English – a language with a long colonial trajectory. The point of English as a colonially-imposed language of record is an historical fact, as we discussed when considering the history of the language of record predating the arrival of Jan van Riebeeck in the Cape.

De Vos's (2010) outlook of the future of transformation as a concept in South Africa is dull, yet true in every sense. He states that "transformation has become a hollow and empty word, devoid of any real meaning". A search for literature on transformation in the legal system is flooded with articles on transformation of the judiciary in South Africa. The literature is written with specific reference to the legal system and is thus applicable. Transformation of the legal system is about embracing and enforcing the principles of a new legal order (Wesson & Du Plessis, 2008:5). Transformation of the judiciary is premised on racial and gender transformation and ensuring that, more broadly, the judiciary and legal profession is representative of the racial and gender demographics of South Africa (ibid, 11). By being representative, the legal system must facilitate the creation of a new inclusive society that the Constitution envisages (ibid, 12). This is in accordance with Section 174 of the Constitution, concerning the appointment of judicial officers, where racial and gender demographics must be taken into account when making judicial appointments.

Moerane (2003:716) viewed transformation as a process of change where language is included, i.e., transformation was not limited to race and gender. The issue, however, is that the judiciary does not recognise language as intrinsic to transformation. This was evident from Mogoeng Mogoeng's identified process of transforming the judiciary. Four of the five points are relevant to the discussions, namely:

> ...the importance of demographic representation; being aware of the injustices, which occurred under Apartheid; the inaccessibility of courts and the notion of real justice for Black persons; and abiding by the constitutional values for an equal and just legal system (Ntlama, 2014:15).

Although language is not explicitly mentioned, Docrat (2017a) argues that language is intrinsically linked to these points, with specific mention of the inaccessibility of the courts and attaining justice for persons speaking languages other than English. Docrat (2017a) went further and explained that there is no possible way in which an accessibility argument cannot include language playing a pivotal role. The legal system is accessed through a language: you present your case, defend yourself, or act as a witness. In all three instances, communication is key, so language has the power to include or exclude you from proceedings. The language of the prosecutor and presiding officer influences how you answer the questions and present your *viva voce* evidence. According to Docrat (2017a), linguistic transformation is key to a functioning legal system.

'Transformation' has become a prevalently used concept for change in the legal system; it has also been used in the context of universities, where Badat (2010), commissioned by the Development Bank of Southern Africa, submitted a report on the challenges of transformation in higher education institutions in South Africa. Badat (2010:31) noted that the institutional cultures, specifically at historically White universities, perpetuated a conscious and subconscious exclusion of students and younger academics who do not fit the stereotypical image of being White, from a privileged background, and where English was the medium of tuition and administration. According to Badat (2010:31), this can be exclusionary and disempowering.

The institutional cultures at universities may well have an impact on prospective and current students enrolling for degrees in African languages. Badat (2010:15) records that enrolments for language studies, especially the African languages, is declining at universities and this has a direct negative impact on the maintenance of multilingualism in South Africa. As a recommendation, Badat (2010:16) states that African languages should receive the concerted attention and protection of the Higher Education Ministry; this is vital for the promotion of multilingualism beyond the confines of universities and has a broader role in safeguarding the humanities and social sciences in South Africa.

Kaschula (2016:199-200) identified five points raised by Badat at a seminar on Africanisation and higher education. These are:

> Firstly, he asked whether a university can Africanise without transforming – in other words, what are we really talking about by using these terms? Secondly, how do we decolonise universities? This includes a de-gendering and de-masculinizing in building new academic cultures that embrace social inclusion and justice. Thirdly, one must debate the extent to which universities have critically analysed their traditions and cultures and engaged with pedagogic innovation at an epistemological level. Fourthly, university research and curricula need to engage with issues of transformation; lest universities simply remain in the mode of reproducing what already exists. Lastly, universities need to engage with producing students who show social accountability and who use their skills as instruments of the economy in an alternative manner to the neo-liberal globalisation epoch – students who produce fresh ideas, rather than those who simply reproduce what they are taught. Essentially, this means finding an African voice in both the political and pedagogic sense of the word.

Kaschula (2016:200) responded to these questions and points by arguing that they can be addressed by assessing the way in which language is used to teach and what is taught. Kaschula (2016) argues that a debate on decolonisation of the curriculum and transformation of higher education cannot take place where language is not part of the discussion. It is noticeable how Kaschula (2016) uses the words "decolonisation" and "transformation" in different senses in one sentence, leading one to the conclusion that the two are different processes. Kaschula (2016) explains that decolonisation of the university curriculum is not the mere change of reading materials; instead, it involves learning, teaching and expressing oneself in the language of one's choice, whether that be an African language or English. The point is that universities categorise language into confined boxes, for example, the language of learning and teaching is English-only. There is no reason why other languages cannot be used in a transforming and empowering way. This will encourage greater participation in lectures and tutorials while creating a culture of inclusivity, where a student is able to express themselves in a language they fully understand and the student, another student, or a lecturer, is able to provide an English summary where necessary.

Kaschula (2016:202) explains that decolonisation should rather be couched in the term 'Africanisation' which, in itself, represents a perspective through the medium of African languages. This will be a positive change as part of the transformation agenda. Africanisation will enable South African universities to move out of the racialised binary that has been created (Kaschula, 2016:209). Kaschula (2016:209) explains that intellectual domination is linked to English hegemony; language thus has an important role to play in changing this domination, where knowledge is informed by African experiences. Kaschula (2016) holds that decolonisation and transformation need to be defined according to each institution and that specific context, where language forms part of the decolonisation and transformation debates.

Higher education legislative and policy framework

The legislative framework, including the 'new transformative' of the Legal Practice Act (2014) pertaining to legal practitioners, fails to recognise the important role of language as a means of effective communication, access to justice, the level of substantive justice achieved, and employment opportunities through the creation of incentives. The focus of this chapter now shifts to language at universities.

The linkage between university legislative and policy frameworks and that of the legal system is the need to graduate linguistically competent LLB students who can positively affect the legal system in this transformation age in which we find ourselves.

The HEA (1997) is the primary legislation for regulating higher education in South Africa. To a certain extent, we have identified and explained the legislative and policy developments in the preceding discussions of this chapter. The HEA (1997) enables the drafting of subordinate legislation and language policies at university level. Section 27(2) is the provision that enables this. We quoted this provision earlier in this chapter (see 'Language planning in higher education') and repeat it here for convenience of discussion:

> Subject to the policy determined by the Minister, the council, with the concurrence of the senate, must determine the language policy of a public higher education institution and must publish and make it available on request.

According to Section 27(2), an institution's language policy cannot be inconsistent with the Ministerial Policy. Further, it must conform to the LPHE (2002) and read together with the National Language Policy Framework (2002). This was explained earlier. At this stage of the discussion, we are briefly advancing the relevant provisions, as the legislative and policy frameworks will be engaged with in greater depth further on. It must be noted that, although the HEA (1997) is the primary legislation regulating higher education, the Languages Act (2012), being the primary language legislation for the entire country, is also applicable. The Department of Higher Education and Training (DHET) is a government department and, as with the Department of Justice and Constitutional Development, is required to draft a language policy in accordance with the Languages Act (2012). The point is that the policies we have referred to above are to be read with the updated language policy.

The Revised Language Policy for Higher Education (2018) currently remains in draft form as the final comments are still being incorporated. The following extracted provisions (2018:9) are relevant:

Introduction and Background

1. Language has been and continues to be a barrier to access and success in higher education, both from the perspective that indigenous official languages have structurally not been afforded the official space to function as academic and scientific languages.
2. The majority of students entering higher education are not fully proficient in the present dominant languages of teaching and learning in higher education and are not even skilled and proficient – to the required level – in the language they call their tongue or choose as their preferred language of learning and teaching (LOLT).
3. Moreover, since the inception of democracy, the South African higher education system has experienced and accelerated increase in linguistic and cultural diversity in terms of student population, and therefore gradually becoming multilingual. For this reason, the country's higher education system is confronted with a challenge of ensuring the simultaneous development of a multilingual environment in which all our official languages are used as languages of scholarship, research, teaching and learning, while at the same time ensuring that the existing languages of offering do not serve as a barrier to student access and success.
4. Thus, mindful of the historically orchestrated underdevelopment and undervaluing of indigenous official languages prior to democracy, and the disinclination to empower these languages in the present dispensation, conditions must be created for the valuing of indigenous languages as languages of meaningful academic discourse, as well as sources of knowledge in the different disciplines of higher education…

Purpose

13. The purpose of the policy is to:
    13.1. guide higher education institutions to evolve relevant strategies, policies, implementation plans for strengthening indigenous official languages of South Africa as languages of teaching, learning, research, innovation and science; …

14. The policy therefore seeks to address the following:
    14.1. the language or languages of learning (medium or mediums of instruction) in higher education institutions, bearing in mind the fundamental right of persons to receive education in the official language or languages of their choice in public educational institutions, where it is reasonably practicable to do so, and the duty of the state to ensure effective access to and implementation of this right (section 29(2) of the Constitution)…

Policy Framework

25. The policy framework recognises the important role of higher education in the promotion of multilingualism for social, cultural, intellectual, and economic development…

- **The domain uses of the languages**
31. *Language of instruction*: This policy recognises the linguistic diversity of the student make-up of our higher education institutions and the value of language as a means of epistemic access. Universities must diversify the languages of instruction to include indigenous official languages…
- **Enablers:**
34. *Institutional language policy and plans*: Universities must revise their language policies to accord greater importance to the use of African languages for scholarship; teaching and learning; and administrative purposes. They must set up implementation structures that can leverage the opportunities provided by the instruments of this policy. Higher education institutions must indicate in their language policies and plans, strategies they have put in place to promote multilingualism and transformation…
- **Effective Date of Policy**
49. This policy will be effective from 1 January 2019.

These extracted provisions illustrate firstly, the emphasis placed on identifying and acknowledging the historical marginalisation and underdevelopment of the indigenous languages; secondly, the acknowledgement that there is an increase in student diversity; and, with this, that diversity language is key, given the multilingual make-up of students; and, thirdly, there is an instruction that indigenous languages be made languages of learning, teaching and research. The policy does not promote a monolingual language view and the advancement of English-only as a language of economic access. We make this point in light of these: the linkages between language planning and the economy; the selected university language policies presented below; and the case law concerning university language policies.

Selected university language policies

Against the theory presented above, selected practical language policies of South African universities are advanced. In each case, the relevant provisions are extracted.

Rhodes University

The history of RU's language policy commenced with the establishment of the RU Language Committee represented by Deans, administrative heads of department, and representatives from the staff union and SRC, as well as other relevant co-opted individuals internal to the university. The Vice Chancellor formally elected the Language Committee Chairperson. In 2014, the language policy was officially reviewed by a sub-committee comprising members who were knowledgeable in the drafting of language policies. The policy review made use of the process of meaningful engagement (Docrat, 2013) in conducting university-wide consultations on the contents of the policy, thereby adopting a bottom-up approach to language planning (Docrat & Kaschula, 2015).

The language policy is reviewed every three years. The review process commenced in 2017 and followed the same process described above; it was completed and approved by Council in September 2019. The provisions relevant to the discussions at hand include the following:

1.2. Policy Statement
The Language Policy of Rhodes University is predicated on the following principles:
- The University's language of learning and teaching is English, and the University's official business is conducted in English;
- Creation of an environment where language is not a barrier to equity of access, opportunity and success;
- Promotion of multilingualism and furthering the development of academic languages and literacies of the languages of South Africa where necessary and practicable;
- Creation of conditions for the use of particularly isiXhosa as a language of learning and teaching.

In light of historical conditions and contemporary realities:
- Other languages alongside English in a process of translanguaging may be used in teaching and learning e.g., in the tutorial system;…

1.4. Policy Objective/s
The following objectives are recommended where necessary and practicable and subject to the University's resources:
- Promote and support proficiency in isiXhosa, Afrikaans and English through vocation-specific and additional language courses for staff and students.
- Requirements in professions should be addressed through the offering of courses such as conversational isiXhosa in order to produce graduates who can function in a multilingual professional environment.
- Promote the development and literacies of academic languages, particularly of isiXhosa, through teaching, learning and research outputs as part of redressing the previous marginalisation of indigenous languages at departmental level.

Based on these extracted provisions, RU has made clear its intention to use isiXhosa as a LOLT across all subjects in all faculties. Although English is the primary LOLT, the policy dedicates the university's interests and resources to developing further isiXhosa as an academic language. What is also significant of the policy is that it permits the use of translanguaging in teaching and learning processes. According to Section 3, which deals with the definitions of the policy, translanguaging refers to a process which:

> Occurs when bilingual or multilingual speakers draw on a wide range of languages and language varieties to create meaning and to communicate. For example, reading, speaking or writing simultaneously in multiple languages.

This enables students to express their thoughts, ideas and opinions in their mother tongue to enable them to participate fully without being excluded. The process views language as a resource that enables and enhances the acquisition of knowledge and where language is not a barrier to teaching and learning. In doing so, the policy recognises the importance of graduating students who can function in professional multilingual contexts. This point is important for the argument of graduating linguistically competent LLB students.

University of Cape Town

UCT's language policy, enacted in 2013, is relatively short: a two-page document. The policy does, however, take note of the position of UCT as an institution that has an important role to play in the development of the official languages, particularly isiXhosa. The provisions relevant to this book are as follows:

Preamble

The University of Cape Town views language as a resource and recognises the personal, social and educational value of multilingualism, as well as the importance of promoting scholarship in all official South African languages.

The language policy of the University takes as its starting point the need to prepare students to participate fully in a multilingual society, where multilingual proficiency and awareness are essential.

The first objective is the development of multilingual awareness on the one hand, and multilingual proficiency on the other.

The second objective is to contribute to the national goals of developing all South African languages so that they may in the medium-to-long term be able to be used in instruction, and of promoting scholarship in all our languages.

While – given the location of the university in the Western Cape – English, isiXhosa and Afrikaans are all recognised by UCT as official languages, English is the primary medium on instruction and administration. However, although English is an international language, it is not the primary language for many of our students and staff. The third objective is, therefore, to ensure that our students acquire effective literacy in English, by which we understand the ability to communicate through the spoken and written word in a variety of contexts: academic, social, and professional.

Teaching and Examination

English is both the primary medium of teaching and of examination except in language and literature departments where another language is taught and may be used. This applies at all levels, and to dissertations and theses for higher degrees.

There is a definite acknowledgement of using isiXhosa as a LOLT. However, the policy entrenches English, even at postgraduate level, with the production of theses in English, except in departments where another language is the course subject. The policy, as opposed to that of RU, fails to permit the use of translanguaging. The practical components of UCT's vocation-specific courses in professional contexts is discussed further on in this chapter.

University of KwaZulu-Natal

It appears that UKZN's original 2006 language policy was revised in 2014. From the onset, the 2014 language policy unequivocally states that importance of being bilingual:

1. **Purpose statement**
   The University of KwaZulu-Natal identifies with the goals of South Africa's multilingual language policy and seeks to be a key player in its successful implementation. The policy recognises the need to develop and promote proficiency in the official languages, particularly English and isiZulu. The benefits for students becoming proficient in English, the dominant medium of academic communication and of trade and industry internationally, and the *lingua franca* in government and institutions in South Africa, are clear. Proficiency in isiZulu will contribute to nation building and will assist the student in effective communication with the majority of the population of KwaZulu-Natal. This Policy seeks to make explicit the benefits of being fully bilingual in English and isiZulu in South Africa and to inform a corresponding Language Plan.

Further emphasis is placed on isiZulu as an academic LOLT under the purpose statement that includes:

- achieve for isiZulu the institutional and academic status of English;
- provide facilities to enable the use of isiZulu as a language of learning, instruction, research and administration;
- become a national hub in the development of isiZulu national corpus and the development and standardization of isiZulu technical terminology and its dissemination.
- promote the intellectualization of isiZulu as an African language.

Although English is maintained as a LOLT at UKZN, the language policy is the first of its kind in relation to the others we have discussed – and will discuss further in this chapter – that places isiZulu alongside English as a language of learning and teaching:

> The University will continue to use English as its primary academic language but will activate the development and use of isiZulu as an additional medium of instruction together with the resources (academic and social) that make the use of the language a real possibility for interaction by all constituencies in the University.

In the language policy, UKZN validates the above purpose by stating the importance of isiZulu, not only for their current and future students, but for the university as a responsible institution, practically fulfilling the mandate of Section 6(2) of the Constitution:

2.2 At our University, students whose home language is isiZulu form an important and growing language group, reflecting the fact that isiZulu speakers are by far the largest single language group in KwaZulu-Natal. The University therefore has a duty to provide a linguistic and cultural ethos favourable to all students...

2.4 IsiZulu is one of the official South African indigenous languages named in the Constitution, whose 'use and status' have been 'historically diminished'. The University, following the Constitution, is bound to 'take practical and positive measures to elevate the status and advance the use of isiZulu'. The University is also bound to promote the principle of multilingualism i.e., that all official languages of South Africa enjoy parity of esteem and are treated equitably.

2.5 The Language Policy of the University forms part of a wider interconnected strategy at the national level to promote multilingualism and, at the provincial level, to advance isiZulu.

Realistically, UKZN's objectives would require administrative and academic staff who are bilingual in English and isiZulu. The language policy provides for this, stating the following:

5.4.3 The languages of administration will be English and isiZulu.

5.4.4 To enhance the knowledge of existing academic and administrative staff the University will provide language courses for staff who do not have English or isiZulu communication skills.

5.4.5 Candidates for posts in the administrative or academic sectors shall be expected to have knowledge of English and isiZulu. Where knowledge of either language is inadequate for the post, there will be provision for access to communication courses as appropriate.

Given the extensity of UKZN's language policy, a Language Plan (UKZN, 2014) was formulated to accompany the language policy with the aim of ensuring implementation. It is divided into phases, with each phase being implemented over a specific period. The implementation appears to be incremental in nature with two phases: Phase 1 will run from 2015 to 2019, and Phase 2 from 2020 to 2030. The purpose is outlined in the following excerpt:

The Language Plan guides the implementation goals to be achieved within each of the two phases. It also makes reference to the provision and monitoring of the budget and resources necessary for the implementation of the University's Language Policy.

The Language Plan is intended to assist in measuring progress made in the achievement of the goals of the Language Policy.

The Language Plan is divided into eight sub-categories under Phase 1. For the purposes of the discussions at hand, we will advance the relevant categories and only the relevant extracts from each relevant category.

1. Delivery of Services

1.1 An isiZulu language audit will be carried out to identify bilingual staff to ensure that the University has the operational capacity to comply with the Language Plan. Language proficiency records of all staff will be maintained in the University Human Resources database...

6. **Implementation of Policy on Language of Learning & Teaching**
6.1 In Phase 1, the main language of learning and teaching at the University will primarily be English. The use of isiZulu as a medium of instruction will be encouraged but will be at the discretion of the Schools and Colleges in consultation with the University Language Board, depending on their contexts of teaching and learning...
6.2 During Phase 1, students and staff will develop communicative competence in isiZulu and English sufficient for academic interaction.

With regard to receiving education in isiZulu, the language plan is extensive, thus we have extracted the sections relevant to the discussions at hand:

7.1.4 The Colleges will develop the following four main areas of isiZulu medium provision:
- '*Ab initio*' undergraduate provision provided by the discipline of isiZulu.
- High level skills courses, e.g. in translation or in formal written isiZulu.
- Professional/vocational provision for undergraduate students, designed to appeal to a wide audience and with individual disciplines being able to provide subject-specific input for their own students. Such provision will be developed through a gradual and realistic approach, and the possibility of attracting external funding will be explored.
- isiZulu for Adults, the provision of which will be extended in the light of identified student and staff demand.

7.2 The Colleges will appoint language tutors to teach, develop and co-ordinate isiZulu-medium provision throughout their Colleges, building on the current provision offered by the Discipline of isiZulu and drawing on the expertise of the staff of the Discipline...

7.3.2 The University will expand the introduction of modules in professional degrees (e.g., legal and medical isiZulu) that focus on proficiency in isiZulu and English as a priority to facilitate and enhance bilingual professional/vocational practice.

These extracted provisions from UKZN's Language Policy and Language Plan will be engaged with below. Suffice to say at this point, there is an unwavering commitment from the institution to place isiZulu on an equal footing alongside English.

Stellenbosch University

As with the language policies of the UFS and the UP, SU's language policy (2017) was contentiously before the CC in the *Gelyke Kanse and Others* v *Chairperson of the Senate of the University of Stellenbosch and Others* case (2019). The provisions of the language policy relevant to the themes of this book read as follows:

5. **Aims of the Policy**
5.1 To give effect to section 29(2) (language in education) and 29(1) (b) (access to higher education) read with section 9 (equality and the prohibition against direct and indirect unfair discrimination) of the Constitution...
5.4 To promote multilingualism as an important differentiating characteristic of SU.

These aims point to an inclusive, multilingual language policy that will see the use of all three official provincial languages being used as language of learning and teaching. This is, however, not the case for isiXhosa, which has not been incrementally introduced as a LOLT.

7. Policy provisions
The Policy principles above give rise to the following binding Policy provisions:
7.1 Learning and teaching
> 7.1.1 Afrikaans and English are SU's languages of learning and teaching. SU supports their academic use through a combination of facilitated learning opportunities for students, including lectures, tutorials and practicals, as well as learning support facilitated by means of information and communication technology (ICT).

The SU language policy speaks to the role of isiXhosa as an academic language in the section on the promotion of multilingualism and reads accordingly:

> 7.5.4 IsiXhosa as an emerging formal academic language receives particular attention for the purpose of its incremental introduction into selected disciplinary domains, prioritised in accordance with student needs in a well-planned, well organised and systematic manner. The academic role and leadership of the Department of African Languages, through its extensive experience in advanced-level teaching and research in language and linguistic fields, will be harnessed to the full. In certain programmes, isiXhosa is already used with a view to facilitating effective learning and teaching, especially where the use of isiXhosa may be important for career purposes. SU is committed to increasing the use of isiXhosa, to the extent that this is reasonably practicable, for example through basic communication skills short courses for staff and students, career-specific communication, discipline-specific terminology guides (printed and mobile applications) and phrase books.

The scope of isiXhosa is therefore limited to certain courses, particularly vocation-specific courses. It is not implemented across courses and faculties. Important to note, for the purposes of this research, is that there is scope for teaching isiXhosa as part of the LLB degree and this must be borne in mind in relation to the discussions in a section of this Chapter concerning language and the LLB curriculum.

University of the Free State

The UFS language policy (2016) was approved by the UFS Council on 11 March 2016. This policy is discussed in relation to the case of the CC judgment which forms an integral part of our discussions.

The relevant provisions from the preamble include:

> The University of the Free State (UFS) is committed to
> - Enabling a language-rich environment committed to multilingualism with particular attention to English, Afrikaans, Sesotho and isiZulu and, other languages represented on the three campuses.
> - Ensuring that language is not a barrier to equity of access, opportunity and success in academic programmes or in access to the UFS administration.
> - Promoting the provision of academic literacy, especially in English, for all undergraduate students.

- Ensuring that language is not used or perceived as a tool for social exclusion of staff and/or students on any of its campuses.
- Contributing to the development of Sesotho and isiZulu as higher education languages within the context of the needs of the UFS different campuses.
- The continuous development of Afrikaans as an academic language.

It is a known fact that preambles in legislative and policy documents are aspirational in nature, thus it is not surprising that UFS language policy preamble has an aspiratory tone it. There appears to be an intention to create an inclusive multilingual university; however, this is limited by the third goal where the focus is primarily on English. The focus is thus on producing monolingual graduates.

2. Principles
The following principles inform the adoption of this policy:
- Diversity, equity, redress, reconciliation and social justice.
- Practicability, cost effectiveness and justifiability.
- Support for academic literacy development at undergraduate level.
- Support for the development of multilingualism.
- Language as a resource for the university to achieve individual development and integration.

The majority of principles upon which the UFS language policy is premised encourage and celebrate multilingualism; however, this is qualified through the insertion of the second principle of "practicability, cost effectiveness and justifiability". The costs argument, as we have illustrated, is a caveat that will enable the university to state that it is not practicable to have languages other than English as languages of learning and teaching owing to cost implications.

4. Policy statement
Bearing in mind the above commitments, principles and definitions the following policy is accepted:

4.1 English becomes the primary medium of instruction at undergraduate and postgraduate level on all three campuses.

4.2 Multilingualism is supported among other activities by an expanded tutorial system especially designed for first-year students. Tutorials take place in English, Afrikaans and Sesotho in the same class on the Bloemfontein Campus and in English, Sesotho and isiZulu on the Qwaqwa Campus.

4.3 In particular professional programmes such as teacher education and the training of students in Theology who wish to enter the ministry in traditional Afrikaans-speaking churches, where there is clear market need, the parallel medium English-Afrikaans and Sesotho/isiZulu continues. This arrangement must not undermine the values of inclusivity and diversity endorsed by the UFS.

4.4 The primary formal language of the UFS administration will be English with sufficient flexibility for the eventual practice of multilingualism across the UFS.

4.5 Formal student life interactions should be in English, while multilingualism is encouraged in all social interactions.

The entire policy statement above focuses on English as the language of learning, teaching and research. The insertion of 4.5 is gravely concerning where English is to be used in "formal student life interactions". In our opinion, this effectively forces a student to speak in a language other than their mother tongue, given that, in the Free State, the majority of persons do not speak English as their mother tongue. The policy statements are to be implemented by the university which includes, as part of their policy, the implementation goals. Those of relevance are extracted here:

5. Implementation
    5.1 Undergraduate teaching and learning
        5.1.1 Lectures, study materials, examinations and related material will be in English.
        5.1.2 Multilingual study resources will be provided in the context of tutorials in order to support epistemological access for all students.
        5.1.5 Undergraduate programmes offered in English will include as part of their contact time at first- and second-year level tutorials in Afrikaans, English, and Sesotho/isiZulu depending on the campus needs.
    5.2 Postgraduate education
        5.2.1 The language for the writing of theses and dissertations at the UFS is English except in disciplines where languages other than English are taught as subjects of study.
        5.2.2. Specific cases for the use of languages other than English in theses and dissertations is left to the discretion of the head of department and the dean who are accountable for the implementation of this language policy and for the compliance with the academic rules of the UFS regarding external examination of PhD theses.

For undergraduate students, English language learning and teaching is entrenched through course material being produced in English only. Clause 5.1.2 does, however, provide for the use of languages other than English in tutorials. This is limited, as noted in 5.1.5, to first- and second-year tutorials only. One can only ponder and question if the UFS are under the misinformed understanding that students would be fully competent in English when they reach their third year. It is concerning that the language in education right, Section 29(2) of the Constitution is unfairly limited for those students who are not proficient in English.

With the UFS compelling students to produce theses in English only, with the exception of theses produced in specific language courses, it is clear that the institution is not contributing to the development of African languages for terminology and intellectualisation purposes, in accordance with the HEA (1997). Clause 5.2.2, which permits a PhD candidate to produce their thesis in a language other than English, at the discretion of a Dean and head of department, is wholly suspended in the section where it states: "… head of department and the dean who are accountable for the implementation of this language policy and for the compliance with the academic rules of the UFS regarding external examination of PhD theses". If the Dean and head of department permit this, they will be in breach of their duties and act contrary to the language policy objectives; in this way, the production of theses in English-only is secured.

These provisions and related brief discussions are to be borne in mind with the case discussion later in this chapter. The provisions will also inform the conclusions and recommendations of this research in Chapter 10, in terms of what needs to be amended by universities in drafting languages policies. Furthermore, this will highlight the effect that policies such as this UFS language policy have on hindering the promotion, use and development of African languages in accordance with Section 6, read with Section 29(2), of the Constitution.

University of Pretoria

As with the language policy of the UFS, the UP's language policy (2019) is central to the core of this research given that it also informs the case law. The UP is another institution that has adopted an English-only language policy. The provisions relevant to the discussions at hand are extracted from the UP's language policy. Although formulated and approved by Council in 2016, the policy was subject to court processes in the form of an application that was brought to challenge the constitutionality of the policy and review the administrative decision-making process. Implementation of the policy was therefore delayed, and it only became effective from 1 January 2019.

> 1. **Purpose**
> The purpose of this policy is to determine language planning, management and practice at the University of Pretoria in a framework that promotes academic quality, equality and social cohesion, as well as to redress imbalances.

The purpose of the policy emulates the HEA (1997) and the broader mandate of the Constitution to achieve social cohesion and equality, while redressing past discrimination. This, in our opinion, would translate into the policy adopting African languages as languages of learning and teaching alongside English. This is, unfortunately, not what was intended.

> 4. **Policy statement**
> In support of the above considerations, the following policy is adopted:
> 4.1 English is the language of teaching and learning (in lectures, tutorials and assessments) except in cases where the object of study is a language other than English, and in programmes with profession-specific language outcomes, subject to approval by Senate;
> 4.2 The University must identify needs and provide the necessary financial and other resources to facilitate learning in the medium of English;
> 4.3 The University must provide spaces and resources for drawing on students' strongest languages (in particular Sepedi and Afrikaans, but where possible also other South African languages) to assist students in understanding key concepts in their modules; ...
> 4.5 The University must adequately resource the development of Sepedi to a higher level of scientific discourse and must support the maintenance of Afrikaans as a language of scholarship; ...

The policy statement above entrenches English as the sole language of learning and teaching. It is ironic to see, in 4.2, how far the institution is willing to go, and the financial injections being made to ensure the successful implementation of the English-only language policy. Throughout our discussions, we have highlighted the costs argument being used in defence of excluding African languages; yet there is no hesitation in allocating funds to further the promotion and use of English. The policy statement, in our view, is contrary to the purpose, outlined at the beginning of the policy, calling for historical redress, equality and social cohesion. The UP policy goes a step further than the UFS policy by stating that English will also be the sole language used in tutorials. It seems meaningless to state in 4.3 that Sepedi concepts are to be developed for the modules to assist students, as students are not permitted to express themselves in their mother tongue, if that is not English. The 'adequate' resourcing of Sepedi as per 4.5 is vague, with no tangible directive to do so. The policy statement appears to be contrary to the following listed principles:

> 3. Principles
> The University of Pretoria's language policy seeks to:
>> 3.2 promote inclusiveness and social cohesion, while guarding against exclusivity and marginalisation, and in this way contribute to creating an environment where all students and staff feel confident and comfortable and can enjoy a sense of belonging;
>> 3.3 be transformative in attending to historical injustices and promote justice and equality;
>> 3.4 facilitate an equitable learning environment that provides equal access to knowledge and resources; ...
>> 3.6 promote multilingualism in all South African languages, with specific responsibility for the development of Sepedi to the highest level of scholarship; ...

The policy is to be implemented incrementally with regard to phasing out of Afrikaans as a language of assessment, teaching and learning. On the point of assessments, essays at undergraduate level and those at postgraduate level can, according to 5.11 of the policy, be completed in any language where "reasonably practicable".

A critique of selected university language policies

The discussions of language policies at selected South African higher education institutions highlight the importance of the language question in higher education as part of transformation and Africanisation. The practical insights provided alert one to the many issues that continue to exclude students on grounds of language and point to the half-hatched graduates being produced, who, in the case of the legal system, will not be able to give effective meaning to the constitutional language rights. The language policy framework must be in place in order for law faculties and African language departments to change the curriculum positively, as indicated earlier.

From a legislative and policy perspective, the HEA (1997), through Section 27(2) thereof, provides the enabling authority for the drafting of university language policies. The HEA (1997) provides no further directives on the drafting of language policies and merely states that university language policies may not be inconsistent with the Ministerial Policy.

The Revised Language Policy for Higher Education (2018) is very clear on the university mandate applicable when formulating a language policy. The entire policy, in acknowledging the marginalisation and resultant underdevelopment of indigenous official languages in South Africa, accords a positive obligation on universities to revise language policies to change the linguistic landscape. Sections 31 and 34 are of particular importance in the context of the research at hand. Through the word "must", Section 31 obligates universities to "…diversify languages of instruction to include indigenous official languages". Universities enacting language policies where English is the sole LOLT are acting contrary to this obligation where the university language policy is inconsistent with the Revised Language Policy for Higher Education (2018). Having said this, as we noted, the Revised Language Policy for Higher Education (2018) came into effect on 1 January 2019 following the formulation of the monolingual university language policies.

These university language policies have already been challenged legally, with two cases being decided unfavourably in the CC, this being the apex court. The Revised Language Policy for Higher Education (2018) will, however, not be obsolete and will serve to regulate other universities in revising their language policies. This mandate is clarified in Section 34 of the Revised Language Policy for Higher Education (2018): universities, through their language policies, are to revise their previous language policies and language plans "…to accord greater importance…" to using African languages, not only for teaching and learning purposes, but for research and scholarship as well. This speaks to the role universities have to play in intellectualising the African languages.

Section 34 goes further to obligate universities to put strategies in place to promote multilingualism and transformation. These strategies are to be included in universities' language policies. The latter hold universities to account through the inclusion of strategies where the language policy is not theoretical but establishes how the objectives will be achieved. There is also the linkage between language and transformation which is important, given the preceding discussions in this book which illustrate where language has not been identified as a tool to transform.

What follows is an engagement with each of the six university language policies in relation to the HEA (1997) and Revised Language Policy for Higher Education (2018).

RU began revising their language policy in 2018 and completed the process in 2019; we specifically mention the dates, given the gazetting of the Revised Language Policy for Higher Education (2018). Compliance with the latter was thus mandatory. Taking cognisance of the extracts from the RU language policy, we note three points which immediately stand out. Firstly, the policy states that English is the language of learning and teaching and so fails to "diversify the languages of instruction…" by including, for example, isiXhosa as a LOLT, in accordance with Section 31 of the Revised Language Policy for Higher Education (2018). We fully acknowledge that there are arising legal implications for a university to include (an)other language(s); however, efforts need to be made in including (an)other language(s) for teaching and learning purposes, understanding that such implementation is incremental. It is therefore important to include strategies and mechanisms regarding how the policy will be implemented, over what period of time and the cost and staffing implications. This is precisely what Section 34 of the Revised Policy for Higher Education (2018) requires.

The positive attributes, in congruence with the provisions of the Revised Policy for Higher Education (2018), include the recognition of the need to promote multilingualism and further the development of isiXhosa as an academic language. This is, however, qualified by the phrase "where necessary". It is discretionary; and, given that there are no timelines for implementing this, enforceability is minimalised. The same applies to the inclusion of vocation-specific courses as these are subject to university resources. The RU Language Policy does recognise the importance of producing graduates "… who can function in a multilingual professional environment". Many positive developments have been made in RU's Language Policy; and, if mechanisms and timelines are included, the policy, through its future revisions, could include isiXhosa as a language of learning and teaching – that is, if the university is committed to a transformation programme that includes the language question.

From a language policy perspective, in comparison to RU, UCT falls short in equating the African languages alongside English. A positive attribute of RU's Language Policy is the inclusion of translanguaging for students to use to express themselves in their mother tongue without excluding monolingual students. UCT's Language Policy, in recognising the need to use all South African languages as languages of scholarship, pledges to developing languages, so "… in the medium to long term…", the languages can be used as languages of instruction. As with RU's Language Policy, UCT recognises English as the only language of learning and teaching and therefore states that one objective is to ensure that students acquire 'good' English. UCT is yet to revise their language policy following the gazetting of the Revised Language Policy for Higher Education (2018).

Presently, UCT must also be acknowledged for implementing isiXhosa for medical students, a compulsory vocation-specific course which all students have to pass prior to obtaining their medical degree. The University of the Witwatersrand (Wits) has introduced an isiZulu medical course. The course equips medical students with critical language skills that can be used in practice when communicating with isiXhosa- or isiZulu-speaking patients. Corder (2019) stated that the vocation-specific course is an excellent idea and should be implemented in the Law Faculty. In saying so, he acknowledged that logistical issues, such as curriculum space, staffing, and collaboration with the African Languages Department would need to take place. He explained that, as with RU, there was an elective, but students instead opted to learn foreign languages rather than the indigenous South African languages. The same applied to the undergraduate LLB curriculum, where students are required to learn an additional language, and yet opt to learn Spanish or French instead of isiXhosa (Corder, 2019).

The universities need to strike a balance between the provincial languages and English, where English is maintained for international and communicative purposes, while not foregoing the constitutional and legislative responsibility of developing the African languages. A university which has managed (and is managing) to achieve this task, is UKZN. UKZN's language policy was formulated and signed by Council in 2014, prior to the gazetting of the Revised Language Policy for Higher Education (2018). UKZN's language policy differs from all the other selected university language policies in that isiZulu is a language of teaching and learning alongside English. The language policy in its entirety is devoted to advancing isiZulu. By stating that isiZulu is a LOLT, the language policy and language plan acknowledge that, in order to achieve this throughout all colleges (faculties), staff capacity needs to be developed. This, according to the policy, will be achieved by ensuring that current staff are equipped with isiZulu through various language courses; and that new appointees, depending on the nature of the post, will be competent in isiZulu so as to function meaningfully in the academic space.

UKZN's language policy is accompanied by a well-formulated Language Plan (2014) which envisages objectives in the language policy being achieved through two phases. Each phase is accorded specific timelines for realisation and implementation. The phases outline proactive strategies and mechanisms to achieve the objectives and are constantly reviewed to account for budget changes and so forth. The Language Plan, furthermore, creates employment opportunities where isiZulu, as an African language, is used as an incentive in employing tutors and relevant persons for the vocation-specific and other language-related courses.

A key attribute of the language policy is the development of an isiZulu corpus via which terminology can be disseminated and the language be intellectualised for use in high status domains and professional contexts. We stated earlier that this development is critical for the use of African languages as languages of record in courts. This development can also be juxtaposed to the judgment of *State* v *Damani* (2016) where a lack of terminology was cited as a reason to maintain an English-only language of record policy for courts. Furthermore, as opposed to the other five selected universities, UKZN has made it compulsory for all students, regardless of their degree, to pass isiZulu prior to graduating. This applies to both mother tongue and non-mother tongue students. This has been validated through the policy, based on Section 6 of the Constitution. As well as affording students their right to be taught in their mother tongue, as espoused in Section 29(2) of the Constitution, this recognises the fact that the majority of people in KwaZulu-Natal speak isiZulu as their mother tongue.

UKZN's language policy has come under criticism, particularly for the specific aspect of all students having to pass isiZulu before graduating. On 31 March 2019, the *Sunday Times* newspaper (Bhengu, 2019) reported in a front-page headline: "Taking Zulu module won't boost marks – even for mother tongue students", referring to the compulsory isiZulu module at UKZN. The newspaper article focused on a journal article (Murray, 2019) published by a UKZN academic in the sciences. The article is based on a statistical analysis of students' marks in the isiZulu module, as opposed to their marks across other courses. Upon closer engagement with the article (Murray, 2019), problematic points of discussion can be highlighted. Each of these points forms the basis of Murray's (2019) article.

The first point identified is that the six-month module does not provide students with proficiency at academic level; this is according to a student, as per the newspaper article (Bhengu, 2019). There is no possible way in which any language course for a six-month period could provide a student with full academic proficiency in that language. The student should be posed the question of whether taking a law module for six months results in one becoming an attorney, or well versed with all components of the law. The simple answer would be 'No'. Why, then, where languages are concerned, are students of the idealistic and misinformed perception that learning isiZulu for a period of six months will result in full academic proficiency in that language? There is a notion that, as mother tongue speakers, an easy credit can be sought by learning that language at university level.

The argument that Murray (2019) provides, that mother tongue speakers are prevented from taking alternative courses as a result of the isiZulu module, is baseless, given that isiZulu mother tongue speakers are exempt from registering for the compulsory course and can do so voluntarily. Murray (2019:2) goes further to argue that student time spent learning a new course is time wasted for other courses. The statement presents a one-sided view. As with any course, time needs to be invested by each student to achieve results. It is inaccurate and unfair to blame a language module for a student's time management and poor performance. The study fails to advance proof that the language module is to blame. The student quoted in the newspaper article (Bhengu, 2019) provides her own perception of the course; and one student alone does not mean the entire course is a failure. It is concerning that mother tongue African language students are interested in studying only a six-month module for an easy credit. This undermines not only the status of African languages but also creates the mistaken impression that African language modules and degrees are not worthy of academic study and should be an 'easy' credit. One would rarely find an English mother tongue student who is studying an English module at university level saying they are there for an easy credit; nor would the difficulty or intensity of the module be questioned or blamed for a lack of performance in other courses. There is no evidence to suggest that African language mother tongue students are underperforming as they are battling to use English, the medium of instruction, as Murray (2019) states.

The entire article in both cases (journal and newspaper) portrays isiZulu in a negative light, with factual inaccuracies and misperceptions; and English emerges as a unifying language to solve all problems. In fact, Murray (2019:3) makes no qualms about suggesting that English be made compulsory for all African language mother tongue speakers. The point is that this form of criticism needs to be addressed internally. Based on the contents of UKZN's language policy, there are mechanisms for reviewing implementation to address practical challenges when these arise.

The remaining three selected university language policies present a negative outlook of non-inclusion and non-development for the African languages.

SU's language policy, ironically, states that the policy aims to give effect to Section 29(2), as well as Section 29(1) (b) and Section 9 of the Constitution. After engaging with the policy, however, it is clear to us that access to higher education is, according to the policy, achieved through English as the primary language of learning and teaching, with Afrikaans used in certain domains. This enables 'equal' access and does not discriminate against a potential student on grounds of language. Again, this speaks to an earlier point we made regarding the skewed understanding of 'equal access' and discriminating fairly against everyone; yet English mother tongue students are not discriminated against, fairly or unfairly.

The language policy, in promoting the importance of multilingualism, recognises isiXhosa as an "emerging formal academic language" which will be implemented incrementally, in selected domains. In essence, there is then a qualification restricting the implementation of isiXhosa as a LOLT. As opposed to UKZN's language policy, SU, in its language policy, fails to assign timelines and strategies for the implementation of this objective. Further noteworthy inclusions, as with the other university language policies, include vocation-specific courses for students, as well as isiXhosa courses for staff.

UFS's language policy also entrenches English as the primary language of instruction at undergraduate level. The language policy makes an exception at postgraduate level, subject to the head of department or dean's discretion. This is contrary to what occurs at RU where, for example, at postgraduate level, regardless of the faculty in which the student is registered, a thesis can be completed in any language. English, as a primary language of instruction, is further strengthened given that it must be used in all lectures, study materials and examinations at undergraduate level. It is ironic, then, that the language policy states that language must not be a barrier to access; and that the policy only speaks to the African languages in the context of promoting isiZulu and Sesotho on the three UFS campuses.

UP, in their language policy, went a step further by stating that financial and other resources be made available to facilitate the learning of English – this in support of English as the primary language of learning and teaching. The same financial support is not afforded to Sepedi even though it must be developed, according to the language policy.

The language question at selected universities

We have advanced the relevant provisions of the language policies of each of the six selected universities, all of which are located in a South African province where English is not the majority spoken language, as evidenced in the language statistics captured in Table 3.1. It would thus be practical for the selected universities to have formulated or revised language policies that are reflective of the language demographics of the respective provinces. This would also have ensured constitutional compliance with Section 6 of the Constitution. Unfortunately for three (UFS, UP and SU) of the six selected universities, monolingual language planning models were formulated and adopted.

What was severe was the fact that each of these universities was previously a bilingual institution where English and Afrikaans were both recognised as languages of teaching and learning. Having had experience with bilingual learning and teaching and recognising the issues associated with a bilingual language policy, the universities were poised to amend these policies successfully to include an African language spoken by the majority of the province. For Rhodes and UCT, being monolingual English institutions since their establishment, there is a commitment towards multilingualism and the recognition of isiXhosa and Afrikaans as provincial languages. The pace at which these institutions are moving regarding the language question appears to be moderate.

From the six selected institutions, UKZN is the only institution pursuing a bilingual LOLT policy, with the entire focus of both the Language Policy and Language Plan on developing isiZulu and placing it on an equal footing alongside English. This gives practical meaning to the language demographics of the province, where the overwhelming majority, 77.8% of the province, speak isiZulu as their mother tongue (see Table 3.1). The point we are conveying links back to discussions concerning decolonisation and transformation at institutions of higher learning.

Applying the definitions and theoretical underpinnings of decolonisation to the language policies of universities, the UFS, the UP and SU would, in our opinion, fall short. The term 'decolonisation' in itself refers directly to colonialism, so it is nonsensical to adopt a monolingual English language policy when English was the language of the colonisers.

There is undoubtedly a skewed interpretation of what decolonisation at universities should be. This skewed interpretation and rationalisation would then preclude the language question and only concern aspects such as name changes and symbolic statues. Kaschula's (2016) proposal that the term 'Africanisation' be used in place of decolonisation is a sound one, as language is then included, plus the focus is on African principles rather than colonialism. In the context of UCT, the #FeesMustFall and #FreeDecolonisedEducation Campaigns from 2015 to 2017 placed emphasis on the removal of statues. Other symbols and slogans such as 'Decolonise the curriculum' were used where there was a plea to exclude 'western' textbooks and research; but the language question failed to feature prominently.

Motinyane (2020) argues that attitudes towards language played a major role in the protests. The protests, with calls to decolonise the curriculum, swept across universities; however, it was concerning and questionable to see protest placards written in English rather than in African languages. There was no increase in the number of students registering in African languages at these respective institutions (RU, UCT and SU). None of these universities indicated that there had been a sudden increase in numbers following the protests; instead, they maintained that numbers had remained high.

From a bottom-up approach, there was no student voice permeating these protests on the right to be taught in their mother tongues and the power of their languages in decolonising and transforming the universities. Similarities can be sought with the Soweto Uprisings of 1976 in South Africa concerning the power associated with English: schoolchildren, in protesting against the use of Afrikaans, failed to mobilise power around their mother tongues (African languages) and opted for English instead.

Language as part of the LLB curriculum

With the legal system transforming, one would expect that the LLB curriculum would be reflective of this changing landscape. This is not the case, however, given that both the legal system and universities are moving towards English-only language policies, forsaking their collective responsibility for social justice and abandoning the constitutional ideals.

We have made mention of the 2017 proposal by then chairperson of the Parliamentary Justice and Corrections Oversight Committee, Mathole Motshekga, that all LLB students pass one of the indigenous languages before being awarded a law degree (Ndenze, 2017:4). The proposal was made with the aim of transforming the legal system. Debate raged on for months, with many voicing their dissent at the proposal on a number of grounds, including the practical relevance of doing so and how learning a language as part of an LLB degree was irrelevant and time-consuming in an already onerous law curriculum. As we have argued, law is not a profession that exists in isolation from broader society where interaction with other people is minimal or non-existent; it is, in fact, the complete opposite for legal professionals who practise the law.

The proposal would require university language policies to create mechanisms for ensuring all students graduate with an African language, i.e., register for the subject and major in it, either at mother tongue or second language level, or complete the vocation-specific course, if offered as part of the LLB programme. The specifications would need to be determined by every university if not dictated by policy at national level. This would require collaboration between the various African language departments, as well as the law faculties at universities.

The question then arises as to where such a course would fit into the curriculum. There is a constant defence mechanism that the curriculum is already 'full'. At RU, for example, students completing the two-year LLB degree, having completed an undergraduate degree majoring in Legal Theory, are required to do a course called Legal skills. One of the objectives of this course is to equip students with practical aspects of legal practice. There are a number of components in the course, including a writing course, maths skills and a practical component that entails working for a semester at the RU Legal Aid Clinic. Docrat, having completed her degrees at RU, including her LLB during 2014-2015, offered the views, as set out in this paragraph:

> The legal skills course is undertaken in the penultimate year of the two-year LLB degree. The class of students is divided into two groups, with each group working in the Rhodes University Legal Aid Clinic for a semester. You are assigned to smaller groups at the Rhodes University Legal Aid Clinic under the tutelage of an attorney. The long and the short of it is that you are then required to consult with the indigent people seeking legal advice on civil law issues. During my semester, my group comprised three students: one was a foreign student; and the other was from outside the Eastern Cape Province (where Rhodes University is located). Given that I am proficient in isiXhosa I did not require the assistance of an interpreter, student colleagues would require interpretation, as would the vast majority of the entire class, given that they could not communicate in isiXhosa. There was no legal interpreter of any sort, so either the receptionist or the person who attends to the cleaning needs at the clinic would be called in to 'act' as an interpreter during consultations. In my case, communication was direct, in isiXhosa; the client appeared to be at ease, communicated freely and appeared to trust me immediately. Somehow, the power relations appeared relaxed or non-existent, given the absence of language barriers. The point is that it would be of immense benefit for both the students and, more specifically, the clients accessing the services, if legal personnel were able to communicate directly in their clients' mother tongue, which are primarily either isiXhosa or Afrikaans, or both.
>
> As part of the LLB curriculum, in the final year of the LLB degree, elective courses are offered, one of which is isiXhosa for Law. It is a vocation-specific course which aims to equip students with legal terminology and language skills to communicate effectively in isiXhosa. During final year, a specific number of electives (all voluntary) is to be undertaken. IsiXhosa for Law is not offered to students who have majored in the language or who are mother tongue speakers of the language. The positioning of the course as an elective in final year offers no benefit to the legal skills course in the penultimate year. This speaks to the positioning of the course and the need for

> management structures of both the Law Faculty and African Languages Departments to act positively on the language question. If learning an additional language (African language) is compulsory for other degrees such as journalism and pharmacy, why is law excluded? The bottom line, in my opinion, is the intention of those in authority: their commitment towards the African languages; and graduating students who are linguistically aware and competent.

With reference to UCT, Corder (2019) acknowledged that learning an African language and collaboration with the African Languages Department, would be beneficial and that there could be overlap with their legal aid clinic on the UCT campus. Simply put, collaboration is needed and the curriculum question, in light of decolonisation and transformation, needs to be revisited. By formulating these courses in professional contexts, universities will contribute to terminology development and thus the intellectualisation of the African languages. This terminology would be central for a legal system as was stated in the case law, there is no language corpus in the African languages for use in the legal system, so terminology is lacking. This speaks to the role of universities in society and the intersections between language, law and, in this case, higher education. This also speaks to the broader mandate of universities concerning the language question which Alexander (2005:30) summarised thus:

> The basic idea is that a university or group of universities would be given the task of developing specific languages such as isiZulu, or isiXhosa, or Sesotho, or Setswana and over a period of 10 to 15 years…a step-by-step development and implementation plan should be formulated…such that…it will be clear when they will be able to be used as languages of tuition in specific disciplines. The decision, however, about when to begin using the languages for specific functions will be the prerogative of the relevant institutional community.

The concept is not a foreign one if one takes the development and implementation of Afrikaans as an example. African language speaking legal academics and legal practitioners would need to dedicate the time to producing research in their mother tongues, where textbooks are written in the African languages. According to Froneman J (2019), this is not impractical nor impossible; and if the Afrikaans speaking academic community could do so, why is the same intention not shared by African language academics? The latter points speak to transforming the curriculum, where content is in one's mother tongue, making the curriculum more accessible for all. This is needed by many students entering universities with limited reading and writing skills in English. At a 2019 forensic linguistics colloquium, hosted at RU under the theme 'New courtroom languages', the book, *New frontiers in forensic linguistics: New themes and perspectives in language and law in Africa and beyond* (Ralarala et al., 2019), Volume I in this book series, was launched. At this colloquium, an isiXhosa mother tongue Master's student in forensic linguistics explained the difficulty she continuously experiences when engaging with academic texts. The student provided an emotional account of how she had to read books and journal articles multiple times, firstly to understand the English, then to comprehend the concepts. She explained that the aforementioned book had lessened the burden considerably, given that the level of English was accessible. She advocated for knowledge and research to be produced in the African languages to provide students with equal access to knowledge enjoyed by English mother tongue speaking students.

Maseko (2008, 2014) has advocated for vocation-specific courses in professional contexts at university level, where the language question is far more deep-rooted than merely learning and teaching in a language. When taking account of the demographics we have presented, the majority of people, being African language speakers, do not exist in a vacuum separate from their culture and identity, which is essentially informed through language. Maseko (2008) summarises this point:

> Part of this transformation deals with the notion of identity negotiation. The challenge at most South African universities is to negotiate an identity of belonging for students. Language and culture are important in this process, and acknowledgement thereof can create an environment conducive to inclusivity rather than exclusivity. Furthermore, an individual's self-identification through language opens up interaction with other cultures, thereby deepening a unified sense of voice rather than voiceless silence and cultural alienation. Developing mother tongue and second-language vocation-specific courses is integral to fostering this sense of acceptance and inclusion.

Kaschula (2016:208) contextualises the importance of vocation-specific courses in South African universities in the transformational age, taking into account previous discussions we have advanced that link language, law, power and the economy:

> When it comes to the teaching of African languages as second languages, generic first additional language or second-language courses do have their place. However, there needs to be a more integrated social approach to the teaching of these languages as part of transforming university curricula and culture, creating the "mindfulness" discussed earlier in this article. Furthermore, the development of vocation-specific courses is vital at this time in South Africa's socio-political history. There remains little evidence of a normalised, integrated, transformed, multilingual society, at least from a linguistic point of view. Instead, what exists now is a "linguistic fault line" which divides the "haves" and the "have-nots" into a three-tier economic system, based on those citizens who are communicatively competent in English, those who have a partial knowledge of the language, and those who speak no English at all.

This excerpt takes cognisance of the language question at universities in relation to the evolving sociopolitical and cultural spectrums, where universities are no longer exclusively for what has been stereotyped, as English mother tongue speaking students.

Analysis of the higher education language policy cases

What emerges from the cases in Chapter 7 is that university management structures are propelling English-only language policies under the guise of transformation, which, in our opinion, is completely the opposite of what a university transformation agenda should be enabling. In the *Gelyke Kanse and Others* v *Chairperson of the Senate of the University of Stellenbosch and Others* (2019) case, the costs argument weighed heavily in arguments and the determination of the standard of reasonable practicability with the implementation of Section 29(2) of the Constitution. The court held that it was not the burden of a university to develop or sustain a language. We disagree with this point in light of the reasoning throughout this entire book. In addition, UKZN, as seen from the earlier discussions, has been abundantly clear in their language policy: universities have a central role to play in developing the languages in accordance with the constitutional mandate so that the African languages in particular can be used in all domains in society. Froneman J (2019:66) comments on this issue and raises the important point of the need to identify whose responsibility it is do so:

> The first judgment candidly declares that "[e]ndorsing the University's 2016 Language Policy as conforming with section 29(2) comes at a cost. Our judgment must acknowledge it". It recognises that the "flood-tide of English" is a real threat to minority languages, including Afrikaans. It proceeds then to state that this risk is not Stellenbosch University's burden, nor is the fact that Afrikaans has all but vanished as a language of instruction at other tertiary institutions.

In terms of accessing education in your mother tongue, as Section 29(2) enables, this will now be significantly diminished based on the judgments in Chapter 7. It is also concerning that the CC, through its majority judgments, has endorsed this position, as Froneman J (2019:para. 75) also pointed out in the *Gelyke Kanse and Others* v *Chairperson of the Senate of the University of Stellenbosch and Others* judgment. Alexander (2013:84) stated that English enjoying a hegemonic position globally would not guarantee educational equity at tertiary level if it were the language of instruction. In fact, the scales will be tipped in favour of the already privileged mother tongue speakers and proficient second language speakers of English. Thus, the vast majority will remain disadvantaged, as Hendricks J correctly pointed out in the UFS judgment (*AfriForum and Another v Chairman of the Council of the University of the Free State and Others,* 2016) of the court *a quo.*

What is glaringly disturbing in Mogoeng CJ's judgment in the *UFS* (*AfriForum and Another v University of the Free State,* 2018) case is the constant reference to Afrikaans as a medium of instruction fostering racism. Froneman J pointed out that this would imply that all other official languages (African languages) other than English divide a university along racial and ethnic lines. Froneman J appeared to have reiterated this point in the *Gelyke Kanse and Others* v *Chairperson of the Senate of the University of Stellenbosch and Others*

(2019:para. 76) case. A point of critique is that Mogoeng CJ, in the *UFS* (*AfriForum and Another v University of the Free State*, 2018) case, failed to engage with the sentiments on the point of language, race and ethnicity outlined by Alexander (2013:84), who stated:

> An Afrikaans-dominant or a Zulu-dominant university does not have to be an ethnic university. Because an entire university community is Zulu speaking, they cannot be said to be ethnicist or even racist. The language of tuition does not determine whether or not a course or a university is racist or tribalist. It is what is taught that is decisive.

The majority in both CC judgments, as well as Kollapen J in the *UP* case (*AfriForum and Another v Chairperson of the Council of the University of Pretoria and Others*, 2017), are clearly conflicted as to whether African languages will have any relevance in the transformation of higher education and society more broadly. It is also concerning that African language voices and organisations have not been vocal on these issues and have not considered joining proceedings as *amicus curiae*.

The dissenting judgments and differing reasoning offer positive glimpses that there is hope for all official languages to be treated equally. Furthermore, the dissenting judgments, in the South African context, can be equated with those of Wilson J in the Canadian case study presented in Chapter 7.

The *UNISA* case (2020) offered a new perspective on language rights at universities and the need to guard against accepting a weak, cost-based argument for the removal of a language in favour of English only. There are three points from our discussion in Chapter 7 that need to be noted at this point in Chapter 9: the obligation conferred on institutions through the right in Section 29(2) of the Constitution; the cost-based argument; and the importance of statistics in informing the language planning process and justifiably limiting a right.

Maya P in the *AfriForum NPC v Chairperson of the Council of the University of South Africa and Others* case (2020:paras30-34) held that UNISA's argument and understanding of its responsibility under Section 29(2) was "fallacious", where it was of the view that it was not liable to ensure the effective access to, and implementation of, the right concerned. Maya P (2020), in relying on the *Ermelo* judgment (*Head of Department: Mpumalanga Department of Education and Another v Hoërskool Ermelo and Another*, 2010), pointed out that the right was already in existence at UNISA where students were able to elect to be taught in Afrikaans in over 300 modules. The right in Section 29(2) and its parameters were clearly established, with Maya P adopting a purposive approach to the interpretation of the right in the context of UNISA. UNISA's obligation, in terms of the right in Section 29(2), was thus clearly outlined and could not merely be removed on the basis of practicability where no appropriate justification was provided.

On the point of appropriate justification in removing the right of Afrikaans-speaking students, UNISA employed the costs-based argument, which the court rightfully dismissed. As opposed to the *UFS* (*AfriForum and Another v University of the Free State*, 2018) and *Gelyke Kanse and Others* v *Chairperson of the Senate of the University of Stellenbosch and Others* (2019) cases, the court in the *UNISA* case (*AfriForum NPC* v *Chairperson of the Council of the University of South Africa and Others*, 2020:para37) held that:

> ... it would have been equitable comparing the commercial viability of the 300 Afrikaans modules to the 300 least profitable modules offered in English as part of the exercise – this was not done.

Maya P (2020:para. 38) rightfully accepted the argument that UNISA failed to explain why the Afrikaans modules could not have been cross-subsidised by the English modules, as was done with Philosophy and French. The point of language being of strategic and national importance must be highlighted.

The third and final point of statistics is important when limiting the right as per the sliding scale formula. UNISA's argument was weak and failed to provide a source for the statistics which were used to validate the decision to remove Afrikaans as a LOLT. Important to note is that the court agreed with the applicants that 30,000 existing and prospective students was a large number and could not be ignored when removing an existing right.

Conclusion

This chapter advanced both theoretical discussions and practical enactments in the form of the selected university language policies. This was followed by a critique of the language policies and language planning processes of the selected universities, explicated further through analysis of the relevant case law.

Numerous reports, committees and commissions have been established with the aim of advancing recommendations for the implementation of the indigenous languages at universities in South Africa. As we have noted throughout this book, South Africa is an example of policy implementation failure, especially where language policies and legislation are concerned.

The mandate and subsequent discussions following all the reports and recommendations are subsumed under the transformation and decolonisation agenda. 'Transformation' has been the sweeping word and trend in the legal system; however, this has been to the exclusion of language. Instead, the legislative framework for the legal system has focused on gender and race, while promoting a monolingual English approach with the argument that English enables greater access to justice. This represents a skewed and, in our opinion, incorrect line of thinking. Similarly, universities, adopting the trend of decolonisation, have largely chosen to exclude the language question from ongoing debates.

The higher education legislative and policy framework promotes the use of multilingualism in a cautious manner, one which enables universities to adopt the default English-only approach. This was evident in many of the university language policies which we presented. There is a move towards English-only for purposes of teaching and learning at the UFS, UP and SU. RU and UCT have attempted to promote multilingualism; however, UKZN leads by example in both theory and practice and is a model that can be emulated by other South African universities.

As this chapter has illustrated, there are, of course, opposing voices from both academics and management at universities. However, the point of concern is the judicial endorsement of English-only language policies at universities. As seen in the case law concerning university language policies, the judiciary has projected their own English-only agendas, as well as supported and endorsed arguments by universities for English-only language policies.

While this portrayal of the current challenges that South Africans are facing regarding linguistic inclusion and equality is negative, we are of the opinion that all hope is not lost and that there are positives which can be drawn upon in ensuring positive linguistic change. The following chapter covers our recommendations for a new, equalised linguistic order in South Africa, influenced by the African and international comparative case studies presented in earlier chapters.

CONCLUSIONS AND RECOMMENDATIONS

The way forward

Introduction

This chapter provides an overview of the book in its entirety in relation to the goals and objectives as outlined in Chapter 1. Furthermore, this chapter provides seven recommendations that are informed by the discussions put forward. The chapter ends with an overall conclusion to the discussions, themes and issues raised.

Overview

In this book, we commenced with the objective of critiquing the monolingual language of record policy directive by the Heads of Courts against the constitutional and legislative language rights frameworks. In doing so, we found parallels between the selected higher education language policies that affect the language of record through the graduation of multilingual LLB students. The other objectives identified were formulated in the context of the research problem, as outlined in Chapter 1. Furthermore, the research was established within the parameters of the discipline of forensic linguistics. This was important, given that this is a relatively 'new' discipline in Southern Africa.

This research proceeded by providing a historical account of the development of the language of record in South Africa, where the relationship between language, law and power was highlighted. The historical account traced the language of record in courts in the pre-Apartheid era where the indigenous languages of the South African people were excluded in favour of Dutch and English. The political power of the elite dominated, influenced the use of language and led to the marginalisation of the indigenous languages. With time, as the research has illustrated, this linguistic exclusion and discrimination was perpetuated during Apartheid where, once again, political power influenced the language policies of the day. The dominance of the official languages at the time was also entrenched at universities and ultimately led to the development and use of the languages at an intellectualised level.

This research has explained the unfortunate lack of political will to include and advance the African languages during the CODESA talks. The negotiated settlement appeared to have included the previously marginalised African languages, as reflected in the Interim Constitution and the Final Constitution, but this was obviously not the case.

The research has illustrated that there were numerous missed – or intentionally neglected – opportunities to deal adequately with the language question in South African and in the courts in particular. This was a constant outcome, given the lack of implementation dating back to LANGTAG (1996). The resultant effect was the continuous cycle of English and Afrikaans usage in courts and at universities. Legislation and language policies mimicked this cycle; and, although language requirements for legal professionals were removed, this failed to remedy the position regarding the non-inclusion of African languages.

The above historical account and subsequent legislative and policy developments concerning the language of record in South African courts was informed by African and international case studies. The African case studies on Kenya, Morocco and Nigeria illustrated that South Africa was not unique in following an English-only model at universities and in the legal system on the African continent. Each of the African case studies illustrated the effects of political situations on the language question in courts and at universities. The case studies, particularly the Nigerian one, highlighted the issues of interpretation in the courts where English was the language of proceedings and record.

Chapter 3, comprising international case studies focusing on Australia, Belgium, Canada and India, again illustrated the marginalisation of indigenous languages. Such marginalisation was inherent in Australia and India, where indigenous people were excluded from, or unfairly disadvantaged in, courts and from accessing justice as a result of language. In India, the situation is compounded, as English is a minority spoken language in a multilingual country. As illustrated in the chapter, the issues are deep-rooted, with a political elite pursuing an agenda that continues to divide India. Canada and Belgium are clearly models to emulate in enacting bilingual and multilingual language policies for courts and universities; and these countries provide much-needed guidance and hope for linguistic inclusivity and equality for the languages and the speakers thereof. We will return to discussing Canada and Belgium further on in this chapter as part of the recommendations.

The discussions are brought together through the concurrent themes in the legislation, language policies, case law, language surveys and statistics for both the legal system and higher education. The supposed transformative framework in the form of the Legal Practice Act (2014), language policies enacted in accordance with the Languages Act (2012), and the language policies of universities (with the exception of UKZN), support an English-only agenda, contrary to reflecting and giving meaning to the constitutional provisions, as well as the language statistics presented.

Recommendations

The discussions that follow comprise seven identified and explained recommendations. The seven recommendations are interlinked while also related to the theme that runs through the book. This theme will become apparent with the advancement of each recommendation. These recommendations are formulated for the South African model; however, they are informed by the African and international comparative case studies. It is also important to note that, with South Africa implementing these recommendations, a new trajectory will be established on the African continent, one which could be emulated by other African countries, as identified in Chapter 2. The recommendations focus on reversing the monolingual English approach in South Africa with the aim of strengthening the indigenous languages and proving that these are powerful resources for development on the African continent.

What follows are the seven recommendations, each of which are advanced in relation to the discussions throughout Chapters 1 to 9.

Declaratory order

The Constitution is the starting point, given that it is the supreme law of the country, providing the framework upon which legislation and policies need to be drafted to ensure the successful implementation of the language rights and other language provisions, including Section 6. As we have advanced in preceding chapters, the constitutional provisions need be given further meaning through legislation and when being interpreted and applied in practical situations. There is a level of ambiguity in the form of discretionary words and phrases, detracting from the implementation of the language rights and provisions. Perry (2004:131) has critiqued the constitutional language rights and provisions, focussing on the ambiguity of the discretionary words and phrases, while noting the sentiments of retired CC Judge Albie Sachs, who stated the provisions of Section 6 are "…messy, inelegant and contradictory". The case law presented in Chapter 7 has advanced conflicting interpretations of the constitutional language provisions and, more specifically, language rights. The point is that there needs to be clarification on the parameters of the language rights.

A declaratory order is a constitutional remedy. Constitutional remedies, according to Currie and De Waal (2013:177) are:

> The remedies flowing from a direct application of the Bill of Rights to law and conduct governed by ss8 and 38 of the Constitution.

We have previously advanced the provisions of Section 8 of the Constitution (while Section 38 of the Constitution is also relevant in advancing this specific recommendation) whereby anyone has the right to approach a court, alleging that a right in the BOR has been infringed or threatened; and, in response, the court may grant appropriate relief, including a declaration of rights.

In light of the current situation concerning Section 35 of the Constitution, this research has presented a negative outlook for language rights of accused, arrested and detained persons. This situation has been exacerbated by the monolingual language of record announcements in the form of 'directives'. Simply put, a language of record policy for courts will not only adversely affect one individual, but also society as a whole. The same applies to the constant limitation of Section 29(2) of the Constitution, where, through the case law, monolingual teaching and learning language policies are endorsed as being constitutionally sound. A constitutional remedy would therefore address these issues in providing clarity. Currie and De Waal (2013:181) capture this point in the following excerpt:

> The harm caused by violating constitutional rights is not merely a harm to an individual applicant, but a harm to society as a whole; the violation impedes the realisation of the constitutional project of creating a just and democratic society. Therefore, the object in awarding a remedy is not only to grant relief to the litigant before the court but also to vindicate the Constitution. The judiciary therefore bears the burden of striking effectively at the source of the infringement.

This positive, forward-looking remedy and explanation thereof by Currie and De Waal (2013:181) brings into question the intention of the heads of courts. In the first place, they had no authority to determine the language of record policy for courts, let alone proceeding, nonetheless, to limit the constitutional rights of society by furthering an English-only, elitist agenda.

In explaining the reasons for granting a declaratory order, Currie and De Waal (2013: 96) state that it is both a flexible and valuable remedy in a constitutional democracy, "… as it allows the courts to clarify and declare a right on the one hand while leaving the decision on how best to realise the rights to other branches of the state". Therefore, a declaratory order comprises the court establishing the parameters of rights and provisions. Muller (2015) explains that a declaratory order is an order by which a dispute over the existence of some legal right or obligation is resolved. The right or obligation can either be existing or prospective (Muller, 2015). With an existing right or obligation, the declaratory order would be brought to seek clarification (meaning) from the court.

With a prospective right abstract review (without reference to a specific case), is provided where interpretation may be unclear. The declaratory order is not enforceable unless the applicant also applies for an enforcement order, such as an interdict. In the context of our discussions, the declaratory order would describe with precision what the breach or infringement of a right is and, through inference, what the parameters of the right are.

Lourens (2012:275) advanced that, although the declaratory order needs to be coupled with an enforcement order, the state would be bound by the provisions that would have been clarified. This, in our opinion, would be important given the failure to determine adequate language policies that provide clarity on the language question and provide further for the implementation of the language rights for all and not a minority English elite. The Language Policy of the Department of Justice and Constitutional Development (2019) fails in this mandate, leaving the language of record for courts to be undecided and for the Heads of Court to take it upon themselves, without the requisite authority, to determine the policy.

Depending on the ambit of the application for a declaratory order, it would be interesting and important to see the function of PanSALB explicated further. To this end, we refer to the role of PanSALB as being to play an active role in developing and advancing the use of the African languages in accordance with Section 6(2) of the Constitution. Furthermore, the role of PanSALB is to ensure that effective language policies are drafted in creating a linguistically-inclusive legal system. It is our opinion that PanSALB should be playing an active role in challenging monolingual language decisions and policies through legal and other engagement forums. The latter is discussed further with the recommendation for meaningful engagement.

Statutory and constitutional interpretation methods: purposive interpretation

One of the reasons for recommending a declaratory order is to ensure judicial officers do not adopt restrictive interpretations of the constitutional language provisions, given the ambiguity that enables such interpretation. As seen in the case law presented in Chapter 7, judicial officers have interpreted the language rights provisions restrictively. The exception was the case of *State* v *Pienaar* (2000), where the court adopted a purposive approach in giving meaning to the constitutional language rights in a practical situation.

Adopting a restricted and restrictive interpretation and the courts shying away from interpreting the constitutional language provisions is not confined to South Africa. This was also evident in the Canadian model presented in Chapter 3, with the interpretation adopted in the trilogy of cases. The case of *MacDonald* v *Montreal (City)* (1986:462) is specifically relevant, where the Supreme Court of Canada (SCC) held it is "... not the court's responsibility under the guise of interpretation, to improve upon, supplement or amend this historical constitutional promise". This, in our opinion, is contrary to the role of the courts in providing a purposive interpretation to ensure that the rights are fully realised. It is our opinion, further, that the courts' narrow interpretation is contrary to Section 8(3) of the Constitution which obliges a court to apply and develop the law where necessary.

As we explained in Chapter 3, concerning the Canadian model, the courts eventually moved on from the trilogy of cases and began adopting a more purposive approach to the language rights and other language-related provisions. Simply put, the Canadian jurisprudential model shows that purposive interpretation is possible, following years of exclusion and restrictive interpretation. Simply put, South Africa must emulate the Canadian model where judicial officers have clarified the importance of interpreting language rights purposively. This was evident in Wilson J's (1986:463) dissenting judgment in *MacDonald* v *Montreal (City)* (1986), where he explained that discretionary words such as 'may' and 'either' were inserted, not for the state to hold that there is a discretion on the state to choose the official language in which to conduct the case, but rather that it is up to the litigant before court to choose the official language in which to be tried.

In this light, South African judicial officers, when interpreting the constitutional language provisions, must adopt the reasoning evident in the Canadian case of *R* v *Beaulac* (1999:770) where the court held that interpretation must be guided by the preservation and development of official languages, while noting, importantly, that language rights are substantive and procedural in nature. This is the complete opposite of what judicial officers interpreting language rights in South Africa have done (and continue to do), where the language right in Section 35(3) (k) is seen as a procedural right, one which forms part of the substantive right to a fair trial. The case law presented in Chapter 7 illustrates the granting of appeals and reviews, where procedural irregularities have resulted from restrictive interpretation and the failure to implement the language rights. Purposive interpretation is therefore recommended for future interpretation of language rights and legislative provisions regulating the use of language in the legal system and for higher education.

Legislative interpretation is not simply the reading of the words contained in the statute. In the context of this research, it involves interpreting and applying the provisions of legislation. Thus, in order to interpret legislation, the interpreter requires an understanding of the legal principles and legal language in comprehending the meaning conveyed in the legislation. The methods of statutory interpretation and, more specifically, the rules, overlap to a certain extent. The extent of the overlap, if any, is dependent on the facts and the interpreter's understanding. The latter entails an element of subjectivity with interpretation occurring in real-life contexts.

In applying the methods and rules of statutory interpretation, the court's function is to interpret and not to make law, as held in the Latin maxim, *judicis est dicere non dare*. This is important to note in the context of the judgments in Chapter 7. Interpretation of legislation, or what is referred to as 'statutory interpretation', consists of two main approaches, namely the literal and purposive approaches (Burger, 2015:25).

The literal approach, also known as the orthodox text-based approach, is where an interpreter focuses on the literal meaning of the provision. The meaning of the words in the statute would be clear and unambiguous in conveying the meaning and intention (Botha, 2004:47). If the literal approach results in what Botha (2004:47) refers to as "absurd results", the court must then deviate from the literal meaning. Deviation in this instance is referred to as the golden rule of interpretation. The literal meaning is then sourced from secondary aids of interpretation, namely the long title of the statute, chapter headings and sections, and the text in the other official language (ibid).

The second approach is the purposive, or text-in-context, approach focusing on the purpose or object of the legislation, which is the prevailing factor in interpretation. At the centre of the purposive approach is the mischief rule (Botha 2004:51) which takes into account external aids, such as the common law prior to the enactment of the legislation, to assist in the interpretation of the statute (ibid).

There is an overlap between the methods employed for statutory interpretation, explained above, and constitutional interpretation. There are five constitutional interpretational techniques identified by Du Plessis and Corder (1994:73-74). Grammatical interpretation is the first technique, acknowledging the importance of the language in the legislation and constitutional provisions. This will include taking careful account of words, phrases, sentences and other structural components of the text. According to Botha (2004:58), this is different from the literal approach as it is merely an acknowledgement of the text. The second technique is systematic or contextual interpretation, which involves reading the sentence in question within the context of the entire statute and the social and political context in which the legislation has been drafted and exists (Botha, 2004:59). Third is teleological interpretation which emphasises the constitutional values when interpreting the legislative provisions (ibid). The fourth is historical interpretation, taking historical account of the circumstances which gave rise to the drafting of the legislation (ibid). Historical interpretation cannot be the only technique used for interpretation; it must be coupled with one of the other techniques. The amended legislative texts in the form of the Attorneys Amendment Act (1993a) and the Admission of Advocates Amendment Act (1994b), were originally drafted and enacted during Apartheid and, as such, inherited the official languages at the time. Historical interpretation is, furthermore, important for the discussion pertaining to the situation, which engendered the drafting and enactment of the Languages Act (2012) and the implications of these factors on the contents and overall effect of the legislation.

The fifth and final technique is comparative interpretation, whereby the court, which is interpreting the legislation or constitutional provisions, looks at international interpretation or foreign courts interpretation of similar legislation (Botha, 2004:59). As we have indicated, foreign legislation and interpretation of constitutional language provisions and legislation by foreign courts is discussed in Chapters 2 and 3, as well as foreign case law, in which these techniques of interpretation have been employed.

It is clear from the preceding discussion that there are similarities between statutory and constitutional interpretation.

Language audit

The statistics provided do not represent and record the language demographics of legal practitioners. More specifically, the NPA does not have in its possession statistics that concern the language competencies of their prosecutors, nor does the judiciary have statistics recorded on the language competencies of judicial officers. The absence of these statistics was seen in the case law presented in Chapter 7, specifically the cases of *State* v *Damoyi* (2004), *State* v *Damani* (2016) and, most recently, in the case of *State* v *Gordon* (2018). In the case of *State* v *Damoyi* (2004), we advanced that Yekiso J made an enquiry at provincial level where some form of language demographics was provided. In the case of *State* v *Damani* (2016), as advanced in Chapter 7, the pilot project referred to issues of dialect that would also need to be considered in the undertaking of a language audit. In the case of *State* v *Gordon* (2018), Thulare J stated that this would result in 'shopping' for judges; except that his reasoning saw him confining language to race. Furthermore, as we argued in Chapter 7, judges will not be discriminated against on grounds of language and race. The same model as applies in Canada and Belgium will apply; and this would be implemented incrementally in phases, as UKZN have done in the context of higher education.

The language survey conducted by De Vries and Docrat (2019) is precisely what is needed, but not as a voluntary exercise. The Department of Justice and Constitutional Development at national level will need to facilitate this audit or survey. There is no reason why various organisations such as the NPA, the Law Society of South Africa, General Council of the Bar and the office of the CJ cannot individually conduct the survey and submit the findings to the Department of Justice for further consolidation and to be publicised. Throughout our discussions, we have illustrated the importance of collective efforts to avoid duplication and simultaneously ensure that all stakeholders are participating and aware of the audit and the purpose thereof.

This language audit or survey will then provide precise statistics on the language competencies of legal practitioners and judicial officers, plus the levels of competency for each language spoken; and this can be recorded. As seen in Chapter 3 Belgium follows this model; and South Africa could emulate this. These statistics will be vital in the drafting of bilingual and multilingual language policies for courts in each province. The drafting and amending of existing policies is discussed in the following recommendation in this chapter.

Amendment of existing legislation and policies

South Africa has many statutes and policies that either duplicate mandates, fail to give effective meaning to the constitutional provisions or, in many instances, are not implemented. The failures to address the language question appropriately begin with the language practices of the SAPS Draft Language Policy (2015) which exclude or disadvantage people on grounds of language. A collective effort is needed where experts (forensic linguists) assist in the development of policies and training programmes for the police. We will expand on the latter point further along in this chapter. This is important: as we explained, the criminal justice system commences with the SAPS. With the legal system, there is a failure to address the language requirements of legal practitioners. Given the failure to include African language requirements in the Attorneys Amendment Act (1993a) and the Admission of Advocates Amendment Act (1994b), there is an inherent need to include language requirements where legal professionals are competent in at least one of the indigenous languages. This should have been dealt with in the Legal Practice Act (2014) given its mandate.

The absence of language requirements for legal practitioners is supported through the failure to deal with the language of record for courts in the Language Policy of the Department of Justice and Constitutional Development (2019). The executive must therefore seek to amend this position with immediate effect through the implementation of a series of actions that we are outlining as part of these recommendations. The executive must act swiftly and positively in changing this position of a monolingual language of record.

The Canadian model is one which South Africa can emulate in this regard, especially the legislative and policy framework of the Province of New Brunswick. Again, as we have indicated throughout the discussions, the entire system needs an overhaul, given that the statutes and policies for the legal system directly affect higher education and vice versa. As with the legislation and policies governing the legal system, the HEA (1997) does not provide much directive besides the fact that universities must adopt a language. Until the gazetting of the Revised Language Policy for Higher Education (2018), the language policies and numerous reports on the language question in higher education, advanced in Chapter 2 of this book, were not implemented, or the mandate was duplicated.

Simply put, the Revised Language Policy for Higher Education (2018) provides much-needed directive for the implementation of the African languages as languages of learning and teaching, in addition to their being languages of research and scholarship. It will result in the development of the African languages and the intellectualisation of the previously marginalised African languages, placing them on an equal footing with English.

This, however, requires that universities implement this policy through their respective institutional language policies. As Chapters 6 and 7 illustrate, the selected universities, with the exception of UKZN, are either moderately or extremely slow in doing so and may perhaps be accused of paying lip service to the Revised Policy for Higher Education (2018) by promoting the use of African languages and the development thereof. Worse, however, is the situation at the universities of UFS, UP and SU where English-only language policies have been formulated on the basis of their being transformative and enabling equal access for all.

The recommendation is that there is an urgent need to revise these language policies through understanding whose interpretation of transformation is actually being pursued. The university language policies need to be reflective of the language demographics of the provinces in which they are located and the broader language demographics of South Africa. Universities, through their language policies, have to facilitate a process through which graduates leave university with a sound knowledge of another language (particularly an African language) that equips them to function in that language in various professional domains such as the legal system. This will ultimately support the language policies of the Department of Justice and Constitutional Development in instituting language requirements, as well as formulating language of record policies for courts on a provincial basis, taking into account the language demographics.

Each province for the MC(s) and High Courts can have either bilingual or multilingual policies formulated, where the African languages and Afrikaans, or both, are languages of record alongside English, given the majority spoken languages in each province. Translation services can be employed, as with the Canadian model, to translate the record for appeal and review processes. This is a long-term recommendation that needs to be formulated by all relevant stakeholders identified in the discussions advanced above.

Within university structures, the LLB curriculum needs to be revised to factor in language and the need to graduate linguistically competent professionals, as UCT is doing with medical students. This would also require collaboration between the respective law faculties and African languages departments in formulating courses that are of benefit to students in a professional context.

Universities also have a further role to play in ensuring that proficient and academically qualified interpreters are graduated. There is a need to offer legal interpretation and translation courses to produce interpreters specifically for the courts. This will assist in improving the quality and consistency of legal interpretation in courts and assisting the police, given the discussions indicating that the SAPS Draft Language Policy (2015) includes interpretation services. We expand on the point of legal interpreters further on in this chapter.

Having a bilingual language policy at universities, where one of the languages is an African language, is possible; and a model that can be emulated is that of UKZN, as is Canada for the legal system. Indeed, these policies would need to be introduced incrementally as UKZN is doing through their extensive language plan, implemented through two phases. Further to UKZN in South Africa, Belgium is a further model that universities could emulate. As presented in Chapter 3, universities' geographical position determines the languages of learning and teaching and the languages in which LLB students must graduate. The Belgian model is one that can be applied in the South African context and reflected in policy and legislative works.

Meaningful engagement

Following on from the recommendations presented thus far, we note that there is a need for legal reform. The recommendation to amend existing legislation and policies illustrates that the legislature, at national level, has failed to address the language question; instead, a top-down approach has been adopted in the legal system and higher education. Statutes and policies are formulated without taking into account the language demographics of the country and are imposed on the people (litigants) and students. What is needed is a bottom-up approach, as discussed with reference to Alexander (1992). Common ground needs to be sought; and the ill-informed policies need to be redressed, with experts, persons affected by these policies, and those drafting and implementing the policies, finding solutions.

The concept of 'meaningful engagement' originated in the socioeconomic rights cases of *Joe Slovo Community Western Cape* v *Thubelisha Homes* (2010) and *Occupiers of 51 Olivia Road, Berea Township, and 197 Main Street, Johannesburg v City of Johannesburg* (2008:212). Meaningful engagement is defined as a two-way process in which government and the affected persons are required to find a common understanding in terms of which issues can be addressed and solutions and or agreement achieved. Meaningful engagement is grounded on effective consultation and mediation. It is to occur in good faith, transparently, with mutual understanding and sympathy and the necessary skill to achieve the stated objectives (Chenwi & Tissington, 2010:4).

These definitions and explanations of meaningful engagement make the concept relevant in the context of language planning. As with socioeconomic rights, language planning involves a fair level of emotiveness, given that it concerns who we are as a people. The concept of meaningful engagement, as a tool, was expanded upon and developed in the realm of language planning in ensuring the realisation of the constitutional language rights. Docrat and Kaschula (2015a:4) encapsulate the applicability of meaningful engagement in relation to language legislation in the reasoning here:

> Applying the concept of meaningful engagement to language legislation to support the language reality within the country and promote the...goals of the legislation is both necessary and desirable. The concept of meaningful engagement builds on Alexander's (2013) observation that in the case of language policy and implementation, if we cannot provide negotiated solutions we should not criticise.

As part of the process of meaningful engagement, and building on the definitions of meaningful engagement, forensic linguists will have a central role to play in informing the amendments, and drafting of new legislation and polices where necessary, from both a theoretical and practical perspective. This was acknowledged by Turi (1993) who states that legislation must be drafted by experts with an understanding of law and language. Meaningful engagement will be vitally important in engaging with the Heads of Courts and the CJ in fleshing out the issues from a point of practice, where, from an academic and practical side, solutions can be found. PanSALB will have an important role to play in facilitating the process of meaningful engagement with all these stakeholders identified in this research.

Linguistic training programmes and forensic linguists as expert witnesses in South African courts

This research, in critiquing the monolingual language of record policy directive by the Heads of Courts and the solidifying directive by Hlophe JP, has highlighted the need for forensic linguists in South Africa to advise in the process of formulating sound policies. The case law has also illustrated the need for expert evidence to be led concerning the language rights in courts. This research has illustrated that the language question either is an afterthought or considered insignificant. Expert evidence led in court is confined to ballistics, entomology and pathology, amongst others, to the exclusion of forensic linguists. There is a misconception when it comes to language – the analysis of language through documents, text messages, language rights, and other forms of evidence – that every police officer, legal practitioner and judicial officer is an expert in the field and possesses the necessary expertise to assume the role of a forensic linguist. This is again evident in the case law presented in Chapter 7, as well as the monolingual language of record and the discussion following therefrom.

A further point of substantiation of this point of critique is the fact that judicial officers believe language proficiency of witnesses and accused persons can be 'tested' and determined by asking them is they understand English. As we have recommended above, forensic linguists have a meaningful and important role to play at the beginning of the criminal justice system with the SAPS and their training and investigative techniques. This is being done successfully in Australia, where support and advise is offered to police during investigations in formulating and refining techniques for questioning accused persons, analysing statements and other evidence. In the United Kingdom, the Forensic Linguistics Centre at the University of Aston provides critical support during investigative stages in analysing evidence and providing expert evidence in courts.

Simply put, the point being conveyed is that these are only two countries which are maximising all efforts and expertise in the legal system through language and the specialised field of forensic linguistics. Thus, there are models which South Africa can follow. The research area of forensic linguistics is continuously growing in South Africa and universities are developing this field. The legal system can benefit there from and this will have a positive impact on the lives of citizens relying on their constitutional rights to attain justice.

Having said this, we recommend, firstly, that, in the interim, while the long-term recommendations presented above are being further discussed and implemented, training programmes commence for police officers, prosecutors and judicial officers. Training programmes are needed to sensitise these professionals to the linguistic and resultant cultural barriers experienced by complainants, accused persons and litigants on a daily basis. Secondly, there is the need to unpack the complexity surrounding the use of language in courts of law. Thirdly, there is a need to understand the effects of interpretation on oral evidence and, ultimately, the record. Fourthly, there has to be a realisation of the importance of interpreting language rights and provisions in a purposive manner, where the rights are realised rather than limited where English is the threshold. Fifthly, it is vital to enlighten these professionals about the research area of forensic linguistics and the role of forensic linguists in assisting during investigations and providing expert evidence in courts.

Linguistic justice

Each of the recommendations above is aimed at ensuring linguistic equality for the official languages and the speakers of these languages, as well as ensuring the attainment of linguistic justice. Linguistic justice is a concept that was first coined by Philippe van Parijs, a Belgian political philosopher and political economist. In the context of South Africa, based on this research, linguistic justice favours those with competency in English, as opposed to the majority of South Africans. Given the recent CC judgments concerning university language policies, linguistic justice appears to be an unattainable myth for African language speakers and currently also for Afrikaans speakers.

We are therefore recommending that the concept of linguistic justice be part of the meaningful engagement discussions, training programmes and long-term policies. This, foremost, requires an understanding of the concept, which Van Parijs (2002) advanced in relation to other societal influencers, including the economy, political power, societal social circumstances and an individual's mother tongue. What is clear from this research is that linguistic communities and speakers of languages other than English are treated indifferently. The level of indifference is often determined by a multitude of accompanying social, political and economic factors. The situation is no different in South Africa, as discussed in this book. According to Van Parijs (2002:60), a person's linguistic competency affects their life chances and earning power. This links to the language and economics argument by Grin (2010) and Kaschula (2004, 2019), and how this ultimately affects the level of education attained where language policies promote English only.

According to Van Parijs (2002:60), linguistic justice must be seen as "...a form of intercommunity cooperative justice. This, in our opinion, needs to take place in South Africa from a community perspective; and if the legal system and higher education language policies are adopting top-down approaches, they need to lead by example and act in the best interests of all. An inclusive community-based approach was also referred to by Froneman J in the *Gelyke Kanse and Others* v *Chairperson of the Senate of the University of Stellenbosch and Others* case (2019: para. 96) where the following was stated:

> Imagine a Stellenbosch University where the current emotional and often odious public oppositional discourse is displaced. Imagine a Stellenbosch University where there is a community working together to ensure that the university alumni and other sympathetic supporters raise awareness of the plight of less-resourced isiXhosa and Black and brown Afrikaans speaking communities that need access to its academic excellence. And then do something "reasonably practical" about it, by raising funds for the progressive institutionalisation of isiXhosa, Afrikaans or English as their choice of medium of instruction on an equal basis.

The quotation above speaks to achieving linguistic justice where proactive measures are adopted and pursued and where separate treatment on the basis of different mother tongues is excluded (Van Parijs, 2002:70). This is what is needed at all institutions and in the legal system, for linguistic justice to be achieved through community-based concerted efforts. The legal system, and in particular the judiciary can play an active role promoting the use and development of the African languages by writing judgments in their mother tongues alongside English. Froneman J also proposed this in the *Gelyke Kanse and Others* v *Chairperson of the Senate of the University of Stellenbosch and Others* case (2019:97):

> And imagine a Constitutional Court where judgments are written not exclusively in English, but in a variety of the indigenous official languages, with simultaneous translations in English in the column next to it, as in the Canadian law reports.

In the South African context, judgments have been written in isiXhosa and isiZulu, as seen in Chapter 7; and with ongoing terminology development programmes at UKZN and other institutions, this can surely be a reality, one that will become the norm, where the constitutional provisions are fully realised. This would be the true attainment of linguistic justice where fairness is the primary criterion (Van Parijs, 2002:71).

We are delighted to note that bilingual judgments are being produced in South Africa where the SCA has begun setting the trend and emulating the Canadian model of the Province of New Brunswick. Having a bilingually written judgment at the level of the SCA offers significant insights as to the development of African languages in the legal system. The bilingually written judgments illustrate that African languages have the capacity to be used in high status domains and ensure judgments are accessible to a wider number of South Africans. This contributes not only to the transformation of the legal profession and legal system but also to terminology development for the African languages in high status domains and provides greater access to justice. The *UNISA (AfriForum NPC v Chairperson of the Council of the University of South Africa and Others,* 2020) judgment and the judgment in the case of *Mgijima* v *The Premier of the Eastern Cape Province and Others* (2020), both bilingually written by Maya P, illustrates her commitment to linguistic transformation of the legal system, enhancing access to justice, and promoting, using and developing the African languages. Maya P's stance should be emulated by other judges across all courts in South Africa and proves that, if judges are willing and committed to using the African languages as languages of record and in judgments, it can be done and is both practicable and practical.

Conclusion

This interdisciplinary book, located in the research area of forensic linguistics, presents African and international case studies, all of which have been selected on the basis of presenting a holistic view of the use of language in the respective countries' legal and higher education systems. The purpose thereof is to provide models that can be emulated by South Africa. As explained in Chapter 1, the research and discussion we have undertaken were prompted by the increasingly unequal use of English only in the South African legal and higher education system. The monolingual language of record policy in South African courts is, in our opinion, cementing an English-only approach and unfairly discriminating against the majority of the population, where access to justice for African language speakers becomes difficult, if not unattainable.

In critiquing the monolingual language of record policy directive for courts, we have identified that the executive has failed in their duty to determine the language of record through legislative and policy means. From the post-Apartheid era (1994) to the present, there has been a continued game of avoidance employed where the language of record has been constantly overlooked. This has pointed to the gaps which this research has identified and highlighted with regard to the systemic failure of language legislation and, further, the failures of policy implementation.

With the executive failing in their mandate, we have, through this research, proved that the Heads of Courts decision, under the leadership of Mogoeng Mogoeng CJ, has occurred without the requisite legislative and administrative authority to make a directive on the language of record. There is also no authority under which Hlophe JP or any other Judge can determine the language of record. The monolingual language of record policy is a blatant abandonment of the constitutional values and provisions and unfairly limits the language rights of African language and Afrikaans speaking litigants in favour of English speaking litigants. This decision/directive has had a ripple effect on the status, use and development of African languages, in contrast to what was warranted through Section 6 of the Constitution.

The sole use of English in courts and in the legal system more broadly has resulted in the promotion and elevation of English to a 'super official language'. This has been supported by the growing trend in universities, with the exception of UKZN, to retain English-only language policies, paying lip service to multilingualism and the African languages. Universities are abandoning previous bilingual language policies in favour of English as the sole medium of teaching and learning under the intentional guise of transformation and equal access. The reasoning of 'everyone being fairly discriminated against' is a shallow excuse that illustrates the true intention of promoting English only, at the expense of the African languages.

This research has illustrated that people in authority tasked with upholding the Constitution are failing in their mandate to do so; and the silence of our people and those who should – and can – hold them to account, endorses the English-only position. This silent endorsement is contributing to the continued undermining of the African languages and the prevention of African language speakers from mainstream society being able to access and attain justice and from being afforded equal opportunities to participate at universities and obtain equal access to education (Kaschula, 2016:201). The costs are both intellectual and cultural in nature, a loss which cannot be recouped, if we continue on this path.

Organisations such as the PanSALB, Black Lawyers Association, Advocates for Transformation, and the African language membership organisations such as the African Languages Association of Southern Africa, by failing to challenge the status quo and legislative and policy means, are benefiting from an unequal system. There is no reason why these organisations cannot join as *amicus curiae* for the position of African languages to be considered and be made known. We cannot expect Afrikaans speaking litigants to litigate on behalf of African language speakers as well, when there are organisations who have this mandate and the resources to do so, but not the intention.

In South Africa, the language question is problematised. We have substantiated this point throughout this research, where this form of problematising is evident in the legal system and higher education. There is a cloud of negativity in attitude that accompanies discussions concerning language and, in particular, the African languages. These negative attitudes are captured in the survey by de Vries and Docrat (2019). There is lack of willingness to act, regardless of the fact that the Legal Aid Survey (2017) and Census language statistics prove that the majority of South Africans speak an African language as their mother tongue. The majority do not speak, read, write or understand English with sufficient levels of proficiency to facilitate necessary cognition and understanding in complex legal settings.

In South Africa, language is seen as a problem, not as a right or a resource (Ruíz, 1984). Language planners therefore need to engage with Ruíz's (1984) three orientations to language planning: language as a problem; language as a right and language as a resource. This will allow the costs defence to be addressed through the work of Grin (2010) and Kaschula (2004, 2019) in relation to language planning and the economy.

In this research, we have explicated the economic advantages under the fourth tier of language planning, namely opportunity planning (Antia, 2017). As part of the recommendations above, there are numerous employment opportunities that can be created by the legal system and universities through the establishment of curriculum reform for legal interpretation and translation degrees that will positively affect the rights of people in the pursuit of justice. There is a further need for the development of forensic linguists in South Africa to assist the police and legal system, as well as play an active role in the formulation of legally- and linguistically-sound language legislation and policies. There is therefore a correlative need in South Africa for universities to develop this research area that can serve to assist the continent as whole. This is achievable where the intention to do so is rightfully positioned. The African case studies in Chapter 2 have proven that there is a need for South Africa to lead from the front in charting a new course of social justice and linguistic inclusivity. The international models in Chapter 3 serve as a basis of what to avoid, how to overcome challenges, and how to achieve a linguistically inclusive legal system supported by universities who graduate multilingual professionals.

We do not think all hope is lost, but it is no longer about finding ways to "…sjambok the people to paradise", as Alexander (1997:90) rightfully pointed out. What has happened instead is that, collectively, as a society, and as South Africans, we have failed to realise our constitutional aspirations and we need to consider what we have not achieved since 1994 (Alexander, 2013). Instead, there is an incessant justification of why English is practicable rather than how the African languages can be used in practice.

In our view, as South Africans, we erroneously think that we are pursuing a transformative agenda (including that of language use), when the very statute, the Legal Practice Act (2014), fails even to mention language in its provisions.

> Sadly, few lawyers and judges have embraced this vision of a transformative constitutional project. While most pay lip service to the need for transformation and claim to endorse the transformative vision of the Constitution, it is as if the old had colonised the new by co-opting them in the oppression of the majority of citizens. The concept of "transformation" is now often used – so it seems to me – as a Band-Aid to hide and legitimise the continued injustice and inequality that is perpetuated by the old business elite and the new political business elite (De Vos, 2010).

De Vos (2010), through this quotation, summarises the current position in a concise, factually sound and unapologetic manner. We are the silent voice who are benefitting from an unjust system and we need to acknowledge this, break the silence and challenge a status quo that benefits an English elite at the expense of our African languages.

The current position concerning language selection and usage in the legal system can be one of equality and inclusivity, where international language planning models are emulated, as presented in the Belgian and Canadian case studies. What South Africa needs to avoid is continuing on this monolingual trajectory that has the power of strengthening the position of English on the African continent at the expense of the African languages. This will most certainly happen, as other African countries look to South Africa as a model to emulate, based on practicality for an English speaking minority elite. The dangers thereof are already present on the African continent, as well as internationally. The racial and linguistic inequalities perpetuated in the Australian and Indian case studies prove to be more than warning signs for South Africa and the African context more broadly. What is needed is the equal promotion and development of African languages alongside English in ensuring equal access to legal and educational justice for greater social justice.

REFERENCES

Abioye, F.T. 2011. Rule of law in English speaking countries: The case of Nigeria and South Africa. Unpublished PhD Thesis. Pretoria: University of Pretoria.

Alexander, N. 1992. Language planning from below. In: R.K. Herbert (ed.). *Language and Society in Africa*. Johannesburg: Witwatersrand University Press. 143-149.

Alexander, N. 1993. *Language policy and national unity in South Africa/Azania*. Cape Town: Buchu Books.

Alexander, N. 1997. Language policy and planning in the new South Africa. *African Sociological Review*, 1(1):82-92.

Alexander, N. 1999. *English unassailable but attainable: The dilemma of language policy in South African education*. Cape Town: PRAESA.

Alexander, N. 2005. *The intellectualisation of African languages*. Cape Town: PRAESA.

Alexander, N. 2013. *Thoughts on the New South Africa*. Johannesburg: Jacana.

Antia, B.E. 2017. University multilingualism: Modelling rationales for language policies. In: R.H. Kaschula, P. Maseko & H.E. Wolff (eds.), *Multilingualism and intercultural communication: A South African perspective*. Johannesburg: Wits University Press. 157-181. https://doi.org/10.18772/22017050268.16

AUS (Australian Government). 1901. *Immigration Restriction Act 17 of 1901*. https://bit.ly/3eTEPgG [Accessed 6 October 2020].

AUS (Australian Government). 1986. Evidence Amendment Act 107 of 1986. https://bit.ly/33XzrTm [Accessed 6 October 2020].

AUS (Australian Government). 1991. Commonwealth Attorney-General's Department, Access to Interpreters in the Australian Legal System, Report. https://bit.ly/3eYulNj [Accessed 13 November 2020].

AUS (Australian Government). 1995. *Evidence Act 1995. Federal Register of Legislation*. https://bit.ly/3hyHRJ2 [Accessed 6 October 2020].

Badat, S. 2010. The challenges of transformation in higher education and training institutions in South Africa. https://bit.ly/3uXaxzr [Accessed 12 October 2020].

Baker, C. 2006. *Foundations of bilingual education and bilingualism*. 4th Edition. Clevedon: Multilingual Matters.

Baldauf, R.B. 2004. Language Planning and Policy: Recent Trends, Future Directions. American Association of Applied Linguistics Conference. Portland Oregon. 1-4. https://bit.ly/2T0fKID

Bambust, I., Kruger, A. & Kruger, T. 2012. Constitutional and judicial language protection in multilingual states: A brief overview of South Africa and Belgium. *Erasmus Law Review*, 5(3):211-232. https://doi.org/10.5553/ELR221026712012005003006

Bamgbose, A. 1999. African language development and language planning. *Social Dynamics: A Journal of African Studies*, 25(1):13-30. https://doi.org/10.1080/02533959908458659

BEL (Belgium Government). 1935. Law of June 15, 1935.

Bhengu, L. 2019. Taking Zulu module won't boost marks- even for mother tongue students. *Times Live*. https://bit.ly/2SOH8ZR [Accessed 21 October 2019].

Boes, M. & Deridder, L. 2001. Language legislation in the judiciary in Belgium: Legal principles. In: K. Deprez, T. du Plessis & L. Teck (eds.), *Multilingualism, the judiciary and security services*. Pretoria: Van Schaik. 49-56.

Botha, C. 2004. *Statutory interpretation. An introduction for students.* 4th Edition. Cape Town: Juta.

Burger, A.J. 2015. *A guide to legislative drafting in South Africa*. Cape Town: Juta.

Busch, B., Busch, L. & Press, K. 2014. *Interviews with Neville Alexander*. Pietermaritzburg: UKZN Press.

CA (Canada). 1867. Founding Constitution Act of 1867.

CA (Canada). 1867 (rev. 2011). *Canada's Constitution of 1867 with Amendments through 2011.* Constitute. https://bit.ly/3ftewwW [Accessed 6 October 2020].

CA (Canada). 1969. Official Languages Act of 1969. https://bit.ly/3ymgg3S [Accessed 7 October 2020].

CA (Canada). 1870. The Manitoba Act – Enactment No. 2. https://bit.ly/3bCU9MS [Accessed 7 October 2020].

CA (Canada). 1982a. Canadian Charter of Rights and Freedoms in 1982. (*Constitution Act, 1982*). https://bit.ly/3hzl9Ax [Accessed 7 October 2020].

CA (Canada). 1982b. Official Languages Act of Canada (1988). Justice Laws Website. https://bit.ly/3uXg3C3 [Accessed 7 October 2020].

CA (Canada). 2000. *Alberta Languages Act of 2000*. https://bit.ly/2RvJBrM [Accessed 13 November 2020].

CA (Canada). 2002. New Brunswick Official Languages Act, 2002. https://bit.ly/3f1H0iB [Accessed 7 October 2020].

Cameron, E. 2013. Constitution holding steady in the storm. *Sunday Times*, 30 June:13.

Cassim, F. 2003. The right to address the court in the language of one's choice. *Codicillus*, 44(2):24-31.

Chenwi, L. & Tissington, K. 2010. *Engaging meaningfully with government on socio economic rights: A focus on the right to housing*. Belville: Community Law Centre, University of the Western Cape. https://bit.ly/3bxBbHu [Accessed 3 October 2020].

Constitutional Court Rules. 2003. Juta's Statutes Editors. 2015. *Superior Courts Act & Magistrates' Courts Act and Rules*. Cape Town: Juta.

Cooke, M. 2009. Anglo/Aboriginal communication in the criminal justice process: A collective responsibility. *Journal of Judicial Administration*, 19(1):26-35.

Cooke, M. 2019. E-mail interview, 31 August. In: Z. Docrat, *A critique of the language of record in South African courts in relation to selected university language policies*. Appendix H. PhD Thesis. Grahamstown: Rhodes University.

Cooper, R.L. 1989. *Language planning and social change*. New York: Cambridge University Press.

Corder, H. 2019. Formal interview, 6 March, Cape Town. In: Z. Docrat, *A critique of the language of record in South African courts in relation to selected university language policies*. Appendix I. PhD Thesis. Grahamstown: Rhodes University.

Coulmas, F. 1992. *Language and economy*. Oxford: Blackwell.

Coulthard, M. & Johnson, A. (eds.). 2010. *The Routledge handbook of forensic linguistics*. London: Routledge. https://doi.org/10.4324/9780203855607

Council of Europe. 1995. Framework convention for the protection of national minorities and explanatory report. https://bit.ly/2RvKX5Q [Accessed 13 October 2020].

Cowling, M.J. 2007. The tower of Babel – Language usage and the courts. *South African Law Journal,* 124(1):84-111. https://bit.ly/2T0huSb [Accessed 3 October 2020].

Crystal, D. 2003. *English as a global language*. 2nd Edition. Cambridge: Cambridge University Press.

Currie, I. & De Waal, J. 2005. *The Bill of Rights Handbook*. 5th Edition. Cape Town: Juta.

Currie, I. & De Waal, J. 2013. The *Bill of Rights Handbook*. 6th Edition. Cape Town: Juta.

De Vos, P. 2001. A bridge too far? History as context in the interpretation of the South African Constitution. *South African Journal on Human Rights,* 17(1):1-33. https://doi.org/10.1080/02587203.2001.11827615

De Vos, P. 2008. All languages equal but English (and Afrikaans) more equal? Constitutionally Speaking, 30 April. https://bit.ly/3eWEiur [Accessed 8 June 2016].

De Vos, P. 2010. What do we talk about when we talk about transformation? *Constitutionally Speaking*, 12 August. https://bit.ly/33WupXv [Accessed 10 February 2016].

De Vries, A. 2018. Attorneys experiences of language issues in the South African judicial system. Unpublished research survey. Pretoria: Vereniging van Regslui vir Afrikaans (VRA).

De Vries, A. & Docrat, Z. 2019. Multilingualism in the South African legal system: Attorneys' experiences. In: M.K. Ralarala, R.H. Kaschula & G. Heydon (eds.), *New frontiers in forensic linguistics: Themes and perspectives in language and law in Africa and beyond*. 89-112.

Docrat, Z. 2017a. The role of African languages in the South of African legal system: Towards a transformative agenda. Unpublished Master's Thesis. Grahamstown: Rhodes University.

Docrat, Z. 2017b. The fissure between law and language in a multilingual constitutional democracy exposed in the case of Lourens v Speaker of the National Assembly and Others. In: M.K. Ralarala, K. Barris & S. Siyepu (eds.), *Interdisciplinary themes and perspectives in African language research in the 21st Century*. Cape Town: Centre for Advanced Studies of African Societies. 279-298.

Docrat, Z. 2019. *A critique of the language of record in South African courts in relation to selected university language policies*. PhD Thesis. Grahamstown: Rhodes University.

Docrat, Z. & Kaschula, R.H. 2015a. Meaningful engagement: Towards a language rights paradigm for effective language policy implementation. *South African Journal of African Languages*, 35(1):1-9. https://doi.org/10.1080/02572117.2015.1056455

Docrat, Z. & Kaschula, R.H. 2015b. Strategy for Multilingual Success. *Mail & Guardian: Getting Ahead Supplement*. 6 March. https://bit.ly/2QqPTIM

Docrat, Z., Kaschula, R.H. & Ralarala M.K. 2017a. The exclusion of South African sign language speakers in the criminal justice system: A case based approach. In: M.K. Ralarala, K. Barris & S. Siyepu (eds.), *Interdisciplinary themes and perspectives in African language research in the 21st Century*. Cape Town: Centre for Advanced Studies of African Societies. 261-278.

Docrat, Z., Kaschula, R.H., Lourens, C.J.A., Bailey, A., De Vries, A. & Ralarala M.K. 2017b. Courts should promote all languages. *City Press* via *News24*. 17 September. https://bit.ly/3w8V92W [Accessed 3 October 2020].

Doucet, M. 2012. Language rights in New Brunswick. The pursuit of substantive equality: Myth or reality? In: C. Brohy, T. du Plessis, J.G. Turi & J. Woehrling (eds.), *Law, language and the multilingual state. Proceedings from the 12th International Conference of the International Academy of Linguistic Law*. Bloemfontein: African Sun Media. 159-193.

Du Plessis, T. 2001. *Towards a multilingual policy in the judiciary and security services in South Africa*. In: K. Deprez, T. du Plessis & L. Teck (eds.), *Multilingualism, the judiciary and security services*. Pretoria: Van Schaik. 95-105.

Du Plessis, T. 2012. A language act for South Africa? The role of sociolinguistic principles in the analysis of language legislation. In: C. Brohy, T. du Plessis, J.G. Turi & J. Woehrling (eds.), *Law, language and the multilingual state: Proceedings of the 12th International Conference of the International Academy of Linguistic Law*. Stellenbosch: African Sun Media. 195-213.

Du Plessis, L.M. & Corder, H. 1994. *Understanding South Africa's Transitional Bill of Rights*. Durban: Juta.

Eades, D. 1994. Forensic linguistics in Australia: An overview. *Forensic Linguistics*, 1(2):113-132. https://doi.org/10.1558/ijsll.v1i2.113

Eastman C.M. 1992. Sociolinguistics in Africa: Language planning. In: R.K. Herbert (ed.), *Language and society in Africa: The theory and practice of sociolinguistics*. Johannesburg: Witwatersrand University Press. 95-114.

El Kirat El Allame, Y. & Laaraj, Y. 2016. Reframing language roles in Moroccan higher education: Context and implications of the advent of English. *Arab World English Journal*, 43-46.

Fabunmi, J.O. & Popoola, A.O. 1990. Legal education in Nigeria: Problems and prospects. *Law and Politics in Africa, Asia and Latin America*, 23(1):34-55. https://doi.org/10.5771/0506-7286-1990-1-34

Foucher, P. 2012. The right to linguistic autonomy in Canadian constitutional law. In: C. Brohy, T. du Plessis, J.G. Turi & J. Woehrling (eds.), *Law, language and the multilingual state. Proceedings from the 12th International Conference of the International Academy of Linguistic Law*. Bloemfontein: African Sun Media. 227-248.

Froneman, J. 2019. Formal interview, 21 October, Grahamstown. In: Z. Docrat, *A critique of the language of record in South African courts in relation to selected university language policies*. Appendix K. PhD Thesis. Grahamstown: Rhodes University.

FW de Klerk Foundation. 2011. SA Languages Bill 2011 falls short: Draft legislation makes no provision to promote indigenous languages. *Politicsweb*, 21 December. https://bit.ly/3uTFAfk [Accessed 9 October 2020].

Getman, J.G. 1969. Development of Indian legal education: The impact of the language problem. *Journal of Legal Education*, 21(5):513-522.

Gibbons, J. 1986. Courtroom application of second language acquisition research. *Australian Review of Applied Linguistics*, 3:131-133. https://doi.org/10.1075/aralss.3.09gib

Gibbons, J. 1994. *Language and the law*. London: Longman. https://doi.org/10.1177%2F096394709500400207

Gibbons, J. 2003. *Forensic linguistics. An introduction to language in the justice system*. Oxford: Blackwell.

Goldflam, R. 2012. *Ngayulu nyurranya putu kulini: The legal right to an interpreter*. Paper presented at the Northern Territory Language and Law Conference, May 2012, Supreme Court NT. https://bit.ly/3hAdJx2 [Accessed 5 May 2019]

Grant, T. 2017. The usefulness of investigative linguistic analysis in the Courts and beyond. New Challenges for Forensic Linguists. 13th Biennial Conference of the International Association of Forensic Linguists. Conference paper. Porto, Portugal: University of Porto.

Grin, F. 2010. Managing languages in academia: Pointers from education economics and language economics. Paper presented at the conference, *Professionalising Multilingualism in Higher Education*. Luxembourg, 4 February. https://bit.ly/3eUIKda [Accessed 5 October 2020].

Hartle, B. 2019. Formal interview, 20 June, Grahamstown. In: Z. Docrat, *A critique of the language of record in South African courts in relation to selected university language policies*. PhD Thesis. Grahamstown: Rhodes University.

Haugen, E. 1965. Construction and reconstruction in language planning: Ivar Assens's Grammar. *Word*, 21(2):188-207. https://doi.org/10.1080/00437956.1965.11435423

Heugh, K. 1995. *Multilingual education for South Africa*. Johannesburg: Heinemann.

Heugh, K. 2002. Recovering multilingualism: Recent language-policy developments. In: R. Mesthrie (ed.), *Language in South Africa*. Cambridge: Cambridge University Press. 449-475. https://doi.org/10.1017/CBO9780511486692.025

Hlophe, J.M. 2004. Official languages and the courts. *South African Law Journal*, 117(4):690-696.

Hoexter, C. 2012. *Administrative law in South Africa*. 2nd Edition. Cape Town: Juta.

IND (India). 1858. The Government of India Act of 1958. https://bit.ly/3hN2TUD [Accessed 13 October 2020].

IND (India). 1949. Constitution of India. https://bit.ly/3hy6e9R [Accessed 7 October 2020].

IND (India). 2011. Census of India 2011. Report on post enumeration survey. https://bit.ly/3fowO2A [Accessed 13 October 2020].

JCCD (Judicial Council on Cultural Diversity). 2017. Recommended National Standards for Working with Interpreters in Courts and Tribunals. https://bit.ly/3tWxyRM [Accessed 6 October 2020].

Joyner, T. 2018. Aboriginal defendants are pleading guilty due to language and cultural barriers, legal officials warn. *ABC News*, 27 September. https://ab.co/3eVHh6s [6 October 2020].

Kamwendo, G. & Ndimande-Hlongwa, N. 2017. Language planning in South Africa: A history. In: R.H. Kaschula, P. Maseko & H.E. Wolff (eds.), *Multilingualism and intercultural communication: A South African perspective*. Johannesburg: Wits University Press. 157-181. https://doi.org/10.18772/22017050268.11

Kaplan, R.B. & Baldauf Jr, R.B. 1997. *Language planning from practice to theory*. Clevedon: Multilingual Matters.

Kaschula, R.H. 2004. South Africa's National Language Policy revisited: The challenge of implementation. *Alteration*, 11(2):10-25.

Kaschula, R.H. 2016. In search of the African voice in higher education: The language question. *Stellenbosch Papers in Linguistics Plus*, 49 199-214. https://doi.org/10.5842/49-0-658

Kaschula, R.H. 2019. Econo-language planning and transformation in South Africa: From localisation to globalisation. In: R. Hickey (ed.), *English in multilingual South Africa: The linguistics of contact and change*. Cambridge: Cambridge University Press. https://doi.org/10.1017/9781108340892.010

Kaschula, R.H. & Maseko, P. 2012. Intercultural communication and vocational language learning in South: Law and healthcare. In: C.B. Paulston, S.F. Kiesling & E.S. Rangel (eds.), *The handbook of intercultural discourse and communication*. New Jersey: Willey-Blackwell. 313-336. https://doi.org/10.1002/9781118247273.ch16

Kaschula, R.H. & Ralarala, M.K. 2004. Language rights, intercultural communication and the law in South Africa. *South African Journal of African Languages*, 2(4):252-261. https://doi.org/10.1080/02572117.2004.10587242

Kerr, D.H. 1976. *Educational policy: Analysis, structure, and justification*. New York: David McKay.

KY (Republic of Kenya). 1967. Judicature Act 16 of 1967 Chapter 8. Revised Edition, 2018. 1-9. https://bit.ly/3huFcQG [Accessed 14 November 2020].

KY (Republic of Kenya). 2010. *The Constitution of Kenya, 2010*. https://bit.ly/3wdPw3B [Accessed 5 October 2020].

KY (Republic of Kenya). 2012. Criminal Procedure Code Chapter 75. C44-201, Issue 1:1-317. https://bit.ly/3hzvdtt [Accessed 5 October 2020].

Law Society of South Africa. 2015. *Statistics for Legal Education and Development (LEAD) and the Legal Profession 2014-2015*. https://bit.ly/3tYiHGc [Accessed 12 October 2020].

Legal Aid South Africa. 2017. Language Survey 2017. https://bit.ly/3tWXLj1 [Accessed 10 October 2018].

Leung, J.H.C. 2019. *Shallow equality and symbolic jurisprudence in multilingual legal orders*. New York: Oxford University Press. https://doi.org/10.1093/oso/9780190210335.001.0001

Lourens, C. 2012. Language rights in the constitution: The "unborn" language legislation of subsection 6(4) and the consequences of the delayed birth. In: C. Brohy, T. du Plessis, J.G. Turi & J. Woehrling (eds.), *Law, language and the multilingual state. Proceedings of the 12th International Conference of the International Academy of Linguistic Law*. Bloemfontein: African Sun Media. 269-290.

Lubbe, H.J. 2008. The right to language use in court: A language right or a communication right? *APP International Conference 16-19 July 2008*. https://bit.ly/3fxgkoW [Accessed 10 February 2016].

MacFarlane, J., Kurt, C.S., Heydon. G. & Roh, A. 2019. Multilingualism in the South African Legal System: Attorneys' Experiences. In: M.K. Ralarala, R.H. Kaschula, & G. Heydon (eds.), *New frontiers in forensic Linguistics: Themes and perspectives in language and law in Africa and beyond.* 51-70.

Malan, J.J.K. 2009. Observations on the use of official languages for the recording of court proceedings. *Tydskrif vir die Suid-Afrikaanse Reg (TSAR)*, (1):141-155. https://bit.ly/33Udkxe [Accessed 3 October 2020].

Marley, D. 2005. From monolingualism to multilingualism: Recent changes in Moroccan language policy. In: J. Cohen, K.T. McAlister, K. Rolstad & J. MacSwan (eds.), *Proceedings of the 4th International Symposium on Bilingualism.* Cascadilla Press, Somerville, MA.

Maseko, P. 2008. *Vocational language learning and how it relates to language policy issues.* Master's Thesis. Grahamstown: Rhodes University.

Maseko, P. 2014. Multilingualism at work in South African higher education: From policy to practice. In: L. Hibbert & C. van der Walt (eds.), *Multilingualism in South Africa: Reflecting society in higher education.* Bristol: Multilingual Matters. https://doi.org/10.21832/9781783091669-005

Maurais, J. 1991. A sociolinguistic comparison between Quebec's Charter of the French language and the 1989 language laws of five Soviet republics. *Journal of Multilingual and Multicultural Development*, 12(1/2):117-126. https://doi.org/10.1080/01434632.1991.9994452

Mbangi, Y. 2019. E-mail interview, 26 July, Bisho. In: Z. Docrat, *A critique of the language of record in South African courts in relation to selected university language policies.* PhD Thesis. Grahamstown: Rhodes University.

McConnachie, C. 2019. Formal interview, 13 June, Grahamstown. In: Z. Docrat, *A critique of the language of record in South African courts in relation to selected university language policies.* Appendix N. PhD Thesis. Grahamstown: Rhodes University.

McLean, D. 1992. Guarding against 'the Bourgeois Revolution': Some aspects of language planning in the context of national democratic struggle. In: R.K. Herbert (ed.), *Language and Society in Africa: Theory and practice of sociolinguistics.* Johannesburg: Witwatersrand University Press. 151-161.

Meakins, F. 2015. Some Australian Indigenous languages you should snow. The Conversation, 7 May. https://bit.ly/3u6jN33 [Accessed 6 October 2020].

Moerane, M.T.K. 2003. The meaning of transformation of the judiciary in the new South African context. *South African Law Journal*, 120(4):708-718. https://bit.ly/33R439l [Accessed 3 October 2020].

Motinyane, M. 2020. Decolonising our minds, decolonising our languages: A mentalist approach to language attitudes. In: R.H. Kaschula & H.E. Wolff (eds.), *The transformative power of language: From postcolonial to knowledge societies in Africa.* Cambridge: Cambridge University Press. 67-82. https://doi.org/10.1017/9781108671088.005

MR (Kingdom of Morocco). 2011. *Morocco's Constitution of 2011.* https://bit.ly/3u1Swyl [Accessed 5 October 2020].

Muller, G. 2011. "Conceptualising 'meaningful engagement' as a deliberative democratic partnership". *Stellenbosch Law Review*, 22(3):742-758.

Muller, G. 2015. "Declaratory orders and interdicts" Constitutional litigation LLB elective course notes. Grahamstown: Rhodes University.

Murray, M. 2019. Exploring the unintended consequences of learning a new language at a South African university. *PLOS ONE*, 14(3):1-11. https://doi.org/10.1371/journal.pone.0213973

Naidu, S.M.V. 2018. The language used in courts should be understood by the petitioners who are seeking justice. *Press Information Bureau Government of India Vice President's Secretariat.* https://bit.ly/3bBPrPf [Accessed 7 October 2020].

Namakula, C.S. 2019. When the tongue ties fair trial: The South African experience. *South African Journal on Human Rights*, 35(2):219-236. https://doi.org/10.1080/02587203.2019.1615383

Nambiar, V. 2019. India Supreme Court judgments to be published in multiple languages. *Jurist*, 4 July. https://bit.ly/3ylbp2L [Accessed 8 July 2019].

Ndenze, B. 2017. No law degree without fluency in indigenous language proposed. *Herald*, 30 March:4.

Ndlovu, T. 2002. Black languages and the South African courts. *De Rebus*, April.

NG (Federal Republic of Nigeria). 1960. *Criminal Procedure Code*. https://bit.ly/3ospebl [Accessed 5 October 2020].

NG (Federal Republic of Nigeria). 1979a. *Constitution of the Federal Republic of Nigeria*. https://bit.ly/3uZHCuj [Accessed 5 October 2020].

NG (Federal Republic of Nigeria). 1979b. *Police Act 23 of 1979*. https://bit.ly/3yn0CoC [Accessed 13 November 2020].

NG (Federation of Nigeria). 1990. Criminal Procedure Act, Chapter 80. https://bit.ly/3fqrdZl [Accessed 5 October 2020].

NG (Federal Republic of Nigeria). 1999. *Constitution of the Federal Republic of Nigeria*. https://bit.ly/3fpEX6I [Accessed 5 October 2020].

Ngcukaitobi, T. 2013. Equality. In: I. Currie & J. de Waal (eds.), *The Bill of Rights Handbook*. 6th Edition. Cape Town: Juta.

Nombembe, P. 2017. Afrikaans sentenced to death: English now sole court official language. *Sunday Times*, 16 April. https://bit.ly/33Vw7rX [Accessed 8 October 2020].

Ntlama N. 2014. Transformation of the judiciary: A measure to weaken its capacity. Paper delivered at International Workshop entitled: Constitutional rights, judicial independence and the transition to democracy: twenty years of South African constitutionalism. Organised by the New York Law School, held on 13-16 November 2014, New York, United States of America.

Odhiambo, K., Kavulani, C.K. & Matu, P.M. 2013. Court interpreters view of language Use in subordinate courts in Nyanza Province, Kenya. *Theory and Practice in Language Studies*, 3(6):910-918. https://doi.org/10.4304/tpls.3.6.910-918

Ogechi, N.O. 2003. On Language Rights in Kenya. *Nordic Journal of African Studies*, 12(3):277-295.

Olanrewaju, F.R. 2009. *Forensic linguistics: An introduction to the study of language and the law*. Muenchen: Lincom Europa.

Olsson, J. 2004. *Forensic linguistics: An introduction to language, crime and the law*. New York: Continuum.

Olsson, J. 2008. *Forensic linguistics*. 2nd Edition. New York: Continuum.

Orman, J. 2014. Language policy and identity conflict in relation to Afrikaans in the post-apartheid era. In: A. Alexander & A. von Scheliha (eds.), *Language policy and the promotion of peace: African and European case studies*. Pretoria: Unisa Press. 59-76.

Perry, T. 2004. *Language rights, ethnic politics: A critique of the Pan South African Language Board*. Cape Town: PRAESA Occasional Papers No. 12. https://bit.ly/3oCVGb7 [Accessed 3 October 2020].

Pretorius, J.L. 2013. The Use of Official Languages Act: Diversity affirmed? *Potchefstroom Electronic Law Journal*, 16(1):281-319. https://doi.org/10.4314/pelj.v16i1.9

Ralarala, M.K. 2012. A compromise of rights, rights of language and rights to a language in Eugene Terre-Blanche's (ET) trial within a trial: Evidence lost in translation. *Stellenbosch Papers in Linguistics*, 41:55-70. https://doi.org/10.5774/41-0-43

Ralarala, M.K. 2019. Identifying anomalies in police record construction and sworn statements. 2nd Forensic Linguistics Colloquium: New Courtroom Languages. Keynote. Grahamstown, South Africa: Rhodes University.

Reagan, T.G. 1986. Language ideology in the language planning process: Two African case studies. *South African Journal of African Languages*, 6(2):94-97. https://doi.org/10.1080/02572117.1986.10586658

Robertson, K., Hohmann, J. & Stewart, I. 2005. Dictating to one of 'us': The migration of Mrs Freer. *Macquarie Law Journal*, 5:241-275.

RSA (Republic of South Africa). 1882. *Constitution Ordinance Amendment Act 1 of 1882.*

RSA (Republic of South Africa). 1884. *Dutch Language Judicial Use Act 21 of 1884.*

RSA (Republic of South Africa). 1925. *Union Act 8 of 1925.*

RSA (Republic of South Africa). 1927. *Act 8 of 1927.*

RSA (Republic of South Africa). 1964. *Admission of Advocates Act 74 of 1964. Government Gazette Extraordinary.* 111-121. https://bit.ly/33WzXRP [Accessed 8 October 2020].

RSA (Republic of South Africa). 1979. 53 of 1979: Attorneys Act. *Government Gazette*, 168(1168):1-72.

RSA (Republic of South Africa). 1983. *Republic of South Africa Constitution Act 110 of 1983.* https://bit.ly/3hBysAu [Accessed 8 October 2020].

RSA (Republic of South Africa). 1986. *Act 110 of 1986.*

RSA (Republic of South Africa). 1993a. Attorneys Amendment Act 115 of 1993. *Government Gazette*, 337(14981):1-10. https://bit.ly/3uZFGSC [Accessed 3 October 2020].

RSA (Republic of South Africa). 1993b. Act No. 200 of 1993. *Constitution of the Republic of South Africa.* (Interim Constitution). State President's Office, No. 185. https://bit.ly/33QTfrG [Accessed 8 October 2020]

RSA (Republic of South Africa). 1994a. Judicial Service Commission Act 9 of 1994. *Government Gazette*, 349(15850):1-6. https://bit.ly/3tWPonu [Accessed 3 October 2020].

RSA (Republic of South Africa). 1994b. Admission of Advocates Amendment Act 55 of 1994, *Government Gazette*, 354(16132):1-13.

RSA (Republic of South Africa). 1995. Pan South African Language Board Act 59 of 1995. (PanSALB). *Government Gazette*, 364(16726):1-20. https://bit.ly/3ydHGsu [Accessed 9 October 2020].

RSA (Republic of South Africa). 1996a. *Constitution of the Republic of South Africa,* 1996. https://bit.ly/3eU06qH [Accessed 14 November 2020].

RSA (Republic of South Africa). 1996b. Bill of Rights, *Chapter 2 of Constitution of the Republic of South Africa,* 1996. https://bit.ly/3oCX11D [Accessed 3 October 2020].

RSA (Republic of South Africa). 1997. Higher Education Act 101 of 1997 as amended, Higher Education Amended Act of 1999, 2000, 2001, 2002. *Government Gazette*, 390(18515):1-47.

RSA (Republic of South Africa). 2000a. Promotion of Equality and Prevention of Unfair Discrimination Act 4 of 2000. *Government Gazette*, 416(20876). https://bit.ly/2S7uAMI [Accessed 8 October 2020].

RSA (Republic of South Africa). 2000b. Promotion of Administrative Justice Act 3 of 2000. (PAJA). *Government Gazette*, 416(20853):1-9. https://bit.ly/3uZJHX9 [Accessed 8 October 2020].

RSA (Republic of South Africa). 2012. Use of Official Languages Act No. 12 of 2012. *Government Gazette*, 568(35742):1-12. https://bit.ly/3yjvGWI [Accessed 3 October 2020]

RSA (Republic of South Africa). 2013. The Superior Courts Act 10 of 2013. *Government Gazette*, 578(36743):1-56. https://bit.ly/3eSFRJT [Accessed 3 October 2020].

RSA (Republic of South Africa). 2014. Legal Practice Act 28 of 2014. *Government Gazette*, 591(38022):1-68. https://bit.ly/3ymoau4 [Accessed 3 October 2020].

RSA DAC (Republic of South Africa, Department of Arts and Culture). 2002. National Language Policy Framework. 1-21. https://bit.ly/3tW80Eb [Accessed 8 October 2020].

RSA DAC (Republic of South Africa, Department of Arts and Culture). 2003. Implementation Plan: National Language Policy Framework. 1-33. https://bit.ly/33Tx2Jv [Accessed 8 October 2020].

RSA DACST (Republic of South Africa. Department of Arts, Culture, Science and Technology). 1996. *Towards a National Language Plan for South Africa. Final Report of the Language Plan Task Group.* LANGTAG (Language Plan Task Group). Pretoria.

RSA DHET (Republic of South Africa, Department of Higher Education and Training). 2008. *Report of the Ministerial Committee on the Development on Transformation and Social Cohesion and the Elimination of Discrimination in Public Higher Education Institutions.* https://bit.ly/2Rqv7JK [Accessed 2 December 2020].

RSA DHET (Republic of South Africa, Department of Higher Education and Training). 2018. Revised Language Policy for Higher Education. *Government Gazette No. 41463.* https://bit.ly/2Qt5EPz [Accessed 13 November 2020].

RSA DoE (Republic of South Africa, Department of Higher Education). 2002. Language Policy for Higher Education. *Government Gazette*, 449(24101). https://bit.ly/3yiBlfn [Accessed 12 October 2020].

RSA DoE (Republic of South Africa, Department of Higher Education). 2003. *Report of the Ministerial Committee on the Development of Indigenous African Languages as Mediums of Instruction in Higher Education.* https://bit.ly/3yiwn2h [Accessed 2 December 2020].

RSA DOJ & CD (Republic of South Africa). 2019. Language Policy of the Department of Justice and Constitutional Development. 26 April. *Government Gazette*, 646(42422):1-32. https://bit.ly/3uX8Z8o [Accessed 9 October 2020].

RSA SAPS (Republic of South Africa. Department of Police). 2015. Language Policy of the South African Police Service. Use of Official Languages Act, 2012 (Act no. 12 of 2012), Draft language policy of the South African Police Service. *Government Gazette*, No. 39308:4-14. https://bit.ly/2RkJwaE [Accessed 5 October 2020].

RSA SSA (Republic of South Africa. Statistics South Africa). 2011 Census. https://bit.ly/33RaNDV [Accessed 21 October 2016].

RU (Rhodes University). 2014. Language Policy. https://bit.ly/3ow6rf1 [Accessed 13 October 2020].

Ruíz, R. 1984. Orientations to language planning. *Journal of the National Association for Bilingual Education*, 8(2):15-34. https://doi.org/10.1080/08855072.1984.10668464

Saadoun, A. 2015. Moroccan court proceedings: Towards an Amazigh language of rights. *The Legal Agenda*. https://bit.ly/2T3FWCh [Accessed 22 March 2019].

Schwikkard, P.J. & Van der Merwe, S.E. (eds.). 2010. *Principles of evidence.* 3rd Edition. Cape Town: Juta Press.

Shohamy, E. 2006. *Language policy: Hidden agendas and new approaches.* London: Routledge. https://doi.org/10.1080/14790710903411816

Sonewal, S. 2016. Is Hindi feasible in all courts of India? *India Legal*, 15 September. https://bit.ly/3fsykk7 [Accessed 7 October 2020].

Stewart, W. 1968. A sociolinguistic typology for describing national multilingualism. In: J.A. Fishman (ed.), *Readings in the sociology of language.* The Hague: Mouton. 531-545. https://doi.org/10.1515/9783110805376.531

Strydom, H. 2001. Democratic security in multicultural societies – the South African case. In: K. Deprez, T. du Plessis & L. Teck (eds.). *Multilingualism, the judiciary and security services.* Pretoria: Van Schaik. 106-114.

SU (University of Stellenbosch). 2017. Language Policy. https://bit.ly/3w9imlA [Accessed 13 October 2020].

Theophilopoulos, C., Van Heerden, C.M. & Boraine, A. 2012. *Fundamental principles of civil procedure.* 2nd Edition. Durban: LexisNexis.

Turi, J.G. 1993. The importance of the conference theme: Language and equality. In: K. Prinsloo, Y. Peters, J.G. Turi & C. Van Rensburg (eds.), *Language, law and equality.* [Proceedings of the Third International Conference of the International Academy of Language Law (IALL) held in South Africa, April 1992]. Pretoria: University of South Africa (UNISA). 5-24. https://bit.ly/2QyA4Qw [Accessed 3 October 2020].

Turi, J.G. 2012. Law, language and the multilingual state. In: C. Brohy, T. du Plessis, J.G. Turi & J. Woehrling (eds.), *Law, language and the multilingual state. Proceedings of the 12th International Conference of the International Academy of Linguistic Law.* Bloemfontein: African Sun Media. 269-290.

UCT (University of Cape Town). 2013. Language Policy. https://bit.ly/3ykU5ek [Accessed 13 October 2020].

UDLR (Universal Declaration of Linguistic Rights). 1998. https://bit.ly/3eUkNCT [Accessed 13 October 2020].

UFS (University of the Free State). 2016. University of the Free State Language Policy. https://bit.ly/3vb9oo5 [Accessed 12 October 2020].

UKZN (University of KwaZulu-Natal). 2014. Language Plan of the University of KwaZulu-Natal. https://bit.ly/3bC2DUf [Accessed 12 October 2020].

UKZN (University of KwaZulu-Natal). 2014. Language Policy. https://bit.ly/3bvWaub

UN (United Nations). 1948. Universal Declaration of Human Rights. https://bit.ly/3weMewX [Accessed 13 October 2020].

UN (United Nations). 1995. Framework Conventions for Protection of National Minorities. https://bit.ly/3byT9t9 [Accessed 14 November 2020].

UN: OHCHR (United Nations: Office of the High Commissioner on Human Rights). 1996. International Covenant on Civil and Political Rights, Assembly resolution 2200A (XXI) of 16 December. https://bit.ly/3opXhAE [Accessed 6 October 2020].

Uniform Rules of Court. 2013. In: Juta's Statutes Editors. 2015. *Superior Courts Act & Magistrates' Courts Act and Rules.* Cape Town: Juta.

Union of South Africa. 1909. South Africa Act, 1909. https://bit.ly/3hwkj7H [Accessed 8 October 2020].

Union of South Africa. 1925a. Official Languages of the Union Act, 1925. *Government Gazette Extraordinary*, No. 1477. https://bit.ly/33QBngJ [Accessed 8 October 2020].

Union of South Africa. 1925b. Magistrates' Courts Act 32 of 1944. *Union Gazette Extraordinary*, 32:1-30. https://bit.ly/3uU6rla [Accessed 3 October 2020].

UP (University of Pretoria). 2019. Language Policy. https://bit.ly/3oscQYz [Accessed 12 October 2020].

Van Niekerk, G. 2015. Multilingualism in South African courts: The legislative regulation of language in the Cape during the nineteenth century. *Fundamina*, 21(2):372-391. https://doi.org/10.17159/2411-7870/2015/v21n2a10

Van Parijs, P. 2002. Linguistic justice. *Politics, philosophy and economics*, 1(1):59-74. https://doi.org/10.1177/1470594X02001001003

Webb, V. & Kembo-Sure. 2000. *African Voices. An introduction to the languages and linguistics of Africa.* Cape Town: Oxford University Press.

Wei, L. (ed.). 2013. *Applied linguistics.* Hoboken, NJ: Wiley Blackwell.

Wesson, M. & Du Plessis, M. 2008. The transformation of the judiciary: Fifteen year policy review. *South African Presidency.* https://bit.ly/3eTyguG [Accessed 12 February 2016].

Williams, C.H. 2012. In defence of language rights: Language commissioners in Canada, Ireland and Wales. In: C. Brohy, T. du Plessis, J.G. Turi & J. Woehrling (eds.), *Law, language and the multilingual state. Proceedings from the 12th International Conference of the International Academy of Linguistic Law.* Bloemfontein: African Sun Media. 45-69.

Woolman, S. 1998-2003. Limitations. In: M. Chaskalson, J. Kentridge, J. Klaaren, G. Marcus, D. Spitz & S. Woolman (eds.), *Constitutional Law of South Africa*. 1st Edition. Cape Town: Juta Law. 12-1 – 12-66. Loose-leaf publication.

Wynants, A. 2001. Basic principles of language legislation in the judiciary in Belgium. In: K. Deprez, T. du Plessis & L. Teck (eds.), *Multilingualism, the judiciary and security services*. Pretoria: Van Schaik Publishers. 41-48.

Case Law

AfriForum and Another v *Chairman of the Council of the University of the Free State and Others* 2016 ZAFSHC 130.

AfriForum and Another v *University of the Free State* 2018 (2) SA 185 (CC).

AfriForum and Another v *Chairperson of the Council of the University of Pretoria and Others* 2017 (1) SA 832 (GP).

AfriForum NPC v *Chairperson of the Council of the University of South Africa and Others* 2020 ZASCA 79 (30 June 2020).

Bato Star Fishing (Pty) Ltd v *Minister of Environmental Affairs and Others* 2004 (4) SA 490 (CC).

Bilodeau v *Manitoba (Attorney General)*, [1986] 1 S.C.R. 449. [Canadian law reports]

Ford v *Quebec (Attorney General)*, [1988] 2 S.C.R. 712 (Can). [Canadian law reports]

Gelyke Kanse and Others v *Chairman of the Senate of the Stellenbosch University and Others* 2017 (1) SA 119 (WC).

Gelyke Kanse and Others v *Chairperson of the Senate of the University of Stellenbosch and Others* [2019] ZACC 38.

Head of Department: Mpumalanga Department of Education and Another v *Hoërskool Ermelo and Another* 2010 (2) SA 415 (CC).

Jones v *Attorney General of New Brunswick*, [1975] 2 S.C.R. 182 (Can). [Canadian law reports].

Lourens v *President of the Republic of South Africa and Another* 2013 (1) SA 499 (GNP).

Lourens v *Speaker of the National Assembly and Others* 2015 (1) SA 618 (EqC).

Lourens v *State Party: Republic of South Africa* case number 3178/2018 (United Nations Human Rights Committee).

MacDonald v *Montreal (City)*, [1986] 1 S.C.R. 721. [Canadian law reports]

Mgijima v *The Premier of the Eastern Cape Province and Others* [2020] ZASCA 139 (30 October 2020).

Mthethwa v *De Bruin NO and Another* 1998 (3) BCLR 336 (N).

Occupiers of 51 Olivia Road, Berea Township, and 157 Main Street, Johannesburg v *City of Johannesburg* 2008 (3) SA 208 (CC).

Omotoso and Others v *State* (2018) ZAECPEHC 81 (30 October 2018).

R v *Beaulac*, [1999] 1 S.C.R. 768 (Can). [Canadian law reports]

R v *Pooran & Vaillant*, [2011] ABPC 77 (Alb.P.C). [Canadian law reports]

Reference re: Manitoba Language Rights, [1985] 1 S.C.R. 721 (Can). [Canadian law reports]

Residents of Joe Slovo Community Western Cape v *Thubelisha Homes* 2010 (3) SA 454 (CC).

Societe des Acadiens du Nouveau Brunswick v *Association of Parents for Fairness in Education*, [1986] 1 S.C.R. 549 (Can). [Canadian law reports]

State v *Damoyi* 2004 (1) SACR 121 (C).

State v *Damani* 2016 (1) SACR 80 (KZP).

State v *Gordon* 2018 ZAWCHC 106 (29 August 2018). https://doi.org/10.1093/ejil/chy068

State v *Lesaena* 1993 (2) SACR 264 (T).
State v *Manzini* 2007 (2) SACR 107 (W).
State v *Matomela* 1998 (3) BCLR (Ck).
State v *Ndala* 1996 (2) SACR 218 (C).
State v *Ngubane* 1996 (2) SACR 218 (C).
State v *Pienaar* 2000 (2) SACR 143 (NC).
State v *Sikhafungana* 2012 Mount Frere Magistrates' Court (Unreported judgment).
State v *Siyotula* 2003 (1) SACR 154 (E).
State v *Van Breda* 2018 ZAWCHC 87 (7 June 2018).